T0360666

Corporate Political Responsibility

Behind closed doors, many large companies quietly use their political clout to influence public policy on social and environmental issues – often in a negative direction. This book seeks to create a new norm for responsible political behavior by corporations. It brings together leading scholars of corporate political responsibility with leading organizations that have been working to support companies in adopting more responsible political practices. The contributors present new evidence on what motivates firms to become more responsible and how markets view corporate "dark money" spending. They also explain how activists have pressed companies to play a more responsible role in politics. With a particular focus on climate change and the important role of corporate lobbying in supporting or blocking climate policy, this volume leads the way forward for researchers, activists, and citizens who seek a future in which corporate political influence is transparent, accountable, and responsible.

THOMAS P. LYON holds the Dow Chair of Sustainable Science, Technology and Commerce at the University of Michigan, Ann Arbor, with appointments in the Ross School of Business and the School for Environment and Sustainability. He is a leader in the field of corporate sustainability, and coined the phrase "corporate political responsibility" (CPR) in an award-winning article. Under his leadership, the University of Michigan's Erb Institute is bringing CPR into the world of business practice.

"Corporations not only need to follow the 'rules of the game', they need to act responsibly and transparently in their efforts to shape the rules of the game through corporate political actions. This book points the way toward enlisting business leaders themselves in the cause of corporate political responsibility."

Ed Dolan, Senior Fellow, Niskanen Center

"This collection tackles one of the central problems of our time: namely whether, given that a significant number of corporations are already vigorously engaged political actors, firms should be required to be responsible citizens and – if so – can they be made so? Carefully researched, thoughtfully presented and eminently practical, this is a masterful introduction to a critically important subject."

Rebecca Henderson, Natty and John McArthur
University Professor, Harvard University.

"This book is the first of its kind on one of the most critical topics of our day: the billions of dollars in so-called 'dark money' that US companies pour into political coffers and how to create much needed transparency and accountability around these massive corporate expenditures. Lyon has gathered contributions from a broad array of experts in the field (himself included) and offers thoughtful solutions in the face of the ongoing failure of politicians and regulators to step up to this challenge. I highly recommend this book to both corporate executives and those who invest in their firms."

Allison Herren Lee, Former Acting Chair, Securities
and Exchange Commission

"The great challenges of the modern era – from affordable health care, to climate change and functional democracy – are inextricably tied to profit. That makes the question at the heart of this book – the proper role of business in society – the essential stuff of our time. I can think of no better guide than Tom Lyon, one of our leading thinkers on the topic."

Auden Schendler, Senior Vice President of Sustainability at Aspen Skiing
Company and author of Getting Green Done: Hard Truths
from the Front Lines of the Sustainability Revolution.

"As a former U.S. Congresswoman, who served on perhaps the first Campaign Finance Reform Task Force, I assure you our democracy would be enhanced if corporate campaign contributions ended and companies assumed 'political responsibility'. I have long felt that the G of ESG (Environment, Social & Governance) needed to incorporate measures of political responsibility in how corporations govern themselves. Tom Lyon and his co-authors clarify the criticality of doing so, especially at this moment in time."

Claudine Schneider, Former Congresswoman (R-R.I.)

"In a world that is overheating dangerously fast, it's no longer enough for companies to simply reduce their own social and environmental impacts. The systemic changes we need require companies to step up and use their political clout not for narrow self-interest, but to advocate for the policies that drive innovative solutions to our biggest challenges. This is the first book on this critical topic, and it brings together leading scholarly voices with accounts from the front lines by leading practitioners. This is essential reading for understanding the challenges companies will face in the decade ahead."

Andrew Winston, Sustainability strategist and best-selling
author of Net Positive and Green to Gold

Corporate Political Responsibility

Edited by

THOMAS P. LYON
University of Michigan

CAMBRIDGE
UNIVERSITY PRESS

CAMBRIDGE
UNIVERSITY PRESS

Shaftesbury Road, Cambridge CB2 8EA, United Kingdom

One Liberty Plaza, 20th Floor, New York, NY 10006, USA

477 Williamstown Road, Port Melbourne, VIC 3207, Australia

314–321, 3rd Floor, Plot 3, Splendor Forum, Jasola District Centre, New Delhi – 110025, India

103 Penang Road, #05–06/07, Visioncrest Commercial, Singapore 238467

Cambridge University Press is part of Cambridge University Press & Assessment, a department of the University of Cambridge.

We share the University's mission to contribute to society through the pursuit of education, learning and research at the highest international levels of excellence.

www.cambridge.org
Information on this title: www.cambridge.org/9781009420839

DOI: 10.1017/9781009420815

© Cambridge University Press & Assessment 2023

First published 2023

A catalogue record for this publication is available from the British Library

Library of Congress Cataloging-in-Publication Data
Names: Lyon, Thomas Peyton, 1959– editor.
Title: Corporate political responsibility / edited by Thomas Peyton Lyon.
Description: 1 Edition. | New York, NY : Cambridge University Press, 2023. | Includes bibliographical references and index.
Identifiers: LCCN 2023016407 (print) | LCCN 2023016408 (ebook) | ISBN 9781009420839 (hardback) | ISBN 9781009420815 (ebook)
Subjects: LCSH: Social responsibility of business. | Corporations – Political activity. | Business ethics.
Classification: LCC HD60 .C6387 2023 (print) | LCC HD60 (ebook) | DDC 658.4/08–dc23/eng/20230605
LC record available at https://lccn.loc.gov/2023016407
LC ebook record available at https://lccn.loc.gov/2023016408

ISBN 978-1-009-42083-9 Hardback
ISBN 978-1-009-42084-6 Paperback

Contents

Figures

Tables

Contributors

SAMANTHA DARNELL, University of Pennsylvania

MAGALI A. DELMAS, UCLA Institute of the Environment and Sustainability

ELIZABETH A. DOTY, Corporate Political Responsibility Taskforce, the Erb Institute, University of Michigan

ALVISE FAVOTTO, Adam Smith Business School, University of Glasgow

BRUCE F. FREED, Center for Political Accountability

HENRY L. FRIEDMAN, UCLA Anderson School of Management

YAMIKA KETU, Ceres

KELLY KOLLMAN, University of Glasgow

WILLIAM S. LAUFER, Wharton School of the University of Pennsylvania

THOMAS P. LYON, University of Michigan

WILLIAM MANDELKORN, University of Michigan

MARY-HUNTER MCDONNELL, Wharton School of the University of Pennsylvania

FRASER MCMILLAN, University of Glasgow

STEVEN ROTHSTEIN, Ceres

KARL J. SANDSTROM, Perkins Coie LLP

ANDREAS GEORG SCHERER, University of Zurich

CHRISTIAN VOEGTLIN, ZHAW School of Management and Law

DAVID VOGEL, University of California, Berkeley

EDWARD T. WALKER, University of California, Los Angeles

TIMOTHY WERNER, McCombs School of Business, University of Texas at Austin

Preface

This book is the culmination of an unexpected turn of intellectual events. Around 2014, I found myself having a series of conversations with other corporate sustainability leaders that all ended up with the same conclusion: businesses had largely exhausted the opportunities for "win/win" solutions that reduce environmental damages at the same time that they increase profits. The only way to unlock further improvement was through systemic change – changing the rules of the game rather than seeking incremental change within the existing rules.

But what role could companies play in that process? Could they actually lead systemic change for sustainability? The only example I could think of was "DuPont and Freon Products," the 1980s tale of a company that had an R&D lead in alternatives to ozone-depleting chlorofluorocarbons (CFCs) and persuaded regulators to accelerate the transition away from CFCs. But were there others? With the generous support of the Borchard Foundation, I worked with long-time colleagues Magali Delmas and John Maxwell to organize a retreat at the Château de la Bretesche to explore the role of the corporation in sustainability transitions. We convened ten additional scholars from the Alliance for Research on Corporate Sustainability (ARCS) and spent several intense days sifting through the evidence for a corporate leadership role in systemic change. At the end of the event, we left a bit disappointed – we had found little evidence that corporations lead systemic change. But we had found copious evidence that firms often block systemic change through their political clout. This was a far cry from where we had hoped to end up.

Flying home from the Château, I banged out a 2-page "Bretesche Manifesto" (as David Vogel later christened it) about the importance of Corporate Political Responsibility as a complement to Corporate Social Responsibility. Magali and John suggested we flesh out the argument and submit it to a journal, which we did with the help of all 13 members of the group. The resulting paper "CSR Needs CPR: Corporate Sustainability and Politics," went on to be selected as the best paper of 2018 in *California Management Review*. It argued that stakeholders concerned with sustainability should pay at least as much attention to what companies do politically as to what they do in their own supply chains. We aimed to raise the bar for what is considered responsible corporate political action by recognizing that it is in the long-term self-interest of the business sector to support healthy market rules of the game, a sustainable planet, and a functioning democracy. And we did so under the banner of a phrase – CPR – that seemed to resonate for most people.

A slogan does not make a movement, however. More work was required to flesh out what precisely were the political responsibilities of business, so I reached out to some of the best scholars working in this space to enlist their help exploring various dimensions of transparency, accountability, and responsibility – the three cornerstones of CPR. The result is this volume. I hope it serves to advance and deepen the discussion of CPR, an idea that seems more and more necessary every day.

As the chapters in this volume were taking shape, I received an email out of the blue from Elizabeth Doty, a Harvard Business School graduate and private consultant who had read "CSR Needs CPR" and believed it was possible to create a taskforce that would bring CPR into the public dialogue. Two conversations later, I brought Elizabeth into the Erb Institute at the University of Michigan (of which I am the Faculty Director) as the inaugural Director of our CPR Taskforce (CPRT). Our goal was twofold: to help companies deal with the rising tide of political challenges they faced in a polarized world and to create a new norm of responsible behavior that would percolate throughout the private sector. Elizabeth's chapter of this volume describes our initial steps along this journey to create a social movement for CPR within the business sector itself. More information on the CPRT's accomplishments since that time can be found at https://erb.umich .edu/partner-with-erb/corporate-political-responsibility-taskforce/

An edited volume like this would not have been possible without the support of many individuals. First and foremost, I thank the authors who contributed their thoughtful insights to the various chapters of the book. They have been a delight to work with. Particular thanks are due to Magali Delmas and David Vogel, who helped to carry the Bretesche vision into this new volume. I also want to acknowledge the support of Wharton's Eric Orts and Bill Laufer, who helped connect me with the Zicklin Center at Wharton and the Center for Political Accountability in DC. Bruce Freed at the Center for Political Accountability has been an ongoing inspiration for his high-impact leadership in making transparency around campaign spending a new norm in America. Steve Rothstein and Yamika Ketu at Ceres were generous in sharing their experience helping companies to align their climate advocacy with their other climate commitments. Erb Managing Director Terry Nelidov threw his support behind the idea of the CPRT and has been instrumental in making Erb a powerful incubator of this new idea. And Erb Institute students Adam Kerlin, Isha Goel, and Meg Cleary provided invaluable research and administrative support. Finally, I thank Cambridge University Press editor Valerie Appleby for her interest in and support of this project. Thanks to you all for helping to birth the new norm of CPR.

Foundations of Corporate Political Responsibility: Metrics for Disclosure and Good Governance

1 | The Meaning of Corporate Political Responsibility

THOMAS P. LYON

To America's watch-me-woke-it-up CEOs I say: When the time comes that you need help with a tax break or a regulatory change, I hope the Democrats take your calls, because we may not. Starting now, we won't take your money either.

Senator Ted Cruz (R-TX)[1]

This may be the most openly corrupt thing any Senator has said. It's the part everyone knows: these crooks sell access. Others have the sense not to admit it. This is why our republic is broken. Immoral politicians selling power we've entrusted to them like it's theirs to sell.

Walter Shaub, Former Director, Office of Government Ethics[2]

1.1 Introduction

It is commonly said that business is a "game" and that the role of a "player" (business firm) is to "win" (maximize profits) subject to playing by the "rules of the game" (whatever is legal). The implicit idea is that business and politics are separate realms, the first designed to serve private interests through the provision of goods and services, and the second to serve public interests through the provision of national security, a functioning set of legal and political institutions, efficient rules for market competition, and a healthy natural environment. Yet as the abovementioned epigraphs suggest, business and politics are far from separate; they are deeply intertwined through flows of money and information, and business often plays a key role in setting the rules of the game it plays.

---

[1] https://twitter.com/tedcruz/status/1388111012008706057?lang=en
[2] Ted Cruz's warning to "woke CEOs" blasted by former government ethics boss, The Independent, May 3, 2021. www.independent.co.uk/news/world/americas/us-politics/ted-cruz-woke-ceo-republican-b1841356.html

In theory, if the public sector sets appropriate rules, then aggressive pursuit of self-interest by the private sector produces socially beneficial outcomes, as Adam Smith (1776) argued two centuries ago, Kenneth Arrow and Gerard Debreu (1954) proved mathematically seventy years ago, and Milton Friedman (1970) preached in the *New York Times Magazine* fifty years ago. Yet despite a constant flow of rhetoric about the wonders of the "free market," Americans increasingly question whether their system of capitalism is delivering the goods. They see average Americans struggling to get by, while the media debate when the world's richest man, Jeff Bezos, will become the world's first trillionaire (Molina, 2020). They see government providing tax cuts to corporations and the rich and seeming impotent to rein in the market power of technology titans like Amazon, Apple, Facebook (now Meta), Google (now Alphabet), and Twitter. They are convinced the system is rigged against them, and that money buys favors in Washington, DC.

In the face of all this, it is not surprising that there is a growing movement to demand more accountability from business about its role in politics, that is, to demand corporate political responsibility (CPR) as a key complement to corporate social responsibility (CSR) (Lyon et al., 2018). More and more companies face proxy votes on disclosing their political spending. Institutional investors with concerns about environmental, social, and governance (ESG) issues are demanding more information about corporate spending on politics, and what it accomplishes. Activist groups increasingly call for companies to put their professed "purpose" into action by aligning their political activity with their mission, vision, and values. Environmentally conscious consumers want to know whether the companies they patronize for their "net zero" commitments secretly lobby against regulations to address climate change. As a recent article put it: "Ready or not, the era of corporate political responsibility is upon us" (Lyon, 2021).

In common parlance, the word "responsibility" has two very different meanings. The first reflects causality, that is, the extent to which one thing causes another. The second reflects character, that is, the extent to which an individual or organization is mature and wise in its actions. The two meanings are related, in the sense that a responsible adult takes into account the impacts of his or her actions on others. In legal usage, a "responsible adult" is a guardian of a minor, who is expected to act on behalf of the well-being of the minor. More generally, a responsible adult grants others some degree of moral weight in decisions that may involve personal gains at the expense of costs imposed on others.

Both meanings of responsibility are relevant for CPR. If corporations have no influence on political outcomes, they can hardly be held responsible for them. But if corporations have no influence on politics, why do they spend billions of dollars each year on campaign contributions and lobbying? Thus, the second meaning is of primary interest here. What would it mean for corporations to be responsible participants in the political process? Is it appropriate for them to lobby for policies that would increase their profits at the expense of the broader public?

This chapter offers an initial exploration of the meaning of CPR, from both perspectives. It seeks to open rather than to settle a profound conversation about the appropriate role of business in our modern political system and about the appropriate form of capitalism itself. It begins by defining a set of key terms, and then turns to the first definition of responsibility, briefly surveying the evidence of corporate influence on government policy. It pivots to the second definition of responsibility, highlighting three key pillars that are essential if business is to fulfill its role as a "responsible adult" in the political realm: transparency, accountability, and responsibility. Finally, it provides an overview of the remainder of the volume.

1.2 Defining Key Terms

Although definitions seldom make for riveting reading, it is important to define some key terms before proceeding.

Corporate political activity (CPA) includes any attempts by a company to influence the political process. When ordinary people think of corporate political engagement, they often use the term "lobbying" as a blanket word to capture any attempts to influence government. That usage is far too broad, however, and it is necessary to make additional distinctions about influence activities. CPA encompasses a wide range of influence tactics, as shown in Figure 1.1.

Political spending is composed of a variety of different types of financial contributions to political campaigns and independent expenditures, or "outside spending," all meant to influence the electoral process. As outlined by OpenSecrets.org, these can include, but are

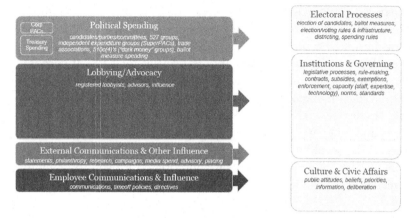

Figure 1.1 Forms of political influence

not limited to, contributions to political action committees (PACs) and so-called Super PACs, different types of political committees that raise and spend money to support or defeat candidates or legislation. Social welfare organizations (501(c)(4)s), which can engage in political action as long as that is not their "primary" activity, labor and agricultural organizations (501(c)(5)s), who generally spend some, but not all, of their money on political activities, and business leagues (501(c)(6)s), like the US Chamber of Commerce, which, like social welfare organizations, may not make political action their "primary" activity, are all active in the political arena, and are often referred to as "dark money groups" for their lack of donor disclosure requirements. Their political activity ramped up after the *Citizens United v. Federal Election Commission* ruling in 2010, which held that the use of independent expenditures by corporations, like money spent from corporate treasuries for electioneering communications, is protected speech. Figure 1.2 shows that outside spending has grown sharply since the Supreme Court's *Citizens United* decision in 2010, from about $500 million in the 2010 election cycle to about $3.3 billion in the 2020 election cycle, nearly a factor of 7. The vast bulk of this spending is done by "Super PACs" organized under section 527 of the tax code. These organizations are required to disclose their spending and their donors. However, the figure underemphasizes the role of 501(c)(4) "social welfare" organizations and 501(c)(6) trade associations, both of which can raise unlimited amounts of cash anonymously, but have

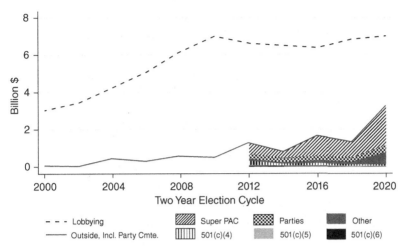

Figure 1.2 Lobbying expenditures and outside spending by election cycle
Notes: Only includes outside spending reported to FEC. 501(c)(4): social
welfare; 501(c)(5): unions; 501(c)(6): trade associations. Other includes
"corporations, individual people, other groups, etc."
Source: OpenSecrets.org.

to ensure their overtly political activities are not seen as their "primary" activity in order to keep their tax-free status. Thus, they are often used as a way to raise "dark money" which they then give to a 527 Super PAC to do the actual spending, without triggering disclosure requirements. Companies may also spend unlimited amounts to influence the outcomes of ballot measures.

The other form of CPA included in Figure 1.2 is lobbying expenditures, which dwarf campaign spending. These funds are spent on either a firm's internal lobbyists or a third-party lobbying firm, both of whose main goals are the provision of information to government officials. As lobbyists attempt to convey the likely effects of proposed policies and to shape these policies to benefit their clients, they are required to submit to some basic disclosure requirements. These mandated disclosures show that lobbying expenditures have increased dramatically since the early 2000s, with business interests dominating this arena (Drutman, 2015). Moreover, the figures probably greatly underestimate true spending on lobbying, as they do not include the "shadow lobbying" industry, composed of individuals who perform essentially the same tasks as lobbyists, but categorize themselves as "advisors" and escape mandatory lobbying disclosure rules; although data are scarce, it is estimated that the "shadow lobbying" business may be as large as the disclosed lobbying business (Thomas and LaPira, 2017).

Meanwhile, external communications and other outreach can include spending on "informational" campaigns to shape public opinion, such as the organized doubt creation orchestrated by members of the oil industry (Oreskes and Conway, 2011) or "grassroots" lobbying groups (astroturf lobbying) that appear to be spontaneous uprisings of individuals, but are actually funded and directed covertly by business groups (Lyon and Maxwell, 2004; Walker, 2014). Support for think tanks, some of which are simply partisan advocates (Chiroleu-Assouline and Lyon, 2020) and philanthropic giving, which may be deployed strategically by companies in need of political support (Bertrand et al., 2020), serve as two other methods of influence, while ballot initiatives, which can be influenced by most of the above-mentioned methods, have their own distinct dynamics of influence.

Lastly, employee communications and influence that encourages employees to be politically active is yet another way for corporations to influence the political process. Some of these efforts may be politically neutral "get out the vote" messages, but after *Citizens United*, there is no federal protection for workers against employer pressure to fund or vote for particular candidates or take public positions viewed as beneficial to the company.

Although public disclosure policies vary across the different types of CPA, as discussed in more detail by Lyon and Mandelkorn (2023), in general, these policies are so lax that it is impossible to get an accurate assessment of total spending on CPA. Nevertheless, publicly disclosed data provide a lower bound on spending on political influence.

With caveats regarding the limitations of available data, it is clear that the role of money in US elections continues to grow. As shown in Figure 1.3, the total cost of federal elections (i.e., spending by candidates' campaigns, political parties, and independent interest groups) grew steadily from the 2000 election cycle through the 2016 election cycle, from about $3 billion to $6 billion, and then jumped sharply upward to $14 billion during the 2020 election cycle. In general, total spending on congressional races exceeds that for presidential races. Figure 1.3 also shows that lobbying spending has grown apace with electoral spending, from about $3 billion total across 1999 and 2000

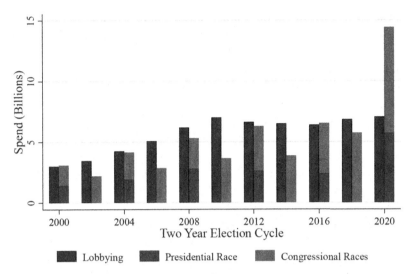

Figure 1.3 Lobbying and election spending
Source: OpenSecrets.org.

to about $7.5 billion total across 2009 and 2010, and stayed around $7 billion per two-year election cycle through 2020.

Corporate social responsibility means corporate efforts that go beyond compliance with legal requirements on either the environmental or social dimensions of performance. This could include corporate commitments to reduce greenhouse emissions or achieve "net zero" carbon emissions by a certain date, initiatives to create opportunity for historically underrepresented minorities, or policies to support human rights in developing countries.

CPR means transparency and accountability of corporate lobbying and other political influence, as well as a commitment to advocate publicly for policies that sustain the systems upon which markets, society, and life itself depend. The latter would include advocating for the elimination of market failures and special-interest subsidies, which undermine the performance of the capitalist system, and for the maintenance of the Earth's climate, a functioning representative political system, and planetary biodiversity.

Political corporate social responsibility (PCSR) holds that firms have a responsibility to fill in gaps in global regulatory governance where the nation-state has failed to do so and to make "a more intensive

engagement in transnational processes of policy making and the creation of global governance institutions" (Scherer and Palazzo, 2011,
p. 910). Thus, firms may provide public health benefits, address AIDS,
and promote societal peace and stability. PCSR emphasizes Habermas's
concept of "deliberative democracy," which explores the formation and
"transformation of preferences" through dialogue and analyzes the conditions under which deliberation "will lead to more informed and rational results, will increase the acceptability of the decisions, will broaden
the horizon of the decision maker, will promote mutual respect, and
will make it easier to correct wrong decisions that have been made in
the past" (Scherer and Palazzo, 2007, p. 1107). The authors distinguish
PCSR from mere corporate responses to stakeholder pressure, arguing
that PCSR calls for moral leadership from companies.

Relative to CPR, PCSR is a broader and more encompassing concept,
and includes corporate participation in both private and public politics.
CPR, in contrast, focuses on corporate engagement in public politics. An
example that illustrates the difference is the Forest Stewardship Council
(FSC), which puts forward voluntary standards for forest management that many companies have adopted. Companies also participate
in the governance of the FSC and the articulation of the standards it
promotes. Scherer and Palazzo (2007) use this as an example of PCSR,
but it would not be an example of CPR because it does not involve
the public political process. Scherer and Palazzo (2007) laud corporate
engagement with FSC as "a corporate move into the political processes
of public policy making" (Scherer and Palazzo, 2007, p. 1110), but we
do not consider FSC to be a public policy process at all because there
are no governments involved. Moreover, simply engaging with a voluntary standards organization provides no assurance that a firm is actually
enhancing sustainability outcomes. Instead, it may simply be driving
standards down, which would not count as CPR, in my view.

Corporate citizenship (CC) means "the role of the corporation in
administering citizenship rights for individuals" (Matten and Crane,
2005, p. 173). They elaborate:

With regard to social rights, the corporation basically either supplies or does
not supply individuals with social services and, hence, administers rights
by taking on a providing role. In the case of civil rights, the corporation
either capacitates or constrains citizens' civil rights and, so, can be viewed
as administrating through more of an enabling role. Finally, in the realm
of political rights, the corporation is essentially an additional conduit for

the exercise of individuals' political rights; hence, the corporation primarily assumes administration through a channeling role. (p. 174)

This conception is quite different from the conception of CPR as describing the way in which a corporation exercises its own rights within the political system.

1.3 Is Corporate Political Activity Responsible for Government Outcomes?

In practice, the worlds of business and politics are not neatly separated, despite appeals for business to stay out of politics altogether (Reich, 1998). There is a widespread perception that the US political system has been corrupted by money and corporate influence, so that the "players" are setting the rules, to the detriment of the rest of society. Politicians from across the political spectrum decry the capture of our government by the wealthy. Independent Bernie Sanders says, "A few wealthy individuals and corporations have bought up our private sector and now they're buying up the government. Campaign finance reform is the most important issue facing us today, because it impacts all the others."[3] At the other end of the political and credibility spectrum, Republican Donald Trump also claims "the system is rigged," at least whenever he loses. And closer to the middle of the political spectrum, Democratic Senator Sheldon Whitehouse warns that "corporations of vast wealth and remorseless staying power have moved into our politics to seize for themselves advantages that can be seized only by control over government."[4]

Ordinary Americans largely agree with these assessments. Even in 2009, before the *Citizens United v. FEC* ruling removed constraints on corporate political spending, 80 percent of Americans agreed with the following statement: "I am worried that large political contributions will prevent Congress from tackling the important issues facing America today, like the economic crisis, rising energy costs, reforming health care, and global warming." In the first presidential contest after the *Citizens United* decision, 84 percent of Americans agreed that corporate political spending drowns out the voices of average Americans, and 83 percent believed that corporations and corporate

[3] "Better World Quotes – Bernie Sanders on Campaign Finance Reform" n.d.
[4] "Corporate Capture Threatens Democratic Government" n.d.

CEOs have too much political power and influence. This aligns with more recent research showing that 84 percent of people think government is benefiting special interests, and 83 percent think government is benefiting big corporations and the wealthy.[5]

Moving beyond public opinion, numerous books suggest that American government has been captured by business, from Whitehouse's own *Captured: The Corporate Infiltration of American Democracy* to Lee Drutman's *The Business of America Is Lobbying* to Alyssa Katz's *The Influence Machine: The US Chamber of Commerce and the Corporate Capture of American Life*. All of these books suggest that corporate influence has successfully raised profits by cutting taxes on business, weakening antitrust enforcement, allowing the outsourcing of American jobs to low-wage countries, undermining environmental law, and limiting corporate tort liability for social harms such as defective products, lung cancer from tobacco use, and climate change.

Economic data indeed document that corporate market power and the concentration of wealth have been rising: market concentration, price/cost markups, profits, and capital's share of income relative to labor have all risen sharply over the past four decades. In the United States, aggregate price markups over marginal cost rose from 21 percent in 1980 to 61 percent in 2019, while the average profit rate rose from 1 to 8 percent. This is consistent with the decline in labor's share of income from around 62 percent in 1980 to 56 percent in 2019 (DeLoecker et al., 2020). The top 10 percent of Americans captured 33 percent of net income (excluding capital gains) in 1980 but 41 percent by 1998, while the top 1 percent saw their share rise from 8 percent to 14 percent (Piketty and Saez, 2003). Wealth is even more highly concentrated: the top 10 percent held 77 percent of the wealth in the United States in 2018, up from about 65 percent in 1980. At the other extreme, the average real disposable cash income of the bottom 50 percent in the United States rose only slightly from $16,000 in 1980 to $18,600 in 2016 (Saez and Zucman, 2020).

But is this growing concentration of wealth and profits the result of CPA, or is it the "natural" outcome of broader trends such as globalization and technological change? This is the $64 million question, but it is very difficult to answer authoritatively, in part because so much of CPA is intentionally hidden from the public. Bessen (2016)

---

[5] "Corporate Capture Threatens Democratic Government" n.d.

attempts to address the question directly and concludes that both corporate investment in intangibles and CPA have played a role in rising profits, but since 2000 political action has been the more important factor; in addition, he finds that the relatively few major extensions of regulation have raised corporate profits significantly. At the same time, the highly publicized work of Princeton political scientists Gilens and Page (2014) finds that "economic elites and organized groups representing business interests have substantial independent impacts on U.S. government policy, while average citizens and mass-based interest groups have little or no independent influence." This is consistent with polling data showing that many policies supported by a wide majority of Americans die in committee. According to recent polling by Data for Progress and Civis Analytics, the majority of Americans support expanded paid family leave policies, corruption reforms to rein in conflicts of interest among lawmakers, and the government manufacture of out-of-patent generic drugs, all of which have been introduced in recent bills that have failed to pass.[6] Lawrence Lessig (2015) argues that the role of money in politics is to edit public choices by ensuring that the only candidates who can afford to compete for election are those acceptable to moneyed interests.

Although it is conventional wisdom among political scientists that money buys access to politicians, recent research advances have documented the effect clearly: randomized field experiments demonstrate that money does indeed buy access to politicians (Kalla and Broockman, 2016). As if to prove this point, Senator Ted Cruz (R-TX) wrote a sneeringly self-righteous opinion piece in the *Wall Street Journal* that sternly told companies not to object to Republican-sponsored bills to protect "election integrity" in the wake of Trump's false claims that the 2020 election was "stolen" (Cruz, 2021). For those with short attention spans, he also tweeted the quote that introduces this chapter.

None of the foregoing proves conclusively and scientifically that corporate capture of the political process is the root cause of growing market concentration, rising economic inequality, and the inability of ordinary people to influence their own government. In fact, some observers argue that business has been held hostage by greedy career politicians whose notion of the public interest is limited to keeping themselves in power (Crow and Shireman, 2020). A related view is

---

[6] "The New Progressive Agenda Project" n.d.

that the fundamental problem in US politics is the lack of competition in the US electoral system, with only two viable parties to choose from (Drutman, 2020; Gehl and Porter, 2020). Since the Supreme Court unleashed unlimited amounts of anonymous political spending in 2010, the parties have had an insatiable demand for cash to fund vicious and uninformative attack ads that can be used to destroy the other side. And Corporate America makes an easy mark for politicians like Cruz who openly admit that their votes are for sale.

If Big Business has been corrupted by immoral politicians, though, it seems to have gone to the Dark Side willingly. Tom Donohue, former president of the US Chamber of Commerce, bragged in 2010 about what was reported as the Chamber's "hard-hitting $75 million ad campaign to elect a Republican House" and he promised to spend "closer to a hundred million" on the 2012 elections (Katz, 2015, p. 177). Unfortunately, it is impossible to conduct the requisite empirical research to disentangle the complex web of political influence without data on the role of business in the political sphere – and Congress intentionally prevents those data from being made public.[7]

1.4 The CPR Movement

In light of the dysfunctional state of US politics, the strong circumstantial evidence of corporate capture of the policy process, and the growing role of "dark money" in American politics, it is small wonder that a movement has emerged to hold companies accountable for their role in the political process. Companies are accustomed to stakeholder demands for CSR, and this new movement can be seen as an extension reflecting the awareness that "CSR Needs CPR," as one recent article puts it (Lyon et al., 2018).

In some issue areas, such as climate change, the extension of CSR into CPR is a natural outgrowth. Climate activists have been increasingly frustrated since the failure of the Lieberman-Warner bill to pass in 2009. They have watched with disgust as companies such as Exxon funded doubt-mongering strategies through "think tanks" such as the George C. Marshall Institute and the Competitive Enterprise Institute

---

[7] In a recent example, Congress has explicitly blocked the IRS from attempting to determine whether "social welfare organizations" make politics their "primary" activity, which means that strictly partisan political 501c4s can receive taxpayer subsidies with no fear of having their tax-free status revoked (Miller, n.d.).

(Oreskes and Conway, 2011), the latter of which once produced a gauzy TV ad with the tag line: "Carbon dioxide: they call it pollution, we call it life." They have watched with anger as the Chamber of Commerce took not a "lowest common denominator" approach to climate lobbying, but simply a "lowest possible" approach. In the spring of 2008, as Lieberman-Warner was in committee,

[T]he Chamber sponsored an apocalyptic TV and Internet ad campaign aimed at the senators who would decide. On the screen of one ad, a man bundled in a scarf and coat prepared his morning eggs in a pan held over burning candles, before he joined a pack of commuters jogging down the highway to work. "Climate legislation being considered by Congress could make it too expensive to heat our homes, power our lives and drive our cars," warned the voice of God in the ad. "Is this really how Americans want to live? Washington politicians should not demand what technology cannot deliver. Urge your senator to vote no on the Lieberman-Warner climate bill." (Katz, 2015, p. 116)

And activists watched with despair from the sidelines as coal executive Robert Murray donated $300,000 to Donald Trump's inauguration shortly before he sent Trump his "Action Plan" for the new Administration, and sat back and saw much of it get enacted (Friedman, 2018). It is no wonder climate activists are focusing on how fossil fuel companies block climate policy.

In other issue areas, however, the calls for CPR are more of a surprise. The unprecedented January 6, 2021, assault on Congress led many companies to "pause" their funding of legislators who refused to certify the legitimacy of the 2020 presidential election. And the slew of voter registration bills moving through state legislatures in the wake of the 2020 election have also drawn rebukes from many corporate leaders who accept the claims of the Black community that the bills will disproportionately make it harder for Black Americans to vote. Both of these issues came into existence solely due to the losing candidate's repeated falsehoods that the election was "stolen" by massive amounts of voting fraud. Only corporate executives with a keen sense of history and awareness of the parallels between the fire in the Reichstag in February 27, 1933, and the assault on Congress would have had any hope of predicting the emergence of these new CPR issues.[8]

---

[8] Chairman of the Joint Chiefs of Staff Mark Milley feared that the January 6 assault would be America's Reichstag moment, a reference to the day in 1933

These calls for CPR have arisen more frequently, not only in public, but in shareholder meetings as well. According to recent reporting by the *New York Times*, in 2019 there were fifty-one political spending proposals at S&P 500 companies, which received an average of 29 percent support and zero proposals passed (Livni, 2021). In 2020, six of the fifty-five political spending proposals at S&P 500 companies 2020 passed, with average support rising to 35 percent. As of June 2021, of the thirty resolutions introduced that year, five of the seven proposals put up for a vote had passed. In the face of relatively few political spending reporting guidelines as mandated by law, more successful shareholder political spending resolutions could lead to much needed transparency surrounding corporate political activities.

1.5 The Three Levels of CPR

The concept of CPR was articulated in an article by Lyon et al. (2018). Transparency, accountability, and responsibility comprise the three tiers of CPR, as illustrated in Figure 1.4.

Transparency covers whether or not a firm discloses their political activities to the relevant parties. While some elements of CPA, like lobbying expenditures, must be disclosed legally, others forms, like contributions to 501(c)(4) "social welfare organizations" and 501(c)(6) trade associations, need not be disclosed at all. Firms can voluntarily report these activities, with more firms recently choosing to release political engagement reports, as discussed in more depth by Lyon and Mandelkorn (2023), but production of these reports is currently limited and there are no accepted norms of best practice yet. Some organizations like Vigeo Eiris and Influence Map are helping to lead a charge toward more widespread, careful analysis of CPA, but much work remains to be done with regard to measuring transparency.

Accountability focuses on whether firms' political activities are "aligned with [their] values, purpose and commitments to all stakeholders." Like the transparency tier below, it is difficult to measure and evaluate whether a firm is being "accountable." Not only is data needed to accurately measure a firm's CPA, but additional data and

---

when arsonists (whom some historians believe to have been associates of Hitler) set fire to the German parliament, which Hitler then used as a pretext to impose emergency rule (Thiebault, 2021).

Figure 1.4 The three tiers of corporate political responsibility

analysis is needed to measure the congruence between a firm's CPA and its stated values. Organizations like CPA-Zicklin are working hard to improve accountability for the political spending elements of CPA, developing a "Model Code" to help guide corporate political expenditures and advocacy and ensure that firms do not exercise their political clout at the expense of shareholders, employees, or other stakeholders. This work represents an important advance, yet further efforts are required to ensure full accountability across the private sector, as described in more detail in Lyon and Mandelkorn (2023).

Lastly, responsibility centers on the firm's role in the public sphere, especially on whether a firm's political activities "support the systems on which markets, society and life depend." At first glance, it may seem that responsibility is too subjective an idea to be useful in practice. For example, customers who believe climate change is a Chinese hoax (as claimed by ex-president Trump[9]) or oil-industry employees whose jobs are at risk may think it irresponsible for a company to support

[9] "PolitiFact | Yes, Donald Trump did call climate change a Chinese hoax" n.d.

climate policy, while customers who see climate change as an existential threat to life on Earth (as claimed by the vast majority of climate scientists) may find it irresponsible not to support climate policy. But a facile "post-truth" position serves only the narrowly self-interested and the peddlers of falsehoods. A more thoughtful, and practical, perspective can be grounded in the market failures approach to business ethics (Heath, 2014). This approach begins from the observation that maximizing profits is justified when markets are competitive because doing so increases overall social welfare. However, when the conditions for perfect competition fail, and we observe market failures like market power, externalities, public goods, and asymmetric information, there is no guarantee that free markets, or profit-maximization, promote welfare. Hence profit-maximizing firms arguably have a responsibility to support the conditions that make markets competitive, and to eschew CPA that exacerbates market failures (Heath, 2014). Of course, it is impossible to assess whether a given company is undermining markets or practicing CPR without the first two pillars of transparency and accountability.

Much of the analysis in the rest of this book focuses on the first two tiers, transparency and accountability, both because they are necessary to assess the third tier and because the analysis of market failures and planetary systems requires deep and issue-specific work. However, in the case of climate change, there is already a rich literature on which to draw for assessing CPR, so the book includes an entire section devoted to the topic of responsibility in this particular context. The following section explains the plan of the volume in more detail.

1.6 Overview of the Rest of the Volume

The rest of the book is divided into four main sections, plus a final chapter on the implications for practice. Section I offers insights into the underpinnings of CPR, with an emphasis on the importance of transparency as the foundation stone. Freed, Laufer, and Sandstrom describe the creation and current activities of the Center for Political Accountability, a Washington, DC, nonprofit they helped launch that is the leader in the movement for greater transparency and accountability around corporate spending on electoral campaigns. Lyon and Mandelkorn position corporate election spending within the larger universe of corporate political activity (CPA), and show how holes in the current disclosure system make it impossible to answer many of the most important questions about the influence of business on politics.

Section II focuses on the foundation stone of transparency, providing the latest findings on the causes and consequences of corporate disclosure from two of the leading empirical researchers on CPA. Walker studies the drivers of disclosure, presenting early results of research funded by the National Science Foundation, while Werner studies how investors react to disclosure and what we can learn from their reactions.

Section III moves up the pyramid of CPR one level, turning to corporate accountability to stakeholders for CPA, with a focus on the links between CSR and CPR, especially around employees. Favotto, Kollman, and McMillan test whether firms with better reputations for CSR offer higher-quality information to legislators, using data from corporate testimony before the UK Parliament. Darnell and McDonnell test whether firms with better reputations for CSR elicit more employee contributions to the corporate Political Action Committee. Scherer and Voegtlin take a normative perspective, arguing that multinational companies should connect their Human Resources Management policies to their CSR, with the goal of being both good stewards of employee well-being and good enablers of employee political expression.

Section IV reaches the top tier of the CPR pyramid, tackling the issue of political responsibility in the context of climate change, one of the areas where irresponsible CPA has been the most glaring. Ketu and Rothstein present the perspective of Ceres, a nonprofit that (among other things) rates the world's 100 largest companies on whether their climate advocacy is responsible or not. Vogel relates the past quarter-century of corporate political engagement around climate change in the United States, showing that "business" is not a monolith and that fundamental principles of political science go a long way toward explaining corporate responsibility and irresponsibility in climate politics. Delmas and Friedman provide empirical evidence suggesting strongly that business firms lobby on both sides of the climate issue, and they shine a light on the gaps in disclosure that make it difficult to hold companies responsible for their political activity around climate policy.

The concluding chapter explores the opportunities and challenges of implementing CPR in practice. Doty draws upon the experience of the Corporate Political Responsibility Taskforce (CPR) at the University of

Michigan's Erb Institute, offering illuminating insights into why CPR is difficult for companies and why it can produce big payoffs if done right. A more detailed overview of the remaining chapters follows.

Section I Foundations of Corporate Political Responsibility: Metrics for Disclosure and Good Governance

Freed, Laufer, and Sandstrom focus on corporate political spending on elections (either through contributions to politicians or through spending on independent, direct political communications). They draw heavily on the experience of the nonprofit Center for Political Accountability (which the authors were instrumental in founding) and its use of "private ordering" (informal, non-state suasion and advocacy) to drive greater accountability around corporate electoral spending. The Center is generally viewed as the most effective organization promoting political accountability, so its story is central to understanding where CPR stands today. The Center's success is attributable in part to its consistent focus on electoral spending (as opposed to lobbying) and accountability to shareholders (as opposed to the full range of stakeholders affected by corporate political activity). Future efforts to encompass a broader range of corporate political activity and stakeholder impacts would do well to learn from the experience of the Center.

Lyon and Mandelkorn discuss the thorny issue of measuring CPR. They present an overview of the various forms of corporate political action (CPA), and the requirements in the United States for disclosure of each form. They organize the discussion around the metrics needed to assess the three levels of CPR: transparency (disclosing CPA), accountability (ensuring that firms are accountable to their stakeholders for CPA), and responsibility (corporate advocacy for public policies that are consistent with a company's stated mission, purpose and values, and that strengthen the systems on which markets, states, and life itself depend). They describe the efforts of existing organizations to evaluate CPR, expose information gaps where lax disclosure requirements make it impossible to evaluate CPR today, and suggest improvements needed in order to make it possible for stakeholders to assess whether or not CPA is responsible.

Section II Transparency: Causes and Consequences

Walker presents findings from a large-scale empirical study of the factors driving firms to disclose their political activity. He points out that public politics has largely failed to require thorough disclosure of CPA, and hence private politics has been the main driver of change, consistent with the argument of Freed, Laufer, and Sandstrom. He goes on to examine two key empirical questions: (1) which companies get targeted by shareholder activists seeking greater voluntary CPA disclosure and (2) how have those targeted companies responded? Among his findings are that, overall, companies are targeted by shareholders for CPA-related shareholder resolutions on the basis of their prior political activities, financial characteristics, their history of facing past shareholder resolutions, and other qualitative factors including their reputational challenges, history of engagement on ESG issues, and whether their CPA might appear to be misaligned with other value commitments. Companies, in turn, tend to be more likely to make reforms after facing CPA resolutions in prior years and also, particularly, if and when they become constituents of the S&P 500 Index, as membership in that Index causes a firm to draw considerably greater scrutiny.

Werner offers a set of empirical insights into how markets respond to corporations engaging in dark money expenditures. Studying covert CPA would seem to be an impossible challenge, but Werner is able to shed light on dark money by making use of accidental disclosures of corporate involvement with it. He shares findings from several different studies, and finds that investor responses to accidental disclosure of covert CPA are nuanced. The Supreme Court's decision in *Citizens United* did not produce abnormal financial returns for politically active firms, suggesting that investors did not think there was much value in opening the floodgates of corporate political spending. Accidental disclosure of corporate giving to the Republican Governors Association, a highly partisan group, raised share prices for corporate contributors. However, accidental disclosure of giving to the American Legislative Exchange Council (ALEC), whose bland name belies its hard-right activist agenda, caused share prices for corporate contributors to fall. Thus, the effects of corporate engagement with dark money groups seem to be contingent on a variety of factors that require further analysis. Werner holds out little hope that further strides toward CPR can be made through private politics. Instead, he argues that reform efforts should move beyond disclosure and instead focus on constitutional changes that will permit greater regulation of money in politics.

Section III Accountability: Linking Corporate Social Responsibility, Employee Relations, and Corporate Political Responsibility

Favotto, Kollman, and McMillan move beyond disclosure to provide valuable empirical insight into accountability and responsibility, and whether better CSR translates into better CPR. They find consistent differences in the quality of the testimony offered to parliament by high- and low-CSR companies. High-CSR companies were more willing to discuss state interventions into the market in their testimony, more likely to support state regulation and more likely to offer committee members sophisticated justifications for their policy stances than low-CSR companies. The high-CSR firms also tended to use a broader array of reasons for their policy stances and did not focus solely on market interests as low-CSR companies tended to do. Thus, high-CSR companies' lobbying efforts do appear to be more aligned with the goal of sustainability.

Darnell and McDonnell also explore the links between a company's CSR and its CPR. More specifically, they examine whether a better reputation for employee relations, or for CSR more broadly, is related to the level of employee contributions to the firm's corporate political action committee (PAC). They find that a firm's reputation for employee relations, but not its overall social reputation, is positively associated with employee support of a firm's PAC. Although these findings do not speak directly to whether a firm's CPA is responsible, they do illustrate a link between a firm's informal and formal nonmarket strategies and demonstrate a potential constraint on corporate political influence.

Scherer and Voegtlin delve further into the links between employee relations and CPR, by focusing on the human resource management (HRM) practices of multinational firms in a globalizing world. They propose that HRM should be extended to include a political agenda through two functions: (1) as a "steward" looking out for the wellbeing of the firm's work force, and (2) as an "enabler" making organizational members competent for helping others. This is consistent with the observation that employees are often the strongest stakeholder group calling for more CPR from their employer, and that employee support for CPR can legitimize and strengthen the firm's position in the political domain, as shown by Darnell and McDonnell. They also serve as a strong reminder that issues of CPR go beyond the climate crisis and include human and labor rights, and that a deliberative approach that pays close attention to corporate engagement in dialogue (as shown by Favotto et al.) can be a productive avenue for illuminating and possibly strengthening CPR.

Section IV Responsibility: Corporate Political Responsibility and Climate

Ketu and Rothstein share their experience working to elevate companies' policy engagement around climate. The authors are both part of Ceres, a nonprofit organization working with influential investors and companies to drive Responsible Policy Engagement on climate change. Recently Ceres produced a report rating the 100 biggest corporations on how well they align their political action with their CSR activities. Although most companies have a long way to go to become leaders in constructive climate policy, there is considerable heterogeneity within the S&P 100. The authors share the key elements they see as part of Responsible Policy Engagement, and suggest ways to accelerate the diffusion of these practices throughout the C-suites of the most influential companies.

Vogel focuses on climate lobbying, from a historical perspective that goes back to the Kyoto Protocol, includes the Waxman-Markey and Lieberman-Warner bills, the Obama administration's proposed Clean Power Plan, and the international Paris Agreement. He shows that "business" is not a monolithic block when it comes to climate policy. Vogel pays particular attention to the role of collective action, both through trade associations and a wide range of ad hoc climate coalitions. He reminds us that energy companies have strong, even existential, incentives to block climate policy, while the rest of the private sector generally has weak incentives to support it. This raises important questions about the depth of commitment expressed by the many companies that now speak out on behalf of climate policy, and about the limits of what can be accomplished through encouraging business climate advocacy.

Delmas and Friedman focus on corporate lobbying on climate change, which consumed over $2 billion between the years 2000 and 2016. Although such spending is largely perceived as a strategy by industry to oppose regulation, the authors show that there is a U-shaped relationship between greenhouse gas (GHG) emissions and lobbying expenditures, suggesting strongly that both dirty and clean firms are active in lobbying. Unfortunately, limitations on legal requirements for detailed disclosure make it impossible to clearly infer corporate positions on policies and fail to capture the full array of CPA. However, there are a number of initiatives aimed at increasing disclosure, coming from investors and asset managers, NGOs, public institutions such as the EU, nonprofits, and academics. The authors offer a series of potential improvements to mandatory disclosure of climate-related political activity, including consideration of content, timing, disclosure channels, users, potentially relevant US regulators, and the value of third parties in aggregating, interpreting, and disseminating information gleaned from disclosures.

Section V Implementing Corporate Political Responsibility: Opportunities and Challenges

Doty returns us to the practitioner perspective, drawing upon the experience of the Erb Institute's CPR Taskforce (CPRT). She suggests that the new emphasis on CPR heralds a larger conversation about the role of business in society, and argues that if such a conversation is to have legitimacy and lasting impact, it must understand and incorporate the perspectives of practitioners. Like Favotto et al. and Scherer and Voegtlin, Doty presents the principles of deliberative democracy as guidance for this larger conversation. She provides fascinating quotes from participants in Erb CPRT discussions, which shed new light on how businesses think about CPR. Company leaders find the concept of CPR intuitive but scary, and lament the lack of venues for discussing it without the bitter polarization that too often passes for discourse. This, of course, was precisely the rationale for forming the CPRT. Doty sees CPR as likely to find a home within the "G" of Environmental, Social and Governance (ESG) criteria for investors. She also suggests that firms may need to address governance issues around CPR before they are willing to undertake more disclosure. Finally, she offers a set of ideas for moving CPR into mainstream business practice, and using it as an opening for a renewal of the social contract. If CPR can perform these functions, it will truly be a transformative concept.

1.7 Conclusions

Today, growing numbers of people feel disenfranchised from the political process. In some countries, corporations and outside groups can spend unlimited amounts on elections, but many individuals find it increasingly difficult even to vote. They have seen tax cuts and financial bailouts enacted that benefit large corporations and wealthy individuals at their expense. Americans are convinced the system is rigged, and it is precisely these groups, large corporations and the ultra-wealthy, that they blame. They have seen mega-donors like Sheldon Adelson spend hundreds of millions of dollars every year to elect their preferred candidates, and trade associations like the US Chamber of Commerce spend billions of dollars lobbying to bend legislation to the liking of certain corporate members. In a world increasingly shaped by the wealthy few, many ordinary Americans are looking for ways to hold large corporations accountable for their political actions.

Americans, especially younger ones, care about the political positions taken by the companies from which they purchase and invest. They want the companies they patronize to support progressive climate policies, or cease giving to those who supported the January 6 insurrection. In short, they want firms to exhibit corporate political responsibility.

Unfortunately, as the following chapters document, the current level of disclosure mandated by law in the United States provides a woefully incomplete picture of corporate political activity, rendering it difficult to distinguish the responsible from the irresponsible. Nevertheless, while serious measurement issues remain, great research is being done in this area. The remainder of this volume serves to document some of this research, along with some of the improvements that could be made in CPA metrics to improve our understanding of CPA and CPR.

Even if we cannot answer all of our questions about CPA currently, the need for more firms to demonstrate CPR remains clear. We need enough transparency and disclosure concerning electoral spending and lobbying that one can monitor the scope of a firm's political influence activities. We need companies to have policies governing the lobbying and political contribution process, with specific officers and boards actively engaged and carefully overseeing their political influence activities. Finally, as some of the most powerful actors in politics, companies must take more responsibility for the health of the governmental systems in which they participate. Public demands are growing for companies to change their role in politics, with increased transparency of electoral spending and lobbying, accountability for corporate political activity within companies, and responsibility for the political system within which they operate serving as the three main levers through which firms can exhibit more CPR, and begin to effect positive change in the political process. This book is an attempt to sharpen academic and practitioner understanding of CPR, and support its emergence into the world of practice.

Appendix A

The CPA-Zicklin Model Code

1 Political spending shall reflect the company's interests, as an entity, and not those of its individual officers, directors, and agents.
2 In general, the company will follow a preferred policy of making its political contributions to a candidate directly.
3 No contribution will be given in anticipation of, in recognition of, or in return for an official act or anything that has appearance of a gratuity, bribe, trade or quid pro quo of any kind.
4 Employees will not be reimbursed directly or through compensation increases for personal political contributions or expenses.
5 The company will not pressure or coerce employees to make personal political expenditures.
6 All corporate political expenditures must receive prior written approval from the appropriate corporate officer.
7 The company will disclose publicly all direct contributions and expenditures with corporate funds on behalf of candidates, political parties, and political organizations.
8 The company will disclose dues and other payments made to trade associations and contributions to other tax-exempt organizations that are or that it anticipates will be used for political expenditures. The disclosures shall describe the specific political activities undertaken.
9 The board shall require a report from trade associations or other third-party groups receiving company money on how it is being used and the candidates whom the spending promotes.
10 The board of directors or an independent committee of the board shall receive regular reports, establish and supervise policies and procedures, and assess the risks and impacts related to the company's political spending.
11 The company shall review the positions of the candidates or organizations to which it contributes to determine whether those positions conflict with the company's core values and policies. This review should be considered by senior management and the full board of directors annually.
12 The board of directors shall, independent of this review, consider the broader societal and economic harm and risks posed by the company's political spending.

References

Abramoff, J. (2011). *Capitol Punishment: The Hard Truth about Washington Corruption from America's Most Notorious Lobbyist.* Chicago, IL: WND Books.

Arrow, K. J., & Debreu, G. (1954). Existence of an Equilibrium for a Competitive Economy. *Econometrica*, **22**, 265–90.

Bertrand, M., Bombardini, M., Fisman, R., & Trebbi, F. (2020). Tax-Exempt Lobbying: Corporate Philanthropy as a Tool for Political Influence. *American Economic Review*, **110**(7), 2065–102.

Bessen, J. E. (2016). Accounting for Rising Corporate Profits: Intangibles or Regulatory Rents? *Boston University School of Law, Law and Economics Research Paper*, 16–18.

Chiroleu-Assouline, M., & Lyon, T. P. (2020). Merchants of Doubt: Corporate Political Action When NGO Credibility Is Uncertain. *Journal of Economics & Management Strategy*, **29**(2), 439–61.

Coase, R. (1960). The Problem of Social Cost. *Journal of Law and Economics*, **3**, 1–44.

Crow, T. S., & Shireman, B. (2020). *In This Together: How Republicans, Democrats, Capitalists and Activists Are Uniting to Tackle Climate Change and More.* Marlton, NJ: Affinity Press.

Cruz, T. (2021). Your Woke Money Is No Good Here. *Wall Street Journal*, April 28.

Delmas, M., Lim, J., & Nairn-Birch, N. (2016). Corporate Environmental Performance and Lobbying. *Academy of Management Discoveries*, **2**(2), 175–97.

Delmas, M., & Lyon, T. P. (2018). When Corporations Take Credit for Green Deeds Their Lobbying May Tell Another Story. *The Conversation*, July 17.

De Loecker, J., Eeckhout, J., & Unger, G. (2020). The Rise of Market Power and the Macroeconomic Implications. *Quarterly Journal of Economics*, **135**(2), 561–644.

Drutman, L. (2015). How Corporate Lobbyists Conquered American Democracy. *The Atlantic*, April 20.

Drutman, L. (2020). *Breaking the Two-Party Doom Loop: The Case for Multiparty Democracy in America.* New York: Oxford University Press.

Drutman, L., & Mahoney, C. (2017). On the Advantages of a Well-Constructed Lobbying System: Toward a More Democratic, Modern Lobbying Process. *Interest Groups & Advocacy*, **6**(3), 290–310.

Friedman, L. (2018). How a Coal Baron's Wish List Became President Trump's To-Do list. *New York Times*, January 9.

Friedman, M. (1970). The Social Responsibility of Business Is to Increase Its Profits. *The New York Times Magazine*, September 13.

Gehl, K. M., & Porter, M. E. (2020). *The Politics Industry: How Political Innovation Can Break Partisan Gridlock and Save Our Democracy*. Boston, MA: Harvard Business Press.

Gilens, M., & Page, B. I. (2014). Testing Theories of American Politics: Elites, Interest Groups, and Average Citizens. *Perspectives on Politics*, 12(3), 564–581.

Heath, J. (2014). *Morality, Competition, and the Firm: The Market Failures Approach to Business Ethics*. New York: Oxford University Press.

Hodgson, S., & Witte, D. (2020). *Responsible Lobbying: An Evaluation Framework*. Carnstone Partners, Ltd.

Kalla, J. L., & Broockman, D. E. (2016). Campaign Contributions Facilitate Access to Congressional Officials: A Randomized Field Experiment. *American Journal of Political Science*, 60(3), 545–58.

Katz, A. (2015). *The Influence Machine: The US Chamber of Commerce and the Corporate Capture of American Life*. New York: Random House.

Lessig, L. (2015). *Republic, Lost: How Money Corrupts Congress – And a Plan to Stop It*. New York: Grand Central Publishing.

Livni, E. (2021). On Voting Rights, It Can Cost Companies to Take Both Sides. *The New York Times*, June 5.

Lyon, T. P. (2021). Ready or Not, the Era of Corporate Political Responsibility Is upon Us. *The Hill*, April 10.

Lyon, T. P., Delmas, M. A., Maxwell, J. W., et al. (2018). CSR Needs CPR: Corporate Sustainability and Politics. *California Management Review*, 60(4), 5–24.

Lyon, T. P., & Maxwell, J. W. (2004). Astroturf: Interest Group Lobbying and Corporate Strategy. *Journal of Economics & Management Strategy*, 13(4), 561–97.

Lyon, T.P., & Mandelkorn, W. (2023). Measuring Corporate Political Responsibility. Chapter 3 in *Corporate Political Responsibility*, T.P. Lyon (editor), Cambridge University Press.

Matten, D., & Crane, A. (2005). Corporate Citizenship: Toward an Extended Theoretical Conceptualization. *Academy of Management*, 30(1), 166–79.

Molina, B. (2020). Jeff Bezos Could Become World's First Trillionaire, and Many People Aren't Happy About It. *USA Today*, May 14. www.usatoday.com/story/tech/2020/05/14/jeff-bezos-worlds-first-trillionaire-sparks-heated-debate/5189161002/

Oberholzer-Gee, F., & Yao, D. A. (2018). Integrated Strategy: Residual Market and Exchange Imperfections as the Foundation of Sustainable Competitive Advantage. *Strategy Science*, 3(2), 463–80.

Oreskes, N., & Conway, E. M. (2011). *Merchants of Doubt: How a Handful of Scientists Obscured the Truth on Issues from Tobacco Smoke to Global Warming.* New York: Bloomsbury Publishing.

Piketty, T., & Saez, E. (2003). Income Inequality in the United States, 1913–1998. *Quarterly Journal of Economics*, **118**(1), 1–41.

Reich, R. B. (1998). The New Meaning of Corporate Social Responsibility. *California Management Review*, **40**(2), 8–17.

Saez, E., & Zucman, G. (2020). The Rise of Income and Wealth Inequality in America: Evidence from Distributional Macroeconomic Accounts. *Journal of Economic Perspectives*, 34(4), 3–26.

Scherer, A. G., & Palazzo, G. (2007). Toward a Political Conception of Corporate Responsibility: Business and Society Seen from a Habermasian Perspective. *Academy of Management Review*, 32(4), 1096–120.

Scherer, A. G., & Palazzo, G. (2011). The New Political Role of Business in a Globalized World: A Review of a New Perspective on CSR and Its Implications for the Firm, Governance, and Democracy. *Journal of Management Studies*, **48**(4), 899–931.

Smith, A. (1776). *The Wealth of Nations.* London, UK: W. Strahan and T. Cadell.

Thiebault, R. (2021). Joint Chiefs Chairman Feared Potential "Reichstag moment" Aimed at Keeping Trump in Power. The *Washington Post*, July 14.

Thomas, H. F., & LaPira, T. M. (2017). How Many Lobbyists Are in Washington? Shadow Lobbying and the Gray Market for Policy Advocacy. *Interest Groups & Advocacy*, **6**(3), 199–214.

Walker, E. T. (2014) *Grassroots for Hire: Public Affairs Consultants in American Democracy.* Cambridge, UK: Cambridge University Press.

World Economic Forum. (2020). *Measuring Stakeholder Capitalism: Towards Common Metrics and Consistent Reporting of Sustainable Value Creation*, www.weforum.org/reports/measuring-stakeholder-capitalism-towards-common-metrics-and-consistent-reporting-of-sustainable-value-creation

2 | Targeting Private Sector Influence in Politics
Corporate Accountability as a Risk and Governance Problem

BRUCE F. FREED, WILLIAM S. LAUFER,
AND KARL J. SANDSTROM

2.1 Introduction

Over the past two decades, American politics has become increasingly polarized. Partisan deadlock has prevented the nation's elected leaders from acting on many critical public policy issues that confront the country, most notably climate change. In the rare instance when deadlock is broken, such as with the Affordable Care Act, it is done along party lines and with the slimmest of margins. A prime example of this failure is the inability of Congress to pass any campaign finance legislation.[1] The need for such legislation became evident following the Supreme Court's decision in *Citizens United v Federal Election Commission* 538 U.S. 310 (2010). Here the Court overturned a century-old law that prohibited corporations from using their treasuries to make contributions and expenditures in connection with federal elections.

Corporations may now spend unlimited amounts of company funds to promote management's preferred candidates without shareholder approval and without disclosure. Disclosure could be easily eluded under the decision by routing company spending through third parties, including trade associations and "social welfare" organizations, also known as nonprofits or 501(c)(4) groups. As a consequence of this decision and a shift of company money to several partisan, state-focused committees known as 527s,[2] public companies have become a

---

[1] See David B. Magleby and Candice J. Nelson, *The Money Chase: Congressional Campaign Finance Reform* (Washington, DC: Brookings, 2010).

[2] These committees are governed by Section 527 of the Internal Revenue Code, hence the shorthand name. Disclosure of contributions to these committees is partial since only the recipient is required to do so, not the donor.

dominant source if not the dominant source of political money at the state and federal levels. Unlike a company's political action committee contributions, made from voluntary contributions by employees and limited and fully disclosed, contributions from corporate treasuries can be unlimited and undisclosed. Company contributions in the six- and seven-figures are not uncommon.[3]

The distortive effects of large unaccountable corporate political expenditures on our politics are evident, and the opportunity for corrupting our politics is clear. The lack of disclosure and accountability puts these contributions beyond the supervision of shareholders and other stakeholders. In addition, large undisclosed corporate contributions pose a threat to a well-functioning marketplace. Corporate contributions foster rent-seeking and unearned economic rewards through favorable legislative and regulatory action and policy decisions.

In this chapter, the challenge of addressing corporate political spending through the informal, non-state suasion and advocacy of the nonprofit Center for Political Accountability (CPA) is explored. CPA

---

[3] Public companies and their trade associations accounted for 44.4 percent (or $750.6 million) of the $1.7 billion raised by six partisan state-focused 527 committees between the 2010 and 2020 election cycles. The next largest source of money was individuals, accounting for $377.3 million, followed by private companies at $255.4 million. Three of the 527 committees – the Republican Governors Association, the Republican State Leadership Committee, and the Republican Attorneys General Association – were the largest recipients of money. Democratic 527s also received public company money but to a much lesser degree than their Republican counterparts. The Democratic 527s also raised less money for each cycle. Over the decade, the Republican 527s raised $1,058.3 billion compared to $632.9 million for the Democratic 527s. (See Conflicted Consequences, pp. 32–35, for comparison of donations raised by the Democratic and Republican 527s from the 2010 to 2020 election cycles.) In the 2018 election cycle, top donors to the RSLC included Altria ($1.2 million), British American Tobacco ($1.1 million), Berkshire Hathaway ($581,078), Anthem ($460,500), Wellcare ($458,593), the U.S. Chamber of Commerce ($2 million), and the Rent Stabilization Association of New York ($1.1 million). In the same election cycle, top donors to RAGA included Anadarko Petroleum ($1.5 million), Altria ($665,000), NextEra Energy ($525,855), PDC Energy ($350,000), Anthem ($285,350), the U.S. Chamber of Commerce ($1.7 million), and the Pharmaceutical Research and Manufacturers of America ($305,500). During this decade, the Republican groups played a major role in reshaping state and national politics and policy through their spending at the state level. The foreword by political scientists Jacob Hacker and Paul Pierson describes the unique impact of contributions to and spending by the 527 committees. See Center for Political Accountability, Conflicted Consequences, Conflicted-Consequences.pdf (politicalaccountability.net), pp. 2, 17, 22 and 32–59.

is a case study in successful private ordering and non-state regulation, prompting companies in the S&P 500 to disclose corporate political spending to shareholders; to develop policies that will ensure good compliance and governance; to adopt codes of conduct to reflect and inspire pro-accountability behavior; and to successfully compete with other firms for best disclosure and accountability practices.

Below we explain the need to go outside of the political process to achieve corporate political disclosure and accountability. This explanation is followed by a discussion of the challenges and necessary strategies for this kind of non-state regulation: (1) the problem of unbridled, undisclosed and unaccountable corporate political influence; (2) the failure over the last two decades of reliance on legislative change to bring broad disclosure and accountability; (3) using incentives and pro-accountability competition; (4) grounding the construct of accountability and successful demonstration of accountability in orthodox compliance terms, metrics, and measures; (5) maturing the conception of corporate political accountability as practices evolve; and (6) considering how accountability, in practice, may be increasingly authentic and genuine.

CPA's goal is to leverage shareholder and related engagement to successfully encourage publicly traded companies to agree to disclose their political contributions and adopt accountability practices that assure their contributions are consistent with company values and public positions. By using corporate governance and shareholder engagement, CPA believes that the role of corporate money in U.S. politics can be addressed, and corporate political disclosure and accountability can, over time, become the norm. The vehicle, as noted earlier, is a form of private ordering, where a critical mass of companies voluntarily engage, act, and turn a practice into a norm and standard. This kind of informal regulation has now led to significant changes in the political spending behavior of companies and how they engage in the political process.

Founded in 2003, the CPA has framed political spending as a corporate governance and risk management issue, harnessed shareholder activism and corporate engagement to drive change, and developed the policies and practices that companies are adopting to manage and mitigate the legal, reputational, and bottom-line risks posed by political spending. What has been achieved, and the foundation that has been laid, offer a case study of how to realize substantive and normative change in the face of political paralysis. There are lessons here for other regulatory objectives that must, out of necessity, be addressed outside of the conventional and formal political process.

2.2 The Problem: Unbridled, Undisclosed, and Unaccountable Corporate Political Influence

The political money landscape changed dramatically beginning in 1995 when Republicans took control of Congress. Following the election, an effort called the K Street Project[4] was launched by a top Republican operative to entrench Republicans in Washington-based lobbying shops and trade associations and steer political giving by companies and lobbying firms to Republicans. The upshot was that corporate political spending became even more partisan.[5] Companies were being pressed to give to political committees associated with Republican officeholders that these elected politicians, in turn, used to fund their personal and ideological agendas. The groups included Americans for a Republican Majority and Texans for a Republican Majority,[6] both associated with Rep. Tom DeLay (R, Texas), the House Majority Whip, and leadership PACs created by Sens. Rick Santorum (R, Pennsylvania) and Sam Brownback (R, Kansas).[7]

The political committees were vehicles for underwriting conservative social issues as well as changing control of state legislatures. This occurred in Texas in 2005, when Republicans gained majorities in both houses and redrew state legislative and congressional district lines that have shifted the party balance since then. Donations from corporations were solicited and became a major source of money. A significant portion of the money came from corporate or treasury funds.

The introduction of corporate or treasury funds created a serious risk for companies and their shareholders because of the issues and outcomes with which the companies became associated. Moreover, it posed a particular problem for certain large shareholders such as public pension funds that found that their money was being used

---

[4] For an overview of the K Street Project, see Nick Confessore, "Welcome to the Machine," *Washington Monthly*, July/August 2003. Welcome to the Machine | Washington Monthly.

[5] Until the Republican takeover of Congress in 1995, the rule of thumb for political contributions had been a 60–40 split between the party in control and the out party. That changed then and contributions moved to an 80–20 split or, in some cases, to giving only to candidates of the party in control.

[6] For an overview of Americans for a Republican Majority, see Jan Reid and Lou Dubose, "The Man with the Plan," *Washington Monthly*, August 2004. The Man with the Plan – Texas Monthly.

[7] Center for Political Accountability, *The Green Canary*, Layout 1 (nmcdn.io), 2005, pp. 21–26.

to pursue agendas that conflicted with their interests or concerns. This was the case with SBC Communications, BellSouth, Altria, and the Union Pacific railroad, whose contributions to Americans for a Republican Majority in the 2002 election cycle were used, in turn, for a contribution to the Traditional Values Coalition, a California-based conservative social organization headed by Rev. Louis Sheldon.[8]

Another example of companies being associated through their contributions with controversial issues involves the Restore America PAC, a leadership PAC affiliated with then Sen. Sam Brownback (R, Kansas). As recounted by the Center for Political Accountability's *Green Canary* ("Green Canary") report, Restore America PAC acted as a funnel for corporate political money to "controversial" organizations. An independent political committee, it raised $95,000 in 2000 and $126,000 in the 2002 election cycles. Public companies supporting it in these two election cycles included PepsiCo, SBC Communications, Union Pacific, and Coors Brewing. These are largely consumer product companies whose reputations are a significant source of shareholder value. Some of these companies embraced progressive personnel policies that reflected employee diversity, offered partner benefits, and contributed to education and the arts to enhance their image. Soft money contributions to Restore America PAC promoted contrary policies in a number of organizations, including Kansans for Life, an anti-abortion group affiliated with the National Right to Life Committee, and the Christian Coalition. The Christian Coalition, for example, opposed domestic partner benefits and prohibiting discrimination based on sexual preference. It supported parental choice in education and protecting the display of the Ten Commandments in public buildings.[9]

These developments were followed later by the Supreme Court's 2010 *Citizens United* decision that opened the floodgates to unlimited contributions from companies and other entities, independent expenditures, and "dark money." As noted above, the decision overturned legislation enacted in 1907 that barred corporations from using their corporate treasuries to support candidates for federal office.[10] That legislation had been adopted after the 1904 presidential election,

---

[8] Center for Political Accountability, *The Green Canary*, Layout 1 (nmcdn.io), 2005, pp. 22–23.

[9] Ibid., pp. 24–25.

[10] Tillman Act of 1907 | The First Amendment Encyclopedia (mtsu.edu); Robert E. Mutch, *Campaigns, Congress, and Courts: The Making of Federal*

which saw an election victory principally financed by the major trusts of the era. *Citizens United* removed the safeguards that the law had in place to protect shareholders and to inform the public regarding the sources of election financing. Unless Congress acted, public companies henceforth would be free to deploy corporate funds to influence election outcomes without shareholders and the public knowing it. Companies would also be exposed to shakedowns by powerful politicians who could take actions that had an impact on their bottom lines.

Today, public companies are a dominant, if not the dominant, source of political money. While precise numbers are difficult to come by because of gaps in disclosure, the following figures provide a sense of scale of corporate versus other money. According to the Center for Responsive Politics (the Center), business political action committees outspent labor PACs by more than three to one and ideological PACs by six to one in the 2018 election cycle.[11] CPA research into the sources of money for six partisan 527 committees active in state-level spending[12] found that public companies and their trade associations accounted for 44 percent (or $750.6 million) of the $1.7 billion raised by the groups between the 2010 and 2020 election cycles.[13]

Money raised by the Republican State Leadership Committee (RSLC) in the two elections preceding the decennial redistricting highlights the impact of contributions from public companies and their trade associations. The RSLC is important because of the role it played in reshaping state and national politics in the 2010 election through its spending that was crucial for changing control of a large number of state legislatures. Following that election, state legislative and congressional districts were redrawn, in many cases giving the

Campaign Finance Law (New York: Praeger Publishers, 1988), 1–8, and *Buying the Vote: A History of Campaign Finance Reform* (New York: Oxford University Press, 2014), 45–57

[11] Opensecrets.org, Why corporate PACs have an advantage • OpenSecrets

[12] CPA looked at six Republican and Democratic groups focused on electing governors, attorneys general, and state legislatures. The groups are the Republican and Democratic Governors Associations, the Republican State Leadership Committee and the Democratic Legislative Campaign Committee, and the Republican and Democratic Attorneys General Associations. These nonprofit, tax-exempt groups are called 527 organizations for the section of the Internal Revenue Code that governs them.

[13] Conflicted Consequences, Conflicted-Consequences.pdf (politicalaccountability.net), p. 36; see footnote 1 for details on corporate and other donors to the 527s committees for 2010 to 2020 election cycles.

Republicans a significant advantage. In the 2010 election cycle, the committee raised $29.4 million, a record amount up to then. Public companies and trade associations accounted for 60.9 percent of that (or $17.8 million). A decade later, the RSLC raised $59.2 million, 43 percent of which (or $25.3 million) came from public companies and trade associations. This money was crucial for Republicans retaining control of many of the state legislatures and positioning them to shape state legislative and congressional redistricting based on the 2020 census. In both cases, the largest source of money was from public companies and their trade associations.[14]

Consider also the Republican Attorneys General Association (RAGA), which helped elect state attorneys general who filed suits challenging the Affordable Care Act and California's clean car emissions standards following the 2018 elections. An attorney general who took the lead in the suits was Ken Paxton of Texas. An amount of $650,000 was donated to or spent by RAGA on the Paxton campaign in the 2018 election cycle. Public companies and their trade associations were the dominant source of money in the 2018 cycle. Of the $39.6 million raised, 49.4 percent (or $19.6 million) came from those two sources.[15] In comparison, the Democratic Legislative Campaign Committee, which focuses on state legislative elections, raised $8.7 million in the 2010 cycle and $45.4 million in the 2020 cycle. The Democratic Attorneys General Association raised $19.7 million in the 2018 cycle.

In this post–*Citizen's United* world, unbridled, undisclosed, and unaccountable corporate political influence remains a problem in need of a solution. CPA focuses on this problem in the glaring absence of legislative remedies.

2.3 The Folly of Banking on Legislative Change to Ensure Accountability

Following the enactment of the Bipartisan Campaign Reform Act in 2003, Sen. Mitch McConnell (R, Kentucky) made the legislative route for addressing the problem of money in politics, and corporate political money in particular, a likely dead end. A member of the Senate Republican leadership since 2003, McConnell has been a staunch opponent of campaign finance laws. Through his words and actions,

---

[14] Ibid., pp. 42, 59.   [15] Ibid., pp. 16–17.

he made it clear that he would block any further campaign finance legislation and any effort to expand disclosure of political contributions and spending.[16]

Staunch Republican leadership opposition left only one option for reform: working outside the political system and using corporate governance and shareholder engagement to persuade companies to voluntarily adopt political disclosure and accountability policies. What followed was the development of the innovative strategy of using corporate governance, shareholder engagement, and risk management to bring transparency and accountability to corporate political spending. Shareholder resolutions were used to open the door to dialogues with companies that would lead to the adoption of political disclosure and accountability policies in return for the withdrawal of the resolution.

Resolutions were filed by the Center's partners. They included the New York State Common Retirement Fund, whose sole trustee is New York State Comptroller Thomas P. DiNapoli; Newground Social Investment, Trillium Asset Management, Clean Yield, Mercy Investment Services, the Unitarian Universalist Association, and Friends Fiduciary Corporation.

Individual investors also have played an important role in filing shareholder resolutions at companies and working with them to adopt political disclosure and accountability policies. James McRitchie and John Chevedden, California-based individual investors, are leaders in filing CPA model resolutions at companies and negotiating withdrawals in return for company adoption of strong disclosure and accountability policies. In the 2021 proxy season, the resolution McRitchie filed with Netflix received a record 80.7 percent vote, while the resolution Chevedden filed with Chemed received an 80.1 percent vote. A resolution filed by Chevedden at Alaska Air Group was withdrawn following substantial improvement in policies by the company.

Proxy advisory firms have been critical to reinforcing the role of investors. They review shareholder resolutions and make recommendations to clients, primarily institutional investors, about how to vote their proxies. This has a significant influence over the outcome of shareholder resolutions. The dominant firms are Institutional Shareholder Services (ISS) and Glass Lewis. ISS's decision in the summer of 2005 to

---

[16] The role of Senate Republican leader Mitch McConnell (Kentucky) will be examined in a forthcoming book on the senator by Ira Shapiro.

change its policy for the 2006 proxy season to recommend on CPA's resolution on case-by-case basis was a turning point in the movement for corporate political disclosure and accountability. Previously, ISS's policy was to oppose social resolutions, which included the CPA's political disclosure resolutions.

The strategy advanced the larger goal of working with companies on the adoption of policies for disclosure and accountability. The dual objectives are very important. Disclosure without accountability does not address risk and does not bring about change in the way companies approach political spending. Accountability is essential for the adoption of policies governing a company's political spending, setting parameters for the spending, and the exercise of oversight to evaluate the legal, reputational, and business risk posed by the spending. The voluntary approach was also important because of the need to work with companies, get their input and acceptance, and lead companies to change how they manage and govern their political spending. CPA's effort focused on company use of corporate or treasury funds, not political action committee money raised from company employees, for political spending.

The results today as seen in shareholder votes and company actions demonstrate the success of shareholder engagement in laying a foundation for company adoption of corporate political disclosure and accountability policies. In 2003, when CPA began its effort, few, if any, companies had those policies. The year 2004 opened with CPA's model political disclosure resolution filed at twenty-three companies. The resolution received a vote of 10 percent or more at twelve of the companies, with 15 percent at two. The average vote for the twenty-three resolutions was 9 percent. Those were considered successful votes for a first-time shareholder resolution.

The resolution was filed again for the 2005 proxy season. In response to a filing, Morgan Stanley became the first company to agree to adopt political disclosure and accountability policies. What followed was a steady year-by-year increase in the number of companies reaching agreements with shareholder filers in return for the resolution's withdrawal. Beginning with two companies in the 2005 proxy season, the number of agreements reached 63 by the 2009 proxy season, 128 by the 2014 proxy season, and 177 by the 2019 proxy season. By the close of the 2021 proxy season, the number of agreements totaled 195 (Table 2.1).

Table 2.1 *Corporate political disclosure and accountability policies*

Proxy Season	Agreements
2004	0
2005	2
2006	8
2007	24
2008	17
2009	12
2010	12
2011	12
2012	14
2013	16
2014	11
2015	15
2016	11
2017	7
2018	3
2019	13
2020	8
2021	10
Total	195

The increase in company agreements was paralleled by a jump in the average vote for the CPA resolution. Following the decision by Institutional Shareholder Services, the leading proxy voting advisory service, to make vote recommendations on CPA's resolution on a case-by-case basis beginning in the 2006 proxy season, the average vote spiked to 21.8 percent in 2006 and rose to 32.7 percent in 2011, 33.3 percent in 2016, 36.4 percent in 2019, 41.9 percent in 2020, and 48.1 percent in 2021. The change in vote recommendation policies by both ISS and Glass Lewis, the other leading proxy advisory service, played a critical role in boosting support for CPA's resolution.

The number of companies with disclosure and/or accountability policies, however, was significantly greater. This was a result of companies acting on their own or in response to their measurement by an annual index developed through a collaboration between the CPA and the Wharton School's Zicklin Center for Business Ethics Research. The

Index, a benchmarking measure of political disclosure and account-ability policies of the S&P 500 companies, was launched to promote greater transparency and accountability through the incentives that come from competition. According to the 2021 Index, well more than three-fifths of the S&P 500 had some level of disclosure and one-half had some degree of board oversight of election-related spending with corporate funds.

Beyond those overall figures, the Index has shown an increase in companies earning top scores for their political disclosure and account-ability policies. Indeed, the number of Trendsetter companies (those with scores of 90 or above) more than tripled from twenty-eight in 2015, when the Index was expanded to the entire S&P 500, to eighty-seven in 2021.

Significantly, as the Index gained acceptance and credibility, CPA found companies strengthening their policies to achieve Trendsetter status, that is, top scores on the Index (Figure 2.1). Some saw it as a matter of good governance, while others saw it as a way to repair reputational challenges or as having political benefits. This judg-ment is based on CPA's interactions with companies and what it has learned from outside sources. Companies moving to Trendsetter sta-tus included Boeing, JPMorgan Chase, Merck, Prudential Financial, AT&T, Noble Energy, and several leading public utilities such as Dominion Energy, Exelon, Ameren, and Sempra Energy.

Strikingly, company adoption of political disclosure progressed in the face of attacks by the US Chamber of Commerce, the *Wall Street Journal*'s editorial and op-ed pages, and Koch brothers–funded groups such as the Center for Competitive Politics and the Manhattan Institute. The *Wall Street Journal* opened its assault on November 10, 2011, with an op-ed by former Federal Election Commission Chair Bradley Smith.[17] It was followed over the next six years by at least ten editorials and op-eds[18] and a book-length attack by Kimberley Strassel of the paper's editorial board.[19]

---

[17] *Wall Street Journal*, Nov. 10, 2011.
[18] *Wall Street Journal* editorials, Dec. 28, 2011; March 18, 2012; May 31, 2012; May 25, 2014; Oct. 21, 2014; op-eds, Oct. 21, 2013; Sept. 29, 2014; and July 7, 2017; and Kimberley Strassel Potomac Watch column, May 31, 2012.
[19] Kimberley Strassel, *The Intimidation Game*, 2016. Pp. 235–36, 237, 238, 239, 240, 243, and 255.

TRENDSETTERS IN POLITICAL DISCLOSURE AND ACCOUNTABILITY

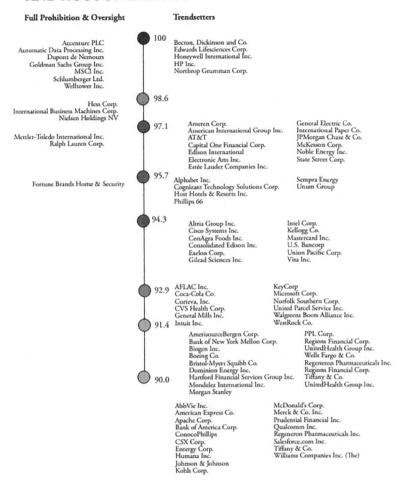

Full Prohibition & Oversight — **Trendsetters**

100
Accenture PLC
Automatic Data Processing Inc.
Dupont de Nemours
Goldman Sachs Group Inc.
MSCI Inc.
Schlumberger Ltd.
Welltower Inc.

Becton, Dickinson and Co.
Edwards Lifesciences Corp.
Honeywell International Inc.
HP Inc.
Northrop Grumman Corp.

98.6
Hess Corp.
International Business Machines Corp.
Nielsen Holdings NV

97.1
Mettler-Toledo International Inc.
Ralph Lauren Corp.

Ameren Corp.
American International Group Inc.
AT&T
Capital One Financial Corp.
Edison International
Electronic Arts Inc.
Estée Lauder Companies Inc.

General Electric Co.
International Paper Co.
JPMorgan Chase & Co.
McKesson Corp.
Noble Energy Inc.
State Street Corp.

95.7
Fortune Brands Home & Security

Alphabet Inc.
Cognizant Technology Solutions Corp.
Host Hotels & Resorts Inc.
Phillips 66

Sempra Energy
Unum Group

94.3
Altria Group Inc.
Cisco Systems Inc.
ConAgra Foods Inc.
Consolidated Edison Inc.
Exelon Corp.
Gilead Sciences Inc.

Intel Corp.
Kellogg Co.
Mastercard Inc.
U.S. Bancorp
Union Pacific Corp.
Visa Inc.

92.9
AFLAC Inc.
Coca-Cola Co.
Corteva, Inc.
CVS Health Corp.
General Mills Inc.

KeyCorp
Microsoft Corp.
Norfolk Southern Corp.
United Parcel Service Inc.
Walgreens Boots Alliance Inc.

91.4
Intuit Inc.

WestRock Co.

AmerisourceBergen Corp.
Bank of New York Mellon Corp.
Biogen Inc.
Boeing Co.
Bristol-Myers Squibb Co.
Dominion Energy Inc.
Hartford Financial Services Group Inc.
Mondelez International Inc.
Morgan Stanley

PPL Corp.
Regions Financial Corp.
UnitedHealth Group Inc.
Wells Fargo & Co.
Regeneron Pharmaceuticals Inc.
Regions Financial Corp.
Tiffany & Co.
UnitedHealth Group Inc.

90.0

AbbVie Inc.
American Express Co.
Apache Corp.
Bank of America Corp.
ConocoPhillips
CSX Corp.
Entergy Corp.
Humana Inc.
Johnson & Johnson
Kohls Corp.

McDonald's Corp.
Merck & Co. Inc.
Prudential Financial Inc.
Qualcomm Inc.
Regeneron Pharmaceuticals Inc.
Salesforce.com Inc.
Tiffany & Co.
Williams Companies Inc. (The)

Figure 2.1 2021 CPA-Zicklin Index/Trendsetters in political disclosure and accountability
Reproduced with the permission of the Center for Political Accountability (CPA)

The main thrust of the attacks on the Center was that corporate political disclosure aimed at stifling corporate free speech. In his *Wall Street Journal* op-ed, former federal Election Commission Chair Smith called the CPA effort "another union attack on corporate speech."

Wall Street Journal editorials followed the same theme. A journal op-ed by University of Rochester Professor David Primo called the push for corporate political disclosure a political attack on shareholder value. Others accused the Center of intimidating companies.

The Chamber's attacks ran from 2010 to 2015 and included articles, blog posts, tweets, and op-eds on corporate political disclosure and the CPA-Zicklin Index and a campaign by former Securities and Exchange Commissioner Paul Atkins to discredit corporate political disclosure and the Center for Political Accountability's efforts.[20] The Chamber's activities were detailed in a *Huffington Post* article.[21] The attacks, which focused on CPA's shareholder resolutions and on the CPA-Zicklin Index, were similar to those mounted in the *Wall Street Journal*. Thus, Atkins charged that corporate political disclosure aimed at restricting corporate free speech. A joint letter dated October 13, 2015, from the US Chamber, the Business Roundtable, and the National Association of Manufacturers criticized the methodology of the CPA-Zicklin Index and said it aimed to "silence the business community's voice."

From the start, the limitations of voluntary adoption of disclosure and accountability policies were recognized by CPA. The voluntary approach laid a foundation to build upon. By 2010, as more companies adopted disclosure and accountability policies to varying degrees, it was clear that regulation, in this case an SEC political disclosure rule, would be the necessary next step to make political disclosure and accountability uniform and universal and create a level playing field. This was reinforced by the call of Noble Energy's then–general counsel and corporate secretary Arnold Johnson for disclosure and accountability to apply to all companies.[22] Privately, a number of companies have told CPA they agreed with Johnson.

CPA decided to work directly with companies and to do so within the context of corporate governance and risk management. The first

---

[20] Paul Atkins, "Efforts to Restrict Corporate Speech," June 10, 2014. Slide deck used for the US Chamber of Commerce.

[21] Paul Blumenthal, *Huffington Post*, April 22, 2015. www.huffingtonpost .com/2015/04/22/chamber-of-commerce-transparency_n_7111022.html

[22] Noble Energy General Counsel Arnold Johnson remarks at 2015 Corporate Political Accountability Roundtable at New York University's Stern School of Business, Special Second Corporate Political Accountability Roundtable Edition of Spotlight on CPA – February 2015 (nmcdn.io).

report by the Center entitled *The Green Canary* framed the issue as one of risk.[23] Released in early 2005, it laid out how corporate political spending posed a risk to shareholder value and cast political spending using treasury funds as a risk management issue. It did so in a series of case studies on Enron, Global Crossing, WorldCom, Qwest, and Westar Energy, companies where political spending was a factor in corporate mismanagement. It also detailed contributions by companies such as SBC Communications, BellSouth, Altria, PepsiCo, and Union Pacific that created reputational challenges. Focusing on the risks companies faced from political spending removed partisan overtones from requests for disclosure and from the analysis of corporate participation.

CPA expanded on its risk analysis by looking at company contributions through third-party groups and the conflicts this posed for companies. One area examined was the contributions of companies with strong diversity policies that scored high on the Human Rights Campaign's Equality Index. CPA found that some of the companies were donating to the campaigns of state judicial candidates who were running homophobic campaigns, a clear conflict with the donating companies' diversity policies. In another case, a contribution was uncovered from a leading pharmaceutical company to a Mississippi state Supreme Court candidate alleged by the state's leading newspaper to be running a racist campaign.[24]

Beyond the shareholder engagement and votes, a key move in gaining the attention and buy-in of companies was the involvement of The Conference Board and the publication of its *Handbook on Corporate Political Activity* in 2010.[25] CPA was the lead co-author.[26] These factors were central to framing corporate political spending as a matter of risk management and putting the imprimatur of the nation's leading business research organization on both political spending as a risk and on the policies and practices companies needed to adopt to manage and oversee it.

---

[23] Center for Political Accountability, *The Green Canary*, 2005, Layout 1 (nmcdn.io).
[24] Time, Secrets of Corporate Giving, March 14, 2006.
[25] The Conference Board, Handbook on Corporate Political Activity, 2010, Handbook on Corporate Political Activity (nmcdn.io).
[26] The other co-authors were Paul DeNicola, Director of the Conference Board's Governance Center, and Stefan Passantino, a Republican campaign finance lawyer then with McKenna, Long & Aldrich.

The *Handbook* reinforced what already was being recognized and accepted, that political spending by companies using corporate or treasury funds posed a substantial risk that required robust policies to manage. One of the areas covered by the report dealt with the risks posed by spending through third-party groups such as trade associations and "social welfare" organizations, also known as nonprofits or 501(c)(4) groups. In a sidebar on political spending by trade associations, the report warned, "Companies should therefore be aware of whether their membership in trade associations accurately represents the company's interests and policy positions and manage these relationships accordingly."[27]

That admonition was followed by a thorough discussion of director responsibilities, board oversight of company political spending, and the elements of an effective program to manage and oversee company political spending. As the *Handbook* concluded,

A board-approved process in close coordination with senior managers may be needed to review the political spending program, but it is management's responsibility to design and implement a program that best serves the company's needs while protecting it against unnecessary risk. Periodic internal and external legal and audit reviews may be needed to reduce the risks inherent in political activity, especially since such reviews can be a mitigating consideration when companies face legal sanctions for political spending violations. When political spending mistakes are made, they should be quickly addressed and, when appropriate, publicly acknowledged.[28]

Investors, particularly socially responsible investment firms and large public pension funds, have been crucial for raising the profile of the issue and spurring companies to act. They created the critical mass by filing CPA's model resolutions at several hundred public companies and beginning the engagement process. This culminated in political disclosure and accountability being recognized as the norm.[29]

Beyond The Conference Board, CPA's investor partners and the proxy advisory firms, the Center's affiliation and consultation with academics has played a central role in making corporate political disclosure and accountability the norm and bolstering CPA's efforts. The most significant development was the construction of the CPA-Zicklin Index. The first Index, released in 2011, covered S&P 100 companies.

---

[27] Ibid., p. 16.   [28] Ibid., p. 24.
[29] Robert Yablon, "Campaign Finance Reform without Law," 103 *Iowa Law Review* 185 (2017).

It was expanded to the S&P 500 in 2015. The Zicklin Center's imprimatur was critical for giving the Index stature and credibility. That was also the case with the CPA-Zicklin Model Code of Conduct for Corporate Political Spending (Figure 2.2).

Biennial roundtables on Corporate Political Accountability held at New York University's Stern School of Business and the introductions academics have written to CPA reports – Collision Course, Conflicted Consequences, and Corporate Enablers – and the CPA-Zicklin Index have been important for framing the issue.[30] They have also joined the Center as co-authors of op-eds. Two in *USA Today* and the *Boston Globe* that were co-authored by Harvard Business School Prof. Michael E. Porter and CPA President Bruce Freed unveiled the Model Code of Conduct for Corporate Political Spending.[31]

The significance of CPA's effort and its impact in the context of "private ordering" were increasingly recognized. Robert Yablon wrote that "Private ordering may not be a panacea, but neither is public regulation. The choice among institutions 'is always a choice among highly imperfect alternatives.' If private ordering might achieve something that public regulation, with all its institutional baggage, cannot, then it deserves a closer look."[32]

---

[30] Academics writing the forewords include Yale School of Management's Constance Bagley (Collision Course), Yale Prof. Jacob Hacker and UC Berkeley Prof. Paul Pierson (Conflicted Consequences), Harvard Business School Prof. Rebecca Henderson (2020 CPA-Zicklin Index), University of Michigan Ross School of Business Prof. Thomas P. Lyon (Corporate Enablers), and Wharton Prof. William S. Laufer (2021 CPA-Zicklin Index).

[31] Michael E. Porter and Bruce Freed, "Big Businesses Say They Are Responsible, but Too Often They Fuel Conspiracy Theories," *USA Today*, Jan. 19, 2021, Corporate political spending and rhetoric do not match (usatoday.com); "Companies Need to Reevaluate the Full Range of Their Political Spending," *Boston Globe*, Jan. 26, 2021, Companies need to reevaluate the full range of their political spending.

[32] CPA's achievement was recognized in work by University of Wisconsin Law Prof. Robert Yablon who noted that "the fallout from *Citizens United* has placed corporate spending in the public spotlight, prompting shareholders and others to prioritize the issue and to become more organized. Advocacy groups like the Center for Political Accountability, for example, have led a coordinated push for greater transparency and accountability in corporate political spending through shareholder activism…. Comparatively speaking, an important virtue of private ordering is that it frees campaign finance reformers from the shackles that jurisprudence and politics place on public regulation…. [P]rivate ordering give[s] private reform a significant edge over public regulation in terms of freedom and flexibility. Reformers can pursue private solutions without getting

The takeaway – and significance – of CPA's effort was to move corporate political disclosure and accountability forward in a decidedly hostile political and legislative environment. By eschewing the political process and using corporate governance to work directly with companies, the Center made corporate political disclosure and accountability the norm and established the policies that companies are following for disclosing, managing, and overseeing their political spending with corporate funds.

The seminal impact of the Center's work is seen in The Conference Board's *Under a Microscope* report released in March 2021. Its analysis of the risks companies face from political spending, its discussion of how companies have changed the way they manage their political spending, and its recommendations for the policies companies should adopt and actions companies should take to manage the risks and more effectively govern how they approach political spending draw on CPA's reports and the Model Code of Conduct.[33]

Much work remains to make corporate political disclosure uniform and universal, but political spending is now accepted as a risk that companies need to manage, and a firm and deep foundation has been laid for disclosure and accountability policies to do that. Beyond this, the groundwork has been laid for changing how companies look at and engage in political spending. This is important as companies grapple today with broader issues such as their role, responsibilities, and obligations as members of society and participants in the democratic process and the ethical implications of their political spending and its consequences.

2.4 Narrowing the Scope of Possible Influences by Avoiding Intractable and Intransient Problems, for Example, Lobbying

At the outset, CPA made a strategic decision to focus laser-like on company political spending with corporate funds. The reason was

---

mired in legislative and bureaucratic quagmires, thwarted by constitutional constraints, or hemmed in by jurisdictional boundaries. Avoiding those obstacles may open the door to more holistic approaches and enable more efficient responses to emerging issues." "Campaign Finance Reform without Law," *Iowa Law Review*, Vol. 103, Issue I, 2017.

[33] The Conference Board, *Under a Microscope: A New Era for Scrutiny of Corporate Political Activity*, March 2021.

rather simple. Disclosure and contribution and spending limits were already in place for political action committees. On the other hand, while some disclosure was required for spending using corporate funds, there were major gaps involving trade associations and "social welfare" organizations. A gray area involved 527 committees where contributions were disclosed by the recipient but not the donor. That made it more difficult to track money to the committees.

Also, the spending decisions involving corporate funds were made by company executives, tying the company much more closely to the spending and its consequences. The amounts of money involved were much greater, as noted above. This drew much greater attention to the company's actions and raised the level of risk, whether it be reputation, legal, or bottom line. The unlimited expenditures enabled by contributions with corporate funds also heightened the corruption risk faced by companies.

CPA decided against including lobbying spending for two reasons. First, lobbying has a large degree of required disclosure and covers a wide range of activities, from local zoning changes to national health policy. Unlike political spending, lobbying spending is more difficult to evaluate. Whether a company is for or against particular legislation is often difficult to assess or act upon. Lobbying positions by their very nature are dynamic. That's not the case with political spending, which is focused on a clear choice to support or oppose a candidate. The decision thus was made to concentrate the corporate political disclosure effort on election-related spending because of its significant areas that are dark or have only partial disclosure. These pose a growing risk for companies and investors and a growing threat to democracy.

A related reason why election-related spending deserves special attention is its central role in forming relationships and building influence with elected officials and helping to shape outcomes and facilitating rent-seeking. This is examined in research on the importance of political contributions in building relationships with members of Congress and the return to companies in terms of favorable legislative action. One recent study found political contributions delivered a greater ROI than lobbying spending. According to Marian Currinder, "There is no shortage of research linking political contributions with access to politicians. Jennifer Brown found that companies pursuing a long-term, contribution-based approach to building relationships with lawmakers fare better in lowering their tax rates than companies that relied chiefly on lobbying. Contributions buy a point of entry and, over time, regular access for those who lobby."[34]

Engagement of companies by CPA and its partners directly or through the filing of proxy resolutions, and the benchmarking of companies in the CPA-Zicklin Index, have been instrumental in making corporate political disclosure and accountability the norm and laying the foundation for changing how companies approach and manage their spending. Since 2004, these have been mutually reinforcing. A crucial development was company acceptance of political disclosure and accountability as an essential part of risk management. This was the result of CPA's work with The Conference Board and its Governance Center and CPA's reports and articles on corporate political spending and risk. This made possible the push for an SEC political disclosure rule, suggested by CPA and proposed in August 2011 by a committee of law professors, and laid the foundation for the broader effort based on the Model Code of Conduct for Corporate Political Spending that is leading companies to change their political spending behavior.[35]

Given the obstacles to reform faced in the political process and the goal of achieving a deeper change in the way companies approach and manage their political spending, broader strategies have been required and are having an impact. The Index has played a key role in helping CPA track and measure changes in company policies and practices over the past decade.

The idea behind the Index was, at least in part, to offer a benchmark of corporate progress toward disclosure and accountability in a competitive setting where companies are incentivized to do better and to receive public recognition for that by achieving Trendsetter

---

[34] "Corporate Campaign Contributions Add Up to Lower Tax Rates," March 23, 2015, http://research.wpcarey.asu.edu/uncategorized/corporate-campaign-contributions-add-up-to-lower-tax-rates/?utm_source=SilverpopMailing&utm_medium=wpc_email&utm_campaign=Research%20and%20Ideas%20-%20March%202015%20(1)&utm_content=&spMailingID=10983680&spUserID=NDYwODIyMjYzOAS2&spJobID=501846353&spReportId=NTAxODQ2MzUzS0; Marian Currinder, "Putting the Political Spending Horse before the Lobbying Cart," *Roll Call*, May 28, 2015. http://blogs.rollcall.com/beltway-insiders/time-to-put-the-political-spending-horse-before-the-lobbying-cart-commentary/?dcz=].

[35] CPA-Zicklin Model Code of Conduct for Corporate Political Spending, CPA-Zicklin-Model-Code-of-Conduct-for-Corporate-Political-Spending.pdf (politicalaccountability.net).

(scores of 90 or above) status. Over the past decade, CPA found that competition and incentives create the kind of change that it could not have achieved otherwise. The Center can point to multiple illustrations of firms climbing the index ranks – all toward a collective norm of accountability.

For example, companies now cite their Trendsetter status or at least a first-tier score (80 or above) to show that they are good corporate citizens. CPA has been told that this is important for image and reputation. Companies doing this include Dominion Energy, Altria, Prudential Financial, and JPMorgan Chase. Companies also see the Index's 24 indicators as providing the template for the disclosure and accountability policies they are adopting. This is a common refrain not only from executives but also from outside lawyers advising companies on the policies to adopt.

Companies do not like being cited for low Index scores. Edwards Life Sciences and DuPont are two cases where low scores moved senior executives to direct the company to adopt robust political disclosure and accountability policies to make them Trendsetters.[36]

2.5 Codifying the Construct of Accountability

Today, adopting the Model Code of Conduct for Corporate Political Spending would be seen a major step in a company's committing itself to changing how it manages political spending. The Code builds on the Index's 24 indicators measuring company policies and practices, and it provides a framework for companies to approach political spending, assess its impact and risk, and view their role and responsibilities as members of society and participants in the democratic process. The purpose of the Model Code is to lead companies to follow and internalize a broader approach to risk management, political spending decision-making and evaluation, and a three-dimensional view of their obligations and responsibilities as members of society and participants in the democratic process.

The heightened risk posed by engaging in political activity makes it paramount that companies adopt a code of conduct to govern their political participation. Whether a company is directly contributing to

---

[36] Edwards Life Sciences became a CPA-Zicklin Index Trendsetter in 2016. Dupont jumped to Trendsetter status in the 2020 Index.

or spending in elections or indirectly participating through payments to political or advocacy organizations, a code commits senior management and directors to responsible participation in our nation's politics. The code is a public commitment to employees, shareholders, and the public to transparency and accountability. It not only mitigates risk but also demonstrates the company's understanding that its participation in politics must reflect its core values, its respect for the law, and its responsibilities as a member of the body politic.

With investors and the wider public placing ever more emphasis on companies being responsible members of the broader society and accountable participants in the democratic process, a code becomes an essential tool for meeting those demands. It is also an element of Corporate Social Responsibility and Corporate Political Responsibility. An indication of the importance of this is the Business Roundtable's Statement on the Purpose of a Corporation (August 2019) which addresses the relationship companies should have with a full range of stakeholders.

The scrutiny that a company's election-related spending is receiving, how the spending aligns with a company's values, and how it affects the wider society and other stakeholders require the board and senior management to pay close attention to where the company's money goes and its wider consequences. In the end, directors and officers are responsible and accountable for the political choices and broader impact that may result from their company's election-related spending, no matter how financially immaterial it may seem.

The Model Code is intended as a guide for companies that seek to:

- Be responsible members of society and participants in the democratic process and responsive to the range of stakeholders, in both letter and spirit,
- Be recognized for their leadership in aligning corporate integrity and accountability with codified values,
- Prudently manage company resources, and
- Avoid the increased level of reputational, business, and legal risk posed by the seismic shifts in how society engages with and scrutinizes corporations. The risk is exacerbated by the evolution of social media and a resurgence of activism in civil society.

Companies are encouraged to develop standards and procedures beyond those outlined in the model code that demonstrate their commitment to ethical behavior as they engage in political activity.

Model Code
1.   Political spending shall reflect the company's interests, as an entity, and not those of its individual officers, directors, and agents.   2.   In general, the company will follow a preferred policy of making its political contributions to a candidate directly.   3.   No contribution will be given in anticipation of, in recognition of, or in return for an official act or anything that has appearance of a gratuity, bribe, trade or quid pro quo of any kind.   4.   Employees will not be reimbursed directly or through compensation increases for personal political contributions or expenses.   5.   The company will not pressure or coerce employees to make personal political expenditures.   6.   All corporate political expenditures must receive prior written approval from the appropriate corporate officer.   7.   The company will disclose publicly all direct contributions and expenditures with corporate funds on behalf of candidates, political parties and political organizations.   8.   The company will disclose dues and other payments made to trade associations and contributions to other tax-exempt organizations that are or that it anticipates will be used for political expenditures. The disclosures shall describe the specific political activities undertaken.   9.   The board shall require a report from trade associations or other third-party groups receiving company money on how it is being used and the candidates whom the spending promotes.   10.   The board of directors or an independent committee of the board shall receive regular reports, establish and supervise policies and procedures, and assess the risks and impacts related to the company's political spending   11.   The company shall review the positions of the candidates or organizations to which it contributes to determine whether those positions conflict with the company's core values and policies. This review should be considered by senior management and the full board of directors annually.   12.   The board of directors shall, independent of this review, consider the broader societal and economic harm and risks posed by the company's political spending.

Figure 2.2 CPA-Zicklin model code of conduct for corporate political spending
Reproduced with the permission of the Center for Political Accountability (CPA)

2.6 Maturing the Conception of Corporate Political Accountability as Practices Evolve

Private ordering and reaching the point of being able to develop a serious, comprehensive Model Code of Conduct for Corporate Political Spending are key signs of the maturation process. The Model Code builds on the Index, the best practices that companies are adopting and the change in the view of risks.

CPA was first to document the risks to companies posed by the consequences of political spending that conflicted with their core values and positions. In an incendiary new political and digital media environment, corporations face a heightened and dangerous risk to their reputations and brands when they spend political money. Corporations have an opportunity to protect their reputations by enacting corporate governance safeguards to align their political activity with their brands, core values, and positions.[37]

Consider the many examples of conflicted company spending:

Racial justice/voting rights:

As CPA detailed, the battle over attacks on voting rights in key states has rapidly escalated following the 2020 election with calls for corporations to take a stand. If they do, many companies face a reckoning whether their principled stance conflicts with their past political spending. Here's why: From the treasuries of corporations that have endorsed diversity efforts, millions of dollars have flowed to groups or campaigns supporting election of officeholders who sponsored, advanced or will be acting on voting restriction or nullification legislation in seven battleground states.

The money trail reveals that 182 of these companies and 17 trade associations pumped at least $79 million in the 2018 and 2020 election cycles into these groups and campaigns, and over $21.5 million of that amount went to supporting election of these legislators and two governors in Georgia, Texas, Florida, Michigan, Pennsylvania, Arizona, and Iowa.

The donor companies include such well-known US corporate leaders as NextEra Energy, Coca-Cola, Chevron, Altria, AT&T, Comcast, Walmart, Visa, Wells Fargo, T-Mobile, and Delta. This money trail matters, even though the $21.5 million sum expended is not large by itself. This record confronts companies operating in today's polarized political environment with questions about bankrolling attacks in state capitals on voting rights.[38]

2.6.1 Climate Change

CPA reported that ten nationally known companies including Walmart, Amazon, and Alphabet pumped hundreds of thousands of dollars of donations into Republican Attorneys General Association in the 2018 election cycle. RAGA paid money in support of election

---

[37] Center for Political Accountability, Collision Course, Collision-Course-Report. pdf (politicalaccountability.net), 2018, p. 9.

[38] Center for Political Accountability, Corporate Enablers, Corporate-Enablers. pdf (politicalaccountability.net), 2021, p. 6.

of seven Republican state attorneys general who were among those signing an amicus (friend-of-the court) brief in 2020 that supports the Trump administration's rollback of clean-car emission standards.

These ten companies signed a statement after the 2020 elections regarding confronting climate change and US membership in the Paris accord setting goals for fighting global warming, opening them to questions about a conflict between their political spending and their core values. The statement read:

"As major companies across diverse sectors of the U.S. economy, we are committed to meeting the profound challenge of climate change. We support the United States' return to the Paris Agreement, and we urge President-elect Biden and the new Congress to work together to enact ambitious, durable, bipartisan climate solutions." At the direction of Trump, the United States withdrew from the Paris accord. Under Biden, the United States rejoined the agreement in February 2021.

2.6.2 The Affordable Care Act

Amid a pandemic killing hundreds of thousands of Americans and threatening millions more, the foremost effort to dismantle the Affordable Care Act was a lawsuit forged by a coalition of Republican state attorneys general, led by Texas's Ken Paxton. The eighteen state attorneys general contended the Affordable Care Act was unconstitutional. The Trump administration sided with the states' lawsuit, which was filed in 2018. An estimated twenty million people would become uninsured if the Supreme Court found the entire Affordable Care Act to be unconstitutional. In a 7–2 decision, the Court rejected the challenge in 2021.[39]

Public companies and their trade associations have contributed generously to the RAGA, which supported the election of the attorneys general who brought suit to strike down the Affordable Care Act (see Figure 2.3).

Public companies typically make public statements supporting health care access for Americans. They may not have believed that

[39] For an analysis of the decision, see "The Affordable Care Act Survives Supreme Court Challenge: What Happens Next?" June 21, 2021. The Affordable Care Act Survives Supreme Court Challenge: What Happens Next? | K&L Gates LLP – JDSupra.

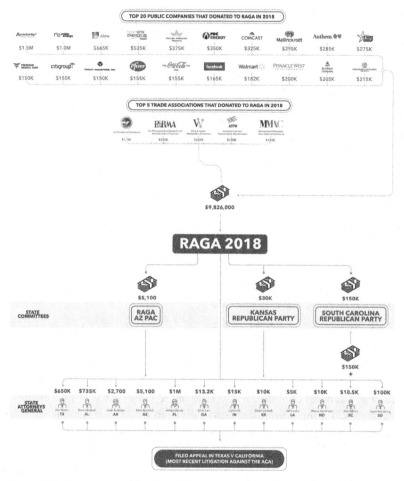

Figure 2.3 Donations to the Republican Attorneys General Association 2018
Source: Reproduced with the permission of the Center for Political
Accountability (CPA).

their political donations could one day help threaten the denial of
health care access for millions. If the Affordable Care Act had been
dismantled, these companies would have shared responsibility for
this denial.[40]

---

[40] Center for Political Accountability, Conflicted Consequences, p. 16.
Conflicted-Consequences.pdf (politicalaccountability.net).

2.6.3 LGBTQ Rights

In another striking example of companies getting scrutiny over political donations, leading US companies were accused of hypocrisy on LGBTQ rights. Publicly criticized were companies that had donated to the Republican State Leadership Committee (RSLC) in 2010 and who voiced opposition in 2016 to North Carolina's infamous "bathroom bill" banning antidiscrimination protections based on sexual orientation.

"Corporations Opposed to North Carolina's Anti-LGBT Law Helped Elect Its Supporters," a *Huffington Post* headline declared in 201629 about corporations donating to the RSLC, which helped flip the North Carolina legislature from Democratic to Republican control following the 2010 elections, and the "bathroom bill" legislation that the legislature enacted in 2016. There was a national outcry. The backlash included more than 200 corporate CEOs joining a letter demanding repeal of the law, which ultimately occurred.

Many public companies gave to the Republican Governors Association (RGA) in elections from the 2010 to 2018 election cycles, while they also have signed the Human Rights Campaign's Business Coalition for the Equality Act, helped elect gubernatorial candidates who subsequently attacked LGBTQ equality. One of the winning candidates for governor was North Carolina's Pat McCrory, who signed the "bathroom bill" into law.[41]

2.7 Consider How Accountability, in Practice, May Be Increasingly Authentic and Genuine

Accountability needs to be serious. It must result in a substantive change in behavior and a company deciding whether or how to engage in political spending. Companies striving for CPA-Zicklin Index Trendsetter status and citing it in press releases and Corporate Social Responsibility reports are indications that political spending is recognized a significant risk that needs to be managed, as well as a perception that a Trendsetter score bestows the appearance of a good corporate citizen. An example is a leading telecommunications company indicating that its adoption of policies to disclose its nondeductible trade association payments and contributions to "social welfare"

---

[41] Ibid., p. 25.

organizations would make it an Index Trendsetter. Becoming a Trendsetter was recognized as a step in repairing the company's image following its brush with scandal. Significantly, this is the case in the utility industry, which has come under close scrutiny because of its pattern of large contributions. As mentioned previously, several leading utilities, including Dominion Energy, Sempra Energy, and Ameren, have publicly touted their Trendsetter scores.

Media coverage of the risks companies face from political spending and of the Center's efforts has been crucial to encouraging companies to act. The *New York Times*, *Financial Times*, *Wall Street Journal*, and *Boston Globe* reported early on CPA's efforts and the initial successes in company adoption of policies for their political spending. The Center's reports and polling played a key role in generating stories and framing political spending as a risk. The reports included *The Green Canary* (2005), on the risks political spending posed to shareholder value; *Hidden Rivers* (2006) on the shift of company political spending to third-party groups, including trade associations and "social welfare" organizations that are not required to disclose their donors; *Collision Course* (2018) on the heightened risks companies faced from conflicted spending and the rise of social media; and *Conflicted Consequences* (2020/2021) and *Corporate Enablers* (2021) that traced company contributions and their role in enabling gerrymandering, abortion restrictions, and attacks on voting rights and efforts to address climate.

CPA has seen a steady increase in the number of agreements with companies to adopt political disclosure and accountability policies over the past eighteen years. This is the result of shareholder engagement by the Center's partners followed by companies agreeing to adopt policies in return for the withdrawal of the CPA model shareholder resolution. As of the end of 2021 spring proxy season, the number agreements totaled 195. However, this does not capture the full scope of company adoption of political disclosure and accountability policies. That is measured by the annual CPA-Zicklin Index, which found that 370 companies or 75 percent of the S&P 500 had adopted some level of disclosure or prohibition of their political spending and 295 companies or 60 percent of the S&P 500 had some level of board oversight or policies governing their political spending as of the fall of 2021.[42]

---

[42] The figures are from the 2021 CPA-Zicklin Index released on November 29, 2021.

What the Index shows is that political disclosure is the outcome of both shareholder engagement and of companies are acting on their own.

Resolutions, engagement of companies via the CPA-Zicklin Index, media coverage and the New York State Comptroller's books and records lawsuits have spurred internal dialogues within companies and been central to the Center's impact. Consider, for example:

- Qualcomm adopted robust political disclosure and accountability policies in 2013 that made it an Index Trendsetter following the New York State Comptroller's lawsuit and settlement discussions. Qualcomm's leadership was made aware of the company's weak policies on its political spending, prompting management to adopt new policies to settle the suit.
- Edwards Life Sciences and Intuitive Surgical, two Silicon Valley companies, improved their standing in the 2016 CPA-Zicklin Index following release of the Index that highlighted their poor scores.
- A leading company in the food sector adopted robust political disclosure and accountability policies in 2019 following a dialogue spurred by the filing of the Center's model resolution. What prompted the action, the corporate secretary told CPA, was that "We're concerned that a controversial contribution could lead consumers to shift to a competing product."

Through voluntary company disclosure of the nondeductible portion of their trade association payments included on the Center for Political Accountability's TrackYourCompany database,[43] CPA has identified significant declines in the money received by associations that can be used for election-related or lobbying spending following company adoption of political disclosure policies.[44] The fact that they were seen in several prominent companies bears examining to what extent disclosure may have been a factor in the change in the payments. In one case, Prudential Financial cut its annual payment to the US Chamber of Commerce from $1.5 million to under $100,000 over a decade after the company's adoption of trade association payment

---

[43] Why Corporate Political Spending Matters – Political Accountability.
[44] Company payments to trade associations cover a range of activities. Some are deductible as business expenses such as various services provided by the association. However, companies are not permitted to deduct as a business expense the portion of its dues or other payments used for election-related spending or lobbying activities.

disclosure. In another case, Dow Chemical's annual nondeductible payments to the US Chamber dropped from close to $2 million to slightly over $100,000 in the five years following its adoption of trade association payment disclosure. Lastly, Coca Cola trimmed its annual US Chamber nondeductible payment from over $300,000 to below $50,000 in the four years following its adoption of trade association disclosure.

CPA found that disclosure affected candidate decisions on whether to accept company political contributions. Take the case of a mayor's race in a major city. As recounted to CPA by several sources with first-hand knowledge, a company that was a CPA-Zicklin index Trendsetter was asked to donate to a nonprofit, also known as a 501(c)(4) group, affiliated with the candidate. The company responded that it would do so but that it would need to disclose the contribution as required by its political spending policies. The candidate's response was thanks, but no thanks. The incident provided an example of the impact on political spending when a company adhered to its policy committing it to disclosure.

Another important area to examine is companies' pausing political spending following the January 6th insurrectionary attack on the US Capitol. How long will this pause last? Already the indications are not very long.[45] A related matter is how state-level attacks on voting have put companies under scrutiny for their political spending.[46]

---

[45] One company that adopted a policy not to contribute to members of Congress who refused to certify the 2020 presidential election results was Intel. Following is the company's policy posted on its website: "In response to stakeholder feedback, we have further enhanced our review process by adding reviews of public statements to our existing reviews of voting records to better assess alignment with our values. When we identify some degree of misalignment, we communicate directly with contribution recipients. In cases of significant misalignment across our multiple key public policy issues, we take action to realign future funding decisions. For example, following the events at the US Capitol on January 6, 2021, we decided to cease contributions to members of Congress who voted against certification of the 2020 presidential election." For companies restarting political spending following a post-January 6, 2021 pause, see *New York Times*, Companies Donated Millions to Those Who Voted to Overturn Biden's Win – *The New York Times* (nytimes.com)

[46] See the Center for Political Accountability's Corporate Enablers report (2021) for an examination of company political spending in seven states that are battlegrounds in the attacks on voting rights. Corporate-Enablers.pdf (politicalaccountability.net).

Climate change is another exposure point for companies. Companies are being confronted on the broader issue of conflicted spending where the consequences of their contributions are at odds with their publicly stated core values, positions, and policies. CPA's objective: promote authenticity and deny greenwashing.

2.8 Conclusion

At a time of prolonged legislative and government paralysis, CPA's strategy of using corporate engagement has been essential to circumventing the political process and laying the foundation to bring transparency and accountability to corporate political spending and change how companies approach political spending. Ultimately, a government rule will be required to make corporate political disclosure uniform and universal. But this could not be achieved without companies being encouraged and incentivized to act voluntarily, with a critical number of companies making it the norm. Achieving such critical mass is the essence of "private ordering" and creation of private law. Adopting a government rule will codify what companies are already doing and turn private law into a public regulation. By creating a level playing field and discouraging noncompliance, regulation will advance an important government interest.

CPA's strategy offers a model for using corporate governance as a vehicle to press companies to address other important public issues. Under this model, the motivation for change would be articulated from the outside. This can be done if an issue is seen as a "risk" and policies to address it are seen as "risk management." This could apply to issues such as climate change, diversity (including redistricting and gerrymandering), and protecting democracy. Addressing them as risks depoliticizes the issue and the remedy. In the case of political spending, change was achieved by adopting disclosure and accountability policies to manage the risk posed by political money. CPA's early reports casting political spending as a risk to shareholder value and The Conference Board's *Handbook on Corporate Political Activity* were key to achieving this.

As CPA's experience has shown, using both the shareholder resolution and the engagement of companies has brought change. They have made political spending an issue that companies needed to address, have prompted them to act, and have led them to reach agreements or act on their own to adopt political disclosure and accountability policies. Companies would not be dealing with political spending and adopting political disclosure and accountability policies without CPA and its shareholder partners putting it before them and creating a framework for a thoughtful response. This observation is based on CPA's first-hand experience.

Building on the political disclosure and accountability policies CPA has put in place, the Model Code of Conduct aims at changing the political spending behavior of companies. It takes the next step of providing a framework for companies to approach political spending. The framework reflects the broader business, political and societal environment that companies need to grow, thrive, and compete and ethical considerations that should be motivating factors in how companies approach political spending. It also recognizes the importance of democracy to business and the need for companies to make that a paramount consideration in political spending decisions.[47]

The progression of CPA's effort shows how corporate governance and "risk management" can be used to promote both internal and external dialogue on an important public policy issue. Change that many might have thought impossible by government action has instead been achieved by engagement and the willingness of companies to reassess their approach political spending in light of shareholder concerns, and to assume greater responsibility for the societal and broader political consequences of their action.

Bibliography

(2011). *Wall Street Journal*, December 28.
(2012a). *Wall Street Journal*, March 18.
(2012b). *Wall Street Journal*, May 31.
(2013). *Wall Street Journal*, October 21.
(2014a). *Wall Street Journal*, May 25.
(2014b). *Wall Street Journal*, September 29.

---

[47] See Practical Stake, the Center for Political Accountability's report on corporations, political spending, and democracy released in April 2022. Practical-Stake.pdf (politicalaccountability.net). It examines the stake that companies have in democracy, the role of their political spending in enabling the attack on democracy and the climate of intimidation that has followed, and actions companies should take to protect themselves and democracy.

(2014c). *Wall Street Journal*, October 21.

(2017). *Wall Street Journal*, July 7.

(2021). Track Your Company. *Center for Political Accountability*, August 23.

Bitzer, J. M. (2009). Tillman Act of 1907. The First Amendment Encyclopedia.

Blumenthal, P. (2015). The Chamber of Commerce Is Fighting Fiercely to Stop the Scourge of Corporate Transparency. *HuffPost Politics*, April 22.

Bross, D., & Johnson, A. J. (2015). 3 Business Leaders Speak about Transparency's Importance at CPA Co-sponsored Roundtable. *CPA Newsletter*, February 2015, 3.

Carnevale, A., Hamscho, V., Lawless, T., & Page, K. S. (2021). The Affordable Care Act Survives Supreme Court Challenge: What Happens Next? *JD Supra*, June 21.

Confessore, N. (2003). Welcome to the Machine. *Washington Monthly*, July 1.

Evers-Hillstron, K. (2020). Why Corporate PACs Have an Advantage. *Open Secrets*, February 14.

Freed, B. F., & Porter, M. E. (2021). Big Businesses Say They Are Responsible, but Too Often They Fuel Conspiracy Theories. *USA Today*, January 19.

Freed, B., et. al. (2005). The Green Canary and the Shareholder. *CPA Report 2005*, 5–6.

Freed, B. et. al. (2020). Conflicted Consequences. *Center for Political Accountability*, July 21.

Laufer, W. S. (2021). Amid Political Turmoil, Continued Attacks on Democracy, 2021 CPA-Zicklin Index Finds Companies Tightening Oversight of Political Spending. *Center for Political Accountability*, November 29, 4.

Magleby, D. B., & Nelson, C. J. (1990). *The Money Chase: Congressional Campaign Finance Reform* (Washington, DC: Brookings).

Porter, M. E., & Freed, B. F. (2021). Companies Need to Reevaluate the Full Range of Their Political Spending. *The Boston Globe*, January 26.

Rappeport, A., Ngo, M., & Kelly, K. (2022). Corporations Donated Millions to Lawmakers Who Voted to Overturn Election Results. *New York Times*, January 6.

Reid, J., & Dubose, L. (2004). The Man with the Plan. *Texas Monthly*, August.

Smith, B. (2011). *Wall Street Journal*, November 10.

Strassel, K. (2012). *Wall Street Journal*, May 31.

Strassel, K. (2016). *The Intimidation Game: How the Left Is Silencing Free Speech* (New York: Grand Central Publishing).

Switzman. (2020). CPA-Wharton Zicklin Model Code of Conduct for Corporate Political Spending. *Center for Political Accountability*, October 13.

3 | Measuring Corporate Political Responsibility

THOMAS P. LYON AND WILLIAM MANDELKORN

3.1 Introduction

Every year, corporations spend vast amounts of money to influence the political process. From the millions some firms spend on Super PAC contributions to the combined over $3 billion spent annually on lobbying in recent years,[1] corporate political activity (CPA) is a big business, with the large expenditures suggesting there are large benefits to shaping policy. But where does this money go, how does it affect policy, and are corporations participating in the political process in a responsible manner? This chapter assesses the state of the art in metrics for CPA and corporate political responsibility (CPR), without which none of the foregoing questions can be answered.

Corporate political activity certainly grabs headlines. In 2021, as reported by the *New York Times*[2] and the *Washington Post*,[3] firms and trade associations spent millions of dollars in an attempt to shape the Biden administration's policy proposals, particularly the economic and social spending bill often referred to as "Build Back Better," with the US Chamber of Commerce, the biggest lobbyist of all (see Table 3.1), vowing to "do everything [they] can to prevent this ... reconciliation bill from becoming law"[4] and the chairman of Merck pharmaceuticals explaining that their push to stop the bill was largely due to projected revenue losses.[5] After vowing to cut support to the 147 members of the House of Representatives who objected to certifying the 2020 presidential election results, corporations came under the

---

[1] www.opensecrets.org/federal-lobbying
[2] www.nytimes.com/2021/10/04/us/politics/biden-lobbying-congress.html
[3] www.washingtonpost.com/us-policy/2021/08/31/
business-lobbying-democrats-reconciliation/
[4] www.uschamber.com/infrastructure/us-chamber-vows-defeat-reconciliation-
hails-voting-deadline-bipartisan-infrastructure
[5] www.nytimes.com/2021/10/04/us/politics/biden-lobbying-congress.html

microscope as they quietly resumed giving when the 2022 midterm elections approached, hoping to maintain influence across parties, with one GOP lobbyist commenting that few people would pay attention, since "time heals all."[6]

The foregoing activity is readily visible, but it is only the tip of the iceberg, with firms spending large amounts of "dark money" to influence the political process while leaving little trace in the public record. Occasionally such covert action does come to light, however. For example, pharmaceutical giant AbbVie, after abusing the patent system to maintain monopoly profits on the world's best-selling drug over its nearly twenty-year existence, poured millions of dollars into dark money ad campaigns against prescription drug negotiation and cost cap bills.[7] Less blatantly, the Allied Pilots Association, an American Airlines pilots union, spent millions on townhouses nearby the US Capitol, providing not only a close access point to influence the legislative process, but a venue for events held by members of Congress.[8] All the while, both Democrats and Republicans receive support from donors who exploit loopholes to launder anonymous contributions through dark money groups before sending them along to Super PACs and other organizations with more stringent disclosure requirements.[9]

With so many dollars flowing from corporations into the political process, is this money being spent in a responsible way? Are pharmaceutical companies lobbying against prescription drug bills because these bills really would stifle research that would benefit the public, or simply because these bills would restrict their revenues? Did the US Chamber of Commerce spend over $46 million on lobbying during the first three quarters of 2021[10] in an attempt to improve the reconciliation bill or simply to block the repeal of the Trump tax cuts? Is there even enough data available to be able to tell? In an environment with lax reporting requirements, can we accurately measure CPA, let alone more complex concepts like CPR? What would be required if we wanted to do so?

---

[6] www.politico.com/news/2021/11/08/gop-lobbyists-corporate-america-520026
[7] www.salon.com/2021/05/26/pharma-giant-abbvie-funds-ads-attacking-prescription-drug-bill--after-hiking-prices-up-to-470/
[8] www.politico.com/news/2021/11/23/lobbyists-capitol-hill-real-estate-523246
[9] www.nytimes.com/2022/01/29/us/politics/democrats-dark-money-donors.html
[10] www.opensecrets.org/federal-lobbying/clients/summary?cycle=2021&id=D000019798&name=US+Chamber+of+Commerce

In this chapter, we examine the measurement issues that currently plague analysis of CPA and that must be remedied for CPR to be credible, with a focus on the federal level. Section 3.2 considers political spending to influence who is elected, and Section 3.3 considers lobbying activity to influence politicians when they are in office. In each case, we survey the laws mandating disclosure of these activities, along with what some firms and third parties are doing to shed light on activities that fall outside these reporting requirements. In Section 3.4, we discuss the questions that can be answered with existing data, and the important questions that are impossible to answer due to data gaps. Finally, Section 3.5 concludes by addressing changes to current laws, and to norms of corporate behavior, that could increase transparency and accountability in the world of CPA. Promising developments are being proposed, and we are confident that more widespread adoption of these policies will lead to greater transparency around CPA, and a better understanding of how well firms are exhibiting CPR.

3.2 Political Spending

The first of the two main levers of CPA that firms have at their disposal is political spending, financial contributions to influence electoral processes through any of a variety of channels. Largely organized as tax-exempt groups through sections 501(c) and 527 of the Internal Revenue Code,[11] the forms we describe below comprise the primary channels of electoral spending. Key 527 groups include many state and federal PACs and Super PACs that are created primarily to influence the political process, while 501(c) nonprofits like social welfare organizations, labor unions, and chambers of commerce can engage in the political process, but must have charitable, religious, or other primary purposes. The key channels are the following, with explanations taken from OpenSecrets.org:

- *Political Action Committees (PAC)*: "A PAC is a political committee that raises and spends money to elect or defeat candidates. Most PACs represent businesses, such as the Microsoft PAC;

---

[11] I.R.C. § 501 and 527.

labor unions, such as the Teamsters PAC; or ideological interests, such as the EMILY's List PAC or the National Rifle Association PAC. An organization's PAC will solicit money from the group's employees or members and make contributions in the name of the PAC to candidates and political parties."[12] PACs are required to disclose their donors and their expenditures, and they are limited to giving no more than $5,000 to a candidate in a particular election cycle.

- *Super PACs*: "Technically known as independent expenditure-only committees, super PACs may raise unlimited sums of money from corporations, unions, associations and individuals, then spend unlimited sums to overtly advocate for or against political candidates. Unlike traditional PACs, super PACs are prohibited from donating money directly to political candidates. Their spending is not supposed to be coordinated with that of the candidates they benefit, although enforcement of this requirement has been lax. Super PACs are required to report their donors to the Federal Election Commission on a monthly or semiannual basis — the super PAC's choice — in off-years, and monthly in the year of an election (Federal Election Commission, 2021). As of July 27,2021, 2,276 groups organized as super PACs reported total receipts of $3,427,543,995 and total independent expenditures of $2,128,047,603 in the 2019–2020 cycle."[13]
- *"Social welfare organizations" or 501(c)(4)s*: Nonprofits organized under section 501(c)(4) of the tax code can engage in political action as long as it is not their primary activity. They "are generally under no legal obligation to disclose their donors even if they spend to influence elections. When they choose not to reveal their sources of funding, they are considered "dark money" groups."[14] These 501(c)(4)s are sometimes paired with a Super PAC, with the 501(c)(4) giving up to hundreds of millions of dollars to the Super PAC.
- *Independent expenditures*: The Supreme Court's *Citizens United* decision declared that political spending is protected "speech," so companies can spend unlimited amounts of money from their treasury on "electioneering" communications as long as they are not coordinated with individual political candidates.

[12] www.opensecrets.org/political-action-committees-pacs/2022?party=D
[13] For current data, see www.opensecrets.org/outside-spending/super_pacs/2020?
chrt=2022&disp=O&type=S
[14] www.opensecrets.org/dark-money/basics

• *Trade associations*: Industry trade associations often engage in political action. These associations typically disclose their membership but not the financial contributions of individual members. Thus, members can engage in unlimited covert political spending through such associations, turning trade associations into a form of dark money spending.

As will be discussed throughout this chapter, public disclosure requirements are so lax that it is impossible to get any accurate assessment of total corporate spending on CPA. Current law requires firms to disclose the sources of donations to their corporate PACs, as well as the recipients of funds from these PACs. It also requires firms to disclose direct donations to Super PACs. However, firms can give unlimited amounts of money to so-called "social welfare" organizations organized as 501(c)(4) groups without disclosing their contributions, and the 501(c)(4) groups can make unlimited contributions to Super PACs. Thus, firms can launder unlimited amounts of money to Super PACs through 501(c)(4)s, and Super PACs can then undertake unlimited amounts of "independent" campaign spending with virtually no accountability. Firms can also spend unlimited amounts of money on "independent" election expenditures and ballot measures. As a result, it is possible to construct a lower bound on corporate spending on CPA, but it is impossible to know the level of real spending.

The Center for Political Accountability has led a two-decade-long movement to increase voluntary disclosure of political spending (Freed et al., 2023) Its annual CPA-Zicklin Index (created in collaboration with the Zicklin Center for Business Ethics Research at Wharton) rates companies on the transparency of their electoral spending (The Center for Political Accountability, 2021). Rating companies on twenty-four metrics meant to measure various aspects of a firm's electoral spending, the Index covers political expenditure reports from members of the S&P 500. In 2020, over half of the S&P 500 disclosed some or all of their political spending, while an additional 14 percent had policies against certain types of election-related spending, showing a strong commitment to electoral spending transparency from some of the world's largest firms. CPA-Zicklin also aims to measure firms on their policies governing political spending decision-making, that is, on their accountability to stakeholders. From 2016 to 2020, CPA-Zicklin notes that the number of S&P 500 firms with "policies requiring board oversight of political spending and board committee review of company policy, political expenditures and trade association payment" has risen from 111 to 162. CPA-Zicklin solely scores firms on their electoral spending and disclosure policies, not their political spending objectives or their lobbying spending or activity. A firm publicly disclosing its contributions to Super PACs that engage in climate change denial can score just as highly as a firm publicly disclosing its contributions to Super PACs that advocate for a carbon tax, or firms that publicly disclose their policy to not engage in any election-related spending. In a world with an increasing need for CPR, CPA-Zicklin does not attempt to assess whether a firm is contributing responsibly, instead opting to evaluate firms on whether they provide enough information on their political spending activity to allow others to make that evaluation.[15]

Although CPA-Zicklin does an admirable job of tracking the disclosed political spending by S&P 500 firms, it remains difficult to get a sense of how large a role total corporate contributions may play in the electoral process. To shed some light on this issue, we consider corporate contributions to the largest Super PACS, which must be disclosed. By focusing on a set of large Super PACs comprising roughly half of all federal Super PAC receipts during the 2018 and 2020 election cycles, we can calculate (imperfectly) a rough lower bound on the overall role of corporate contributions to Super PACs.

After limiting ourselves to the largest Super PACs (the smallest set that will comprise 50 percent of all federal Super PAC receipts),[16] we further limited our count of corporate contributions to those donors reporting an "organization" entity type, and manually removed any non-corporations (trade associations, dark money groups, Native American tribes, etc.) before summing their total contributions. For comparison, we also included in the table contributions from individuals who contributed more than a certain threshold (either one million or ten million dollars, in separate calculations) to these selected Super PACs. Overall, as shown in Table 3.1, we find that corporations are responsible for roughly 5 and 8 percent of contributions to these top Super PACs, in 2020 and 2018 respectively, with conservative-leaning Super PACs generally receiving a larger portion of their receipts from

[15] https://politicalaccountability.net/hifi/files/2020-CPA-Zicklin-Index.pdf
[16] www.opensecrets.org/outside-spending/summary

Table 3.1 *Contributions from corporations and individuals to top Super PACS*

Super PAC	View	Total Receipts	Percent from Corporations	Percent from Individuals Giving >= $1MM	Percent from Individuals Giving >= $10MM
		2020			
SENATE LEADERSHIP FUND	C	$475,597,989	7.5%	63.0%	41.1%
SMP	L	$316,664,959	3.0%	25.7%	0.0%
CONGRESSIONAL LEADERSHIP FUND	C	$165,638,705	8.4%	65.0%	52.6%
AMERICA FIRST ACTION, INC.	C	$154,971,075	5.0%	70.0%	46.4%
PRESERVE AMERICA PAC	C	$105,491,967	0.1%	99.2%	96.7%
AB PAC	L	$89,561,900	0.0%	33.9%	0.0%
AMERICAN CROSSROADS	C	$81,806,847	3.1%	2.0%	1.2%
CLUB FOR GROWTH ACTION	C	$71,826,672	5.9%	83.6%	67.9%
INDEPENDENCE USA PAC	L	$67,713,621	0.4%	99.4%	99.4%
LCV VICTORY FUND	L	$61,444,629	1.7%	28.5%	6.8%
THE LINCOLN PROJECT	L	$56,762,698	4.6%	6.1%	0.0%
Top 2020 Super PAC		$1,647,481,062			
Overall 2020 Super PAC		$3,427,543,995	48.1%	4.7%	53.5%	35.1%

2018

Super PAC	View	Total Receipts	Percent from Corporations	Percent from Individuals Giving >= $1MM	Percent from Individuals Giving >= $10MM
SMP	L	$158,920,153	2.2%	56.6%	23.9%
CONGRESSIONAL LEADERSHIP FUND	C	$157,783,333	11.0%	58.2%	43.6%
SENATE LEADERSHIP FUND	C	$130,706,345	13.9%	61.9%	44.4%
HOUSE MAJORITY PAC	L	$96,896,532	2.1%	43.7%	19.9%
INDEPENDENCE USA PAC	L	$65,188,915	2.1%	97.4%	97.4%
NEXT GEN CLIMATE ACTION COMMITTEE	L	$64,397,905	3.7%	93.9%	93.9%
WOMEN VOTE!	L	$45,749,746	12.4%	31.5%	4.3%
AMERICA FIRST ACTION	C	$38,308,581	16.6%	62.3%	26.1%
NEW REPUBLICAN PAC	C	$34,104,749	15.6%	49.2%	44.0%
Top 2018 Super PAC		$792,056,258	7.8%	61.1%	42.3%
Overall 2018 Super PAC		$1,567,304,432	50.5%		

Source: FEC. OpenSecrets.org.

corporations. Corporate contributions are dwarfed by money from large individual donors however, with some individuals contributing tens of millions of dollars (e.g., Michael Bloomberg, Timothy Mellon, and Kenneth Griffin), and some contributing hundreds of millions (e.g., Sheldon and Miriam Adelson). It is worth mentioning that these results, focusing on top federal Super PACs, differ substantially from the results of a similar analysis, focusing on six state-based 527 groups, mentioned in Freed et al. (2023). Given the wide range of state and federal groups that are considered 527 organizations, it is possible that similar analyses run on different subsets of 527 groups could yield different results.

Further complicating this analysis is the fact that these estimates constitute lower bounds on corporate contributions, with Super PAC-to-Super PAC contributions inflating the amount of total documented receipts, and contributions from dark money groups to Super PACs shielding possible additional undocumented corporate contributions. The latter is particularly troubling, as the pairing of a dark money group and a Super PAC can result in large sums of money travelling across organizations, while being shielded from some public view. The power of combining a 501(c)(4) with a 527 Super PAC was immediately recognized by Karl Rove, the Republican operative, who helped to form American Crossroads, a Super PAC, and Crossroads Grassroots Policy Strategies (GPS), a 501(c)(4) group, within months of the *Citizens United* ruling. One Nation, another 501(c)(4) associated with Rove, is not required to disclose their donors, but has contributed over $125 million to the Senate Leadership Fund, an independent 527 Super PAC that is required to disclose their donors.

Although corporate influence in some areas, like lobbying, may be large, corporate contributions to Super PACs seem to be relatively small, showing that, while CPA-Zicklin may do a great job documenting electoral contributions from corporations, additional ratings systems may be needed to fully capture the scope of corporate influence.

The Center for Political Accountability has also developed a framework designed to help ensure accountability for political spending. Called the CPA-Zicklin Model Code, it has twelve key elements, which are presented in full in Freed et al. (2023). In general, they call for avoiding agency problems (i.e., pursuing the interests of the company overall rather than those of individual managers), being transparent about corporate spending (including through trade associations and other political organizations), avoiding any appearance or actuality of paying for political favors, having a clear oversight process for corporate political spending that goes up to the Board of Directors, ensuring that political activity is aligned with the company's core values and policies, and considering fully the broader social and economic harm and risks posed by corporate political spending.

This is an admirable set of principles, yet even so it is incomplete as a means of ensuring accountability. For example, it does not cover lobbying expenses, positions, and targets; revolving door activity; or corporate philanthropy and the politicians who benefit from it. Nevertheless, since there is no legal mandate for accountability around corporate political activity, the voluntary CPA-Zicklin Model Code represents the current "gold standard" for corporate accountability practices. It is gaining traction, and over time may become the de facto standard for political accountability. Although some prominent scholars like Michael Porter have begun to "urge businesses to adhere to the principles outlined in the Model Code," there is still a long way to go before adherence to the Model Code becomes the norm for large corporations.[17]

Another promising development in the domain of accountability is the emergence of corporate Political Engagement Reports. Among the companies offering these reports are AT&T, Chesapeake Energy, Ford Motor Company, JP Morgan Chase, and Verizon. There is as yet no norm for the format and content of these reports. For example, Chesapeake Energy's 2019 report is a simple one-page document. Although it does not mention the CPA-Zicklin Model Code, it does state that the firm takes certain actions that are consistent with Code items 1, 5, and 10. For 2019, it discloses $210,240 in PAC contributions, a contribution of $2,845,311 to the American Petroleum Institute (API), and $430,000 in federal lobbying spending and $690,000 in state lobbying spending. It states that it did not provide any funding to candidates, political campaign committees, or Super PACs. It also states explicitly that it does not fund the American Legislative Exchange Council (ALEC).[18] It is unclear whether the firm contributed to any 501(c)(4) "social welfare" groups that might have

---

[17] https://corpgov.law.harvard.edu/2020/11/28/the-cpa-wharton-zicklin-model-code-of-conduct/

[18] www.chk.com/Documents/responsibility/2019-Political-Activity-Report.pdf

then contributed to Super PACs, whether the firm made any "independent expenditures" on elections, or what positions were espoused by its lobbyists on material issues such as climate change.

In contrast, Ford Motor's 2020 report is thirteen pages long. It states explicitly that the firm did not contribute to any 501(c)(4) groups or to 527 Super PACs. It contains a significant discussion of climate change, including the fact that Ford opted to support the California Air Resources Board (CARB) in working on a unified GHG/CAFE policy, at a time when the Trump administration sought to disenfranchise CARB altogether from the enforcement of the Clean Air Act, a role CARB has held since the early 1970s. Ford discloses the trade associations to which it contributes, although it is not explicit about exactly how much it contributes to each. It also shares a short summary of each association's position on climate change. For example, it quotes the Chamber of Commerce's position: "The Chamber stands with every American seeking a cleaner, stronger environment—for today and tomorrow. The Chamber recognizes that our climate is changing and humans are contributing to these changes. Inaction is simply not an option, and American businesses will play a vital role in creating innovative solutions to protect our planet." Ford's comment on this vacuous verbiage is the anodyne "Ford continues to highlight the importance of climate change at the Chamber."[19]

Although these political engagement reports may not be perfect, the companies issuing them are to be applauded for taking these positive steps toward greater transparency and accountability. More will surely follow.

Although the foregoing discussion focuses on federal election spending, growing attention is being paid to the state level as well. As Bruce Freed and Michael Porter mention[20] and Freed et al. (2023) discuss, corporate giving to the Republican Attorneys General Association (RAGA) has remained high despite their encouragement of the January 6 attack on the Capitol and their support of lawsuits aimed at overturning the 2020 presidential election. For example, four companies

---

[19] https://corporate.ford.com/content/dam/corporate/us/en-us/documents/reports/Political-Disclosure-Report-Final-Revised-November-2021.pdf

[20] https://politicalaccountability.net/hifi/files/CPA---Boston-Globe---Companies-need-to-reevaluate-the-full-range-of-their-political-spending---01-26-21---Michael-Porter-Bruce-Freed-op-ed.pdf

that signed a November 2020 letter asking for the Trump administration to accept the election results have given, over just the last two election cycles, over $500,000 each to RAGA, an organization that has supported lawsuits challenging these very same election results.

Werner (2017, 2023) uses an event study framework to examine the impact of the accidental disclosure of contributions to a 501(c)(4) group under the control of the Republican Governors Association (RGA). These contributions would normally go undisclosed, but donor names were accidentally published on a RGA website. Surprisingly, Werner finds positive abnormal financial returns associated with companies being included in this disclosure, perhaps indicating that shareholders view this connection as indicative of having established a closer relationship with RGA and being able to reap the benefits of this relationship, in spite of the fact that RGA-advocated policies may be in conflict with public statements and goals made by these firms. Minefee et al. (2021) examine a similar, whistleblower leak of the American Legislative Exchange Council's (ALEC) corporate sponsors, but find a negative effect on returns for those companies involved, perhaps due to the controversial nature of ALEC.

This research helps to further our understanding of corporate electoral contributions and why firms contribute (a question explored in depth by Walker (2023) in this volume), but points back to the main issue discussed above, a lack of adequate measurement and disclosure of CPA. Clearly, based on market returns surrounding the accidental disclosure of contributor identities, shareholders care about the CPA and CPR of companies they invest in. However, we cannot rely on accidental disclosures to provide us with the data needed to measure CPA, CPR, and firm alignment on stated goals. A better understanding of firms' electoral contributions will require strengthening reporting requirements, third-party data collection and analysis, or firms adopting more stringent reporting requirements and releasing political engagement reports that better document their activities and positions.

3.3 Lobbying

The second major element of CPA is lobbying that involves the provision of information to government officials regarding the likely effects of particular policies. Throughout this chapter, we focus mainly on federal lobbying efforts. Firms employing in-house lobbyists that spend more than $14,000 per quarter on lobbying activities and lobbying firms receiving more than $3,000 per quarter from a client are required by law to disclose which individuals conducted lobbying on their behalf, who the target was (in broad buckets such as "Senate" or "White House Office"), and the broad topic covered (such as "Taxation/Internal Revenue Code" or "Environmental/Superfund").[21]

The total level of spending on lobbying is somewhat better documented than political spending, and in this domain it is clear that business completely dominates all other groups. A few years ago, Lee Drutman, one of the most astute observers of lobbying behavior, wrote:

Corporations now spend about $2.6 billion a year on reported lobbying expenditures—more than the $2 billion we spend to fund the House ($1.18 billion) and Senate ($860 million). It's a gap that has been widening since corporate lobbying began to regularly exceed the combined House-Senate budget in the early 2000s.... For every dollar spent on lobbying by labor unions and public-interest groups together, large corporations and their associations now spend $34. Of the 100 organizations that spend the most on lobbying, 95 consistently represent business. (Drutman, 2015)

Figure 3.1 shows yearly lobbying expenditures for business, labor, and ideological groups, as classified by OpenSecrets.org.[22] Their categorization finds that in 2020 nearly $3 billion and 88 percent of lobbying expenditures originated from business interests. While the exact amounts vary year-over-year, business groups were responsible for greater than 85 percent of lobbying expenditures every year since 2008, with labor interests composing fewer than 2 percent. Echoing Drutman's observation on the imbalance between corporate, labor, and public interest lobbying, business interests are by far the largest spenders in the lobbying sphere.

Mandated disclosures surely underestimate lobbying expenditures. There is estimated to be an equally large "gray market" for "shadow lobbying" conducted by individuals who decline to register themselves as lobbyists, but perform essentially the same services in their capacity as "advisors" (Thomas and LaPira, 2017). The bipartisan Lobbying

---

[21] https://lobbyingdisclosure.house.gov/ldaguidance.pdf
[22] www.opensecrets.org/federal-lobbying/business-labor-ideological

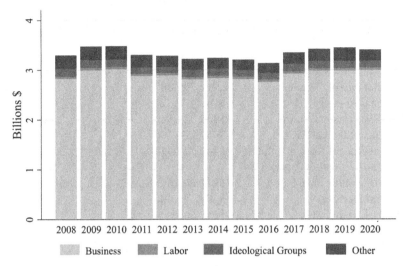

Figure 3.1 Business, labor, and ideological lobbying split
Source: Senate Office of Public Records (2020). OpenSecrets.org.

Disclosure Reform Act of 2020 would eliminate this loophole by updating the definition of what constitutes lobbying.[23]

Lobbying is a crucial part of CPA because it determines the information available to legislators making decisions in complex and rapidly changing conditions. Legislators receive surprisingly little independent information about the bills they vote on, beyond what they receive from the underfunded Congressional Research Service. Congressional staff are few in number and modestly paid, and the positions primarily attract young people looking to break into politics, who bring limited expertise in most dimensions of policymaking. They are often lured away by lobbyists promising to pay them multiple times what they earn in public service. Infamous lobbyist Jack Abramoff, who spent time behind bars for violating lobbying laws, has said that his most powerful tool for controlling congressional staff was to simply say to them, "'You know, when you're done working on the Hill, we'd very much like you to consider coming to work for us.' Now the moment I

---

[23] https://issueone.org/articles/issue-one-applauds-the-introduction-of-the-bipartisan-lobbying-disclosure-reform-act-of-2020-to-increase-transparency/

Table 3.2 *Top spending lobbying*
organizations, January 1998–September 2021

Organization	Spend
US Chamber of Commerce	$1,711,700,680
National Assn of Realtors	$702,477,321
American Hospital Assn	$459,324,560
American Medical Assn	$457,224,500
Pharmaceutical Research and Manufacturers of America	$442,524,550
Blue Cross/Blue Shield	$415,601,601
General Electric	$374,442,000
Business Roundtable	$341,760,000
Boeing Co	$311,308,310
Northrop Grumman	$306,477,213
Lockheed Martin	$292,279,628
AT&T Inc	$281,304,644
Exxon Mobil	$277,912,742
Verizon Communications	$274,330,859
AARP	$259,651,064
National Assn of Broadcasters	$257,358,000
Southern Co	$250,690,694
Edison Electric Institute	$249,121,069
Comcast Corp	$234,389,323
Altria Group	$227,165,200

Source: OpenSecrets.org.

said that to them or any of our staff said that to 'em, that was it. We owned them."[24]

Companies can lobby individually, through industry-specific trade associations such as the American Petroleum Institute (API) and the American Chemistry Council (ACC), or through "peak associations" such as the National Association of Manufacturers (NAM) or the US Chamber of Commerce, which seek to represent the views of broad swaths of the business community. The twenty biggest lobbyists of the past quarter century are presented in Table 3.2.[25] The US Chamber of

---

[24] https://archive.thinkprogress.org/jack-abramoff-explains-how-he-owned-members-of-congress-and-their-staff-8e2dff027c9b/

[25] www.opensecrets.org/federal-lobbying/top-spenders?cycle=a

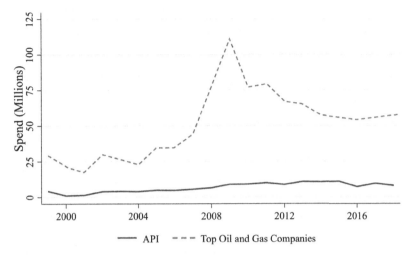

Figure 3.2 API and top oil and gas companies lobbying spend
Notes: Top companies include Royal Dutch Shell, BP, Exxon Mobil, Chevron,
Valero Energy, Phillips 66, Marathon Petroleum, ConocoPhillips, Schlumbeger,
and Enterprise Products Partners.
Source: Lobbying Disclosure Act reports. OpenSecrets.org.

Commerce is by far the highest spending lobbying organization from 1998 through September 2021, spending more than twice as much as the second largest spender during this time. Seven other trade associations make the list, one of them another peak association (the Business Roundtable) and three representing health care providers.

For many industries, individual company spending appears to exceed that of trade associations. Figure 3.2 illustrates this for the case of the American Petroleum Institute, whose annual lobbying expenditures never rise above about $10 million per year. Although this is not a trivial amount of lobbying, it is dwarfed by the combined expenditures of just ten large oil and gas companies, which topped out at just over $111 million in 2009 and have remained above $50 million in every year since then.

Regardless of their spending levels, trade associations are attracting growing attention because they can serve as a sort of "front group" that obscures which companies are really pressing for particular policies. The US Chamber of Commerce is the most notorious for this strategy, working to limit tobacco company liability, block health care

Figure 3.3 The US Chamber versus its members on climate policy, July 2021

reform, and stop progress on climate change – even though the majority of its members might have benefited from policy that improves employee health, reduces their own health care spending, and positions America to compete with countries such as China that are investing heavily in renewable energy (Katz, 2015).

The Chamber likes to present itself as "the voice of business," which suggests that its positions are broadly representative of corporate America. And for many years this was largely true. But under the former president and CEO Tom Donahue, the Chamber adopted a different strategy of taking the positions supported by the subset of its members that were most vehement on an issue, whether or not they were broadly supported by the full membership (Katz, 2015).

The disconnect between the Chamber's position on climate change and that of its non-fossil fuel members is shown dramatically in Figure 3.3.[26] The Chamber aligns itself with those firms whose role in the climate policy space is rated most negatively by independent research organization InfluenceMap, which gives each company a letter grade for its lobbying efforts. (InfluenceMap is discussed in more detail later in this chapter.)

As mentioned in Section 3.2, the CPA-Zicklin Index and Model Code make no attempt to assess or influence a firm's disclosure of its lobbying behavior. This is a very important gap, since firms spend much more on lobbying than they do on direct electoral contributions.

---

[26] https://grist.org/accountability/report-corporations-are-tanking-americas-best-shot-at-fighting-climate-change/

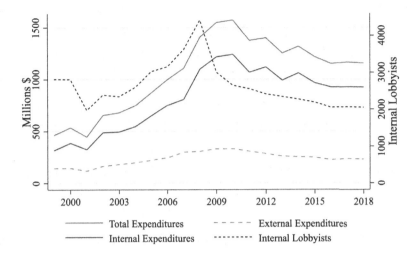

Figure 3.4 Lobbying expenditures and internal lobbyists for firms that ever lobbied on Lieberman-Warner or Waxman-Markey
Source: Lobbying Disclosure Act reports. OpenSecrets.org.

Current law requires all firms that lobby to disclose certain pieces of information, which are typically filed on a quarterly basis: (1) how much money was spent, (2) who conducted the lobbying, either from within the firm or on its behalf by external lobbyists, (3) what general issues were lobbied on, and (4) what general political bodies were lobbied.[27] It is important to note that the responses to items 3 and 4 can be very vague and general, and are all lumped together within a given quarterly report. Thus, there is no way to tell what fraction of the lobbying spend went to any specific issue, nor how much of it went to lobbying the "Senate" as opposed to the "White House Office."

One piece of information that is available on federal lobbying reports is whether firms use in-house lobbyists or hire external lobbyists, a topic examined in depth by Espinosa (2021). Figure 3.4 examines this question for companies that lobbied at any point on the Lieberman-Warner or Waxman-Markey bills on climate change. The data suggest that the vast bulk of lobbying expenditures were for internal lobbyists rather than external ones. The pattern over time

[27] https://lobbyingdisclosure.house.gov/amended_lda_guide.html#section4

is also intriguing, showing a huge increase in internal lobbying from around $300 million/year in 1999 to over $1.2 billion in 2010, and then gradually declining to somewhat more than $900 million/year since that time. These are obviously very large amounts. Moreover, the apparent decline in lobbying spend after 2010 may be illusory, as Thomas and LaPira (2017) argue that the gray market for "shadow lobbying" only took off after the Obama administration passed a rule blocking former politicians from becoming lobbyists. If their estimate is correct that there are at least as many shadow lobbyists as registered lobbyists, then the post-2010 period would show a continued growth in lobbying spend, with a growing shift toward external "advisors" doing a growing amount of lobbying. Furthermore, the even sharper rise and fall in the number of internal lobbyists around 2008 is intriguing as well. Is this evidence of some sort of internal lobbyist preference or ease of changing internal labor forces during times of changing lobbying demand, or is this evidence of a large shift around 2008 toward the labeling of lobbyists as "policy advisors" who lack reporting requirements, as the theory from Thomas and LaPira (2017) might suggest? Unfortunately, given current practices, it is impossible for researchers to confidently settle these debates. Section 3.4 offers a more robust discussion on a few important questions, and the data issues that plague empirical researchers seeking to answer them.

Given the lack of thorough documentation of a firm's exact lobbying activities in federal lobbying reports, there is growing stakeholder interest in third-party ratings of the transparency of a firm's lobbying activities, similar to the way CPA-Zicklin provides a rating of a firm's electoral-related spending disclosure policies. Many consultancies rate firms on their Environmental, Social and Governance (ESG) performance, but ratings provider Vigeo Eiris is the only ESG rater to attempt to evaluate the transparency of corporate lobbying.

Vigeo Eiris rates companies on their "transparency and integrity of influence strategies and practices" metric, which is itself a weighted average of nine metrics measuring firm leadership, implementation, and results.[28] Leadership is measured by a firm's visibility, exhaustiveness, and ownership of their commitment to ensuring transparency and integrity of their lobbying practices. The implementation metric scores a firm on the involvement of their employees in cultivating

---

[28] Data and documents were acquired via an agreement with Vigeo Eiris.

Table 3.3 *Lobbying spend, Vigeo Eiris, and CPA-Zicklin correlations*

	Yearly Lobbying Spend	Vigeo Eiris Responsible Lobbying Score	CPA-Zicklin Score
Yearly Lobbying Spend	1.000		
Vigeo Eiris Responsible Lobbying Score	0.145	1.000	
CPA-Zicklin Score	0.313	0.352	1.000

Source: Lobbying Disclosure Act data. OpenSecrets.org.
Vigeo Eiris. CPA-Zicklin

transparency and integrity in their lobbying process, along with the processes the firm puts into place, and the percent of their operations covered by these processes, that go toward lobbying transparency and integrity. The results score tracks the firm's lobbying budget reporting policies, the severity and frequency of their lobbying controversies, and the firm's responsiveness toward any lobbying controversies. Firms like E.ON and Xcel Energy score near the top of Vigeo Eiris' responsible lobbying metric, while other firms like Volkswagen and Conagra Foods score near the bottom. There is a relatively small correlation between a firm's scores in the categories "overall," "leadership," and "implementation" and the category "results," suggesting that more work is needed to help discover what drives a firm's lobbying results.

There is only a weak relationship between the amount of lobbying done by a company and the transparency of its lobbying as assessed by Vigeo Eiris, as Table 3.3 indicates. Specifically, there is a correlation of 14.5 percent between larger lobbying spend and a higher Vigeo Eiris rating, indicating that big lobbyists do tend to be a bit more transparent than others, assuming that they are not more involved in the "shadow lobbying" market. There is a somewhat greater correlation (31 percent) between lobbying scale and performance on the CPA-Zicklin Index, suggesting that large lobbyists face more pressure to disclose their electoral contributions than to disclose their lobbying activity.

InfluenceMap, a nonprofit rather than a consultancy, is another organization scoring firms and trade associations on their lobbying practices, particularly their climate lobbying activities. InfluenceMap measure firms on two main metrics: a "performance band" score ranging from "A+" to "F" that measures its own and its trade associations' climate policy engagement activities; and an "engagement intensity" score measuring the firm's level of policy engagement.[29] Electric utility Iberdrola is ranked in the "B+" performance band, highest among all firms, while Caterpillar and Marathon Petroleum jointly score in the "F" performance band. Advanced Energy Economy is the highest scoring industry association, and the lone organization to score in the "A+" performance band, while American Petroleum Institute ("E-"), the U.S. Chamber of Commerce ("E-"), NSW Minerals Council ("F"), and National Mining Association ("F") account for the lowest-ranked industry associations.

Engagement intensity is not explicitly tied to a firm's performance band; it is possible for firms to score highly on engagement intensity regardless of whether they are rated in high- or low-performance bands. Royal Dutch Shell, residing in the "C-" performance band, has the highest engagement intensity of any firm at 57, besting even Iberdrola's 53. It is clearly possible for firms to be highly engaged on climate policy, but advocating for unsustainable policies. On the other end of the spectrum, Caterpillar and Foxconn jointly score a 1 in InfluenceMap's engagement intensity rating, illustrating how some firms may score poorly in the performance band metrics, but be too disengaged to advocate strongly for their poorly rated policies.[30] InfluenceMap's rankings shed new light on firms, industry associations, and their relationships with each other and sustainable climate policies. Including Influence Map in the above correlations greatly reduces the number of observations, and results in low correlations, further indicating a weak relationship between the various lobbying and electoral spending ratings.

Figure 3.5 presents a matrix of InfluenceMap climate policy ratings for a selection of firms.[31] Firms in the top-right quadrant of the matrix are considered "climate policy leaders." Predominantly occupied by renewables-friendly energy companies like Iberdrola, SSE, Enel, and

[29] https://influencemap.org/page/Our-Methodology
[30] For current ratings, see https://lobbymap.org/filter/List-of-Companies-and-Influencers#3
[31] https://influencemap.org/climate-lobbying, accessed August 30, 2021.

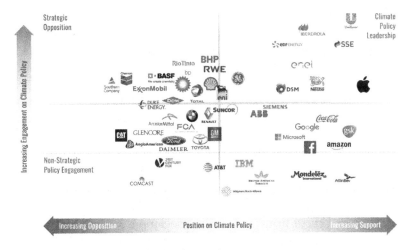

Figure 3.5 Climate policy leadership and engagement

EDF Energy, firms in this quadrant are both supportive of better climate policy and actively engaged in climate policy advocacy. Firms in the top-left quadrant affect climate policy the most negatively: these companies are highly engaged on climate policy, but in opposition to effective climate action. This quadrant is filled with traditional oil and gas giants like Shell, BP, ExxonMobil, and Chevron, although some, like Shell, lie further toward the "supportive" side, primarily due to their support of policies like carbon goals. Less engaged companies include the automobile manufacturers, which are occasionally in opposition to more stringent vehicle emissions policies, and the tech companies, that are generally supportive of climate policies, with cable, internet, tobacco, and alcohol firms least engaged, and running the gamut from opposition to support.

InfluenceMap notes that only 10 percent of firms have "fully aligned their direct climate lobbying practices with the Paris Agreement," while 91 percent of firms have memberships in trade associations that have "climate lobbying practices misaligned with the Paris Agreement." Further, InfluenceMap highlights another disclosure issue plaguing other rating organizations like CPA-Zicklin as well: When disclosure is not mandatory, firms can "cherry pick" what data to release, to obfuscate activities that might be poorly received by investors, employees, or the public. Just as contributions to 501(c)(4) groups need not be disclosed, firms may be hesitant to release their membership in, and funding of, trade associations that lobby for some policies at the expense of the climate. Without further policies regarding disclosure of contributions, lobbying activities, and trade association memberships, it will continue to be difficult to capture the full picture of a firm's influence activities, and whether the behavior of a firm is responsible.[32]

3.4 Why We Can't Know Important Things

As mentioned above, lobbying has become a $3.5 billion per year industry. Some firms and trade associations spend tens, and sometimes hundreds, of millions of dollars per year on lobbying expenses to inform and influence policymakers. Many Americans would like to know how these firms and trade associations are wielding their influence. Whom, specifically, are these firms lobbying? What issues do they care about, and what positions do they take on these issues? Are they lobbying to maintain the status quo, or do their large expenditures lead to substantial policy changes that benefit themselves, perhaps at the expense of the larger public interest? Firms are required to file quarterly lobbying reports, but given the scant information provided in these reports, it is impossible to accurately answer any of the above questions. These quarterly reports are the best source of lobbying information, yet they only provide basic details about the overall spend, lobbyists employed, and the issues and government entities targeted. These reports lack the detail required to answer almost any important lobbying-related question empirically.

To illustrate the limitations of current data, we discuss two research questions below that are hindered by currently data availability. To illustrate the problems involved, we primarily use as our setting lobbying on climate change during the period when the Liberman-Warner and Waxman-Markey climate bills were under consideration.

3.4.1 How Are Expenditures Allocated across Different Issues and Government Entities?

At their core, the federal lobbying reports exist to provide some insight into the flow of money and influence in legislative and regulatory

---

[32] https://influencemap.org/filter/List-of-Companies-and-Influencers#

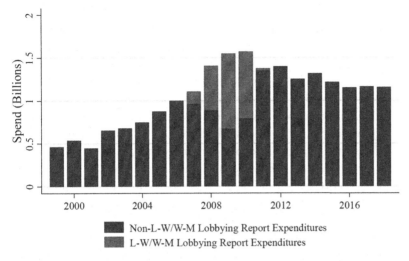

Figure 3.6 Lieberman-Warner/Waxman-Markey lobbying spend
Notes: Limited to companies who lobbied on Lieberman-Warner/
Waxman-Markey.
Source: Lobbying Disclosure Act reports. OpenSecrets.org.

processes. As such, one might be most concerned about two main questions: (1) How much money is spent on lobbying specific items; and (2) which government officials are on the receiving end of these lobbying efforts. While these reports do provide broad insight into who is lobbying and how much they may be spending in total, it can be difficult to ascertain where these efforts are directed most intensely, whether for specific issues or individual policymakers. Continuing our discussion of climate-related lobbying, researchers might well want to know how much of the total lobbying expenditures for firms that lobbied on Lieberman-Warner or Waxman-Markey actually went toward lobbying those two climate bills.

Figure 3.6 shows the yearly lobbying expenditures for all firms who lobbied on Lieberman-Warner or Waxman-Markey, with expenditures from reports mentioning either bill shown in lighter grey. Since the only way to identify lobbying spend on either of those bills is to search in the specific issue field in each report and check for whether the bill name or number appears, what we have constructed is an upper bound that assumes all of a firm's spending was on climate if any of it was. However, we cannot tell the true amount of lobbying on these two bills, only that it most likely falls within the green bars. Is the true amount close to the upper bound, or is it closer to the residual that remains after assuming a linear increase in lobbying expenditures from 2006 through 2011? Without relying on strong assumptions about the distribution of spend across issue codes and specific issues, there is no way to determine an exact amount or a relevant, non-zero lower bound. Even our upper bound on lobbying spend may be inaccurate, if shadow lobbying, as discussed above and in Thomas and LaPira (2017), is truly a large, unreported industry in itself.

To make matters more concrete, consider the 2009 fourth-quarter lobbying report from the US Chamber of Commerce, totaling over $71 million of lobbying expenditures.[33] The "American Clean Energy and Security Act of 2009," the official name of Waxman-Markey, was listed under five separate issue codes: Energy/Nuclear; Environmental/ Superfund; Homeland Security; Government Issues; and Trade (Domestic & Foreign). In total, thirty-nine separate issue codes were listed on this report, with hundreds of individual specific issues listed. How was this $71 million allocated across issues, and specifically, how much spending was directed toward Waxman-Markey lobbying? Without making strong assumptions about spend being divided across the number of issue codes or specific issues, it is difficult to arrive at any estimate other than "the U.S. Chamber of Commerce spent up to $71 million lobbying on Waxman-Markey during the fourth quarter of 2009."

Similar issues plague research attempting to answer specific questions about those on the receiving end of these lobbying activities. As mentioned above, one might like to know which individuals are the targets of these lobbying activities, and perhaps whether their actions are influenced as a result of lobbying. However, the federal lobbying reports do not provide this information, and only require registrants to name which government entities were lobbied on each issue code. Continuing our example from above, on the 2009 fourth-quarter lobbying report from the US Chamber of Commerce, across the five issue codes that mention Waxman-Markey, eighteen different government entities were listed, including the US Senate, the US House of Representatives, the White House Office, the Executive Office of the President, the Environmental Protection Agency, and the Department

---

[33] https://lda.senate.gov/filings/public/filing/d31f1fd6-3d80-4506-b282-6e5503c4fc2b/print/

of Energy. One cannot assume that the Chamber lobbied on Waxman-Markey at all eighteen government entities, either. For example, Waxman-Markey is just one of thirty-six specific issues listed under the "Trade (Domestic & Foreign)" issue code, with sixteen government entities listed for that code alone. While some government entities, like the Senate and House of Representatives, are listed under each issue code, there is no information as to which members of the Senate or House of Representatives were lobbied by the Chamber.

Some academic papers, like Bertrand et al. (2014), have attempted to navigate these challenges by assigning committees to issue codes (e.g., matching the House Budget and Appropriations committees to reports mentioning the Budget/Appropriations issue code) and assuming the members of the relevant committee are the members being lobbied, but this method may have its own set of issues. It is possible a firm directs its lobbying efforts not at the relevant committee, but at the expected pivotal vote in the larger chamber or at a small subset of committee members. There is simply no way to tell the exact reach of a firm's lobbying activities, and exactly which government officials may be on the receiving end.

This issue of how analysts should allocate spend across issues or government entities will plague any empirical work that relies on measuring lobbying spend by issue or government entity targeted. In Delmas et al. (2016), for example, the authors find a U-shaped curve documenting the relationship between a firm's greenhouse gas emissions intensity and its climate lobbying expenditures. This is a fascinating result, but raises questions about how spend on climate lobbying was calculated. To calculate climate lobbying expenditures, the authors simply grouped all reports that mentioned the Lieberman-Warner or Waxman-Markey climate bills or a handful of other climate related keywords, and allocated the entire spend to climate lobbying. However, as illustrated above, it is not realistic to expect that the total spend on each report can be allocated entirely toward climate issues. If a report mentions climate issues, not only will it almost certainly mention a multitude of other issues, but it is impossible to accurately estimate the portion of the spend that went toward climate issues. By limiting themselves to reports that mention climate issues, and allocating the entire spend on those reports to climate lobbying, Delmas et al. (2016) necessarily overestimate the total amount of climate lobbying expenditures. However, since all reports differ in the number of issues they cover, the authors would not overestimate climate lobbying spend consistently across firms either. Since it is impossible to accurately measure the total amount of climate lobbying expenditures at the firm level, the authors can only speculate at a relationship between greenhouse gas emissions and climate lobbying spend. These issues are not unique to this particular paper; they plague all empirical work on lobbying. Until lobbying reporting requirements change, empirical researchers are handicapped in their ability to analyze almost any lobbying-related question, and can at best make educated guesses about a firm's lobbying expenditures.

3.4.2 Are Firm Lobbying Activities Aligned with Their Public Statements?

A particular concern for CPR is when companies take progressive positions on climate in their public statements while lobbying against public policy addressing those issues in private, a form of greenwashing that obscures the true influence corporations have on climate policy. Focusing on ninety-six companies in the S&P 100 as of 2019, a recent Ceres report finds that 92 percent of those companies plan to set goals to reduce emissions and 88 percent charge their boards with a responsibility to oversee sustainability.[34] A full 76 percent of these companies have "publicly affirmed the science of climate change" and 57 percent believe we need new, science-based climate policies. However, 51 percent of companies mention climate change policies only negatively in their financial filings, viewing climate change not as a long-term existential risk, but as a short-term business risk. In fact, 74 percent mention climate change as a risk to their business in their financial filings. In spite of these views, or perhaps because of them, only 40 percent of companies have "engaged directly with lawmakers" on crafting science-based climate policy, with 21 percent of companies having lobbied against these policies. Compounding this issue, seventy of these ninety-six firms are members of the US Chamber of Commerce, a group famously oppositional toward policies to address climate change. Only one of the firms examined has left the Chamber of Commerce over its climate policies, while just 7 percent acknowledge having worked with the Chamber to help "evolve" their climate

---

[34] www.ceres.org/resources/reports/practicing-responsible-policy-engagement-2021

policies. Given the lack of transparency with which companies are allowed to describe the issues on which they lobby in their quarterly lobbying reports, assessing the disparity between a company's public and private statements is essential to understanding the impact that companies have on climate change policy. If we cannot observe a company's true positions on climate change in their lobbying reports, and if their public statements are occasionally "cheap talk," it will be exceedingly difficult to understand which companies are making sincere efforts to influence climate policy positively, and which companies are just trying to greenwash their opposition to it. More detail on Ceres's approach to responsible lobbying on climate can be found in Ketu et al. (2023).

Consider the April 2021 open letter to President Biden advocating for a federal climate target and a commitment to adhere to the Paris Agreement goals, signed by over 400 businesses and investors.[35] Is signing this open letter indicative of the climate policies and positions for which companies lobby? Three notable signatories include Ford Motor Company, General Motors, and Shell. As mentioned above, Ford is one of the few companies to release a Political Engagement Report, which, while lacking granularity about their membership in the US Chamber of Commerce and their efforts to influence the Chamber's positions on climate policy, at least documents Ford's positions on climate in a publicly available way. General Motors provides a voluntary report on political contributions,[36] but their true policy positions are more opaque and may be less in line with their public statements of climate policy support. In October 2019, General Motors joined the Trump administration in pushing for weaker vehicle emissions standards in California,[37] before reversing their position in November 2020 following the election of Joe Biden,[38] perhaps more indicative of their wishes to remain on the "correct" side of the current administration rather than any strongly held beliefs about climate policy. While Shell receives a fairly poor Influence Map performance band score of "C,"[39]

[35] www.wemeanbusinesscoalition.org/ambitious-u-s-2030-ndc/
[36] https://investor.gm.com/static-files/2de4f1bf-8b86-4755-a59f-6cd0f5530883
[37] www.nytimes.com/2019/10/28/climate/general-motors-california-emissions-trump.html
[38] www.reuters.com/article/us-autos-emissions-gm/gm-hits-reverse-on-trump-effort-to-bar-california-emissions-rules-idUSKBN2832HF
[39] https://influencemap.org/company/Royal-Dutch-Shell

Influence Map does note that Shell has "become more positive" in some climate policy areas, having advocated for emissions standards and targets, although they still lobby for supportive fossil fuel production and consumption policies. Moreover, as noted by Influence Map, Shell is still a member of trade associations that "directly contradict" their own climate views. As further documented in a 2020 report from *Unearthed* and the *Huffington Post*,[40] after publicly exiting some trade associations with contradictory climate views, Shell privately remained an active member of at least eight trade associations that lobby against climate regulations. While Shell may be publicly lobbying for better climate goals and regulations, their good work may be undermined by their private support for organizations that seek to prevent any carbon-reduction policies.

3.4.3 What Else Do We Need to Know, and How Does This Impact Research?

The above examples illustrate the difficulties empirical researchers have when trying to glean any important information about a company's lobbying decisions. We are only able to see exactly what companies report on either their quarterly lobbying reports or any voluntary political engagement reports they provide. Given the relatively lenient reporting requirements, there simply is not enough information provided to answer most questions about corporate influence in the lobbying sphere. There is a large, undisclosed "shadow lobbying" industry that may lead researchers to misinterpret a company's true lobbying expenditures. For the lobbying spending that is reported, it is difficult to understand where exactly that money was spent, or even the true policy positions of a given company. It is not possible to calculate what portion of the total expenditure went to lobbying any given entity or on any issue, and even simple questions about which exact members of Congress were lobbied are impossible to answer. Companies list the legislation on which they are lobbying, but do not necessarily mention their positions on each policy. Even if companies provide some sort of political engagement report, it may not document the full extent of their influence, or they may still be funding trade associations with contradictory views. At this point, given the

---

[40] https://unearthed.greenpeace.org/2020/09/28/bp-shell-climate-lobby-groups/

combination of loose federal reporting requirements and relatively few companies providing additional reports voluntarily, there simply is not enough data available to reach meaningful conclusions on many questions surrounding corporate influence in the lobbying and political process.

The above issues tightly constrain the questions addressed in the academic literature. Clever research strategies like that of Delmas et al. (2016), which attempt to get around the lack of disclosure on positions taken by corporate climate lobbyists, must make heroic assumptions about spend allocation in order to get results. Bertrand et al. (2014) use changes in a Congressperson's committee assignments to gain insight into whether lobbyists follow politicians from committee to committee, exploiting personal connections, or remain focused on committees where they can exploit their expertise on issues. Bertrand et al. (2020) combine data on charitable giving with lobbying reports to examine the role of charitable giving as a form of CPA. Again, by exploiting congressional committee assignments and the issues listed on lobbying reports, the authors are able to document a percentage of charitable giving as politically motivated. Across recent lobbying research, we see that despite different levels of mandated disclosure and years of research, scholars are still constrained in the questions we can ask, and hence have a very difficult time establishing how and why money matters in lobbying. Current research is helping to further our understanding of these issues, but changes in the reporting requirements would be a great help in aiding researchers to advance the research on these important questions.

3.5 Conclusion

This chapter has emphasized, perhaps ad nauseam, the gap between current CPA disclosure and the data needed to document the role of money in politics and to assess CPR. Mandated disclosure of certain types of political spending and lobbying activities provides some degree of transparency, and the information aggregation done by third-party organizations like CPA-Zicklin and Influence Map deepens it, but better metrics are needed. While it seems obvious to suggest Congress strengthen political spending and lobbying disclosure policies, such as requiring 501(c)(4) contributions to be disclosed in more detail or requiring lobbying reports to list the exact members of

Congress lobbied, there are a few other, perhaps more feasible, proposals that may lead to much-needed improvements in CPA and CPR measurement.

One practical way to advance meaningful transparency on the content of lobbying messages is for Congress to implement the "Post-Map-Ask" framework proposed by Drutman and Mahoney (2017). This approach is based on the well-established system of making public comments on proposed regulations that is used by all modern regulatory agencies, such as the Federal Energy Regulatory Commission or the Federal Trade Commission. In this framework, the Library of Congress would establish an online portal for all stakeholders to post comments on policy issues of the day. The Library of Congress would then map these comments so that stakeholders could assess which interest groups had weighed in on which issues, and what positions they had taken. Finally, the Library of Congress would ask stakeholders whose interests would be affected by the proposed policy but who had not weighed in for their comments on the policy.

While Post-Map-Ask would help make a firm's positions public, it doesn't necessarily furthering understanding of accountability or responsibility. Since there is no legal requirement for accountability around CPA, best practices currently are offered by the CPA-Zicklin Model Code and the voluntary political engagement reports offered by some companies. While CPA-Zicklin grades firms on their policies surrounding electoral spending disclosure, voluntary political engagement reports can help fill some gaps left after mandatory reporting requirements have been fulfilled. More descriptive than legally required disclosures, these reports can provide additional insight into a firm's political activities, better documenting both the extent and the aims. As norms of best practice emerge for what should be included within the latter reports, they are likely to become an important source of data concerning accountability.

The Responsible Lobbying Framework developed by Carnstone Partners with support from the Meridian Institute presents five criteria that investors can use to determine whether the firms they own are behaving in a responsible fashion (Hodgson and Witte, 2020), the first of which is that "responsible lobbying will never be inconsistent with the public interest." By taking a relatively narrow, market-based approach, we can rely on welfare economics for the propositions that competitive markets serve society well and maximize total surplus or aggregate wealth under certain conditions.[41] However, when the conditions for perfect competition fail, and we observe "market failures," like market power, externalities, public goods, and asymmetric information,[42] there is no guarantee that free markets promote welfare. Thus, an alternative formulation to the Responsible Lobbying Framework's Criterion 1 is "Responsible lobbying will never seek to increase market failures." For example, responsible pharmaceutical firms would not lobby to block competition from generic drug producers, responsible energy companies would not lobby to block the passage of a price on greenhouse gas emissions, responsible defense contractors would not lobby for funding of unnecessary or ineffective weapons systems, and responsible financial firms would not lobby for the "carried interest exemption."[43]

Accordingly, a simple starting point for the assessment of CPR is for the company to report on the alignment between its stated purpose, mission, and values, and the positions it supports in the political arena, that is, with accountability. This at least ensures the company is not practicing corporate hypocrisy by claiming to care about one set of values while lobbying against them behind closed doors in Washington, DC (Delmas and Lyon, 2018).

How should alignment be measured? A promising starting point comes from a recent World Economic Forum report that was prepared in conjunction with the Big 4 Accounting Firms (Deloitte, EY, KPMG, and PwC) entitled *Measuring Stakeholder Capitalism: Towards Common Metrics and Consistent Reporting of Sustainable Value Creation*. They suggest a set of "Core" metrics and disclosures for Governance, as well as a set of "Expanded" metrics and disclosures. In the latter category is Ethical Behavior, the first element of which is the following (World Economic Forum, 2020, p. 54):

---

[41] Of particular importance for perfect competition to hold are the requirements that there are free entry and exit, that consumers are fully informed, and that there are no externalities. Government agencies such as the Federal Trade Commission and the Environmental Protection Agency exist to provide guardrails ensuring those conditions are met.

[42] This is not the place to provide a primer on market failure, but any good undergraduate economics textbook will provide a sound introduction.

[43] On the carried interest exemption, see www.nytimes.com/2017/12/22/business/trump-carried-interest-lobbyists.html.

Alignment of Strategy and Policies to Lobbying: The significant issues that are the focus of the company's participation in public policy development and lobbying; the company's strategy relevant to these areas of focus; and any differences between its lobbying positions and its purpose, stated policies, goals or other public positions. (Emphasis added)

The stated rationale is that

Consistency between corporate activity related to lobbying and the firm's publicly stated purpose and strategy is a core component of alignment on long-term objectives, which in turn is essential for long-term value creation. Monitoring this consistency is an important element of overall transparency and the authentic pursuit of the company's objectives.

This criterion is drawn from GRI Standard 415 on Public Policy(Global Reporting Initiative, 2016), which states that

The reporting organization should report: 1.2.1 the significant issues that are the focus of its participation in public policy development and lobbying; 1.2.2 its stance on these issues, and any differences between its lobbying positions and any stated policies, goals, or other public positions.

In addition

The reporting organization shall report the following information: a. Total monetary value of financial and in-kind political contributions made directly and indirectly by the organization by country and recipient/beneficiary. b. If applicable, how the monetary value of in-kind contributions was estimated.

GRI states explicitly that

Direct or indirect contributions to political causes can also present corruption risks, because they can be used to exert undue influence on the political process. Many countries have legislation that limits the amount an organization can spend on political parties and candidates for campaigning purposes. If an organization channels contributions indirectly through intermediaries, such as lobbyists or organizations linked to political causes, it can improperly circumvent such legislation.

Clearly, CPA and CPR are becoming more important and are having a larger impact on our political process. Lobbying expenditures continue to increase and electoral spending has skyrocketed in the most recent cycle. We know these are important levers of influence, but research is still hampered by the current levels of disclosure, and the data currently available today leads to difficulties when attempting to measure CPA, CPR, and their effectiveness. Yet there are potential positive developments that may lead us to better understand these issues. Organizations like CPA-Zicklin are continuing to do great work in this area, and more and more firms are adopting their Model Code. Political engagement reports are likely to become a more important source of voluntarily disclosed data, and a well-thought-out guide on what should be included could be a valuable resource for firms looking to develop their own reports. Other ideas, like the "Post-Map-Ask" framework proposed by Drutman and Mahoney (2017), provide a promising structure that mirrors a successful system currently used by other regulatory agencies to register a firm's position on current issues. An effective implementation of these proposals could lead to a much greater understanding of the three levels of CPR, providing a method to track a company's positions and actions on important pieces of legislation. Lastly, the World Economic ForumInternational Benchmarking Council metrics are likely to become a more important framework for evaluating a firm's ESG activities. Developed jointly between the World Economic Forum, Bank of America, and the Big 4 accounting firms, these metrics could provide a relatively simple, straightforward, widely accepted way to help measure firm CPR and the alignment between a firm's CPA and their stated goals. While it is clear there is still much work to be done, these third-party proposals and metrics provide a path forward to more accurate measurement of firm CPA and CPR. A combination of reporting rule changes, third-party measures, and firms privately adopting more stringent reporting requirements could finally provide the metrics needed for understanding firm CPA and CPR.

References

Bertrand, M., Matilde, B., Raymond, F., & Francesco, T. (2014). Is It Whom You Know or What You Know? An Empirical Assessment of the Lobbying Process. *American Economic Review*, **104**(12), 3885–920.

Bertrand, M., Matilde, B., Raymond, F., & Francesco, T. (2020). Tax-Exempt Lobbying: Corporate Philanthropy as a Tool for Political Influence. *American Economic Review*, **110**(7), 2065–102.

The Center for Political Accountability. (2021). CPA-Zicklin Index; Raw Data. 2011–2020. www.politicalaccountability.net/cpa-zicklin-index/past-cpa-zicklin-index-reports/. Accessed February 12.

Delmas, M., Jinghui, L., & Nairn-Birch, N. (2016). Corporate Environmental Performance and Lobbying. *Academy of Management Discoveries*, **2**(2), 175–97.

Delmas, M., & Lyon, T. (2018). When Corporations Take Credit for Green Deeds Their Lobbying May Tell Another Story. *The Conversation*, July 17. https://theconversation.com/when-corporations-take-credit-for-green-deeds-their-lobbying-may-tell-another-story-98988.

Drutman, L. (2015). How Corporate Lobbyists Conquered American Democracy. *The Atlantic*, April 20.

Drutman, L., & Mahoney, C. (2017). On the Advantages of a Well-Constructed Lobbying System: Toward a More Democratic, Modern Lobbying Process. *Interest Groups & Advocacy*, **6**(3), 290–310.

Espinosa, M. (2021). Labor Boundaries and Skills: The Case of Lobbyists. *Management Science*, **67**(3), 1586–1607.

Federal Election Commission. (2021). Receipts. www.fec.gov/data/receipts/.

Freed, B., Laufer, W., & Sandstrom, K. (2023). Targeting Private Sector Influence in Politics: Corporate Accountability as a Risk and Governance Problem. In T. Lyon, ed., *Corporate Political Responsibility*. Cambridge: Cambridge University Press.

Global Reporting Initiative. (2016). GRI 415. Public Policy.

Hodgson, S., & Witte, D. (2020). *Responsible Lobbying: An Evaluation Framework*. Carnstone Partners, Ltd.

Katz, A. (2015). *The Influence Machine: The US Chamber of Commerce and the Corporate Capture of American Life*. New York, NY: Random House.

Ketu, Y., & Rothstein, S. (2023). Measuring Climate Policy Alignment: A Study of the S&P 100. In T. Lyon, ed., *Corporate Political Responsibility*. Cambridge, UK: Cambridge University Press.

Minefee, I., McDonnell, MH., & Werner, T. (2021). Reexamining Investor Reaction to Covert Corporate Political Activity: A Replication and Extension of Werner (2017). *Strategic Management Journal*, **42**(6), 1139–58.

OpenSecrets. (2020). Lobbying Tables. www.opensecrets.org/bulk-data/downloads.

Senate Office of Public Records. (2020). Lobbying Disclosure Act Databases. 1998–2020. www.senate.gov/legislative/Public_Disclosure/LDA_reports.htm.

Thomas, H., & LaPira, T. (2017). How Many Lobbyists Are in Washington? Shadow Lobbying and the Gray Market for Policy Advocacy. *Interest Groups & Advocacy*, **6**(3), 199–214.

Vigeo Eiris. ESG Super Premium_Historic_2019_09_EUR_NAM_2011.xlsx.

Vigeo Eiris. The Equitics© Methodology. Guide to the Domains and Criteria of the Equitics Generic Model.

Walker, E. (2023). What Drives Firms to Disclose Their Political Activity. In T. Lyon, ed., *Corporate Political Responsibility*. Cambridge: Cambridge University Press.

Werner, T. (2017). Investor Reaction to Covert Corporate Political Activity. *Strategic Management Journal*, 38(12), 2424–43.

Werner, T. (2023). Promise and Peril: Lessons from Shareholder Reactions to Corporate Political Activity Disclosure. In T. Lyon, ed., *Corporate Political Responsibility*. Cambridge: Cambridge University Press.

World Economic Forum. (2020). Measuring Stakeholder Capitalism: Towards Common Metrics and Consistent Reporting of Sustainable Value Creation.

Transparency: Causes and Consequences

4 | What Drives Firms to Disclose Their Political Activity?

EDWARD T. WALKER

4.1 Introduction

Over the past nearly two decades, the (non-)disclosure of corporate political activity (CPA) has become an area of intense scrutiny and political contestation. Although it has been a long-standing concern among many advocates and investors that the lack of disclosure surrounding CPA is harmful both to democracy and to the interest of transparency in the marketplace, in the period since the 2010 Supreme Court decision in *Citizens United v. Federal Election Commission*, the political foment about undisclosed corporate money in politics has expanded dramatically (e.g., Dawood, 2015).[1] Scores of studies have emerged to help assess the contemporary moment in political science (Dowling & Miller, 2014; Hansen et al., 2015), management (Benton, 2017; Lyon et al., 2018; Skaife & Werner, 2020; Werner, 2017), sociology (Walker, 2014), and, particularly, in law reviews (e.g., Bebchuk & Jackson, 2010; Sachs, 2012). On the advocacy side, numerous reports and white papers have called for greater transparency of corporate political spending, and on a variety of grounds: to more closely align spending with claimed corporate values and reduce risks (Center for Political Accountability, 2018), to be fairer to investors who want to be more fully informed about the risks of such spending (Ahl, 2021), and to understand how companies are shaping democracy writ large (Center for Responsive Politics, 2020). As one legal scholar put it, echoing Justice Kennedy's majority opinion in *Citizens United* about the importance of "corporate democracy," "If we cannot keep corporations out of our democracy, then we must have more democracy in our corporations" (Yosifon, 2015).

---

[1] There are, however, some considerable and well-founded doubts about how much *Citizens United* affected key parts of corporate electoral spending (Hansen et al., 2015) and investor reaction in the marketplace (Werner, 2011).

The question then becomes: What are the means by which such corporate democracy can be expanded and institutionalized? There are two primary routes that could be taken: the public route via government regulations and mandates, or the private route of voluntary corporate actions. A long-standing and rich research literature has examined this distinction between conventional governmental public politics and voluntary corporate private politics (Baron, 2001; Bartley, 2007; Soule, 2009; Vogel, 2008). In the case of disclosure of CPA, both of these are potential routes for changing corporate political disclosure regimes.

The issue, however, is that in the US context, the major efforts at reforming CPA disclosure at the federal level via public politics have, to date, largely failed. A clear case of this has been the consistent struggle over many years to pass the DISCLOSE Act, introduced originally in 2010 after *Citizens United* to require greater disclosure of "dark money" campaign finance by corporations, wealthy donors, and other funders. Designed as a major amendment to the Federal Election Campaign Act of 1971, the Act would markedly expand disclosure requirements for firms, particularly in money paid into a variety of dark money vehicles (e.g., 527 groups, trade groups, 501(c)4 "social welfare" organizations, and more). Although reintroduced in each Congress since 2010 (and since folded into the For the People Act (H.R. 1)), the measure has consistently failed to make it through Congress. Similarly, efforts at rulemaking on the administrative side through the Securities and Exchange Commission (SEC) have been similarly fraught: Although the SEC took up such rulemaking in 2013, progress stalled in 2014 and has since been blocked by a Republican appropriations bill rider that prohibits the SEC indefinitely from engaging in rulemaking to mandate corporate political disclosure (Wheeler, 2015).[2]

Given the failure of public politics to bring about major federal-level corporate reforms in the direction of greater transparency, the private

---

[2] It is possible that congressional and/or SEC actions may change this under the Biden administration and with a Democratic Congress. In January 2021, Rep. Levin (D-MI) introduced the Transparency in Corporate Political Spending Act, which would remove the policy rider prohibiting the SEC from mandating CPA disclosure. There are also separate considerations about whether Gary Gensler (Biden's SEC chair) will himself press for greater disclosure about CPA and other ESG-related transparency measures.

avenue has become appealing to those seeking these reforms. While a regular worry is that private politics may be a weaker mechanism for generating significant and durable corporate change, in a challenging political climate some have found that pressing for voluntary corporate changes may be a fruitful approach (e.g., Short et al., 2020), and that it need not mean that advocates should stop pressing for new governmental regulations. For instance, we know from other cases that public and private politics interact in dynamic ways in generating corporate change (Hiatt et al., 2015).

And, as I document below, many companies are facing pressure from their stakeholders – ranging from organized investors to employees to third-party watchdogs – to become more transparent about their political expenditures. While much more of the pressure has focused on dark-money electoral expenditures, other forms of CPA, including grassroots lobbying (both in its covert form as "astroturfing" and its overt form as mass stakeholder mobilization – see Walker, 2014), have also attracted significant advocacy for greater disclosure (Myers, 2018; Scott, 2019)

This chapter examines two key questions: (1) Which companies get targeted by shareholder-activists seeking greater voluntary CPA disclosure and (2) How have those targeted companies responded?[3] I build from a variety of sources in doing so: evidence from Institutional Shareholder Services (ISS) of shareholder resolutions brought against major public companies over a twelve-year period, findings from a series of in-depth qualitative interviews I conducted with the leading proponents of such shareholder resolutions, additional interviews with field-level experts and watchdogs, media accounts of controversies major companies have faced surrounding the (non-)disclosure of their CPA, and evidence from the annual reports of the Center for Political Accountability, which publishes the CPA-Zicklin Index of corporate political transparency. I find, overall, that companies are targeted by shareholders for CPA-related shareholder resolutions on the basis of their prior political activities, financial characteristics,

---

[3] Note that companies may make changes without facing shareholder resolutions, with the likely mechanisms being either direct (non-resolution-based) engagement with investors and/or they followed the example of other companies in their benchmarking networks such as those in the CPA-Zicklin Index, described below.

history of facing past shareholder resolutions, and other qualitative factors including their reputational challenges, history of engagement on ESG issues, and whether their CPA might appear to be misaligned with other value commitments. Companies, in turn, tend to be more likely to make reforms after facing CPA resolutions in prior years and also, particularly, if and when they become constituents of the S&P 500 Index, as membership in that Index causes a firm to draw considerably greater scrutiny.

4.2 Who Are the Advocates of Corporate Political Responsibility?

Before examining which companies are more likely to take voluntary action to go above and beyond the legal requirements they face for basic political disclosure, it's critical to have a sense about which kinds of constituencies are raising questions about corporate transparency and pressuring companies to improve. This is consequential not only for illuminating which kinds of actors are engaging with companies, but also because the composition of those actors and their claims may affect the ways that targets respond to contentious challenges, as long suggested by scholarship on social movements (e.g., Armstrong & Bernstein, 2008; Walker et al., 2008).

First, it's key to recognize that although companies do face challenges around their CPA practices in a variety of domains, on the whole they only rarely face street protests or boycotts that target political activities; the rare counter-examples are instances in which CPA led to a consumer boycott, such as when Target faced a boycott after donations to a Minnesota gubernatorial candidate seen as anti-LGBT (Montopoli, 2010). The central source of corporate engagement, then, on CPA issues is via shareholder-activism.

Figure 4.1 illustrates the broad patterns of types of shareholder-activists who have brought CPA-related shareholder resolutions at major public companies between years 2007 and 2018. I use data from ISS, which is widely recognized as one of the key sources for data on corporate directorships, proxy votes, and shareholder resolutions in particular. I focus on the years 2007–2018 based on data availability and also because they represent the periods both before and after *Citizens United*; additionally, they capture the later years of the early aughts in which the political activity of undisclosed independent

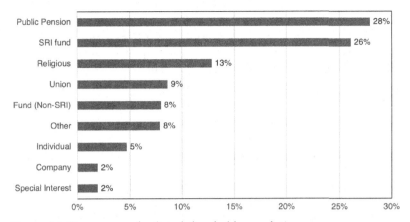

Figure 4.1 Proponents of political shareholder resolutions

expenditure organizations (i.e., 527s) became a major source of social contestation, particularly after the "Swift Boat Veterans for Truth" (a conservative 527 group) incident during the 2004 presidential election.

The data reflect only those shareholder resolutions brought against firms covered in the ISS data – these are firms that were in the S&P 1500 during the period of observation, with the addition of those who exited the S&P index during that period and also a few hundred additional large-cap firms – and I include resolutions coded under the six major ISS classifications for shareholder resolutions related to CPA: codes 2,022 and 2,334 (both around political contributions), 3,220 (request to review political spending), 3,221 (limit political spending), 3,902 (misc. political contributions), and 5,000 (political lobbying disclosure). Using this specification, the data show that CPA-oriented matters constitute 8.3 percent of shareholder resolutions overall, but that attention to CPA has increased notably during the period of observation (from only 4 percent of resolutions in 2005 up to 12 percent in 2018, and there is reason to expect that this has increased further in the years since).

Figure 4.1 makes clear that the majority of politically oriented shareholder resolutions are brought by public pension funds and Socially Responsible Investment (SRI) funds, both of which have been known to be highly active in pressing for greater corporate political accountability (e.g., Guay et al., 2004). These two types of resolution proponents combine to constitute roughly 54 percent of all CPA-oriented resolutions facing major firms. Importantly, this is a much higher representation of these two types of proponents than what one finds for shareholder resolutions overall (including both political and nonpolitical ones), where pensions represent only 13 percent and SRIs are 12 percent. These two types are more active on political than non-political issues in good part because they tend not to be as active on matters such as basic board governance rules (e.g., voting rules surrounding directors), executive compensation matters, and other routine proxy business.

As with other types of ESG-related shareholder resolutions, politically oriented ones also draw in a significant amount of attention brought by religious actors like the Interfaith Center on Corporate Responsibility (ICCR); these actors represent 9 percent of all who brought shareholder resolutions around CPA. Unions were also quite active in the space, consistent with what one analyst refers to as the "rise of the working class shareholder" in which unions have brought pressure against companies through their financial investments during a period of major challenges facing organized labor (Webber, 2018). We also see some representation of conventional (non-SRI) funds, particularly as the movement for corporate accountability has expanded more broadly to new actors. The other types include corporate actors, interest groups, individuals, and a mix of others not elsewhere classified.

4.3 Which Firms Get Targeted, and Why?

Although the concern that large businesses play an outsized role in the American political process is one that is perennial (Bartels, 2016; Hertel-Fernandez, 2019; Mizruchi, 2013; Walker and Rea, 2014), of course some firms play a much more significant role in the political process than others do. A standard – indeed a near truism – finding from studies in political science, political sociology, and nonmarket strategy more generally is that firms that operate in industries with higher levels of government regulation tend to be much more politically active, both individually and through trade associations. Other firms steer clear of the political process and restrict their engagements, whether on the electoral or on the lobbying side. Thus, particularly for less regulated and smaller firms with less of a footprint, it may be easier to agree to political transparency given that, in some instances, they have little or no CPA to disclose. As one of my interviewees – a senior litigator who has built a career working in the realm of CPA-related corporate governance – put it, it's easy for a company to concede to "disclos[ing] every unicorn [they have] on their payroll."

But it is not only on the basis of observable CPA that organized shareholders press companies to become more transparent about their political spending. At times corporate spending gets inadvertently disclosed (Werner, 2017; see also Chapter 5, this volume), which may show that certain firms engage in covert dark-money political spending. Beyond this, we know that those seeking corporate reform also target firms on the basis of other factors, including their previous record of willingness to concede to prior challenges (King and McDonnell, 2012), their reputational sensitivity (King and McDonnell, 2012), CSR commitments (see Chapter 8, this volume), their financial situation (Davis & Thompson, 1994), and/or their worry about the close scrutiny of market observers if the firm has a high enough market capitalization to be listed on one of the major stock indexes (Chiu & Scharfman, 2011).

Table 4.1 presents the results of a fixed-effects panel regression model, using the data from ISS during the period 2007–2018, examining the likelihood that a firm would face a political shareholder resolution in a given year. I estimate the association between facing a CPA-related shareholder resolution with predictors including the firm's legally mandated CPA disclosures (federal lobbying and PAC spending), along with a variety of basic financial indicators (revenue and market value), as well as whether the firm is a constituent of the S&P 500 in a given year, as such index constituency tends to generate significant additional scrutiny of a firm and its political behaviors. I also include indicators of whether the firm faced a variety of different types of shareholder-related resolutions in the prior year: CPA resolutions (autocorrelation term), environment/climate resolutions, basic corporate governance resolutions (i.e., non-ESG), and other social resolutions.

The results presented in Table 4.1 make clear that firms that engage in higher amounts of above-board CPA tend to be more likely to face CPA-related shareholder resolutions. Both reported PAC spending and especially lobbying expenditures increase the likelihood that firms

Table 4.1 *Predicting CPA-related shareholder resolutions (ISS data)*

	Models			
VARIABLES	(1)	(2)	(3)	(4)
Lobbying ($ks, 2016 dollars)	—	—	0.085***	0.052***
			(0.020)	(0.014)
PAC spending ($ks, 2016 dollars)	—	—	0.057+	0.078**
			(0.031)	(0.024)
Revenue ($bs, 2016, logged)	—	—	0.330***	0.203***
			(0.073)	(0.058)
Market value ($bs, 2016, logged)	—	—	0.386***	0.141**
			(0.070)	(0.055)
S&P 500 Constituent	—	—	1.872***	2.285***
			(0.218)	(0.228)
Political Resolutions (t-1, logged)	—	2.364***	—	1.667***
		(0.159)		(0.123)
Climate Resolutions (t-1, logged)	-0.324	0.081	—	-0.089
	(0.520)	(0.163)		(0.108)
Governance Resolutions (t-1, logged)	0.872***	0.787***	—	0.266***
	(0.106)	(0.091)		(0.067)
Other Social Resolutions (t-1, logged)	0.721***	0.299*	—	0.071
	(0.200)	(0.131)		(0.088)
Constant	-3.434***	-3.791***	-6.447***	-6.058***
	(0.079)	(0.070)	(0.186)	(0.211)
Observations	20,251	18,392	19,071	17,181
N Firms	2,042	2,063	2,086	2,058

Robust standard errors in parentheses
***$p<0.001$, **$p<0.01$, *$p<0.05$, + $p<0.1$

will be asked to voluntarily increase their disclosures of other forms of CPA. I also find a strong effect of S&P 500 constituency, indicating that being one of these top firms brings considerable additional scrutiny of CPA, even after adjusting for a firm's revenue and market value (both of which are also significant predictors). As Bruce Freed from the Center for Political Accountability (see his own perspective in Chapter 2 of this volume), perhaps the leading advocacy group in the country pressing for greater CPA disclosure, put it in an interview, this also has to do with a firm's extent of political spending. He said, "our focus has been on the S&P 500. Because they are the largest companies. And it really those maybe the 250 on up, would tend to be the largest spenders. You know, the companies with the lower scores tend to be below the S&P 250... 200 or 250. They engage in much less spending or no spending."

Lastly, there is a strong autocorrelation term, as the same firms tend to get targeted for CPA disclosure year after year; this is consistent with my findings from interviews with shareholder-activists about how they often find that they need to file resolutions for multiple consecutive years in order to have an impact. For the other types of resolutions, I do not find any association between previous year environmental/climate or other social resolutions. I do find that CPA-related resolutions often follow after general corporate (non-ESG) governance resolutions, possibly because earlier scrutiny among investors may provoke additional attention to undisclosed CPA.

How do the shareholder-activists themselves see these actions, and how did they describe their decisions about which firms to target? My interviews highlighted a few themes: evidence of firms' (above-board) electoral and lobbying expenditures, stakeholders' expectations about whether a firm is likely to be open to engagement, reputational issues and company scandals, and considerations about how a firm's CPA may or may not align with other corporate values and stakeholder expectations. I now unpack each of these.

Basic Political Activity. Consistent with the findings from the models above, one of the most straightforward findings from my interviews with leaders in the movement for corporate political accountability was that they target firms that have shown evidence of political activity in their required disclosures. The expectation is generally that these expenditures represent the tip of the iceberg, and that beneath the surface (or partially apparent) are other expenditures on activities like grassroots/astroturf lobbying, funds sent to independent expenditure or 527 groups, trade association payments (501(c)6s), payments to covert "social welfare" nonprofits (501(c)4s), and/or other forms of CPA spending that requires little or no disclosure at the federal or state level.

John Keenan, a corporate governance analyst for the American Federation of State, County and Municipal Employees (AFSCME, the largest public sector union in the United States), who has been heavily involved in the push for greater corporate CPA disclosure, put it plainly when I interviewed him:

There are different levels of screens ... first, you look at level of lobbying and significance of lobbying ... there are resources like Open Secrets, which [reflects] great work by the Center for Responsive Politics. So you'd look up the research and see who's lobbying the most on the federal level. That's one screen. The second screen is what's happening at the state level. And there [are] numerous companies from different industries that also lobby heavily at the state level. And the state lobbying is really submerged. It's kind of goes under the radar. It's under the surface. Because [there aren't] reporters in state capitals anymore. It's a little more sleepy. There [are] only half the states [that] probably have good reporting requirements. California and New York are very good; in some you can't get [CPA] expense data.

Similar remarks came up in other interviews I conducted with shareholder-activists. Tim Smith, who is senior ESG advisor at Boston Trust Walden (formerly Walden Asset Management) and a longtime leader in the area, also put it directly, saying that "the size of the company... the political footprint ... is a key factor," adding that he believes that transparency is about "good governance and every company should do it. [But] if a company is [only] minimally involved in lobbying and political spending, I don't think it's a very good use of our time to be intervening with them." These ideas were reflected consistently in most of additional interviews I conducted.

Expectation of Engagement. Part of the decision about which companies to target for a CPA-related shareholder resolution is about the expected receptivity of the firm to engagement by shareholder-activists. In many instances, before filing a resolution, a potential proponent will reach out directly to the company seeking engagement on the topic, possibly to preempt the need for the resolution to be filed at all. As a number of my interviewees explained, they often prefer not to file a resolution "cold." At the same time, there were others – one SRI firm in particular – that indicated a preference for cold resolutions being filed, on the grounds of holding companies more publicly accountable for their CPA-related disclosure decisions.

And, in general, each type of proponent will have different motivations for engagement: SRI firms are typically only engaging with the firms they have already screened as responsible investments, labor funds will be more likely to engage with companies that are employers of their members, and the like; these factors shape the style of engagement and content of negotiations. As Louis Malizia, a director of corporate and strategic initiatives at the International Brotherhood of Teamsters, put it in my interview with him: "We look at our members' employment or investment in the company by way of the pension fund. We know that our members think there should be better governance in these companies. We also look at ... who are the market leaders and ask whether there could be a ripple effect among their peers from them changing their policies."

Shareholder-activists typically try at first to take a partnership approach in their engagement with companies around CPA issues. As Pat Miguel Tomaino, director of SRI at Zevin Asset Management, described to me:

When you're ... shining a light on companies for disclosure, you have to be constructive and offer them really focused examples of what they can do to improve the positive kind of setup... after all, that's what we are, we're investors in these companies, and that you're not simply a bomb-thrower, or someone who wants to name and shame for the sake of doing that. And as long as you're doing that you're reaching out to a company before you file a shareholder proposal you're offering. Yeah, you're offering a meeting to discuss these concerns before there's a vote to explore areas where there could be a possible negotiation, then, you know, the company is going to understand that even a shareholder proposal, which is something that seems rather challenging, is simply a tool in a process and it's not an expression of animus or opposition.

Similarly, Tim Smith of Boston Trust Walden remarked:

[We would] try to write the company and have a dialogue before we file a resolution. And the resolution is, in essence, and in lots of cases, you file because the company is not going to move far enough, fast enough or move at all. And so you file resolutions that get their attention. But we, the goal is to try to change a company's policies or practices on any issue for diversity, climate change, lobbying, [etc.]. And so obviously, you're going to try to reach out and see if the company is interested in the conversation somewhere.

Oftentimes the highly influential CPA-Zicklin Index (e.g., Goh et al., 2020; Wang & Zhang, 2021), which provides benchmarking of major S&P 500 companies for their degree of CPA transparency – which I will describe further below – strongly shapes shareholder-activists' engagement with companies. Run by the Center for Political Accountability under its director Bruce Freed (see Chapter 2, this volume), the Index has been highly influential in shaping perceptions of political accountability among leading firms, both by shareholder-activists and also by the firms themselves (not to mention other key actors like monitoring groups, investing houses both large and small, and other key policymakers and observers). As Bruce Freed described to me:

In 2011 we started the CPA-Zicklin Index and that's turned out to be absolutely critical for creating the template that companies now use for the political disclosure and accountability policies they're adopting. And we started with the S&P 100, did that for about two years went to 200 to 300. And then four years ago, went to the S&P 500. And we found early on that companies treated the index seriously. [It has been] very, very important that it had credibility.... [We] have these emails that you get with companies that, you know... the index has been so important for shaping what companies are doing. [And others saying they] engage companies, through the shareholder resolution and through the Index.

Reputational issues and company scandals. A company's reputation is a key factor that shapes shareholder engagement around CPA matters. Previous research has found that when a company faces a decline in reputation, this may make them more likely to concede to outside to pressures from stakeholders (King & McDonnell, 2012). An awareness of this kind of susceptibility seemed to be prevalent among shareholder-activists, who were naturally quite cognizant about how reputational pressures can draw in activism.

As John Keenan of AFSCME described it, if a company has any "reputational missteps, [like] AT&T and the undisclosed Michael Cohen payments," that clearly makes them a more likely target for CPA disclosure. He continued, describing that case in saying that "there's [already] been lobbying proposals [at AT&T]. There were already investors who were asking for oversight." Thus, there is a combination of reputational concerns combined with previous requests for CPA disclosure to mount additional pressure.

Keenan extended these ideas further, talking about the fraudulent account scandal at Wells Fargo and remarking,

There's a whole broad range of factors that go [into the targeting decision] but yeah, if's there's been some sort of controversial political position and company drew attention to itself, then there's a likelihood that there'll be a greater focus placed on [the CPA of] that company… when there's a scandal or financial restatement or a lack of board oversight and investors come and say, wait a second, you guys dropped the ball here… engagement tends to be a greater focus. So yeah, Wells Fargo [after the fraudulent account scandal over] last couple [of] shareholder meetings was a great [example].

Contradictory Values/Walking the Talk. Companies are often called out for engaging in political spending that contradicts other corporate values and stakeholder commitments (see Chapters 7 and 12, this volume), and this is often a source of both reputational challenges and other stakeholder grievances in the form of consumer boycotts. Such contradictions were noted very cleanly and clearly in a report entitled *Collision Course* published by the Center for Political Accountability (2018), which called attention to CPA expenditures that violate corporate values.

Bruce Freed, one of the report's key authors, described to me how central CPA disclosure is to corporate ESG issues, arguing that corporate political spending generates a variety of social consequences based on what elected leaders ultimately enact:

Political spending gets to everything, because when a company gives money to a candidate, or to a political committee to bring about an electoral change, you know, that has very serious policy consequences … so, you know, [it] relate[s] to all of that, when a company contributes to a group that helps [bring about] full control of a legislature or elect a governor, and you see the legislative and policy consequences that flow from that. Whether it's racial gerrymandering, or attacking women's reproductive rights, or the attack on LGBT rights, they attack on efforts to address climate change, right? Or, you know, we could look at it more mundanely in terms of the attack on educational systems in states, you take a look at North Carolina, the attack on the University of North Carolina system that you've had, you know, once the Republicans gained full control in 2012.

Freed elaborated on this point, stating that, "All of this relates to risk because if a company takes a position, or company has a business strategy, and their spending underwrites, changes, or results in activities that conflict with it... that poses a very serious risk: reputational, business, and legal, sometimes."

Similarly, Julie Goodridge, CEO of Northstar Asset Management and a prominent leader in the CPA disclosure field, argued to me that a major part of their engagement with companies has been pressing for "shareholder resolution[s] around electioneering contributions ... asking for a shareholder vote for the company to examine to report on the any incongruencies between their stated company values and their electioneering contributions and to allow shareholders to vote on any future contributions." This is a common type of resolution seeking to call out contradictions linked to CPA expenditures.

Echoing the points raised in my other interviews, Pat Tomaino at Zevin described two cases where companies were funding the Chamber of Commerce, conflicting with their other corporate values. First, in the case of Disney, Tomaino noted that

Disney's support for [certain trade] groups may fund in many circumstances, [trade groups'] policy advocacy, which is at odds with Disney's other corporate purposes, and with the interests of shareholders [in the] long term. So for instance, Disney's membership in the Chamber of Commerce, has, it stands to reason, supported that group's lobbying against reasonable climate regulation legislation federally, [and] it has ... supported the Chamber of Commerce's efforts globally to tamp down any tobacco regulation.

Tomaino also raised similar concerns about the biopharmaceutical firm AbbVie, which is also a Chamber member: "And in the case of AbbVie, it's similar, you know... the company can get drawn into policy positions [such as support for tobacco] that are at odds with its public health mission."

4.4 Which Firms Are More Transparent?

Having considered the targeting of firms for CPA disclosure in some depth, the question remains as to which firms tend to respond favorably to such shareholder-activism, as well as through other means (e.g., voluntary changes outside the proxy mechanisms). It is first worth acknowledging that firms are indeed becoming more transparent in their CPA, and that a growing number of companies are disclosing CPA expenditures of varying types. The 2020 CPA-Zicklin Index report found, for instance, that over half of the S&P 500 now discloses some or all of their election-related spending, that many more firms are now subjecting their spending to board oversight, and that there have been consistent increases along these lines for each year since 2015. Some of the largest increases as of 2020 were in the area of disclosing spending to "social welfare" (501(c)4) organizations, but there were also increases in disclosure surrounding 527 groups, other independent expenditure organizations, and also trade groups and spending on ballot measures. The benchmarking work of the Index seems to be an important source of peer pressure encouraging many companies to align with the standards of companies in their reference groups. This may be part of the reason why CPA-related shareholder resolutions that make it onto the proxy ballot without withdrawal have found increasing vote shares in recent years.

To examine firms' likelihood of improving their disclosure practices, here I draw upon two key sources. First, I marshal evidence that a CPA-related shareholder resolution has been withdrawn; such withdrawn resolutions are widely seen as indication that a company has made positive changes in response to a resolution such that the proponent sees the issue as (at least somewhat) favorably resolved (e.g., Graves et al., 2001). And, as in the prior section, I also draw from my aforementioned interviews with shareholder-activists.

Turning to the first of these sources, I again use data from ISS to examine broader patterns, this time examining the correlates of CPA-related shareholder resolutions being withdrawn. Table 4.2 provides these results, using panel regressions with firm-level fixed-effects.

What Table 4.2 makes clear is that only two of the factors I examined were consequential in predicting the likelihood that a CPA resolution would be withdrawn, indicating some likely degree of success in corporate adoption of greater disclosure: S&P 500 Index constituency and whether the company faced a CPA-related resolution in the prior year. I find no significant association between proposal withdrawal and the company's above-board CPA expenditures, nor with company financials or with facing other (non-CPA) shareholder resolutions in the prior year. Of course, it is critical to bear in mind the finding presented earlier: that receiving a CPA-based resolution in the first place is strongly predicted by a firm's political spending and financials.

These findings square with my interviews, which regularly indicated that firms that hold S&P 500 constituency tend to draw much greater

Table 4.2 *Predicting withdrawn CPA-related shareholder resolutions*

VARIABLES	(1)
Lobbying ($ks, 2016 dollars)	0.032
	(0.020)
PAC spending ($ks, 2016 dollars)	−0.005
	(0.052)
Revenue ($bs, 2016, logged)	0.117
	(0.075)
Market value ($bs, 2016, logged)	0.055
	(0.082)
S&P 500 Constituent	1.342***
	(0.305)
Political Resolutions (t-1, logged)	1.045***
	(0.190)
Climate Resolutions (t-1, logged)	0.299
	(0.190)
Governance Resolutions (t-1, logged)	−0.067
	(0.116)
Other Social Resolutions (t-1, logged)	−0.077
	(0.164)
Constant	−4.810***
	(0.283)
Observations	4,026
N Firms	1,001

Robust standard errors in parentheses
***$p<0.001$, **$p<0.01$, *$p<0.05$, + $p<0.1$

scrutiny from investors and other observers. And indeed, as mentioned above, being an Index constituent is what brings a firm under the radar of Bruce Freed and the Center for Political Accountability, thereby introducing new pressures and comparisons against benchmarking groups of other Index constituents. Beyond this, of course, Index constituents also naturally receive more media coverage and close attention from financial analysts, which generates much greater sensitivity (Chiu & Scharfman, 2011). The models make clear that this attention spills over into a significantly higher tendency to improve in political disclosure.

I also find evidence to support the notion that firms get "worn down" by facing repeated CPA resolutions year after year, eventually making it more likely they will enact some reforms. Facing a CPA resolution in the prior year makes it significantly more likely that a CPA resolution the next year will be withdrawn, indicating that the firm has agreed to improve its disclosure practices in some respect. This is consistent with findings from my interviews. As Tim Smith put it,

[Firms are] motivated by what their peers are doing. They're motivated about the public debate about an issue [and] motivated about the business case we can make. And then ambassadors are asking for this information. So oftentimes, a resolution will lead to an agreement, and the resolution itself is withdrawn. And I would say we consider this a success, if a company did join the ranks of corporations that do disclose this information. So Bruce [Freed] has a long list of companies that disclose political spending, right. And he regularly calls those successes. And it is many successes. If a company, maybe they're not going to give you the whole nine yards, but they [concede some points] through the discussion and through their own discernment. [...] We both sign sort of a little letter saying that proponents agree to withdraw the resolution, and then they withdraw it. And the company sends you a note saying, you know, as discussed, we're going to do the following. Okay. And that would be the following: [for example] we asked for 10 things, and they said, well, we're only gonna do eight.

Similarly, Heidi Welsh, the founding executive director of the Sustainable Investments Institute (Si2), put it this way:

Companies don't like shareholder resolutions – they represent a difficulty for them. You are trying to have an annual meeting where you look good. Companies would rather not have this negative attention in the public arena. Proponents, on the other hand, want the attendant publicity. They also often have the goal of moving the needle in public opinion. And, additionally, they want to see the company change and they leverage the company's motivation and they act accordingly. A lot of companies change when it becomes easier to – partly because others in their benchmarking group have done so.... You are seeing this now with political spending. This is Bruce [Freed's] thing. The idea is to compare everybody. And now that a bunch of companies have taken action and will do board oversight and disclosure, some companies might think, "maybe these people will stop troubling us." It's like a lot of other issues.

4.5 Conclusion

The push for greater corporate political responsibility has been mounting for almost two decades now. In the absence of major federal legislation mandating changes to require greater levels of transparency about how corporations are intervening in our democracy, we have seen a powerful growth in investor-based activism to press companies for voluntary changes to their CPA disclosures. While this need not be seen as an either-or decision – voluntary changes to companies' "private politics" surrounding CPA need not circumvent or reduce the chances of meaningful governmental regulations – the voluntary changes have indeed brought about notable improvements in the transparency of major corporations in the United States. As the director of a major national advocacy organization put it to me in an interview, "private ordering fits into broader setting of trying to make change. We see private ordering as complementary to public regulation... we could have a theoretical conversation about whether it's brought about SEC versus companies doing this themselves ... but right now there's not really that choice."

This chapter found that a variety of features shape both the likelihood that a firm will face pressure from organized shareholders to expand their voluntary CPA disclosures, and that a somewhat different set of forces is likely to matter more for whether a company makes reforms in response to those pressures. First, when considering which companies to engage, activists look to a firm's indicators of above-board political activities (both electoral and lobbying), their financials, and whether they are an S&P 500 index constituent; there is also some evidence that prior shareholder resolutions affect present-day ones. My interviews with shareholder-activists provided support for these statistical findings and also helped elaborate that a number of other factors are also very important in deciding which companies to target: the firm's history of stakeholder engagement on social/political issues, whether they have faced major scandals or reputational challenges in recent years, and whether there is any evidence that a firm's CPA spending may be misaligned with other corporate values. Benchmarking networks regarding CPA activities and disclosures, such as those created by the CPA-Zicklin Index, are also critically important both to firms and to a variety of other audiences, including institutional investors and third-party monitoring groups.

When it comes to firms changing their disclosure practices after they are targeted, and conditional upon the aforementioned factors, I find that two major characteristics stand out: being an S&P 500 index constituent and facing CPA-related shareholder resolutions in the prior year. These findings are consistent with my interviews and with other available evidence, which generally suggests that Index constituents receive far greater scrutiny than other firms (including by being monitored by the influential CPA-Zicklin Index) and also that firms do appear to be "worn down" by facing resolutions in prior years. We have seen evidence, for instance, of firms such as AT&T making major concessions on CPA disclosure in recent years after facing shareholder resolutions on the topic in multiple prior years (Repko, 2018).

These findings, in total, when combined with the knowledge that shareholder resolutions around CPA have been more successful and also have been receiving higher vote shares in recent years, would appear to indicate excellent positive potential for major reforms to corporate practices surrounding their political responsibility. And, indeed, the findings of these investigations and also the recent CPA-Zicklin Index reports offer many reasons to have hope. This is not to mention the many – if short-lived (Stanley-Becker, 2021) – commitments that companies made to scale back, discontinue, or otherwise review electoral spending in support of candidates who denied the results of the 2020 election (Dean, 2021).

Yet at the same time, other trends suggest reasons for a more cautious and tentative take-away. In 2020, based in part around pressure from business peak associations like the Chamber of Commerce, the SEC changed the stock ownership thresholds required for a shareholder to file a resolution with a company. The rules, known as Exchange Act Rule 14a-8 (typically just called 14a-8 among shareholder-activists), previously required investors to hold at least $2,000 in stock for one year. After the revision, the requirement is now that one must hold $25,000 in stock ownership for one year before proposing a shareholder resolution or $15,000 for two years. The rule also allows investors who own $2,000 in stock for at least three years to file proposals. For co-filed resolutions, all of these requirements must be met for each of the filers independently (i.e., they can't be aggregated). The reforms to 14a-8 also included a number of revisions that pertain to the resubmission of shareholder resolutions previously received by a company: if a company previously voted on a resolution once, to be considered a second time it must have received at least a 5 percent vote (this used to be 3 percent). If previously voted twice, the threshold shifted from 6 up to 15 percent. If previously voted three times, it shifted from 10 to 25 percent.[4] The SEC also made a number of significant revisions around the allowable role of proxy advisors.[5] Of course it's also worth bearing in mind that the SEC regularly "no-actions" shareholder proposals that they believe are irrelevant, not material, and/ or are overly micro-managing of a company's activities, thus allowing them to exclude the resolution from the proxy ballot; the SEC's propensity to "no-action" resolutions continues to be a moving target.

In sum, these changes at the SEC have worried shareholder activists interested in a wide range of ESG issues, including particularly those pressing for reforms that would make for improved transparency surrounding corporate political engagements. Reforms in the direction of making it more difficult for shareholders to bring resolutions – whether in a single year or in multiple years – would seem to press against the interest of inviting further engagement on CPA reforms.

At the same time, the broader movement for political accountability continues to gain momentum as widespread concerns about corporate influence in politics has only mounted further in the wake of the 2020 presidential election. The risks to democracy have become all the more plain given the misinformation surrounding the election as well as the efforts to scale back voting rights in the states that we have seen in the time since. It seems reasonable to expect that those who are pressing for a more politically responsive corporate sector will need to be all the more emboldened in the years ahead, as they seek out major reforms through both public and private politics.

References

Ahl, A. (2021). *The Risks of 'Business as Usual' Corporate Political Contributions*. Ann Arbor, MI: Erb Institute.

Armstrong, E. A., & Bernstein, M. (2008). Culture, Power, and Institutions: A Multi-Institutional Politics. *Approach to Social Movements. Sociological Theory*, 26(1):74–99. DOI: 10.1111/j.1467-9558.2008.00319.x.

Baron, D. P. (2001). Private Politics, Corporate Social Responsibility, and Integrated Strategy. *Journal of Economics & Management Strategy*, 10(1):7–45. DOI: 10.1111/j.1430-9134.2001.00007.x.

---

[4] See www.sec.gov/corpfin/procedural-requirements-resubmission-thresholds-guide, issued December 28, 2020.

[5] See www.sec.gov/news/press-release/2020-161.

Bartels, L. M. (2016). *Unequal Democracy*. Princeton: Princeton University Press.

Bartley, T. (2007). Institutional Emergence in an Era of Globalization: The Rise of Transnational Private Regulation of Labor and Environmental Conditions. *American Journal of Sociology*, 113(2):297–351. DOI: 10.1086/518871.

Bebchuk, L. A., & Jackson, R. J. (2010). Corporate Political Speech: Who Decides? *Harvard Law Review*, 124(1):83–117.

Benton, R. A. (2017). The Decline of Social Entrenchment: Social Network Cohesion and Board Responsiveness to Shareholder Activism. *Organization Science*, 28(2):262–82.

Center for Political Accountability. (2018). *Collision Course: The Risks Companies Face When Their Political Spending and Core Values Conflict and How to Address Them*. Washington, DC: Center for Political Accountability.

Center for Responsive Politics. (2020). *More Money, Less Transparency: A Decade under Citizens United*. Washington, D.C.: CRP.

Chiu, S., & Sharfman, M. (2011). Legitimacy, Visibility, and the Antecedents of Corporate Social Performance: An Investigation of the Instrumental Perspective. *Journal of Management*, 37(6):1558–85. DOI: 10.1177/0149206309347958.

Davis, G. F., & Thompson, T. A. (1994). A Social Movement Perspective on Corporate Control. *Administrative Science Quarterly*, 39(1):141–73. DOI: 10.2307/2393497.

Dawood, Y. (2015). Campaign Finance and American Democracy. *Annual Review of Political Science*, 18(1):329–48. DOI: 10.1146/annurev-polisci-010814-104523.

Dean, G. (2021). From Cutting All Ties with Trump to Pulling Political Donations, Here's How Corporate America Has Responded to the Capitol Insurrection. Business Insider.

Dowling, C. M., & Miller, M. G. (2014). *Super PAC!: Money, Elections, and Voters after Citizens United*. New York: Routledge.

Goh, L., Liu, X., & Tsang, A. (2020). Voluntary Disclosure of Corporate Political Spending. *Journal of Corporate Finance*, 61, 101403.

Graves, S. B., Waddock, S., & Rehbein, S. (2001). Fad and Fashion in Shareholder Activism: The Landscape of Shareholder Resolutions, 1988–1998. *Business and Society Review*, 106(4):293–314.

Guay, T., Doh, J. P., & Sinclair, G. (2004). Non-Governmental Organizations, Shareholder Activism, and Socially Responsible Investments: Ethical, Strategic, and Governance Implications. *Journal of Business Ethics*, 52(1):125–39. DOI: 10.1023/B:BUSI.0000033112.11461.69.

Hansen, W. L., Rocca, M. S., & Ortiz, B. L. (2015). The Effects of Citizens United on Corporate Spending in the 2012 Presidential Election. *The Journal of Politics*, 77(2):535–45. DOI: 10.1086/680077.

Hertel-Fernandez, A. (2019). *State Capture: How Conservative Activists, Big Businesses, and Wealthy Donors Reshaped the American States – And the Nation.* New York: Oxford University Press.

Hiatt, S. R., Grandy, J. B., & Lee, B. H. (2015). Organizational Responses to Public and Private Politics: An Analysis of Climate Change Activists and U.S. Oil and Gas Firms. *Organization Science,* 26(6):1769–86. DOI: 10.1287/orsc.2015.1008.

King, B. G., & McDonnell, M. H. (2012). Good Firms, Good Targets: The Relationship between Corporate Social Responsibility, Reputation, and Activist Targeting. *Corporate Social Responsibility in a Globalizing World.*

Lyon, T. P., Delmas, M. A., Maxwell, J. W., Bansal, P., et al. (2018). CSR Needs CPR: Corporate Sustainability and Politics. *California Management Review,* 60(4):5–24. DOI: 10.1177/0008125618778854.

Mizruchi, M. S. (2013). *The Fracturing of the American Corporate Elite.* Cambridge, MA: Harvard University Press.

Montopoli, B. (2010). Target Boycott Movement Grows Following Donation to Support 'Antigay' Candidate. *CBS News,* July 28.

Myers, C. (2018). Public Relations or 'Grassroots Lobbying'? How Lobbying Laws Are Re-Defining PR Practice. *Public Relations Review,* 44(1):11–21. DOI: 10.1016/j.pubrev.2017.11.006.

Repko, M. (2018). Trump Lawyer Payments Fuel AT&T Shareholders' Push to Know More about Political Spending. *Dallas News,* June 6.

Sachs, B. I. (2012). Unions, Corporations, and Political Opt-Out Rights After Citizens United. *Columbia Law Review,* 112:800.

Scott, M. J. (2019). Ripping up the Astroturf: Regulating Deceptive Corporate Advertising Methods. *Iowa Law Review,* 105:431.

Short, J. L., Toffel, M. W., & Hugill, H. R. (2020). Improving Working Conditions in Global Supply Chains: The Role of Institutional Environments and Monitoring Program Design. *ILR Review,* 73(4):873–912. DOI: 10.1177/0019793920916181.

Skaife, H. A., & Werner, T. (2020). Changes in Firms' Political Investment Opportunities, Managerial Accountability, and Reputational Risk. *Journal of Business Ethics,* 163(2):239–63.

Soule, S. A. (2009). *Contention and Corporate Social Responsibility.* New York: Cambridge University Press.

Stanley-Becker, I. (2021). American Airlines, Other Companies Resume Donations to Republicans Who Objected to Election Results. *Washington Post,* July 15.

Vogel, D. (2008). Private Global Business Regulation. *Annual Review of Political Science,* 11(1):261–82. DOI: 10.1146/ annurev.polisci .11.053106.141706.

Walker, E. T. (2014). *Grassroots for Hire: Public Affairs Consultants in American Democracy.* Cambridge and New York: Cambridge University Press.

Walker, E. T., Martin, A. W., & McCarthy, J. D. (2008). Confronting the State, the Corporation, and the Academy: The Influence of Institutional Targets on Social Movement Repertoires. *American Journal of Sociology*, 114(1):35–76. DOI: 10.1086/588737.

Walker, E. T., & Rea, C. M. (2014). The Political Mobilization of Firms and Industries. *Annual Review of Sociology*, 40(1):281–304. DOI: 10.1146/annurev-soc-071913-043215.

Wang, J., & Zhang, H. (2021). Political Transparency, Corporate Governance and Economic Significance. *International Journal of Disclosure and Governance.* DOI: 10.1057/s41310-021-00127-z.

Webber, D. (2018). *The Rise of the Working-Class Shareholder.* Cambridge, MA: Harvard University Press.

Werner, T. (2011). The Sound, the Fury, and the Nonevent: Business Power and Market Reactions to the Citizens United Decision. *American Politics Research*, 39(1):118–41. DOI: 10.1177/1532673X10384704.

Werner, T. (2017). Investor Reaction to Covert Corporate Political Activity. *Strategic Management Journal*, 38(12):2424–43. DOI: 10.1002/smj.2682.

Wheeler, L. (2015). Spending Bill Blocks SEC Political Disclosure Rule. *The Hill*, December 16.

Yosifon, D. (2015). It's Law, But It Shouldn't Be. *The New York Times.*

5 | Promise and Peril
Lessons from Shareholder Reactions to Corporate Political Activity Disclosure

TIMOTHY WERNER

5.1 Introduction

On July 21, 2020, David DeVillers, the US Attorney for the Southern District of Ohio, announced the arrests of Ohio State House Speaker Larry Householder and four of his political associates for allegedly having participated in a covert bribery scheme connected to FirstEnergy Corp., the state's largest electric utility. DeVillers argued that in exchange for Householder's work on passing a $1 billion bailout for FirstEnergy's nuclear power plants, the utility provided over $60 million to a Householder-controlled nonprofit 501(c)4 social welfare corporation named Generation Now (Smyth & Seewer, 2020). As with all nonprofits, Generation Now is not required to publicly disclose the identities of its contributors unless they specifically earmark their contributions for political activity, and were it not for the criminal prosecution, FirstEnergy's role in the incident may never have been revealed. DeVillers further alleged that Generation Now used a portion of these illicit funds to support Householder's co-partisans in state legislative elections and that Householder directed another portion to cover expenses at his second home in Florida. In the two days following DeVillers's announcement of the arrests, FirstEnergy's share price dropped over 34 percent, and in the months that followed, shareholders, including some of the largest institutional investors in the United States, filed over a dozen lawsuits against the firm (Eckhouse et al., 2021).

The FirstEnergy event provides firms interested in engaging in corporate political activity (CPA) a stark lesson in the potential perils of doing so. However, as it is an outlier in so many regards – the sums involved, the swift and harsh action by the justice system for an alleged violation of the laws governing CPA, and the dramatic reaction by ordinary and institutional investors – there may be only so many inferences we can draw from it regarding how stakeholders and in particular shareholders react to the disclosure of CPA. Hence, the goal of this chapter is to summarize and synthesize how larger-scale CPA disclosure events inform shareholders' behavior in two ways: by examining shareholder reaction to (i) changes to the legal regulations governing CPA disclosure and (ii) events which involve the inadvertent – whether by accident or via whistleblowing – disclosure of CPA that is otherwise not legally required to be disclosed.

Although disclosure has long been viewed as a minimally intrusive yet effective regulatory tool (Brandeis, 1913; Parkinson, 2003), it is nevertheless essential to explore the impact of CPA disclosure on firms for a host of reasons (see, also, Lyon & Madelkorn, 2023). First, the sheer amount of money in US politics continues to grow: Total federal lobbying expenditures in 2020 set a new all-time high ($3.53 billion), and total expenditures in the 2020 election cycle did so as well ($14.4 billion),[1] suggesting that the stakes of policymaking remain significant for all involved. Further, 7 percent or roughly $1 billion of the total amount spent on elections came in the form of "dark money" (like the funds employed in the opening FirstEnergy example), meaning that the ultimate source of these funds is not subject to mandatory disclosure under federal law (Massoglia & Evers-Hillstrom, 2021).

Second, and perhaps due to the growth of "dark money" ushered in by the US Supreme Court's decision in *Citizens United v. Federal Election Commission* (FEC) in 2010, the role of corporations in the political process and the disclosure of their CPA to both the public and their shareholders has become an increasingly important area for public and private policy, with both federal and state legislation, as well as firm-level shareholder activism, being pursued year after year on this question (DeBoskey & Luo, 2018; Goh, Liu, & Tsang, 2020; Shanor, McDonnell, & Werner, 2022; Walker, 2023). Particular political events, such as the January 6, 2021, insurrection at the US Capitol, have also heightened the salience and risk of CPA, with corporations often coming under pressure to disavow politicians to whom they are connected via prior contributions to the politician from the corporations' affiliated political action committees (PACs).[2] That being said,

---

[1] Statistics sourced from OpenSecrets.org.
[2] See, also, the work of independent journalist Judd Legum, who used his website (https://popular.info/) and Twitter feed both to proactively pressure companies

the effects of such one-off events can be fleeting, as several corporations (e.g., Lockheed Martin, Merck, and Anheuser-Busch) only temporarily halted their contributions to members of Congress that voted against certifying the results of the 2020 presidential election.

Third, disclosure has strong support among the mass public, with over 74 percent of individuals in a 2016 survey agreeing that contribution amounts should be disclosed and over 70 percent of these respondents agreeing that contributor names should also be disclosed (Primo & Milyo, 2020:109); no other potential reform or regulation to money politics commands such broad-based support.

Fourth, in contrast to many other types of regulations on money in politics (e.g., contribution limits/bans; expenditure limits/bans; public financing), disclosure has fared well when challenged judicially, including in *Citizens United* (Shaw, 2016). Although changes in the composition of the Supreme Court may result in a whittling of disclosure's strong legal position (see, e.g., its July 2021 decision in *Americans for Prosperity Foundation v. Bonta*, which creates new limits on and tests for disclosure of contributors to nonprofits), few would argue that any other regulation is likely to supplant it as the most acceptable form of regulation in the current Court's eyes (see, e.g., Jiang, 2019). That being said, actors and scholars increasingly argue that disclosure (and transparency more broadly) is not a purely neutral tool but one that can lead to harassment, from the right or left, of those that participate in politics (Gilbert, 2013) and to rightward ideological drift in underlying substantive regulation (Pozen, 2018).[3]

The remainder of the chapter proceeds by: (i) briefly motivating why firms engage in CPA and why shareholders care about the CPA of the firms in which they invest; (ii) providing background on disclosure as regulatory tool with regard to money in politics broadly and with regard to the specific context of firm-shareholder relations; (iii)

to halt their PAC giving to the 147 Republican members of Congress who did not vote to certify the results of the 2020 presidential election on January 6, 2021, and to monitor whether those firms that adopted such pledges abided by them in the months that followed.

[3] Pozen argues that although transparency was a key tenet of the Progressive movement of the early twentieth-century, by the end of the century, it became captured by corporate and national security interests that exploited transparency requirements to limit the ability of governmental bodies to functional effectively.

introducing the event study methodology employed by social scientists across myriad disciplines to measure shareholder reactions to discrete events that affect corporations; (iv) outlining, in detail, the empirical findings of four published event studies related to CPA disclosure; (v) summarizing the core takeaways of these four studies and articulating their implications for both corporate strategy and public policy; and (vi) concluding with some informed speculation on disclosure's role in the future of CPA.

5.2 Why Do Firms Engage in CPA, and Why Do Shareholders Care?

The principal theoretical lens through which scholars view CPA is public choice, which argues that competition in the shaping of public policy can be analyzed in a similar fashion to competition in a competitive market (see, Buchanan, 1987; Buchanan & Tullock, 1962; Tullock, 1972). Rather than modeling buyers and sellers of a product or service, scholars model policymakers as suppliers and various interests (the mass public, firms, unions, public interest groups, NGOs, etc.) as demanders, with the public institutions the policymakers sit in determining outcomes via a nonmarket mechanism (e.g., a legislative vote or judicial decision) rather than a market mechanism (i.e., price). Although public choice has proven to have remarkable power in explaining policy outcomes, like many political-economic approaches, it is relatively agnostic as to the question of why demanders engage in political markets in the first place (Lenway et al., 2022).

Explicit in the public choice model is that demanders participate in policymaking rationally: thus, in the case of a firm, political engagement has generally been thought to be a form of investment in which firms make lobbying expenditures and employ PACs to make contributions to politicians in the hopes of securing a return in the form of favorable public policies.[4] This investment-centric view has not gone unchallenged, however, with Ansolabehere, De Figueiredo, and

---

[4] These preferred policies need not come at the expense of social welfare; for example, many formal models of lobbying suggest that it represents an important subsidy of the public sector by the private sector (Hall & Deardorff, 2006), as the former suffers from both information overload and information asymmetries which the latter can help address.

Snyder (2003) most prominently arguing that it is likely incorrect with regard to PAC contributions and should be subject to greater testing with regard to lobbying expenditures. With regard to the former, these authors believe that patterns of PAC giving are not consistent with an investment view: Few firms even have PACs, and very few individual contributions from PACs to politicians near the statutory contribution cap; instead, PAC contributions appear to be more a form of consumption than investment (see, also, Hadani & Schuler, 2013). With regard to the latter, although the authors appear to be more sympathetic to an investment-based logic when it comes to lobbying, they and others (e.g., Coates, 2012; Werner & Coleman, 2015; Winkler, 2004) argue that we cannot rule out the possibility that executives are using their firms' CPA to serve their own strategic purposes, which may even be contrary to those of their shareholders (i.e., that CPA is not just a form of consumption but may be subject to a principal-agent problem).

Whether CPA leads to investment gains or agency costs or neither, that either of the former two outcomes is possible means that CPA is clearly relevant to the shareholders of firms that chose to have PACs or engage in lobbying. That is to say, that regardless of the magnitude of a firm's CPA (and whether or not, e.g., it meets accounting definitions of material) and of the direction of CPA's effect, if it has an effect on share price, then the owners of these shares have a clear interest in knowing whether and how managers engage in CPA so as to be able to take any necessary action on the stock exchange as a result.

Further, beyond any immediate pecuniary returns or penalties stemming directly from the firm's impact on public policy, longer-term reputational concerns related to stakeholder management vis-à-vis CPA may also be reflected in a firm's share price. For example, firm engagement in CPA has effects on relationships with not just policymakers (Werner, 2015) but also communities (Minefee, McDonnell, & Werner, 2021), social movements (McDonnell & Werner, 2016), consumers (Panagopoulos et al., 2020), and both current and prospective employees (Burbano, 2021; Darnell & McDonnell, 2023). Additionally, shareholders may also have an interest in holding managers accountable for the CPA they direct the firm to engage in and in ensuring that the firms' CPA aligns with its broader market and nonmarket strategies that seek to enhance long-term shareholder welfare and not just short-term market value (Hart & Zingales, 2017). In the environmental realm, for instance, shareholders may want to prevent management from "talking green while lobbying brown" (Delmas & Lyon, 2018), so as to avoid charges of organizational hypocrisy (Laufer, 2003) and their attendant effects on a firm's reputation.

5.3 Disclosure as a Regulatory Tool in CPA

As a regulatory tool, disclosure has deep roots in the American progressive movement of the early twentieth-century, with future Supreme Court justice Louis Brandeis famously writing, "Publicity is justly commended as a remedy for social and industrial diseases. Sunlight is said to be the best of disinfectants; electric light the most efficient policeman" (Brandeis, 1913: 10). Disclosure of the flow of money in politics, including CPA, has the specific intent of addressing principal-agent problems and informational asymmetries. The principal specific rationale offered in defense of disclosure is that it serves the public policy goal of rooting out corruption and/or the appearance of corruption by serving voters' "informational interest," as balanced against concerns that it degrades contributors' privacy and thus, may "chill" political speech – a concern that has grown with the ready availability of campaign finance information via the internet (Briffault, 2010).[5]

The first application of disclosure to money in politics at the federal level came in the same era that Brandeis wrote, as part of the Publicity of Political Contributions Act of 1910. As this legislation and other early reforms were updated in the 1960s and 1970s for campaign finance and in the 1990s for lobbying, disclosure maintained its prominence.[6] Further, disclosure's importance has only grown in the past fifty years, as the other regulatory tools at the government's disposal in this space (limits/bans on campaign contributions; limits/

---

[5] This is the specific rationale offered for *public* disclosure; of course, *private* disclosure (i.e., between only the contributor/recipient and the government) also serves law enforcement purposes.

[6] See, for example, the following language from President John Kennedy's 1962 Commission on Campaign Costs' final report: "full and effective disclosure is the best way to control excessive contributions on the one hand and unlimited expenditures on the other. Publicity has a cleansing and policing power far more powerful than that of limitations" (President's Commission on Campaign Costs, 1962: 18).

bans on campaign and lobbying expenditures; and public financing of elections) have all run afoul of free speech jurisprudence in the federal courts (Shaw, 2016).

With specific regard to the firm-shareholder relationship, disclosure has had a similarly long history as the means by which investors are provided the information they need to decide whether or not to purchase a given stock (Healy & Palepu, 2001). That is to say, that the New Deal–era Securities Act of 1933 and Securities Exchange Act of 1934 "were not intended to regulate securities based on their merits or financial soundness" (Dalley, 2007: 1098; see, also, Seligman [2003]) but rather to allow investors to decide how to best allocate their scarce capital. Hence, as discussed in the prior section, disclosure of CPA can be thought of as a complement to financial and accounting disclosures in that it can resolve informational asymmetries (and, thus, potentially reduce agency costs) for investors, even though disclosure itself does not directly prohibit firms from engaging in any specific form of political activity.

To be clear, current federal regulations do not impose special disclosure obligations on for-profit, publicly traded corporations when it comes to political activity; rather, they are treated similarly to any other organization seeking to influence either electoral outcomes via campaign finance or policy outcomes via lobbying. Nevertheless, as Table 5.1 adapted from Werner (2017) details, there is considerable heterogeneity in the current federal disclosure regimes across lobbying and campaign finance, and within each of these broad categories, disclosure requirements also vary with the means corporations employ to engage in them.

Due to this variation in disclosure, shareholder protection has been advanced as a justification for regulation in legislative debates and legal cases that touch upon CPA conducted by publicly traded firms. In *Citizens United*, for example, both Justice Anthony Kennedy in the majority opinion and Justice John Paul Stevens in the principal dissent directly addressed it. In Kennedy's case, he argued that since "disclosure permits citizens and shareholders to react to the speech of corporate entities in a proper way,"[7] there was no need for the prohibition on corporate independent expenditures funded from a corporate treasury that *Citizens United* challenged in the case. In contrast, Stevens

---

[7] www.supremecourt.gov/opinions/09pdf/08-205.pdf; p. 55.

argued that disclosure and the subsequent ability of shareholders to divest or challenge management over their CPA (e.g., through shareholder resolutions or derivative suits) was insufficient – and perhaps even a mirage – as a form of regulation, as shareholders' rights would still be violated since they would learn of CPA they disagreed with only once it had already occurred.

Importantly, although the *Citizens United* decision upheld disclosure regulations, it also created a disclosure loophole that would require an act of Congress to address. Specifically, and as detailed in the final section of Table 5.1, if corporations were to make contributions to a 501(c) nonprofit corporation that then made independent expenditures to influence electoral outcomes, then the role of the corporation need not be disclosed. Similarly, and as detailed in the first section of Table 5.1, if corporations were to make contributions to a 501(c) nonprofit corporation that then engaged in lobbying to influence policymaking, then the role of the corporation need not be disclosed.[8] In the wake of *Citizens United*, academic and legal debates over CPA increased in frequency and intensity: questions being addressed include whether corporate political spending that is not subject to mandatory public disclosure ought to be disclosed to shareholders (Bebchuk & Jackson, 2013); whether all forms of CPA should be subject to shareholder approval (Bebchuk & Jackson, 2010); and whether shareholders should have the right to opt out of CPA in similar fashion to how union members can opt-out of their organizations' political activities (Sachs, 2012).

Informing the above debates is an emergent literature on financial market reactions to CPA disclosure that asks whether financial market participants (i.e., shareholders) value disclosure, and what factors explain variation in their opinions on it. These studies examine both changes in disclosure regulation and incidents of inadvertent disclosure to answer these questions; before examining these studies, the next section provides a brief primer on the methodology they employ to analyze shareholders' reactions.

---

[8] To be clear, this lobbying disclosure loophole existed prior to *Citizens United*, which strictly dealt with electoral activity and not lobbying. In general, lobbying is subject to far less regulation than electoral activity, as lobbying is one of three clearly protected professions in the US Constitution. (The other two being press and clergy.)

Table 5.1 *Legal regulations on corporate political activity (excluding individual employees' activity)*

Political spending category/type	Source of funds	Funds given to/spent on	Limits on contributions/ spending	Disclosure of firm's role required?
Lobbying expenditures directly by firm	Corporate treasury	In-house/contract lobbyists, research, informational advocacy	None	Yes, quarterly (post-2007)
via 501(c)	Corporate treasury	Nonprofit, tax-exempt organization that can engage in informational advocacy	None	No
Political action committee (PAC) contributions	Restricted class of employees and shareholders, and their spouses	Candidate, party campaign committees; other PACs (administrative costs of PAC may be paid by firm directly from corporate treasury)	$5,000 to candidate/ election; $15,000 to national party/year	Yes, quarterly
Contributions to a national party committee account directly by firm	Corporate treasury	Local nonpartisan host committee for national party convention	None	Yes, during presidential cycle

via a PAC	Restricted class of employees and shareholders, and their spouses	Recount/legal fees; facilities; national party convention	$45,000 to each party committee (i.e., national, Senate, House)/year	Yes, quarterly
Communications costs	Corporate treasury	Informs employees/ shareholders of political issues, firm endorsements	None	Yes, quarterly and in communication
Issue advocacy (excluding "grassroots campaigns") directly by firm	Corporate treasury	Advocates for a public policy position without expressly advocating for/ against a candidate	None	Yes, quarterly and in advertisement
via 527	Corporate treasury	Tax-exempt organization that advocates for a public policy position without expressly advocating for/against a candidate	None	Yes, quarterly
Independent expenditures (post–*Citizens United*) directly by firm	Corporate treasury	Advertising, etc. that can expressly advocate for/ against a candidate	None	Yes, quarterly and in advertisement

Table 5.1 (*cont.*)

Political spending category/type	Source of funds	Funds given to/spent on	Limits on contributions/ spending	Disclosure of firm's role required?
via "Super PAC"	Corporate treasury	Candidate- or party-affiliated (though independent) or ideological committees that engage in express advocacy	None	Yes, quarterly
via 501(c)(4) or (c)(6)	Corporate treasury	Nonprofit, tax-exempt organization that can expressly advocate for/against a candidate	None, but political activity may not be "primary purpose" of a 501(c)(4)	No, as long as funds are not earmarked for political activity

5.4 How to Measure Shareholder Reaction to CPA Disclosure: Event Study Methodology

The principal means by which scholars across disciplines assess whether or not shareholders react to corporate events is the financial market event study. Event study methodology uses financial market returns around an event to construct expected returns for a focal firm or firms that are "treated" by the event and compares those expected returns to the actual returns of the focal firm(s). The goal of this comparison between expected and actual returns is to uncover what effect, if any, researchers can attribute to the event (McWilliams & Siegel, 1997). As a counterfactual method, financial market event studies proceed in three steps. First, using data from an estimation period prior to the event of interest (typically, a year's worth of trading data), a baseline relationship between the stock market return of the focal firm affected by the event and a market benchmark return is estimated using ordinary least squares regression:

$$FF\_Ret_t = b_0 + b_1 Mkt\_Ret_t \qquad (1)$$

where FF_Ret_t represents returns of the focal firm on day t, and Mkt_Ret_t represents the returns of the benchmark on day t.[9] In the second step, the parameter estimates from equation (1) are used to predict an expected return for the focal firm during the event window, that is, an appropriate period around or following the event, which is chosen by the researcher to reflect when the event's potential impact should have appeared in the focal firm's share price:

$$\widehat{FF\_Ret_t} = \hat{\beta}_0 + \hat{\beta}_1 Mkt\_Ret_t \qquad (2)$$

Researchers then calculate the treatment effect of the event on the focal firm by taking the difference between the firm's expected and actual return for each day, generating an "abnormal" return:

$$FF\_AR_t = \widehat{FF\_Ret_t} - FF\_Ret_t \qquad (3)$$

If a researcher expects an event's effect to unfold across multiple days, they then sum these abnormal returns across the full event window to generate a cumulative abnormal return (CAR). Lastly, the

---

[9] A benchmark can take various one of various forms (e.g., single or multiple factors related to asset pricing) and can be estimated using different samples (e.g., the full market or a relevant subset, such as the focal firm's industry).

researcher assesses whether the effect is statistically significant using one or multiple parametric or nonparametric tests of significance, the choice of which depends upon the nature of the event and the number of firms affected.

In doing the above, event study methodology grounds its counterfactual data generating process in a rational statistical model of financial markets, assuming that the semi-strong form of the efficient markets hypothesis holds (Brown & Warner, 1980). This assumption requires that (i) "all available information [about a given firm] is costlessly available to all market participants" or at least filters very rapidly into the market, and (ii) that "all [market participants] agree on the implications of current information for the current price [of a given firm]" (Fama, 1970: 387). Additionally, the event analyzed must be a "surprise" – that is, the release of new information – to the market participants, otherwise its effects will already be priced in by investors.

Reflecting its robustness as a tool for measuring shareholder reactions to events of all stripes, event study methodology has seen wide applicability in political economy (see, Milyo [2014] for an overview). Political events analyzed using the methodology include close elections (Akey, 2015; Fowler, Garro, & Spenkuch, 2020; Knight, 2007); unexpected party switches in the US Senate (Den Hartog and Monroe, 2008; Jayachandran, 2006); the death of a key policymaker in the US Senate (Roberts, 1990); and current political connections in the United States (Acemoglu et al., 2013; Khurana et al., 2012) and abroad (Fisman, 2001), as well as historical political connections to bygone authoritarian regimes (Ferguson & Voth, 2008).

Event study methodology has also seen application in the narrower realm of the regulation of money in politics. Of greatest relevance, Ansolabehere, Snyder, and Ueda (2004) examine the effects of various events related to the passage and legal challenge of the Bipartisan Campaign Reform Act (i.e., McCain-Feingold), which banned so-called "soft money" contributions from corporations' treasuries to the coffers of political parties. They find that none of the events related to congressional or Supreme Court consideration of the law had any effect on firms that had made such contributions prior to the law's passage. That is to say, the imposition of a ban on a political tactic previously available to firms had no effect on shareholders' perceptions of the anticipated future performance of those firms that had previously made use of the tactic. Although this study examines the regulation of money in politics, it does not specifically focus on shareholder reactions to changes in or acts of CPA disclosure; in the next section, studies of four events that relate to disclosure are reviewed in depth.

5.5 Studies of Shareholder Reactions to CPA Disclosure

5.5.1 *Study One:* Citizens United v. FEC *and Changes in Independent Expenditure Regulation*

As noted above, in 2010, the Supreme Court struck down various campaign finance regulations in its decision in *Citizens United*. Of greatest importance for corporations and their shareholders, the ruling allowed corporations to make unlimited independent expenditures to affect electoral outcomes from corporate treasuries.[10] Although the decision simultaneously upheld various disclosure-related precedents, one consequence of the decision is that these new independent expenditures could take the form of contributions to 501(c) nonprofit corporations that are not obligated to disclose their contributors, provided the contribution is not specifically earmarked for electoral activity. Thus, *Citizens United* created a new opportunity for firms to influence elections in an undisclosed, albeit indirect, fashion.

Werner (2011) examines how shareholders reacted to key events in *Citizens United*, arguing that movements in share prices could capture whether or not (and in which direction) shareholders anticipated that the new means for political engagement allowed by the decision would affect firms' fortunes. To do so, Werner analyzed three key events in the case via an event study of the membership of the Fortune 500, segmenting this sample based upon its political sensitivity as measured by (i) lobbying expenses, (ii) PAC giving, and (iii) contracting levels. The three events were (i) an order for a rehearing in the case on June 29, 2009, (ii) the second oral argument in the case on September 9, 2009, and (iii) the announcement of the decision on January 22, 2010. Across the three measures of political sensitivity and across all three findings, Werner finds that financial market participants did not react

---

[10] Independent in this instance means uncoordinated between the spender and the benefiting party or candidate. Formal coordination is *per se* illegal, but informal coordination (e.g., observing and adjusting tactics in a reciprocal fashion) is not.

differentially based upon firms' prior political engagement. That is to say, Werner finds evidence for a "non-event" or at least no evidence that would support the claim that shareholders anticipated that *Citizens United* would lead to corporations' influence to grow and to result in enhanced performance for those firms with expertise in/ an established sensitivity to politics. (Additionally or alternatively, he also found no evidence shareholders anticipated that the case would result in firms experiencing greater agency problems or greater rent extraction by politicians and thus result in diminished performance for firms with a history of engaging in CPA/a sensitivity to politics.)

Other studies also examined the *Citizens United* decision, employing different samples and analyzing different events. Most significantly, in the samples they employ, Burns and Jindra (2014) find that regulated firms experienced positive CARs around the decision announcement in the case, and Strattman and Verret (2015) also estimate positive CARs around the decision for firms based upon both their prior engagement in electoral politics, as measured via contributions to 527 organizations and their regulation level. These two papers only analyze the decision in *Citizens United*, however, which may be a violation of the assumptions of event study analyses, for as Werner (2011) notes, the final outcome in the case was heavily telegraphed to financial market participants by the Court's order for a rehearing in the case, as well as by the tenor of the second oral argument in the case.

By contrast, one additional study that also exploited *Citizens United* extended Werner's original analysis to explore whether or not corporate governance mechanisms may have moderated market reactions to the Court's actions in the case: Skaife and Werner (2020) found that this was indeed the case, with firms that had powerful chief executive officers (i.e., CEOs who were also chairperson of the board) experiencing more negative CARs, on average, if they had high prior levels of CPA and firms that had more concentrated ownership (i.e., more shares held by five-percent-or-greater blockholders) experiencing less negative CARs, on average, if they had high prior levels of CPA. Skaife and Werner argue that shareholders anticipated that the specific nature of the new, undisclosed CPA that firms could engage in stood to create agency problems within already politically active firms and that this possibility explains why governance mechanisms played such an important moderating role in shareholders' reactions to events in the case.

Despite the different research design choices made by the authors of these event studies of *Citizens United*, one issue that all four face – and one that may be producing these mixed findings from which it is difficult to draw public policy or strategy implications – is that they are all anticipatory studies of shareholders' reactions and do not analyze the actual use of independent political expenditures. The paper summarized in the next section leverages an accidental disclosure of such activity to do just that.

5.5.2 Study Two: Exposure of Covert Connections to the Republican Governors Association

On September 24, 2014, the *New York Times* published an expose of corporate contributors to the Republican Governors' Public Policy Committee, a 501(c)4 nonprofit under the control of the Republican Governors Association (RGA) that makes independent expenditures in support of Republican candidates for governor across the United States. As a 501(c), the committee is not required to publicly disclose its contributors, but it accidentally posted the names of its contributors to a website for its annual meeting, 66 of which were publicly traded firms. These firms spanned industries and included many well-known corporations such as Aetna, General Motors, Microsoft, Verizon, and Walgreens.

Werner (2017) exploited this accidental disclosure to analyze shareholder reactions to the actual use of the new freedoms given to firms by *Citizens United* and not just shareholder reactions in anticipation of their use. As a first step in answering this question, Werner conducted a market-wide event study, in which he examined whether contributing firms experienced CARs that were, on average, different from those of noncontributing firms. Across six different event windows, he finds consistent evidence that shareholders reacted positively to the disclosure of firms' connections to the RGA, with contributing firms experiencing CARs that ranged from +0.36 to +2.13 percent. Werner speculates that shareholders may have had this reaction because the disclosure event revealed that these firms had successfully established access to these governors and their high-level staffers.

To further unpack the mechanisms beyond this shareholder reaction, as a second step in his study, Werner examines the cross-sectional variation in the CARs of just those firms that contributed to the RGA's 501(c). He finds that firms in heavily regulated industries experienced more positive CARs and that firms' CARs were positively correlated with the campaign contributions they previously made to candidates. The former finding is consistent with a long line of research in CPA that suggests that returns to CPA are greater for firms whose market opportunities are subject to greater governmental control (Baron, 2013), and the latter, more novel finding suggests that in the eyes of shareholders at least, independent expenditures appear to serve strategically as a complement to rather than as a substitute for traditional direct contributions to candidates.

One brake on the positive reaction that Werner uncovers relates to shareholder contention: specifically, he finds that firms that had faced a shareholder resolution focused on political spending disclosure in the proxy season (2013) prior to the *New York Times* reporting experienced negative CARs around the release of the news story. Werner argues that this finding suggests that the controversial nature of covert CPA and, in particular, its potential for misuse, moderated shareholders' reactions downward, despite the overall positive stock price effect for firms connected to the RGA.

5.5.3 Study Three: Exposure of Covert Connections to the American Legislative Exchange Council

In an effort to replicate and extend the findings in Werner (2017), Minefee, McDonnell, and Werner (2021), exploit a whistleblower's leak of the American Legislative Exchange Council's (ALEC) corporate sponsors to conduct an event study. ALEC is a conservative 501(c)3 nonprofit that is "dedicated to the principles of limited government, free markets and federalism"[11] and that drafts model bills for its members – mostly Republican state legislators – to introduce and advocate for. As Hertel-Fernandez (2014) documents, in an average year, over 800-ALEC drafted bills are introduced, and approximately 15 percent of these bills have become law. On July 13, 2011, the Center for Media and Democracy, with the help of a whistleblower within ALEC, exposed the names of ALEC's corporate donors on a website it created named "ALEC Exposed." Like the RGA's contributors, ALEC's spanned industries and included prominent firms such as Altria, Bank of America, eBay, Humana, Raytheon, and Time Warner Cable.

Minefee, McDonnell, and Werner exploit this leak and find that firms tied to ALEC experienced negative cumulative abnormal returns

---

[11] See, www.alec.org/about/

around the event. These CARs averaged from –0.06 to -2.66 percent, depending upon the market model they employed to estimate predicted returns and the event window over which they summed abnormal returns. Like Werner (2017), the authors also conduct a cross-sectional analysis of the CARs of just those firms that contributed to ALEC and find that the abnormal returns of ALEC sponsors were more negative for firms that faced shareholder resolutions related to CPA disclosure in the run-up to the event, replicating Werner's finding with regard to the RGA. Extending Werner's findings, they find a similar negative moderating effect for those firms that have liberal-leaning employees and a positive moderating effect for firms engaged in higher levels of institutional corporate social responsibility.

To reconcile their seemingly contradictory results with Werner's, Minefee and colleagues conduct a content analysis of media coverage of both the RGA and ALEC in the one-year run-up to the respective events. They gathered every article in Factiva that mentioned and provided a descriptive phrase for either the RGA (145 articles) or ALEC (71 articles) and then coded whether or not the descriptive phrase included a word from a political controversy dictionary. They found that "words denoting political controversy were used in 0.7 percent of the articles describing the RGA and 5.6 percent of the articles describing ALEC" (1147). Based upon these results, they argue that the more controversial nature of ALEC as an organization led shareholders to react in such a different manner toward the news that firms were connected to it versus the news that firms were connected to the RGA. Additionally, Minefee and coauthors also point toward internal ALEC documents that corroborate this argument, as the organization's own staff blamed its controversial policy stances and behavior for costing it corporate members.

5.5.4 Study Four: A Comparative Perspective on Reforms from Changes to the United Kingdom's Regulation of Political Spending

Following a scandal involving a £1 million donation to the British Labour Party in 1997, the newly elected Labour government of Prime Minister Tony Blair asked the Committee on Standards in Public Life to examine the financing of British political parties and recommend reforms as necessary. In 1998, the Committee recommended a number of reforms related to election administration, campaign contributions, campaign expenditures, third parties, state funding, and referendums. Parliament then enacted these reforms into law via the Political Parties, Elections and Referendums Act (PPERA) 2000. Importantly, PPERA affected CPA conducted by British firms in two ways: (i) It broadened disclosure requirements originally established in 1985 to include not just attempts by firms to influence domestic actors but attempts to influence European Union actors as well, and ii) it required firm managers to obtain pre-approval from shareholders before making any contributions in excess of £5,000 (Fisher, 2001).

Exploiting the initial surprise of the Committee's recommendations, Prabhat and Primo (2019) analyze how financial market participants viewed these simultaneous changes in CPA regulation. To do so, not only do the authors conduct an event study to examine whether politically active British firms experienced abnormal returns around the announcement of the committee's findings, they also examine whether or not market participants (i) viewed these firms as riskier (as proxied by the volatility of their returns around the event) and (ii) viewed these firms as less valuable in the long run (as proxied by Tobin's Q).

In their event study, Prabhat and Primo find no effect for the release of the Committee's recommendations on firms that had previously been politically active, and this null finding parallels Werner's (2011) study above that found no effect for Court announcements in the *Citizens United* case. However, the authors did find statistically significant effects for the Committee report on both of the additional firm-level outcomes they analyzed. Specifically, firms that had previously been politically active experienced higher levels of idiosyncratic, firm-level risk following the Committee report, and in the long-run (i.e., in the two- to three-year period following the report) these firms experienced reductions in their value of 3 to 5 percent.

Prabhat and Primo reconcile their findings by arguing that while shareholders could understand how the reforms that were to eventually come in PPERA would increase risk for politically active firms, these market participants had a harder time anticipating, in the short run, how the reforms would affect firm value. However, over the long run, shareholders (again as proxied by their effect on the market value component of Tobin's Q) viewed this increased risk as detrimental to firm value. Prabhat and Primo speculate as to two possible mechanisms that could explain this effect: (i) The regulations could constrain firm strategy/make it easy for competing firms and/or interest groups to replicate, and/or (ii) disclosure could serve to make politically active firms attractive targets, whether they be of the investor or social movement variety. Unfortunately, due to the limitations of their data, they are unable to discern which (if either) mechanism is indeed in play.

5.6 Empirical Takeaways and Implications for Corporate Strategy and Public Policy

Table 5.2 summarizes the findings of the four papers reviewed in the prior section. The key empirical takeaway of the literature on shareholder reactions to CPA disclosure is that these reactions are highly context dependent. Two factors militate for this conclusion: (i) The two studies that look for effects based upon immediate or forthcoming changes in the regulation of CPA disclosure – Werner (2011) and Prabhat and Primo (2019) – find non-effects in the event studies they conduct; and (ii) the two studies that examine specific and surprising disclosure incidents – Werner (2017) and Minefee, McDonnell, and Werner (2021) – find opposite effects, but the latter reconciles these seemingly disparate findings by demonstrating that even though the context of the events was highly similar in that large, politically active, and publicly traded firms were found to be giving to conservative organizations, the controversial nature of one of the two recipients (ALEC) likely explains why shareholders reacted negatively in that instance.

Based upon these results, the remainder of this section discusses the implications of CPA disclosure for both corporate strategy/stakeholder relations and public policy.

5.6.1 Implications for Corporate Strategy and Stakeholder Relations

The findings of the event studies summarized here provide a mixed bag when it comes to corporate strategy. On one hand, mere changes in the regulation of CPA disclosure appear not to affect share prices, at least in the short run. On the other hand, when firms actually engage in CPA that is not required to be disclosed but subsequently is, reactions are highly dependent upon both the purposes of the CPA and how the specific form of CPA deployed aligns or misaligns with the firms' critical stakeholders, including its shareholders and employees.

Table 5.2 *Summary of CPA disclosure event studies*

Study	Event analyzed	Main effect(s)	Moderating effect(s)
Werner (2011)	US Supreme Court consideration of *Citizens United v. FEC* in 2009–2010	No effect for case's events on the share price of politically active firms (as measured by lobbying)	
Burns and Jindra (2014)	US Supreme Court decision in *Citizens United* in 2010	No effect for decision on the share price of politically active firms (as measured by PAC activity)	More positive abnormal returns for firms in regulated industries and firms headquartered in states with more stringent campaign finance regulation
Strattman and Verret (2015)	US Supreme Court decision in *Citizens United* in 2010	Positive effect for decision on the share price of politically active firms (as measured by 527 activity)	More positive abnormal returns for firms in regulated industries
Skaife and Werner (2020)	US Supreme Court consideration of *Citizens United v. FEC* in 2009–2010	No effect for case's events on the share price of politically active firms (as measured by lobbying and PAC activity)	More negative abnormal returns for firms facing with CEO-chair duality Less negative abnormal returns for firms with more concentrated ownership

Werner (2017)	Accidental disclosure of corporate contributors to the Republican Governors Association's (RGA) 501(c)4 in 2014	Firms connected to the RGA experienced positive abnormal returns (+0.36 to +2.13 percent) around reporting of the connection in the *New York Times*	More positive abnormal returns for firms in heavily regulated industries and firms with higher levels of prior political activity Less positive abnormal returns for firms facing shareholder resolutions
Minefee, McDonnell, and Werner (2021)	Whistleblower's disclosure of corporate contributors to the American Legislative Exchange Council's 501(c)3 in 2013	Firms connected to ALEC experienced negative abnormal returns (−0.06 to −2.66 percent) around the launch of the "ALEC Exposed" website	More negative abnormal returns for firms facing shareholder resolutions and more liberal employees Less negative abnormal returns for firms with higher levels of institutional corporate social responsibility
Prabhat and Primo (2019)	Release of the recommendations of the Committee on Standards in Public Life's report on British political party financing in 1998, including provisions related to corporate contribution disclosure and shareholder approval	No effect for committee's report on share price of politically active firms; however, idiosyncratic risk increased, and long-term firm value (proxied by Tobin's Q) declined 3 to 5 percent	

In particular, firms appear to face the greatest downside when their disclosed CPA seemingly contradicts their primary stakeholders' desires. Thus, when formulating their political strategies, firms would be well advised to consider not just how shareholders will react generally to it, but whether the CPA firms are engaged in has been a "contested" practice that may lead to distrust and further activism, including potential shareholder "exit." In a similar vein, they should also give great weight to whether disclosure of CPA may create issues with regard to employee recruitment and retention (Burbano, 2021), as well as reputationally challenging instances of employee voice, such as recent walkouts that have occurred at both Google and Wayfair over the issues of sexual harassment and immigration, respectively.

5.6.2 Implications for Public Policy

In contrast to the relatively straightforward firm-level value implications of CPA disclosure, as Prabhat and Primo (2019) acknowledge, conducting a social welfare analysis with regard to CPA disclosure's value is extremely difficult, in part because such an analysis would involve tradeoffs across non-pecuniary dimensions, including political power and free speech. Further, analyses of any reform proposals would have to wrestle with Issacharoff and Karlan's (1999) hydraulic claim that money in politics is like water running down a hill and will always find its way into the political system.

Nevertheless, there are conclusions we can draw with regard to disclosure as a regulatory tool vis-à-vis CPA. First, as others have observed, disclosure is primarily a tool of those already well off in the political system, as they have resources both to incorporate and act on the information made public by it (see, e.g., Arnold [1990] on how increased disclosure in congressional lawmaking primarily benefited already active interest groups). This is perhaps less problematic from a shareholder's perspective than that of a member of the general public, but even among shareholders, there are vast differences in resources and power. Second, disclosure often requires informational intermediaries (e.g., stock analysts) to put the disclosed information into context, and they may have conflicts of their own that color what they report on/reveal and how they do so (Dalley, 2007). Third, in the specific context of money in politics, there is the lingering concern that disclosure chills political speech (Gilbert, 2013), and public support for disclosure of political activity, while strong in the abstract, declines when applied to one's own speech (Primo & Milyo, 2020). Lastly, as Pozen (2018) has argued, disclosure is not a neutral tool, and it has in the last century in particular been used as a sop of sorts by right-leaning interests to justify significantly limiting regulations designed to address the underlying economic and/or political activity subject to disclosure mandates.

Thus, turning to potential policy recommendations leaves us in a tricky spot. Leaving regulation to the actors themselves (i.e., allow-ing for self-regulation) and in this context allowing firms to determine whether and how to disclose their CPA would allow for "private order-ing" to occur free of the government's involvement (Yablon, 2017). But, such private ordering rarely occurs absent pressure from investor activists or organizations such as the Center for Political Accountability that specifically targets publicly traded firms (see, Freed, Sandstrom, & Laufer, 2023). Hence, this solution would be underinclusive, as it would be unlikely to succeed in pressuring privately held firms to adopt strong disclosure practices (or other CPA restrictions).

In terms of specific public policy reforms, given the Supreme Court's recent decisions in this space (Shaw, 2016), short of a constitutional amendment, reforms will still have to focus on narrowly tailored dis-closure requirements.[12] Ripe areas for enhancement include beefing up lobbying disclosure by requiring far more detailed and frequent reports from domestically held firms and ending 501(c)-related disclosure loopholes when it comes to specific electoral and/or lobbying activities (for further details on disclosure reform suggestions that are likely to be constitutionally permissible under the current Court, including pass-through requirements, see Shanor, McDonnell, & Werner [2022]).

Beyond disclosure, the US Congress should also take steps to strengthen its internal resources and make itself less reliant on private interests for information (LaPira, Drutman, & Kosar, 2020), and can-didates in congressional races could agree to run campaigns that reject and/or condemn undisclosed money being spent to influence their elec-tion (Sitaraman, 2014). This possibility is subject to the same issue as

---

[12] Such a Constitutional amendment would need not to target the Supreme Court's ruling in *Citizens United v. FEC*, but rather, its 1976 ruling in *Buckley v. Valejo*, which largely established the view that expenditures to influence political outcomes are a form of protected speech and thus subject to few regulations.

private ordering at the firm level, however, in that it is underinclusive because it would only apply on a race-by-race basis. Further, it would also require that outside groups honor the contract reached between the candidates running for office. Finally, similar to the PPERA requirement in the UK, the Congress could adopt a "say on political speech" provision, which would require management to secure shareholders' approval before making any significant political investments.

5.7 Conclusion

Arguments in favor of disclosure and transparency often start with Justice Brandeis' famous quotation that "sunlight is said to be the best of disinfectants," but, as Feldman (2009) points out, this claim is "based on a medical theory now long refuted (alcohol is a much better disinfectant)." Within the context of corporate political activity, a similar argument likely holds: Despite the above calls and recommendations for increased disclosure and transparency, which will likely benefit shareholders, little information that the mass public can make use of is likely to be provided, and as a result, more thorough efforts to heighten CPA disclosure may distort social welfare by undercutting policy proposals designed to address the underlying political-economic distortions CPA causes. Hence, reform efforts should move beyond disclosure and instead focus on constitutional changes that will permit greater regulation of money in politics – regardless of the monies' source – as current jurisprudence is unlikely to allow for serious reform via statutes and attempts at a solution via private ordering by either firms or politicians are underinclusive. A robust public policy response that moves well beyond disclosure is needed to address the concerns regarding the political responsibility of managers and corporations to both shareholders and citizens alike.

References

Acemoglu, D., Johnson, S., Kermani, A., Kwak, J. & Mitton, T. (2013). The Value of Political Connections in Turbulent Times: Evidence from the United States. National Bureau of Economic Research, Working Paper 19701.

Akey, P. (2015). Valuing Changes in Political Networks: Evidence from Campaign Contributions to Close Congressional Elections. *Review of Financial Studies*, **28**(11), 3188–223.

Ansolabehere, S., de Figueiredo, J. M. & Snyder, Jr., J. M. (2003). Why Is There So Little Money in U.S. Politics? *Journal of Economic Perspectives*, 17(1), 105–30.

Ansolabehere, S., Snyder, J. M. & Ueda, M. (2004). Did Firms Profit from Soft Money? *Election Law Journal*, 5(2), 193–98.

Arnold, R. D. (1990). *The Logic of Congressional Action*. New Haven, CT: Yale University Press.

Baron, D. P. (2013). *Business and Its Environment*. Boston: Pearson.

Bebchuk, L. & Jackson, R. (2010). Corporate Political Speech: Who Decides? *Harvard Law Review*, 124, 83–117.

Bebchuk, L. & Jackson, R. (2013). Shining Light on Corporate Political Spending. *Georgetown Law Journal*, 101, 923–67.

Brandeis, L. D. (1913). What Publicity Can Do. *Harper's Weekly*, December 20.

Briffault, R. (2010). Campaign Finance Disclosure 2.0. *Election Law Journal*, 9(4), 273–303.

Brown, S. & Warner, J. (1980). Measuring Security Price Performance. *Journal of Financial Economics*, 8(3), 205–58.

Buchanan, J. M. (1987). The Constitution of Economic Policy. *Science*, 236, 1433–36.

Buchanan, J. M. & Tullock, G. (1962). *The Calculus of Consent*. Ann Arbor, MI: University of Michigan Press.

Burbano, V. C. (2021). The Demotivating Effects of Communicating a Social-Political Stance: Field Experimental Evidence from an Online Labor Market Platform. *Management Science*, 67(2), 1004–25.

Burns, N. & Jindra, J. (2014). Political Spending and Shareholder Wealth: The Effect of the U.S. Supreme Court Ruling in Citizens United. *American Politics Research*, 42(4), 579–99.

Coates, IV, J. C. (2012). Corporate Politics, Governance, and Value before and after Citizens United. *Journal of Empirical Legal Studies*, 9(4), 657–96.

Dalley, P. J. (2007). The Use and Misuse of Disclosure as a Regulatory System. *Florida State University Law Review*, 34(4), 1089–131.

Darnell, S. & McDonnell, M-H. (2023). License to Give: The Relationship between Organizational Reputation and Stakeholders' Support for Corporate Political Activity. In T. Lyon, ed., *Corporate Political Responsibility*. Cambridge, UK: Cambridge University Press.

DeBoskey, D.G. & Luo, Y. (2018). Recent Trends in Corporate Political Disclosure for a Sample of S&P 500 Firms: A New and Emerging Corporate Disclosure Area. *International Journal of Disclosure and Governance*, 15(1), 176–84.

Delmas, M. & Lyon, T. (2018). When Corporations Take Credit for Green Deeds Their Lobbying May Tell Another Story. *The Conversation*, July 17.

Den Hartog, C. & Monroe, N. (2008). The Value of Majority Status: The Effect Jeffords's Switch on Asset Prices of Republican and Democratic Firms. *Legislative Studies Quarterly*, 33(1), 63–84.

Eckhouse, B., Chediak, M., Provance, J. & Henry, T. (2021). Angry Shareholders Pile into Lawsuits That Could Cost FirstEnergy Millions of Dollars. *Associated Press*, January 1.

Fama, E. (1970). Efficient Capital Markets: A Review of Theory and Empirical Work. *Journal of Finance*, 25(2), 383–417.

Feldman, N. (2009). In Defense of Secrecy. *New York Times*, February 10.

Ferguson, T. & Voth, H-J. (2008). Betting on Hitler: The Value of Political Connections in Nazi Germany. *Quarterly Journal of Economics*, 123(1), 101–37.

Fisher, J. (2001). The Political Parties, Elections and Referendums Act of 2000. *Representation*, 38(1), 11–19.

Fisman, R. (2001). Estimating the Value of Political Connections. *American Economic Review*, 91(4), 1095–102.

Fowler, A., Garro, H. & Spenkuch, J. L. (2020). Quid Pro Quo? Corporate Returns to Campaign Contributions. *Journal of Politics*, 82(3), 844–58.

Freed, B., Sandstrom, K., & Laufer, W. S. (2023). Targeting Private Sector Influence in Politics: Corporate Accountability as a Risk and Governance Problem. In T. Lyon, ed., *Corporate Political Responsibility*. Cambridge, UK: Cambridge University Press.

Gilbert, M. D. (2013). Campaign Finance Disclosure and the Information Tradeoff. *Iowa Law Review*, 1847–94.

Goh, L., Liu, X. & Tsang, A. (2020). Voluntary Disclosure of Corporate Political Spending. *Journal of Corporate Finance*, 61, Article 101403.

Hadani, M. & Schuler, D. A. (2013). In Search of El Dorado: The Elusive Financial Returns on Corporate Political Investments. *Strategic Management Journal*, 34(2), 165–81.

Hall, R. L. & Deardorff, A. V. (2006). Lobbying as Legislative Subsidy. *American Political Science Review*, 100(1), 69–84.

Hart, O. & Zingales, L. (2017). Companies Should Maximize Shareholder Welfare Not Market Value. *Journal of Law, Finance, and Accounting*, 2(2), 247–74.

Healy, P. M. & Palepu, K. G. (2001). Information Asymmetry, Corporate Disclosure, and the Capital Markets: A Review of the Empirical Disclosure Literature. *Journal of Accounting and Economics*, 31(1–3), 405–40.

Hertel-Fernandez, A. (2014). Who Passes Business's "Model Bills"? Policy Capacity and Corporate Influence in US State Politics. *Perspectives on Politics*, 12(3), 582–602.

Issacharoff, S. & Karlan, P. S. (1999). The Hydraulics of Campaign Finance Reform. *Texas Law Review*, 77, 1705–38.

Jayachandran, S. (2006). The Jeffords Effect. *Journal of Law & Economics*, 49(2), 397–425.

Jiang, L. (2019). Disclosure's Last Stand? The Need to Clarify the "Informational Interest" Advanced by Campaign Finance Disclosure. *Columbia Law Review*, 119, 487–526.

Khurana, R., Fisman, R., Galef, J. & Wang, Y. (2012). Estimating the Value of Connections to Vice-President Cheney. *B.E. Journal of Economic Analysis & Policy*, 13(3), Article 5.

Knight, B. (2007). Are Policy Platforms Capitalized into Equity Prices? Evidence from the Bush/Gore 2000 Presidential Election. *Journal of Public Economics*, 90(4–5), 751–73.

LaPira, T. M., Drutman, L. & Kosar, K. R. (2020). *Congress Overwhelmed: The Decline in Congressional Capacity and Prospects for Reform*. Chicago: University of Chicago Press.

Laufer, W. S. (2003). Social Accountability and Corporate Greenwashing. *Journal of Business Ethics*, 43(3), 253–61.

Lenway, S. A., Schuler, D. A., Marens, R. R., Werner, T., & Green, C. D. 2022. The Evolving Political Marketplace: Revisiting Sixty Years of Theoretical Dominance through a Review of Corporate Political Activity Scholarship in Business & Society and Major Management Journals. Business & Society, 61(5), 1416–70.

Lyon, T. P. & Mandelkorn, W. (2023). The Meaning and Measurement of CPR. In T. Lyon, ed., *Corporate Political Responsibility*. Cambridge, UK: Cambridge University Press.

Massoglia, A. & Evers-Hillstrom, K. (2021). 'Dark Money' Topped $1 Billion in 2020, Largely Boosting Democrats. *OpenSecrets.org*, March 17.

McDonnell, M-H. & Werner, T. (2016). Blacklisted Businesses: Social Activists' Challenges and the Disruption of Corporate Political Activity. *Administrative Science Quarterly*, 61(4), 584–620.

McWilliams, A. & Siegel, D. (1997). Event Studies in Management Research: Theoretical and Empirical Issues. *Academy of Management Journal*, 40(3), 626–57.

Milyo, J. (2014). Corporate Influence and Political Corruption: Lessons from Stock Market Reactions to Political Events. *The Independent Review*, 19(1), 19–36.

Minefee, I., McDonnell, M-H. & Werner, T. (2021). Reexamining Investor Reaction to Covert Corporate Political Activity: A Replication and Extension of Werner (2017). *Strategic Management Journal*, 42(6), 1139–58.

Panagopoulos, C., Green, D. P., Krasno, J., Schwam-Baird, M. & Endres, K. (2020). Partisan Consumerism: Experimental Tests of Consumer Reactions to Corporate Political Activity. *Journal of Politics*, 82(3), 996–1007.

Parkinson, J. (2003). Disclosure and Corporate Social and Environmental Performance: Competitiveness and Enterprise in a Broader Social Frame. *Journal of Corporate Law Studies*, 3(1), 3–39.

Pozen, D. (2018). Transparency's Ideological Drift. *Yale Law Journal*, 128, 100–65.

Prabhat S. & Primo, D. M. (2019). Risky Business: Do Disclosure and Shareholder Approval of Corporate Political Contributions Affect Firm Performance? *Business & Politics*, 21(2), 205–39.

President's Commission on Campaign Costs. (1962). *Financing Presidential Campaigns: Report of the President's Commission on Campaign Costs*. Boston, MA: John F. Kennedy Presidential Library and Museum.

Primo, D. M. & Milyo, J. D. (2020). *Campaign Finance and American Democracy: What the Public Really Thinks and Why It Matters*. Chicago: University of Chicago Press.

Roberts, B. (1990). A Dead Senator Tells No Lies: Seniority and the Distribution of Federal Benefits. *American Journal of Political Science*, 34(1), 31–58.

Sachs, B. (2012). Unions, Corporations, and Political Opt-Out Rights after Citizens United. *Columbia Law Review*, 112, 800–69.

Seligman, J. (2003). *The Transformation of Wall Street: A History of the Securities and Exchange Commission and Modern Corporate Finance*. 3rd ed. New York: Aspen Publishers.

Shanor, A., McDonnell, M-H. & Werner, T. (2022). Corporate Political Power: The Politics of Reputation and Traceability. *Emory Law Journal*, 71, 153–216.

Shaw, K. (2016). Taking Disclosure Seriously. *Yale Law & Policy Review, Inter Alia*, April 3.

Sitaraman, G. (2014). Contracting around Citizens United. *Columbia Law Review*, 114, 755–806.

Skaife, H. A. & Werner T. (2020). Changes in Firms' Political Investment Opportunities, Managerial Accountability, and Reputational Risk. *Journal of Business Ethics*, 163(2), 239–63.

Smyth, J. C. & Seewer, J. (2020). Ohio House Speaker, 4 Others Arrested in $60M Bribery Case. *Associated Press*, July 21.

Strattman T. & Verret J. W. (2015). How Does the Corporate Political Activity Allowed by Citizens United v. Federal Election Commission Affect Shareholder Wealth? *Journal of Law & Economics*, 58(3), 545–59.

Tullock, G. (1972). The Purchase of Politicians. *Western Economic Journal*, 5(3), 224–32.

Walker, E. T. (2023). What Drives Firms to Disclose Their Political Activity? In T. Lyon, ed., *Corporate Political Responsibility*. Cambridge, UK: Cambridge University Press.

Werner, T. (2011). The Sound, the Fury, and the Nonevent: Business Power and Market Reactions to the Citizens United Decision. *American Politics Research*, **39** (1), 118–41.

Werner, T. (2015). Gaining Access by Doing Good: The Effect of Sociopolitical Reputation on Firm Participation in Public Policy Making. *Management Science*, **61**(8), 1989–2011.

Werner, T. (2017). Investor Reaction to Covert Corporate Political Activity. *Strategic Management Journal*, **38**(12), 2424–43.

Werner, T. & Coleman, J. J. (2015). Citizens United, Independent Expenditures, and Agency Costs: Reexamining the Political Economy of State Antitakeover Statutes. *Journal of Law, Economics, & Organization*, **31**(1), 127–59.

Winkler, A. (2004). Other People's Money: Corporations, Agency Costs, and Campaign Finance Law. *Georgetown Law Journal*, **92**, 871–940.

Yablon, R. (2017). Campaign Finance Reform without Law. *Iowa Law Review*, **103**, 185–243.

Accountability: Linking Corporate Social Responsibility, Employee Relations, and Corporate Political Responsibility

6 Responsible Lobbyists?
Corporate Social Responsibility Commitments and the Quality of Corporate Parliamentary Testimony in the UK

ALVISE FAVOTTO, KELLY KOLLMAN,
AND FRASER MCMILLAN

6.1 Introduction

Corporate political responsibility includes how companies lobby government officials in addition to being transparent about this activity. As outlined in previous chapters, calls for transparency are partially premised on the idea that companies need to give an account of how their policy advocacy is compatible with the organization's stated values and commitments, including the commitments embedded in their well-publicized corporate social responsibility (CSR) programs (Lyon & Mandelkorn, 2023; Walker, 2023). Indeed, academics, civil society organizations and even voices within the global investment community increasingly have argued that the future legitimacy of CSR depends on the alignment of companies' environmental and social commitments with their public policy advocacy (GRI, 2016; Lyon et al., 2018). To avoid accusations – and the common perception – that companies' sustainability efforts are largely CSR-washing, companies need to convince key audiences of the consistency of their lobbying and sustainability positions (Pope & Wæraas, 2016).

Although interest in CSR and lobbying alignment has grown over the past decade, surprisingly little empirical work has examined how companies coordinate their CSR and lobbying activities or how joined up such activities are within large and often politically influential corporations. The paucity of empirical work on the topic no doubt stems in part from the difficulty of measuring such alignment. Large corporations traditionally have preferred to engage with public officials behind closed doors. As such it has proven difficult to gather reliable evidence about the specific policy positions companies' advocate and how consistent these positions are with the company's CSR commitments.

While these data availability challenges are widely acknowledged, there are also less-recognized conceptual difficulties involved in defining CSR and lobbying alignment in the first place. Just as there is a range of views about the types of policies states should adopt to address the climate crisis, there are differences of opinion about the compatibility of companies' climate pledges and their positions on the regulation of greenhouse gas emissions. Different social actors have different views about how aligned a company's CSR and public policy activities are (Favotto & Kollman 2021). Although egregious cases of misalignment are easy to spot and have often been highlighted by the media, accepted standards of CSR-lobbying alignment have to be constructed and broadly agreed upon by the key actors affected by such policies.

For this reason, most scholars writing on the topic define responsible lobbying in terms of how companies engage with the policy process as well as the positions they advocate (Anastasiadis et al., 2018; Lock & Seele, 2016). In addition to aligning their substantive policy positions with an accepted notion of the public good, corporate political responsibility also necessitates that companies align their lobbying activity with the deliberative norms promoted by CSR professionals and activists. This includes not just transparency, but also a commitment from corporate lobbyists to engage in genuine dialogue with relevant stakeholders about the role that state regulation should play in reaching common environmental and social goals (Scherer & Palazzo, 2011; Scherer & Voegtlin, 2023). Such deliberative engagement is not a panacea for creating either CSR-lobbying alignment standards or more effective public policy. But adhering to these norms is likely necessary to forge a broader consensus across social actors about the proper role for public policy within the sustainability paradigm. Responsible corporate lobbying thus entails engaging with these deliberative norms as well as adopting policy positions that are consistent with the company's values and CSR commitments.

In this paper we use this conception of responsible lobbying to evaluate how the large corporations that make up London's FTSE 350 index testify before a selection of UK parliamentary committees, including a general business committee and two committees that scrutinize environmental issues. Specifically, we carry out an in-depth content analysis of this corporate committee testimony over two parliamentary sessions, 2010–2015 and 2015–2017, and compare the deliberative quality as well as the policy positions offered by representatives of high- and low-performing CSR companies. This analysis allows us to evaluate if companies with higher CSR credentials better align their testimony with the norms of the sustainability field as well as if they prove more supportive of state interventions into the market. Put more simply, we investigate whether better corporate social responsibility equates with better corporate political responsibility.

The focus on the UK adds an interesting counterpoint to much of the literature, which to date has concentrated on the nature of corporate lobbying in the US Congress and the institutions of the European Union (EU). The UK context offers insight into another pluralist system in which corporate lobbying is prominent but where corporate sustainability has been widely promoted through government policy as well as broadly endorsed by the business community over the past two decades (Kinderman, 2012). As such companies operating in the UK have come under increasing pressure to demonstrate their CSR credentials to key audiences, including government officials. The extent to which these companies have aligned their lobbying activities with sustainability norms and commitments remains largely unexamined.

We find that there are consistent differences in how high and low CSR companies lobby before the committees of the UK parliament. These differences are most evident in the policy positions and policy deliberations of the two sets of companies. High CSR companies are more likely to discuss and support specific policy measures than their low CSR counterparts as well as to offer more fleshed out justifications for their policy positions. Perhaps unsurprisingly, these high CSR companies are also more likely to underpin their policy-related evidence with information and research drawn from their CSR programs. These findings largely hold across all the three committees we analyzed. Differences between high and low CSR companies were not more pronounced in committee testimony that focused on environmental issues despite the prominence of these issues within the sustainability field. Overall, the findings indicate that high CSR companies do align their policy positions and testimony with the commitments and norms of the sustainability field to a greater extent than low CSR firms. While significant, the magnitude of these differences should not be exaggerated, suggesting that even high CSR companies have some way to go to fully incorporate notions of political responsibility into their CSR commitments.

6.2 Conceptualizing CSR and Lobbying Alignment

As outlined in the volume's introductory chapter, corporate political accountability necessitates that companies align their political activity with the organization's stated values, purpose, and stakeholder commitments (Lyon & Mandelkorn, 2023). In this chapter we examine one aspect of such accountability, namely, the extent to which companies' lobbying activities are aligned with their CSR practices and commitments as measured by environment, social and governance (ESG) ESG ratings.

This analysis complements the discussion of corporate values and public policy alignment offered in the volume's other chapters. For example, Ketu and Rothstein (2023) focus on how well companies' advocacy of climate policy aligns with accepted climate science and the goals of the 2015 Paris Agreement. Similarly, Delmas and Friedman (2023) examine how consistent corporate lobbying on climate change is with stakeholders' positions as well as broader public interest on the topic. Doty (2023), writing on the work of the newly formed Corporate Political Responsibility Taskforce at the University of Michigan, focuses more broadly on how companies' political influence aligns with its stated commitments to purpose, values, sustainability, and stakeholders. We seek to add to this discussion of alignment by examining the extent to which companies with strong CSR credentials engage in more responsible forms of lobbying. We thus offer empirical insight into how well companies with a strong reputation for sustainability translate these commitments into public policy advocacy and corporate political responsibility more broadly.

6.2.1 The Emergence of Corporate Sustainability

Corporate social responsibility is a broad umbrella term that can refer to any nonmarket activity that a company undertakes to address a social issue. Since the 1990s, CSR increasingly has become associated with corporate sustainability (Favotto & Kollman, 2020; McWilliams & Siegel, 2001). This framing of CSR draws from the sustainable development paradigm first introduced by the UN in the 1980s and calls on the business community to measure success according to a triple bottom line of economic, environmental and social performance (World Commission on Environment & Development, 1987), at the time a significant departure from traditional, shareholder-centric conceptions of corporate responsibility. The advent of corporate sustainability has introduced more political forms of CSR in which companies increasingly are expected to provide public goods and engage in different forms of self-regulation (Scherer & Palazzo, 2011).

Corporate sustainability gained prominence throughout the 1990s as a way to counter certain aspects of economic globalization. The advent of global production chains and the large transnational corporations that dominate them have become increasingly difficult for states to regulate effectively. As a result, NGOs and intergovernmental organizations have sought to use the sustainability paradigm to target companies directly and to pressure them to improve their environmental, labor, and human rights practices via codes of conduct such as the UN Global Compact and NGO-led multi-stakeholder initiatives (MSI) such as the Fairtrade logo (Vogel, 2010).

By the early 2000s, the corporate sustainability movement had developed into a recognizable organizational field made up of interactive networks of business organizations, NGOs, and a growing number of standard setting organizations such as ISEAL (International Social and Environmental Accreditation and Labelling; Loconto & Fouilleux, 2014). While the substance of corporate sustainability remains contested, these actors have increasingly come to agree on an underpinning set of norms and best practices to structure the field (Bernstein & Van der Ven, 2017; Van der Ven, 2015). The most prominent of these principles include transparency about corporate social and environmental impacts, credible stakeholder dialogue, and collaborative corporate learning through procedures such as target-setting, internal auditing, and reporting (Loconto & Fouilleux, 2014; Mueckenberger & Jastram, 2010). These practices are now embedded in a growing number of MSIs as well as form the basis for investor ESG rating schemes (Albareda & Waddock, 2018).

6.2.2 Corporate Sustainability and Corporate Political Advocacy

The growing prominence of corporate sustainability raises a number of questions about the relationship between CSR and public policy; most importantly the relationship – and degree of alignment – between companies' CSR practices and the content and effects of their political lobbying. Indeed, both scholars and CSR activists have become increasingly critical of the ways that companies combine their prominent sustainability activities and their less visible political lobbying (Vogel, 2010). Numerous, and often well-regarded, corporations have been found to advocate for policies that appear to directly contradict their publicly stated environmental and social goals. For example, BP and Shell, both of which have portrayed themselves as having progressive climate policies, have been repeatedly criticized for maintaining their membership in and financial support of the American Petroleum Institute, a trade association that has consistently lobbied against policies to reduce greenhouse gas emissions (Ketu & Rothstein, 2023; McGreal, 2021). As these high-profile cases illustrate, large companies, even ones with strong sustainability credentials, often do not include public policy advocacy in their CSR programs or seek to make their organization accountable to key stakeholders for the lobbying that they do (Favotto & Kollman, 2021). This is perhaps not surprising as corporate lobbying has traditionally been viewed as purely instrumental in nature. Lobbying public officials is a time-consuming and expensive enterprise. It is widely assumed that profit-seeking companies generally only engage in such activity to enhance their own, often material, goals (Lock & Seele, 2016).

As many scholars have pointed out, however, lobbying by corporations and other actors is a relational activity and not solely determined by the interests of those seeking to engage with state officials (Walker & Rea, 2015). Policymakers generally only give access and listen to organizations they trust and find to be credible policy interlocutors (Binderkrantz et al., 2015; Coen, 2007). Management scholars have often noted that companies' reputation for trustworthiness is an important intangible resource that helps these organizations to facilitate their political activities (Lawton et al., 2013). Increasingly, a company's CSR activities and the alignment of its lobbying and CSR positions have been seen as an important determinant of a company's reputation (Lyon et al., 2018; Werner, 2015).

A growing number of scholars have argued that companies run the risk of doing serious damage to their organizational reputations and even their broader legitimacy if they are perceived to have misaligned sustainability and lobbying positions (Anastasiadis, 2014; Den Hond et al., 2014; Favotto & Kollman 2021). Such reputational damage is perhaps magnified by the suspicion that companies deliberately use their CSR programs and pledges of self-regulation to enhance their anti-regulatory lobbying and to undermine the case for greater state regulation of market actors (Kinderman, 2012; Lyon et al., 2018). Increasingly, NGOs and sustainability campaigners have encouraged companies to engage in more responsible policy advocacy by applying the transparency and accountability practices promoted within the sustainability field to their lobbying activity. The Global Reporting Initiative (GRI), a leading sustainability reporting standard, for example, has included lobbying disclosure in its standard since 2016 (GRI, 2016). Companies are thus coming under significant pressure to broaden the goals of corporate lobbying beyond purely instrumental ones and to better align their CSR and public policy positions.

6.2.3 Operationalizing CSR-Lobbying Alignment: Policy Substance and Dialogue

The question of how companies combine their CSR and lobbying activities has yet to be addressed by systematic research. Indeed, while most observers agree that CSR-lobbying alignment is central to contemporary notions of responsible lobbying, it remains a difficult concept both to define and to measure empirically. Blatant cases of misalignment such as those noted above are easy to identify. But precisely what constitutes aligned corporate sustainability and public policy advocacy is much harder to pinpoint. Several studies have shown that companies often do not coordinate the work of their CSR and government affairs units and as a result these units are often focused on different policy issues (Anastasiadis, 2014; Favotto & Kollman, 2021). But even when companies' lobbying and CSR activities are focused on the same policy areas, what counts as alignment remains a question of interpretation in many instances. As observers have noted, it is not realistic to expect corporations to endorse or lobby for policies that threaten the organization's survival or seriously undermine its ability to make a profit (Lock & Seele, 2016; Lyon et al., 2018). The extension of corporate responsibility beyond the maximization of shareholder value does not mean this imperative has disappeared. What constitutes a reasonable alignment of a company's CSR and lobbying activity is ultimately a social construction and perceptions are likely to differ across social actors.

For this reason, many scholars have argued that an important element of responsible corporate lobbying lies in how companies engage with policymaking processes in addition to the particular positions they advocate (Anastasiadis et al., 2018; Lock & Seele, 2016). Drawing on deliberative democracy theory, political CSR scholars have argued that companies should engage in genuine dialogue with relevant stakeholders when seeking to contribute to the provision of public goods, including when advocating for public policies, to ensure the legitimàcy of such endeavors (Scherer & Palazzo, 2011; Scherer & Voegtlin, 2023). At a minimum this type of deliberative lobbying would entail dissemination of credible information, transparency about companies' interactions with public officials, accountability to relevant stakeholders for the policy positions companies' advocate, and a commitment to resolving policy disputes in a consensual manner (Anastasiadis et al., 2018; Lock & Seele, 2016). Through such open dialogue, companies would be compelled to give an account of how their lobbying and CSR goals are aligned and to adjust their positions where these accounts are unconvincing to relevant community actors through rational argument (Lock & Seele, 2016).

To be sure, many business and politics scholars, including those that argue for more deliberative forms of lobbying, are skeptical that business actors can be persuaded or compelled to change their policy positions through this type of open dialogue. Numerous scholars have argued that business actors possess discursive power in capitalist democracies that allows them to use market and neo-liberal norms to argue against state intervention in the market (Fuchs, 2013; Gill, 1995). Ultimately the extent to which companies become entangled in their pledges for responsible behavior and can be compelled or persuaded to consider greater state regulation to meet commonly agreed environmental and social goals is an empirical question.

The notion of responsible lobbying that has emerged thus includes both a substantive and a procedural element. The former focuses on the policy positions and the credibility of information companies feed into the policy process, while the latter focuses on the deliberative quality of companies' interventions and their engagement in collaborative dialogue with key stakeholders involved in the policy process. Although scholars have made progress conceptualizing the core elements of responsible lobbying, surprisingly little empirical work has examined the extent to which companies apply these principles or how a company's CSR commitments shape the nature of its engagement in the policymaking process. Similarly, there is almost no research on the extent to which a company's CSR commitments lead it to engage in a genuine dialogue with policymakers about state regulation despite the growing focus on deliberation in the CSR and lobbying literatures.

Such empirical questions are crucial to address, particularly in light of recent findings indicating that companies with strong CSR reputations do indeed gain privileged access to policymakers in some democracies (Favotto et al., 2021; Werner, 2015). In his prominent study of CSR reputation and political access, Werner (2015) not only found that companies with stronger CSR reputations are more likely than low CSR companies to be invited to give testimony to US congressional committees, these companies also mention their CSR activities and include CSR-related policy information more often in their testimony. Werner's findings suggest that companies with strong CSR credentials ultimately do offer better quality, policy-relevant information when lobbying policymakers. Building broadly on this work in a recent article, Van den Broek (2021) finds that high-performing CSR companies are more likely than low-performing companies to support regulatory proposals when lobbying the institutions of the European Union (EU). This again implies that companies that invest in their CSR programs, at least to some degree, align their lobbying positions with these commitments. We seek to extend the insights offered by these studies by using the fuller conceptualization of CSR-lobbying alignment implied by the deliberative lobbying approach. In the sections that follow we analyze the testimony that representatives of large corporations gave to committees of the UK (Westminster) parliament and assess the extent to which their CSR commitments align with the nature and the substance of their testimony.

6.3 Data and Methods

To investigate the question of how aligned the CSR practices and lobbying activities of large corporations in the UK are, we examine the testimony that representatives of FTSE 350 companies gave to the select committees of the UK (Westminster) parliament over two sessions from 2010 to 2017. By focusing on the UK, we help to broaden the current research on corporate lobbying, which largely has focused on the US Congress (Baumgartner et al., 2009) or the EU (Eising, 2007). The committees of the UK parliament are an interesting venue in which to examine corporate lobbying. Like the United States (US), and to an extent the EU, the UK has an elite pluralist interest group system in which business and individual companies frequently engage in lobbying and generally are granted privileged access to policymakers (Geddes, 2018; Hall & Soskice, 2001).

The committee system in the UK parliament, however, is somewhat unique. Unlike the committees of the US Congress, the select committees in Westminster are largely oversight committees with only weak formal powers to amend policy. The select committees shadow government departments and oversee the administration, budget, and legislative work of these ministries. Although the party affiliation of committee members is roughly in proportion to the elected House of Commons, the committees operate independently of the government and are often chaired by members of the opposition party (Benton & Russell, 2013). The select committees gather written and oral evidence to conduct their inquiries and to scrutinize the government's work. When an inquiry is complete the committee publishes a report based on this written and oral evidence, which usually contains concrete recommendations for the government department they shadow. The government is not obliged to implement these recommendations, but it does have to offer a response. Research has indicated that, despite their lack of formal legislative powers, select committees in Westminster are able to influence government bills and often influence the nature of policy debates (Benton & Russell, 2013).

The evidence sessions of the select committees are a particularly interesting setting in which to examine the CSR-lobbying alignment of the companies that testify there. For a number of reasons, organizational reputation plays an important role in building relations with the MPs who sit on select committees in the UK. First, the oral evidence sessions of the select committees are closed. The groups that appear before them do so by invitation, presumably based on their perceived ability to provide the committee with relevant information or because the committee wishes to make the organization accountable for its actions (Helboe Pedersen et al., 2015). Many scholars have noted that oversight committees such as the select committees in Westminster have less need of technical expertise than committees that are focused on drafting and amending legislation. At the same time because of their focus on holding the government to account such committees have greater need to engage with groups that have social legitimacy or are likely to attract media and public attention (Binderkrantz et al., 2015; Chaqués-Bonafont, & Muñoz Márquez, 2016). Thus, the reputation – both good and bad – of the groups who are invited to testify before oversight committees are of greater relevance than in legislatures such as the US Congress that are more focused on drafting technical bills and regulation.

Finally, over the past decade the UK government has adopted legislation, both hard and soft, promoting corporate responsibility and transparency (Favotto & Kollman, 2022). For these reasons the company representatives that appear before select committees in the UK will likely be under some pressure to show that their testimony is aligned with their organizations' sustainability commitments. As such, this case offers a theoretically relevant venue in which to analyze the relationship between a company's CSR commitments and how they engage with public officials.

6.3.1 Data Collection: Committee Testimony of FTSE 350 Companies

We chose to analyze the testimony of FTSE 350 companies because the large corporations that make up this index are the most likely to engage with parliamentary committee inquiries and to be invited to give evidence. More importantly, because the FTSE index gathers and publishes firm-level data of the companies on its lists, we are able to track the CSR ratings of these companies over the eight-year period under investigation as well as other basic firm characteristics such as size, sector and company headquarters. This allows us to evaluate how aligned companies' CSR credentials are with their lobbying positions and the quality of their testimony. We gathered data on companies' CSR credentials using "ESG Peer View," a database provided by Thomson Reuters. ESG Peer View provides systematic information about the environmental, social, and governance performance of over 7,000 publicly listed companies worldwide. This database uses a range of sources to assess a firm's CSR performance including data from publicly available financial and sustainability reports as well as surveys and expert opinion.

After collecting this demographic and CSR information, we gathered data on firm appearances at all House of Commons committees using "formal minutes" and saved the minutes of the oral testimony that representatives of the companies in our database gave to three specific select committees during the two parliamentary sessions under investigation: Business, Innovation & Skills (Business); Environmental Audit; Energy & Climate Change. In addition to being publicly available, the nature of the oral committee testimony is useful for examining companies' policy positions on a range of topics covered by the committee enquiries. Further, the oral testimony in which firm representatives answer questions posed by policymakers as one of several witnesses helps us to gauge the deliberative quality of companies' lobbying efforts. The public nature of committee testimony no doubt shapes how and what corporate managers say at these committee hearings. But as we evaluate how transparent and open to dialogue companies are about their public policy advocacy, this publicness represents a good test of their lobbying quality.

We have chosen to focus on these three particular committees because, given their subject remits, these committees frequently invite companies to give evidence. Not surprisingly, the companies in our database appeared before the Business committee more than any other. We added the testimony given to the Environmental Audit and Energy & Climate Change committees to analyze corporate lobbying in front of committees that focus on issues related to companies' core CSR commitments. Given their thematic similarity we aggregated the content analysis results of the Environmental Audit and Energy & Climate Change committees. We present these results under the label 'Climate Change & Environment' committees.

6.3.2 Coding Frame

We created an original coding structure to analyze the quality of testimony that company representatives gave to the select committees. Because there is little published analysis of companies' committee testimony, we developed this coding frame largely inductively as well as by adapting research instruments used to analyze parliamentary speech (Steiner et al., 2005; Werner, 2015). As outlined in the theory section, we conceptualize responsible lobbying and the quality of corporate committee testimony using two broad constructs: deliberative quality and policy substance. We used the following codes to measure deliberative quality: evasive/noncommittal answers; referencing the questioner/hearing participants; justification of policy positions; stakeholders mentioned. These codes allow us roughly to gauge the willingness of corporate representatives to engage in dialogue with both the committee members during their testimony as well as with the broader set of stakeholders involved in a policy area.

To evaluate the policy substance of company testimony we examined both the quality of the policy-relevant evidence company representatives offered policymakers and the policy positions company representatives took on state regulation and the distribution of state resources including subsidies, state investment policies, and taxation. Specifically, we used the following codes for policy substance: stance on current policy/proposals; stance on regulation; stance on distribution of state resources; stance on self-regulation; policy-relevant evidence (CSR-related evidence; non-CSR-related evidence). The code for stance on current policy/proposals is independent of the codes for stance on regulation and state resource distribution as it is often difficult to distinguish between general statements of policy support and references to specific regulatory or distributional measures in company testimony. These policy codes allow us to evaluate the policy positions that individual company representatives reveal during their testimony as well as the quality of the policy evidence they offer the policymakers on the committee. The unit of analysis is the individual hearing statement or put more simply each uninterrupted answer a company representative gives to a committee member's question.[1] Overall, we analyzed 1,812 hearing statements, 853 of which were given in front of Climate Change & Environment committees, while 959 were made during Business committee hearings.

---

[1] The analysis of the parliamentary testimony was conducted by two coders. To establish inter-coder reliability, both coders independently analyzed a common sample of approximately 10 percent of the hearing transcripts chosen at random. Drawing on Hayes and Krippendorf (2007), we used Krippendorf's alpha to estimate the inter-coder reliability of each of our overarching codes (see Appendix 1). The resulting Krippendorf's alpha scores ranged between 0.78 and 0.97. All scores exceeded the 0.67 threshold required for ensuring adequate inter-coder reliability, and the majority was above the 0.80 required to achieve high reliability.

6.3.3 Analysis

To evaluate the alignment of companies' lobbying quality and CSR commitments we divided the companies in our database into high and low CSR performers using the ESG measure described above. We have designated the companies whose ESG score were above the median score for their industry sector as high CSR performers, while those whose score fell below the median are categorized as low CSR performers, thus allowing us to roughly control for the effect of industrial sector in our analysis (Green & Homroy, 2022). Although we do not formally control for company size or home country, the companies in our sample are broadly similar on these measures; that is, most are large organizations with headquarters in the UK. Similarly, the Conservative Party led the government during both sessions of parliament in our analysis and thus does not vary. We descriptively compare high and low CSR companies against our substantive policy and deliberative quality codes to see if higher CSR companies are more likely than the low CSR companies to support government policies, offer policy-relevant evidence, and engage in dialogue with the hearing participants and relevant stakeholders. We test the significance of the differences between the two groups through parametric (t-test) statistics and note the level of significance in the tables by each code.

6.4 Corporate Committee Testimony in the UK Parliament: Toward Alignment of CSR-Lobbying Positions?

In this section we present the analysis of the testimony that representatives of FTSE 350 companies gave to the Business and Climate Change & Environment committees from 2010 to 2017. We first present the aggregated results from both samples before comparing the results of the Business with the Climate Change & Environment committees. The tables report the frequency with which the different codes appear in the individual speeches of our sample companies. Specifically, we report the differences and associated level of statistical significance in the policy substance (Table 6.1) and deliberative quality (Table 6.2) of high and low CSR companies based on these frequencies.

The results suggest that there are discernable differences in how high and low CSR companies testify before these committees. The

Table 6.1 *Policy substance statements per parliamentary committee (% of all statements)*

	All Committees			Business Committee			Climate Change & Environment Committees		
	High CSR firms $n = 755$	Low CSR firms $n = 1,057$	T-Statistics	High CSR firms $n = 341$	Low CSR firms $n = 618$	T-Statistics	High CSR firms $n = 414$	Low CSR firms $n = 439$	T-Statistics
Policy Position									
Government's policy	22.9	14.8	4.338***	25.2	16.0	3.310***	21.0	13.0	3.126**
Regulation	15.9	4.8	7.450***	13.2	3.7	4.767***	18.1	6.4	5.273***
State resource distribution	10.6	8.1	1.755	10.9	7.8	1.609	10.4	8.7	.859
Self-regulation	4.8	3.2	1.638	5.0	4.0	.661	4.6	2.1	2.060*
Policy Evidence									
CSR mentioned	19.2	10.8	4.887***	14.1	7.8	2.905**	23.4	15.0	3.116**
Evidence from CSR sources	13.8	7.1	4.504***	7.6	2.4	3.317***	18.8	13.7	2.045*

Note: Significance of t-statistics is denoted as *, **, *** for statistically significant results at the 0.05, 0.01 and 0.001 levels respectively.

Table 6.2 Deliberative policy statements per parliamentary committee (% of all statements)

	All Committees			Business Committee			Climate Change & Environment Committees		
	High CSR firms $n = 755$	Low CSR firms $n = 1,057$	T-Statistics	High CSR firms $n = 341$	Low CSR firms $n = 618$	T-Statistics	High CSR firms $n = 414$	Low CSR firms $n = 439$	T-Statistics
Stakeholders mentioned									
Civic society	6.2	7.1	-.729	7.6	10.4	-1.444	5.1	2.5	1.955
Customers	15.8	15.1	.363	13.8	18.6	-1.978*	17.4	10.3	3.023**
Community	4.0	4.0	.000	5.0	5.2	-.130	3.1	2.3	.776
Employees	12.6	16.2	-2.171*	20.2	23.6	-1.205	6.3	5.7	.360
General Public	2.8	1.1	2.414*	2.3	0.8	1.714	3.1	1.6	1.477
Market Actors	46.8	44.3	1.044	54.5	53.9	.197	40.3	30.8	2.932**
Policymakers	28.9	21.6	3.512***	27.3	20.2	2.424*	30.2	23.0	2.219*
Unions	0	0.6	-2.455*	0	0	0.0	0	1.4	-2.464*
Style of deliberation									
Evasive statement	2.4	6.3	-4.238***	0.9	5.7	-4.515***	3.6	7.3	-2.372*
Noncommittal statement	5.3	4.5	.730	4.4	4.2	.140	6.0	5.0	.657

Participant mentioned	15.2	15	.111	20.2	17.6	.990	11.1	11.4	-.128
Pushback statement	3.3	6.5	-3.213**	1.2	2.3	-1.306	5.1	12.5	-3.893***
Questioner mentioned	9.3	11.2	-1.302	7.0	11.5	-2.355*	11.1	10.7	.189
Sophisticated statement	15.8	6.8	5.823***	18.2	7.9	4.349***	13.8	5.2	4.260***
Justifications provided									
Effectiveness of policy	27.7	15.4	6.216***	28.7	17.8	3.776***	26.8	12.1	5.502***
Ethical motives	4.0	2.1	2.262*	4.1	2.6	1.212	3.9	1.4	2.273*
Legitimacy motives	5.4	1.5	4.319***	5.3	1.6	2.784**	5.6	1.4	3.334***
Market or business interest	21.6	14.3	3.958***	28.2	17.0	3.890***	16.2	10.5	2.449*
Public good	1.5	1.0	.776	1.5	0.5	1.383	1.4	1.8	-.428

Note: Significance of t-statistics is denoted as *, **, *** for statistically significant results at the 0.05, 0.01 and 0.001 levels respectively.

most consistent and significant differences can be found in the depth and quality of how high CSR companies discuss policy in their testimony. In general, high CSR companies are more likely to take explicit policy stances and to support specific state regulatory policies than their low CSR counterparts. Differences in the deliberative quality of the testimony between the two sets of companies are more subtle, although in general high CSR firms do engage in more open dialogue than low CSR companies. Somewhat surprisingly, these results do not vary greatly across the two types of committees we analyze, business and environment and climate change. The differences between high and low CSR companies are broadly similar in the more generalist business committee as in the committees that are focused on climate change and environmental issues.

6.4.1 Company Committee Testimony: Aggregate Results

When appearing before select committees, representatives of FTSE 350 companies frequently expressed their positions on current policy and offered the committee members relevant policy evidence in their testimony. Indeed, about one in five of all the statements uttered by company representatives in their testimony pertain to general comments about current policy or a government proposal (see Table 6.1). But the companies only rarely took a position regarding specific proposals related to either regulation or state resource distribution, which appear in approximately 9 percent of the statements respectively.

There are clear differences in how high and low CSR companies discuss these policy issues. Overall, 23 percent of statements uttered by high CSR companies are concerned with general policy issues versus only 15 percent of statements of low CSR companies (see Table 6.1). Similar patterns can be observed regarding the positions that high and low CSR companies offer on specific regulatory and resource distribution policies. Here high performers offer positions on these specific policy measures in 26 percent of their statements given to the committees, while only 13 percent of low performers do so. Perhaps more importantly, a closer look at companies' stances reveals that companies with better CSR credentials are more likely to be supportive of government's policies, both generally and when commenting on specific regulatory or resource distribution measures. Most of the differences between high and low CSR companies are driven by their stances on regulation where high CSR companies are both more likely to offer specific testimony on regulatory measures and more likely to support such interventions into the market.

Interestingly, very few firms regardless of their CSR commitments highlight the role that self-regulation should play in addressing the policy issues discussed before the select committees. Given the focus in the literature on the rise of voluntary regulatory approaches as well as the posited links between such voluntary approaches and state deregulation, it is somewhat surprising that self-regulation is mentioned in just 4 percent of the managers' speeches. This compares with references to state policy in about 20 percent of their contributions. This may reflect the fact that the MPs leading the questioning are more focused on public policy than self-regulatory approaches. But the evidence suggests that companies do not frequently try to persuade these officials of the merits of self-regulation in this testimony. There is also no clear linkage between CSR commitments and mentions of self-regulation. Although high CSR companies do mention self-regulation somewhat more frequently than low CSR companies, this difference is not significant. It is also noteworthy that mentions of self-regulation by the high performers go hand in hand with more frequent mentions of state regulation by these high performers. Thus to the extent that it is mentioned self-regulation appears to be seen as a complement to state regulation by high CSR firms rather than a substitute for it as posited by some CSR-washing accounts.

Both high and low CSR companies that appear before the select committees frequently offer policy-relevant evidence to the committee members. High CSR companies, however, are significantly more likely to cite evidence that is derived from their CSR programs than low CSR companies. In general these high performers both mention their CSR activities and offer evidence related to their CSR programs more frequently than low-performing companies (see Table 6.1). While we cannot say that this CSR-related evidence is necessarily of higher quality than the other policy evidence offered during the committee hearings, it does appear that the CSR activities of high performers shape the nature of the information they offer to committee members in ways that does not appear to be the case for the lower performers.

The differences between high and low CSR companies are more muted when looking at the deliberative quality of testimony offered to the committees in our sample (see Table 6.2). Here we look at a variety of factors, including how company representatives engage with the committee members leading the questioning, how frequently they pick up on the testimony of other participants in the hearing, how often they mention relevant stakeholder groups as well as how and how well they justify their policy positions. In general, the representatives of high CSR companies do not engage with committee members or hearing participants in significantly different ways than representatives of low CSR companies. Similarly, no clear pattern emerges in terms of the number or types of stakeholder groups that the two sets of firms refer to in their testimony.

High CSR companies, however, do offer both more sophisticated and more varied justifications for their stated policy positions than low CSR companies. Representatives of both high and low CSR companies tend to primarily justify their policy positions in terms of market interests or the effectiveness of the measure in question. Very few companies from either group cited ethical commitments, the public good, or their organization's legitimacy when justifying their policy positions. In this way all company representatives tend to rationalize their policy positions in terms of the costs and benefits of the measure rather than in ethical terms or in relation to the public good. However, high CSR companies were significantly more likely to cite the effectiveness of the policy in their justifications than low CSR companies, suggesting that they take a broader view of the policy consequences at stake or at least are more committed to offering committee members a clearer justification of their positions than the low CSR companies. High CSR firms also appear to be somewhat more aware of the legitimacy concerns policy measures may entail for their organization. Low CSR firms tended either to fail to offer clear reasons for their positions or to narrowly justify their policy stances in terms of economic interests.

Overall the differences in the substantive and deliberative quality of the testimony offered by high and low CSR companies are sometimes subtle. But they are consistent across a large number of company representatives and a broad array of policy issues, suggesting that the policy positions and interventions of these high performers are, to a degree, more closely aligned with the commitments and deliberative norms of the corporate sustainability field.

6.4.2 Company Committee Testimony: Business and Environmental Committees Compared

In this section we break down the results presented above and compare the testimony companies gave to the committees that make up the full sample: the business committee and the climate change & environmental audit committees. We use this analysis to compare company testimony given to the generalist Business committee with testimony given to committees that focus on an issue that has been at the heart of corporate sustainability for more than two decades. Given that high CSR companies presumably have deeper and more fleshed out commitments on these environmental issues than low CSR companies, we might expect the differences in the quality of their testimony to the environmental committees to be more pronounced. In fact, as we outline below, the quality of the two groups' testimony varies very little across these committees.

As with the full sample, the most pronounced differences in the testimony of high and low CSR companies in both committee samples lie in the substantive policy positions and justifications offered by the two groups. In the business committee high CSR companies remained more likely than low performers to discuss policy and to support specific regulatory measures (see Table 6.1). High performers discussed government policy and proposals in 25 percent of their utterances before this committee, while low performers mentioned government policy in only 16 percent of their contributions. Similarly, high performers were significantly more likely to discuss and support specific regulatory measures in their testimony, while differences in their support for state resource distribution policies are not statistically significant.

The results in the climate change & environment committees are similar. Here 21 percent of high CSR companies discuss general government policy goals in their testimony, while only 13 percent of their low CSR counterparts do so. High CSR companies remain more likely to discuss and support specific regulatory measures than low CSR companies (18 and 6 percent respectively). The magnitude of this latter difference is very similar to that seen in the business committee. Unlike in the business committee, however, the propensity of high performers to support state regulation in the climate change & environmental committees is complemented by somewhat more frequent mentions of self-regulation by these high performers. The differences between high and low CSR companies in this respect, however, are not large. Again, there is no discernible difference in the positions that high and low performers take on specific state resource distribution policy measures in the climate change & environment committees. Thus while high CSR companies appear more willing than their low CSR counterparts to discuss and support specific regulatory measures in both committees, the differences between high and low performers are not more pronounced in the environmental committees despite the focus on a core sustainability issue. Indeed, high CSR companies were more likely to discuss general policy goals before the business committee than before the environmental committees.

In terms of the policy-relevant evidence offered by companies in their testimony, the differences between high and low CSR companies are not particularly stark in either committee sample. As in the overall sample, high CSR companies are more likely than their low CSR counterparts to mention and to explicitly draw on their CSR activity when offering the committee policy evidence in both types of committees. These differences between the two sets of companies are slightly greater in the testimony given to the climate change & environmental audit committees as we might expect given the prominence of the issue within corporate sustainability activities.

The differences in the deliberative quality of the testimony offered by high and low CSR companies are also similar across the two committee samples. High CSR companies are more likely than low CSR companies to offer both types of committees more sophisticated justifications of their policy positions and to use a wider range of justifications that go beyond narrow market or economic interests. There are some interesting differences between the testimonies offered to the two types of committees, however. High CSR companies are more likely to cite policy effectiveness as a reason for their policy positions in the environmental committees than in the business committee. In addition, these firms appear more likely to mention legitimacy concerns in their testimony when justifying their policy positions.

Interestingly, in the environmental committees, low CSR companies are significantly more likely than high CSR companies to give evasive answers or to push back against MPs' categorizations of their positions rather than engage with the substance of their questions. This may reflect the extent to which companies are being pushed on their climate change and environmental records as well as the willingness of high CSR companies to engage with policymakers about their records in this policy area. In our other measures of deliberative quality, particularly company representatives' engagement with relevant stakeholders, there is little difference in the testimony of high and low CSR companies in either committee sample.

Overall, our analysis of companies' testimony suggests that high CSR companies are more aligned with the commitments and norms promoted by the corporate sustainability field than low CSR performers. Across all venues, these companies appear more willing to discuss and support specific policy and regulatory measures and are more likely to offer evidence drawing from their CSR experiences, suggesting a higher embedding of their CSR commitments in their strategic deliberations. Further high CSR firms are more prepared to be accountable for and justify their positions to policymakers than their low CSR counterparts.

6.5 Discussion and Conclusions

Do companies with stronger CSR credentials lobby in different ways from companies that have not made such commitments? Does stronger CSR translate into greater corporate political responsibility? In this chapter we have sought to address these questions by examining the testimony that large corporations gave to the select committees of the UK parliament and by evaluating the extent to which high CSR companies align their lobbying efforts with the broad norms and commitments of corporate sustainability. We find that there are consistent differences in the lobbying quality of high and low CSR companies. High CSR companies were more willing to discuss state interventions into the market in their testimony, more likely to support state regulation and more likely to offer committee members sophisticated justifications for their policy stances than low CSR companies. These high performers also tended to use a broader array of reasons for their policy stances and did not focus solely on market interests as low CSR companies tend to do. Thus, particularly in terms of their substantive policy positions and their willingness to engage in dialogue about policy, high CSR companies' lobbying efforts do appear to be more aligned with the commitments of the sustainability field than their peers with less developed CSR credentials.

Neither these differences between high and low CSR companies nor the alignment of the former with the norms of the corporate sustainability field should be exaggerated, however. In many respects the differences in the testimony of the two sets of companies are often quite subtle. For example, the deliberative quality of high CSR companies' testimony does not differ significantly from low CSR companies in many key areas despite the strong emphasis put on such dialogue in the sustainability paradigm and the responsible lobbying literature. Both sets of companies reference key stakeholders and engage with other participants at the hearing in a similar manner. Indeed, as the broader literature on lobbying suggests, companies and other interest groups likely need to have these deliberative skills to gain the trust of and access to policymakers in these parliamentary settings (Coen, 1997; Binderkrantz et al., 2015). Similarly, although high CSR companies are significantly more likely than low performers to discuss and support state regulatory interventions in the market, their support for such interventions is not overwhelming. Even in front of environmental policy committees, less than one in five statements by high CSR companies relates to specific regulatory measures. Statements of support for these measures are even less frequent. It is also interesting to note that we did not find significant differences in how high and low CSR companies discuss or support policies that relate to the distribution state resources such as taxation, state subsidies, or state investment in public goods.

If our findings suggest that the corporate political responsibility of high CSR companies is only moderately more developed than that of low CSR performers, these results also suggest that companies are not engaging in the more egregious forms of CSR-washing or strategic misalignment of their CSR and lobbying activity as suggested by some CSR critics (Montgomery et al., 2023; Den Hond et al., 2014). High levels of CSR are not associated with greater levels of de-regulatory lobbying; indeed, the opposite appears to be the case. More tellingly neither high nor low CSR companies appear to emphasize self-regulation in their testimony, although they do occasionally refer to it in their contributions. The fact that high CSR companies discussed both voluntary and state regulation in their testimony with greater frequency than low CSR companies suggests these organizations see these two forms of regulation as complements rather than substitutes. In general references to self-regulation are far less frequent than references to state regulation across both sets of companies and across all the committees we analyzed.

Overall, our findings about the relationship between companies' CSR and lobbying activity in the UK appear broadly to echo the findings of recent research conducted in the EU and the United States. Both Werner (2015), examining business lobbying in the US Congress, and Van den Broek (2021), who examines corporate lobbying within EU institutions, find that companies with higher CSR credentials lobby in subtly different ways than companies with less developed CSR commitments. In Werner's study high CSR companies were found to be more likely to draw on their CSR activity to underpin the policy evidence they supplied to policymakers during committee hearings. In Van den Broek's study, high CSR companies are shown to be more likely to support EU policy proposals than their low CSR counterparts.

Research from all three venues thus indicates that companies with stronger CSR commitments do better align their policy advocacy with the commitments and norms of the sustainability field than organizations with less developed CSR programs. However, these differences are often modest, suggesting that few companies have gone a long way toward incorporating corporate political responsibility into their understandings of CSR. The openings that we do see in our study and the others cited above may indicate that companies are coming under greater pressure to show the consistency of their CSR pledges and policy advocacy. It may also suggest a greater willingness by high CSR performers to engage in genuine dialogue about the role for state regulation in addressing the environmental and social ills that result from market activity. While these outcomes are broadly welcome, more research is needed to examine the extent to which such dialogue shapes policy outcomes and leads to higher welfare outcomes.

Appendix 1

Coding Frame Outline: Corporate Committee Testimony

All codes are scored 00 = not present or 01 = present unless stated otherwise.

1. **Parliament / Session / Committee name/ Party of chair**

2. **Main policy topic area (CAP-UK categories)**
   - 1 = Macroeconomics
   - 2 = Civil Rights, Minority Issues, Immigration and Civil Liberties
   - 3 = Health
   - 4 = Agriculture
   - 5 = Labor and Employment
   - 6 = Education
   - 7 = Environment
   - 8 = Energy
   - 9 = Transportation
   - 10 = Law, Crime, and Family Issues
   - 11 = Social Welfare
   - 12 = Community Development, Planning and Housing Issues
   - 13 = Banking, Finance, and Domestic Commerce
   - 14 = Defense
   - 15 = Space, Science, Technology and Communications
   - 16 = Foreign Trade
   - 17 = International Affairs and Foreign Aid
   - 18 = Government Operations
   - 19 = Public Lands and Water Management (Territorial Issues)
3. **Mention CSR program, activities, policies**
4. **Reveal clear policy positions as follows:**
Code 4.1 and 4.2 as follows:
   - 00 = No stance
   - 01 = Praise or support
   - 02 = Mixed
   - 03 = Criticize or oppose
      4.1. Stance on the current policy
      4.2. Substantive policy position
         4.2.1. Stance on regulation
         4.2.2. Stance on resource distribution (e.g., taxation or state resource provision)
      4.3. Stance on self-regulation as follows:
   - 00 = No mention
   - 01 = General support or unclear purpose
   - 02 = Support as complement to state regulation
   - 03 = Support as a substitute for state regulation
      4.4. Policy code uncertain (must only be used with other policy codes)

5. Offer relevant policy evidence as follows:

  5.1. Relevant evidence derived from CSR program experience or research

  5.2. Relevant evidence based on non-CSR sources (e.g., firm experience, firm research, industry experience or research)

  5.3. Relevant written evidence

6. Mention stakeholder in testimony as follows:

Code all stakeholders as follows:

  - 00 = Not mentioned
  - 01 = Mentioned and valued
  - 02 = Mentioned neutrally
  - 03 = Mentioned and degraded
  - 04 = Mentioned with mixed views (incl. multiple actors in same category)

  6.1. Customers

  6.2. Community

  6.3. General public

  6.4. Market actors (e.g., industry, investors, suppliers, business partners)

  6.5. Policymakers / government officials

  6.6. Civil society organizations / NGOs / Activists

  6.7. Labor unions

  6.8. Employees

  6.9. Other (specify)

7. Deliberative Quality of Testimony

  7.1. Evasive/noncommittal

    7.1.1. Evasive

    7.1.2. Noncommittal

  7.2. Reference to meeting participant / participant's testimony

    7.2.1. Reference to meeting participant / participant's testimony

    7.2.2. Reference to questioner

  7.3. Pushback

  7.4. Sophisticated justification for policy positions

  7.5. Content of justification for policy positions

    7.5.1. None / unclear

    7.5.2. Firm / industry / economic interests

    7.5.3. Public good / costs to the public

    7.5.4. Effectiveness of measure

7.5.5. Ethical commitment to issue
7.5.6. Stakeholder pressure / social legitimacy
7.5.7. Other (specify)

References

Albareda, L. & Waddock, S. (2018). Networked CSR Governance: A Whole Network Approach to Meta-governance. *Business & Society*, 57(4), 636–75.

Anastasiadis, S. (2014). Toward a View of Citizenship and Lobbying: Corporate Engagement in the Political Process. *Business & Society*, 53(2), 260–99.

Anastasiadis, S., Moon, J. & Humphreys, M. (2018). Lobbying and the Responsible Firm: Agenda-Setting for a Freshly Conceptualized Field. *Business Ethics: A European Review*, 27(3), 207–21.

Baumgartner, F. R., Berry, J. M., Hojnacki, M., Leech, B. L. & Kimball, D. C. (2009). *Lobbying and Policy Change: Who Wins, Who Loses, and Why*. Chicago: University of Chicago Press.

Benton, M. & Russell, M. (2013). Assessing the Impact of Parliamentary Oversight Committees: The Select Committees in the British House of Commons. *Parliamentary Affairs*, 66(4), 772–97.

Bernstein, S. & Van der Ven, H. (2017). Best Practices in Global Governance. *Review of International Studies*, 43(3), 534–56.

Binderkrantz, A., Christiansen, P. & Pedersen, H. (2015). Interest Group Access to the Bureaucracy, Parliament, and the Media. *Governance*, 28(1), 95–112.

Chaqués-Bonafont, L. & Muñoz Márquez, L. (2016). Explaining Interest Group Access to Parliamentary Committees. *West European Politics*, 39(6), 1276–98.

Coen, D. (2007). Empirical and Theoretical Studies in EU Lobbying. *Journal of European Public Policy*, 14(3), 333–45.

Delmas, M. & Friedman, H. (2023). Disclosure of Political Responsibility with Regard to Climate Change. In T. Lyon, ed., *Corporate Political Responsibility*. Cambridge: Cambridge University Press.

Den Hond, F., Rehbein, K., de Bakker, F. & Lankveld, H. (2014). Playing on Two Chessboards: Reputation Effects between Corporate Social Responsibility (CSR) and Corporate Political Activity (CPA). *Journal of Management Studies*, 51(5), 790–813.

Doty, E. (2023). Practitioner Views of CPR: Towards a New Social Contract. In T. Lyon, ed., *Corporate Political Responsibility*. Cambridge: Cambridge University Press.

Eising, R. (2007). The Access of Business Interests to EU Institutions: Towards Elite Pluralism? *Journal of European Public Policy*, **14**(3), 384–403.

Favotto, A. & Kollman, K. (2020). An Expanding Conception of Social Responsibility? Of Global Norms and Changing Corporate Perceptions. In H. Hansen-Magnusson & A. Vetterlein, eds., *The Rise of Responsibility in World Politics*. Cambridge: Cambridge University Press, pp. 188–212.

Favotto, A. & Kollman, K. (2021). Mixing Business with Politics: Does Corporate Social Responsibility End Where Lobbying Transparency Begins? *Regulation & Governance*, **15**(2), 262–79.

Favotto, A. & Kollman, K. (2022). When Rights Enter the CSR Field: British Firms' Engagement with Human Rights and the UN Guiding Principles. *Human Rights Review*, **23**(1), 21–40.

Favotto, A., Kollman, K. & McMillan, F. (2021). Is Virtue Its Own Reward? Corporate Social Responsibility and Access to British Policymakers. *Paper presented at the biennial ECPR Regulation & Governance conference held (virtually)*, 23–25.

Fuchs, D. (2013). Theorizing the Power of Global Companies. In J. Mikler, ed., *The Handbook of Global Companies*. Oxford: Wiley & Sons Ltd., 77–95.

Geddes, M. (2018). Committee Hearings of the UK Parliament: Who Gives Evidence and Does This Matter? *Parliamentary Affairs*, **41**(2018), 283–304.

Gill, S. (1995). Globalisation, Market Civilisation, and Disciplinary Neoliberalism. *Millennium*, **24**(3), 399–423.

Global Reporting Initiative (2016). *GRI G4 – GRI Sustainability Reporting Guidelines: Reporting Principles and Standard Disclosures*. Amsterdam: GRI.

Green, C. P. & Homroy, S. (2022). Incorporated in Westminster: Channels and Returns to Political Connection in the United Kingdom. *Economica*, **89**(354), 377–408.

Hall, P. & Soskice, D. (2001). *Varieties of Capitalism: The Institutional Foundations of Comparative Advantage*. Oxford: Oxford University Press.

Hayes, A. F. & Krippendorff, K. (2007). Answering the Call for a Standard Reliability Measure for Coding Data. *Communication Methods and Measures*, **1**(1), 77–89.

Helboe Pedersen, H., Halpin, D. & Rasmussen, A. (2015). Who Gives Evidence to Parliamentary Committees? A Comparative Investigation of Parliamentary Committees and Their Constituencies. *The Journal of Legislative Studies*, **21**(3), 408–27.

Ketu, Y. & Rothstein, S. (2023). Practicing Responsible Policy Engagement: How Large U.S. Companies Lobby on Climate Change. In T. Lyon, ed., *Corporate Political Responsibility*. Cambridge: Cambridge University Press.

Kinderman, D. (2012). 'Free Us Up So We Can Be Responsible!' The Co-evolution of Corporate Social Responsibility and Neo-liberalism in the UK, 1977–2010. *Socio-Economic Review*, 10(1), 29–57.

Lawton, T., McGuire, S. & Rajwani, T. (2013). Corporate Political Activity: A Literature Review and Research Agenda. *International Journal of Management Reviews*, 15(1), 86–105.

Lock, I. & Seele, P. (2016). Deliberative Lobbying? Toward a Noncontradiction of Corporate Political Activities and Corporate Social Responsibility? *Journal of Management Inquiry*, 25(4), 415–30.

Loconto, A. & Fouilleux, E. (2014). Politics of Private Regulation: ISEAL and the Shaping of Transnational Sustainability Governance. *Regulation & Governance*, 8(2), 166–85.

Lyon, T., Delmas, M., Maxwell, J., et al. (2018). CSR Needs CPR: Corporate Sustainability and Politics. *California Management Review*, 60(4), 5–24.

Lyon, T. & Mandelkorn, W. (2023). The Meaning of Corporate Political Responsibility. In T. Lyon, ed., *Corporate Political Responsibility*. Cambridge: Cambridge University Press.

McGreal, C. (2021). How a Powerful US Lobby Group Helps Big Oil to Block Climate Action. *Guardian*, 19 July.

McWilliams, A. & Siegel, D. (2001). Corporate Social Responsibility: A Theory of the Firm Perspective. *Academy of Management Review*, 26(1), 117–27.

Montgomery, A., Lyon, T. & Barg, J. (2023). No End in Sight? A Greenwash Review and Research Agenda. *Organization & Environment*, (early view).

Mueckenberger, U. & Jastram, S. (2010). Transnational Norm-Building Networks and the Legitimacy of Corporate Social Responsibility Standards. *Journal of Business Ethics*, 97(2), 223–39.

Pope, S. & Wæraas, A. (2016). CSR-washing Is Rare: A Conceptual Framework, Literature Review, and Critique. *Journal of Business Ethics*, 137(1), 173–93.

Scherer, A. G. & Palazzo, G. (2011). The New Political Role of Business in a Globalized World: A Review of a New Perspective on CSR and Its Implications for the Firm, Governance, and Democracy. *Journal of Management Studies*, 48(4), 899–931.

Scherer, A. G. & Voegtlin, C. (2023). Multinational Companies as Responsible Political Actors in Global Business: Challenges and Implications for Human Resource Management. In T. Lyon, ed., *Corporate Political Responsibility*. Cambridge: Cambridge University Press.

Steiner, J., Bächtiger, A., Spörndli, M. & Steenbergen, M. (2005). *Deliberative Politics in Action. Analysing Parliamentary Discourse*. Cambridge: Cambridge University Press.

Van den Broek, O. (2021). Soft Law Engagements and Hard Law Preferences: Comparing EU Lobbying Positions between UN Global Compact Signatory Companies and Other Interest Group Types. *Business and Politics*, **23**(3), 383–405.

Van der Ven, H. (2015). Correlates of Rigorous and Credible Transnational Governance: A Cross-Sectoral Analysis of Best Practice Compliance in Eco-labeling. *Regulation & Governance*, **9**(3), 276–93.

Vogel, D. (2010). The Private Regulation of Global Corporate Conduct: Achievements and Limitations. *Business & Society*, **49**(1), 68–87.

Walker, E. (2023). What Drives Firms to Disclose Their Political Activity? In T. Lyon, ed., *Corporate Political Responsibility*. Cambridge: Cambridge University Press.

Walker, E. & Rea, C. (2015). The Political Mobilization of Firms and Industries. *Annual Review of Sociology*, **40**, 281–304.

Werner, T. (2015). Gaining Access by Doing Good: The Effect of Sociopolitical Reputation on Firm Participation in Public Policy Making. *Management Science*, **61**(8), 1989–2011.

World Commission on Environment. (1987). *Our Common Future*. Oxford: Oxford University Press.

7 | License to Give
The Relationship between Organizational Reputation and Stakeholders' Support for Corporate Political Activity

SAMANTHA DARNELL AND MARY-HUNTER
MCDONNELL

7.1 Introduction

While there has been a long history of research interest in nonmarket strategy, defined as "a firm's concerted pattern of actions to improve its performance by managing the institutional or societal context of economic competition" (Mellahi, Frynas, Sun, & Siegel, 2016: 144), a growing body of work has sought to bridge disparate streams of nonmarket strategy research. Several recent review articles have proposed ways in which to integrate research focused on different elements of a firm's overall nonmarket strategy, like corporate social responsibility (CSR) and corporate political activity (CPA), to better elucidate the links and relationships between these sub-strategies (e.g., Dorobantu, Kaul, & Zelner, 2017; Mellahi et al., 2016). In addition, nonmarket strategy researchers have made promising contributions to our understanding of the complementary nature of firms' nonmarket strategies. For example, a more favorable reputation for social responsibility grants a firm increased access to politicians (Werner, 2015), results in firms being perceived by politicians as a lower reputational threat (McDonnell & Werner, 2016), and benefits firms financially by helping them win more lucrative government procurement contracts (Flammer, 2018).

Although many assume firms use their corporate political activity (CPA), or "attempts to manage political institutions and/or influence political actors in ways favorable to the firm" (Lux, Crook, & Woehr, 2011; Mellahi et al., 2016: 144), to achieve private gains, these recent advancements in nonmarket strategy research suggests that firms' actions which burnish their social reputations may help firms overcome this negative societal perception about CPA. In this way, a firm's nonmarket performance among informal institutions signaling the firm's adherence to generally agreed-upon standards of socially accepted behavior (Eesley, Eberhart, Skousen, & Cheng, 2018; Scott, 1995) may reduce stakeholders' hesitancy to embrace the firm as a political actor, strengthening stakeholders' willingness to enable the firm's nonmarket strategy targeting formal regulatory institutions. Because corporations are perceived as pursuing a self-interested, profit-seeking agenda rather than engaging on behalf of society at large (Yue, 2015), many firms choose to bypass the reputational hurdles to openly engaging in CPA by employing "darker" forms of political activity (Freed, Sandstrom, & Laufer, 2023; Lyon & Maxwell, 2004; Walker, 2012; Werner, 2017), since they may lack their stakeholders' support for their political activities and aim to avoid potential backlash. While the collective reputation of the corporate class as profit-seeking constrains the type, and possibly the extent, of a firm's formal nonmarket strategy, a firm's informal nonmarket strategy helps signal to stakeholders that the firm's private goals are more aligned with the public's goals for societal improvement.

While prior work in this area has focused on the effects of firms' informal nonmarket strategy on formal nonmarket performance, an overlooked stakeholder group with significant power to constrain or expand a firm's formal nonmarket strategy is employees. Employees are a central stakeholder in discussions of corporate social responsibility as well as corporate political activity, but have received relatively little research attention (Scherer & Voegtlin, 2023). Seen as a powerful constituency to complement other forms of political activity, firms frequently encourage employees to politically mobilize by contacting representatives or registering to vote in an effort to bolster the firm's impact in the nonmarket arena and increase support for the candidates and policies endorsed by the firm (Hertel-Fernandez, 2018). This type of employee political mobilization can, thus, complement a firm's other formal nonmarket activities. Underexplored in prior research is employees' direct control of a firm's capacity to participate in a specific type of CPA: corporate political action committees (PACs). By increasing or withholding contributions to the corporate PAC, employees expand or contract the firm's ability to influence the policymaking process through direct contributions to political candidates and causes. In light of employees' significant influence over the funds available to disburse, we need a fuller understanding of what drives employees to contribute to their firm's affiliated PAC. This brings us to our motivating research question, "How does a firm's social reputation impact its stakeholders' support of its corporate political activity?"

We propose that firms' overall social reputations as well as their domain-specific reputations for employee relations contribute to employees' perceptions of their employers as trustworthy and lead to more enthusiastic support for their firm's CPA. Superior reputations reduce the uncertainty among stakeholders regarding whether the firm will pursue formal nonmarket strategies in the stakeholders' best interests. In addition, employees may see supporting their firm's CPA as an opportunity to expand their prosocial impact if they believe their firm will act in a socially responsible manner when engaging the nonmarket arena.

Using a unique, hand-collected panel dataset of firms' social reputations and employee contributions to their employers' affiliated corporate PACs from 2007 to 2020, we find evidence that firms' reputations for employee relations is positively associated with employee contributions to their PAC. Contrary to our expectation, firms' overall social reputations are not clearly associated with employee contributions. In addition, we find that the effect of a firm's reputation for employee relations has a stronger association with employee's support than the other elements of a firm's reputation for social responsibility.

We contribute to nonmarket strategy research by examining the relationship between different aspects of firms' informal nonmarket strategies and stakeholders' support for formal nonmarket strategy. We build on recent work studying the effect of organizational reputation on nonmarket access (McDonnell & Werner, 2016; Werner, 2015) and explore whether social reputation indirectly expands a firm's capacity for nonmarket strategy by enhancing stakeholder support. Importantly, we direct focus on employees and demonstrate their collective power to expand or limit their organizations' access to formal regulatory institutions. This chapter also contributes to work on the interplay between CSR and CPA and provides evidence of one way in which these two aspects of nonmarket strategy are complementary (Favotto, Kollman, & McMillan, 2023; Mellahi et al., 2016). An improvement in a firm's reputation for social responsibility complements a firm's political activities by motivating stakeholders to directly enable the firm's formal nonmarket strategy.

7.2 Background

Management research on the antecedents and outcomes of corporate political activity has unpacked the strategies and effectiveness of firms' efforts to access political actors and influence policy (Hillman et al., 2004; Lux et al., 2011). One area of CPA that has received significant scholarly attention and increasing public scrutiny are corporate political action committees (PACs). Corporate PACs are a common element of many firms' CPA, including 75 percent of the S&P 500, and are the primary conduit of firms' financial strategies. This form of CPA stands in contrast to the other major categories of CPA strategies as organized by Hillman and Hitt (1999): informational and constituency. Informational strategies are manifested through lobbying government officials and constituency strategies often involve grassroots organizing or astroturfing (Lyon & Maxwell, 2004; Walker, 2012) to promote a firm's political agenda. While all three strategies may be used in conjunction to constitute a firm's overall political strategy, corporate PACs are subject to strict spending limits and transparency requirements while informational and constituency strategies have no expenditure limits and weak transparency rules. For example, a firm may create a corporate PAC and fund its administrative costs through its treasury funds, but a PAC's direct contributions to political committees can only be funded through contributions from a restricted set of individuals associated with the firm, including executives, managers, shareholders, salaried employees, and their families (FEC, 2018). In addition, the amount of money that can flow through corporate PACs is limited by campaign finance regulations that limit PAC disbursements (a PAC may donate up to $5,000 per candidate and $10,000 per party committee per election cycle) and the willingness of corporate insiders to voluntarily contribute funds (Li, 2018). Lobbying and constituency building activities can be funded directly from the firm's treasury and face no expenditure limits. Finally, donations to federal political candidates and party committees made from corporate PACs must be regularly disclosed to the FEC which provides greater traceability of PAC activities than expenditures for other forms of CPA.

Some scholars have debated the relative importance of corporate PACs compared to other forms of CPA arguing that the effects of campaign contributions on financial performance are unclear (Hadani & Schuler, 2013) and that firms devote roughly ten times as many resources to lobbying as to corporate PACs (Ansolabehere, Snyder & Tripathi, 2002). This ratio is also reflected in our sample as the average total lobbying spend over a two-year election cycle was about US$54M while the average total employee contributions to a PAC was about US $569,000. However, others maintain that the effects of political connections made through corporate PAC donations are substantial and financially meaningful for firms. Given that government officials are more willing to publicly associate with more reputable firms (e.g., McDonnell & Werner, 2016; Werner, 2015), corporate PAC contributions provide evidence of the firm's reputability by creating a fully transparent link between a firm and the politician (Shanor, McDonnell & Werner, 2021). Legislators grant greater access to contributing firms (Kalla & Broockman, 2016) and focus more time on their donors' political priorities (Hall & Wayman, 1990). In facilitating greater access to legislators, campaign contributions complement other forms of CPA, like lobbying, by allowing firm representatives to get a foot in the door (Keim & Zardkoohi, 1988). Firms also maintain full control over CPA executed through their corporate PAC in ways that are diluted when engaging in other prevalent CPA methods such as collective tactics (e.g., contributing to trade associations), or donating through third parties like social welfare associations (e.g., 501(c)(4) organizations).

Although prevalent, corporate PACs have increasingly become a point of contention within the political and corporate class in the United States. Political candidates are pledging to refuse donations from corporate PACs to demonstrate their independence from corporate money (Evers-Hillstrom, 2018) and the events surrounding the 2021 presidential inauguration shone the spotlight on the donation records of many major corporations. Given the attention placed on CPA in early 2021, a handful of firms including Charles Schwab have decided to shut down their PACs (Hirsch, 2021) while more are attempting to justify their continued CPA. Recent public statements made by corporate leaders illustrate how many major corporations approach using their corporate PAC to develop relationships with politicians and how they perceive the relationship between the informal and formal arms of their nonmarket strategy.

In a February 2021 statement, Microsoft President Brad Smith noted that their corporate PAC "plays an important role, not because the checks are big, but because of the way the political process works" (Microsoft, 2021). Smith's statement was made to explain the purpose of their PAC to Microsoft employees after backlash arose from the news that Microsoft's PAC had contributed to the campaigns of members of Congress who either signaled their support for the January insurrection in the US Capitol or had voted to not certify the 2020 presidential election results. That the president of Microsoft was compelled to launch a multifaceted impression management campaign to quell the backlash about the company's CPA, including this statement to employees and several related media appearances, suggests that Microsoft's leadership perceived the recent reputational damage as a threat to the company's image as socially responsible. The statement continued, "I do believe it is important for our company to have this kind of effort (a PAC), and at the same time…make decisions that will continue to reflect where we stand, and the values that we believe are important" (Microsoft, 2021). Smith aimed to publicly reassure Microsoft's employees and other stakeholders that the PAC was necessary to enable the firm to operate effectively and does not diminish Microsoft's commitments to its values. By explaining the instrumentality of the PAC to employees and reaffirming the company's reputation as socially responsible, Microsoft sought to recover its ability to solicit funds from employees for the PAC and, by extension, its ability to maintain this part of the company's formal nonmarket strategy.

This case highlights the relationship between an organization's reputation as socially responsible and its stakeholders' willingness to expand the organization's formal nonmarket influence. In addition, it suggests that corporate leaders recognize how different elements of their overall nonmarket strategy are intertwined, that threats to their firm's reputation signify potential future threats to their formal nonmarket performance, and that employees wield significant power over the firm's ability to deploy its corporate PAC. Since employees contribute the majority of funds for corporate PACs, we focus our attention in this chapter on employees' willingness to support their firm's formal nonmarket strategy.

7.3 Theory and Propositions

7.3.1 Overall Social Reputation

An organization's overall reputation reflects the public's general level of public approval, or "shared perceptions of [its] unique and distinguishing qualities" (McDonnell & King, 2018: 64). A favorable reputation benefits organizations in a variety of ways, particularly in evaluative settings (Rindova et al., 2005). By influencing an audience's expectations for an actor's future performance, an organization's reputation can protect an organization by giving it the benefit of the doubt, particularly in more uncertain situations (e.g., Benjamin & Podolny, 1999; Kim & King, 2014). Reducing the uncertainty among stakeholders about a firm's quality or character can benefit a firm in many domains, including the nonmarket arena. A firm with a more positive social reputation can participate more actively and freely with a variety of nonmarket actors. More reputable firms experience improved access to influence politicians (Werner, 2015) and are insulated from being perceived as having committed wrongdoing (McDonnell & King, 2018). Firms with superior reputations are seen as less tainted than their peers and are granted increased access to influence policymakers since they are less threatening to the policymakers' reputations (McDonnell & Werner, 2016; Werner, 2015). In addition, a more positive reputation benefits firms competing for government procurement contracts since a firm's prior history of social responsibility informs the government's perception that the firm is trustworthy and likely to fulfill its commitments (Flammer, 2018). Overall, firm reputation has been theoretically and empirically associated with helping firms to overcome hurdles in gaining access to and managing relationships with a variety of external nonmarket stakeholders.

The benefits of a more favorable overall reputation are likely to extend to internal stakeholders' perceptions of firms' formal nonmarket activities as well. Since stakeholders are generally skeptical of firms' motives when trying to influence the government (Yue, 2015), a firm's social reputation can communicate its trustworthiness and fair-mindedness (Aguilera et al., 2007) and reduce stakeholders' uncertainty about the potential effects of granting a firm a license to participate actively in the policymaking process. A more favorable social reputation may help internal stakeholders overcome their concerns about enabling their firm's CPA if they perceive the firm as a socially responsible actor. Employees will be more motivated to expand the firm's formal nonmarket impact if they trust the firm will promote prosocial policies.

In addition, we argue that a firm's social reputation will influence employees' support for the firm's CPA by strengthening an employee's identification with the firm and expanding the employee's opportunities for prosocial impact. Prior work has found wide-ranging effects of firms' prosocial cues on employee behavior, such as increasing employee engagement (Flammer & Luo, 2017), reducing wage requirements and increasing motivation (Burbano, 2016); the motivating effects of prosocial cues are particularly strong if employees are able to witness the positive impacts of their work on others (Grant, 2012; Grant et al., 2007). Since cues of congruence between employees' and the organization's values have been shown to increase employee identification (McDonnell & Cobb, 2020; Turban & Greening, 1997), employees within firms with more favorable social reputations will be more motivated to act in ways that expand a firm's formal nonmarket impact. Employees may approach supporting their firm's CPA as a means of extending their personal prosocial impact in a way that is complementary to, but distinct from, direct employee participation in a firm's social initiatives (e.g., Bode, Singh, & Rogan, 2015). If an employee believes her organization has an overall positive impact on society and that its positive impact will also extend to its efforts to influence policy, she may be motivated to further expand its impact by participating in extra-role behaviors to support the firm's political activities.

Proposition: Employees within firms with better overall reputations will support their firm's political activity at higher levels.

7.3.2 Employee Relations Reputation

In addition to the motivating effects of a firm's overall reputation on its employees' support for its formal nonmarket strategy, a firm's domain-specific reputation for human resources ought to be positively related to employee support. While a firm's overall social reputation reflects the public's general level of approval, a firm's reputation as a good or bad employer is informed by the firm's prior treatment of its employees. We contend that the benefits of a firm's reputation for treating its employees well extend to increasing its employees' willingness to support its formal nonmarket strategy. By demonstrating that the firm's and its employees' interests are aligned through a record of good employee treatment, a firm may be better positioned to overcome the reputational hurdle faced by firms due to the perception that its interest in CPA is purely profit-motivated (Yue, 2015).

Employees, a key stakeholder group that constitutes the majority of the contributors to corporate PACs, may perceive that their interests are aligned with their firm's interests if they themselves are treated well. While research examining the effect of a firm's reputation for prosocial activities has found that employees believe they will be treated better by a firm that treats other members of society well (Burbano, 2016; Greening & Turban, 2000), the reverse may also be true. Employees that receive favorable treatment may believe that their employer is more likely to further the employees' own interests and act prosocially when engaging with the government. As firms may be participating in policy discussions or lobbying government officials on issues like minimum wage legislation or anti-union policies that directly affect employees' work experiences and livelihoods, employees who think their employer will push for harmful policies would aim to constrain rather than expand the firm's political influence. Firms with better reputations for employee treatment may be rewarded by their employees through stronger support for their corporate political activity since they are perceived as more trustworthy and as having the employees' best interests at heart.

Treating employees well is more costly for firms (Qian et al., 2020), so more favorable treatment signals to employees that their interests are important to the firm. Firms with a more positive reputation among employees, thus, face a reduced reputational barrier to being accepted by their employees as a responsible actor when trying to influence the government. Since the employer has already demonstrated their concern for the wellbeing of employees, employees who are treated well are more likely to believe that their employer will push for policies that support *the employees'* best interests. Since employees are the largest contributor group to corporate PACs, they determine the extent of influence their firm's corporate PAC can wield. By increasing contributions to the PAC, employees signal their support for their firm's corporate political activity and expand its capacity to influence the policymaking process. In this way, a firm's reputation for good employee treatment reduces the uncertainty about a firm's policy priorities among its employees and increases the likelihood that employees will support the firm's formal nonmarket strategy. Formally, we propose that

Proposition: Employees within firms with better reputations for employee relations will support their firm's political activity at higher levels.

7.3.3 Employee Relations Reputation vs. Overall Reputation

We have argued that overall reputation as well as reputation for employee relations are both positively related to stakeholders' support for the firm's CPA. However, it is likely that the different reputations are not equally as significant drivers of employees' embracing their firm as a political actor. We expect that a firm's reputation for how it treats its employees will be more strongly associated with employees' support for the firm's political activities than a firm's reputation overall because the firm's employee relations reputation is more salient to employees than the firm's overall social reputation.

The theory underlying the proposition that a firm's overall reputation increases employees' support for the firm's CPA outlines an indirect effect of reputation on employee support: Overall reputation enhances employees' organizational identification and provides an additional opportunity for employees to have a prosocial impact, increasing employees' motivation to expand the firm's nonmarket role. In contrast, employees experience the effects of their firm's employee policies and practices directly and on a daily basis. Given that human resources policies and practices directly affect an employee's experience at work, this may have a stronger motivating effect than the more diffuse effects of a firm's overall social responsibility practices. The repeated exposure to signals of a firm's favorable or unfavorable treatment of its employees increases the likelihood that the reputation for employee relations is related to employees' willingness to voluntarily support the firm's CPA. While both the overall reputation for social responsibility and the reputation for employee relations are believed to increase employees' trust that the firm will act in the employees' best interest, employees may put greater weight in their direct experiences of their employer as trustworthy. Thus, the motivating effect of the employee relations-specific reputation is likely to be greater than the effect of the firm's overall reputation.

Proposition: A firm's reputation for employee relations is more strongly associated than a firm's overall reputation with employees' support for their firm's political activity.

7.4 Data and Methods

7.4.1 Sample

To test our propositions, we use a random sample of 100 US-based firms that were a component of the S&P 500 in 2006 and study their reputation and CPA from 2007 to 2020. This time period covers seven two-year congressional cycles and captures periods during which the partisan control of the presidency and Congress varied. There were 532 firms in the S&P 500 at some point during 2006, 370 (70 percent) of which had an active corporate PAC during at least one election cycle from 2007 to 2020. From these 370 firms, we randomly selected 100 firms to constitute our sample. Summary statistics and the correlation matrix for the data are presented in Table 7.1. Due to changes in firm ownership, variation in corporate political activity, and dropped observations due to missing data, this sample results in 543 firm-Congress observations for Models 1 and 4. Since one firm included in the sample lacked an employee relations score for one year, all other Models include 542 observations. The data is structured at the firm-Congress level. The two-year Congress time interval is appropriate because all members of the US House of Representatives are up for reelection every two years and campaign finance regulations set limits on corporate PAC donations to candidates by two-year congressional cycle.

7.4.2 Dependent Variable

The dependent variable in our study is the sum of *Employee contributions to PAC*. We calculate the sum of itemized contributions to the Corporate PAC from individuals who can be identified as employees of the firm based on political donation records accessed from the website of the US Federal Election Commission (FEC; www.fec.gov). For every firm in the sample, we downloaded all itemized contributions to all Corporate PACs affiliated with our focal firms from 2007 to 2020. Since our focus in this chapter is on employees, we included

Table 7.1 *Summary statistics and correlation matrix*

	Mean	SD	Empl. contrib. (log)	Net Social Reput.	Net Empl. Rel. Reput.	Net Other Social Reput.	Lobbying Total (log)	Employees (log)	Tobin's Q	Empl. Ideology	PAC Partisanship	DC Office
Empl. contrib. (log)	12.24	1.75	1.00									
Net Social Reput.	1.62	4.20	−0.062	1.00								
Net Empl. Rel. Reput.	0.56	1.66	0.088*	0.657*	1.00							
Net Other Social Reput.	1.05	3.35	−0.122*	0.927*	0.327*	1.00						
Lobbying Total (log)	13.78	6.46	0.426*	0.069	0.099*	0.037	1.00					
Employees (log)	3.49	1.18	0.468*	0.021	0.005	0.025	0.298*	1.00				
Tobin's Q	1.15	1.05	0.015	0.141*	0.076	0.139*	0.110*	0.066	1.00			
Empl. Ideology	−0.03	0.18	0.039	0.194*	0.170*	0.159*	0.051	0.062	0.206*	1.00		
PAC Partisanship	−0.13	0.18	−0.002	0.111*	0.083	0.098*	−0.018	0.048	0.122*	0.499*	1.00	
DC Office	0.53	0.50	0.343*	0.011	0.136*	−0.054	0.386*	0.163*	0.150*	0.126*	0.088*	1.00

only contributions from individuals who could clearly be identified as employees. To account for the skewed nature of this variable, we added 1 to the sum of contributions and took the natural log. Contributors were classified as employees based on a manual search of the employer and occupation included in the donation record.

Employees' financial contributions to their firm's PAC should be entirely voluntary and corporate political responsibility reform efforts, including the CPA-Wharton Zicklin Model Code of Conduct detailed in Chapter 2 of this volume (Freed et al., 2023), prohibit employers from pressuring or coercing their employees to make personal political contributions. However, some workers have reported feeling pressured to comply with their employer's attempts to politically mobilize employees. Chronicled in Hertel-Fernandez (2018), about 25 percent of workers surveyed had received some type of explicitly political message from their employer including encouragement to register to vote or contact a legislator about a specific policy. The extent to which employers pressure their employees to contribute to the PAC specifically is still unclear, although we contend that these types of explicit employee political mobilization efforts are more likely to occur within firms with large political footprints. In addition, the resources dedicated to firms' fundraising efforts vary. A 2019 report by the Public Affairs Council, a trade association for public affairs professionals, noted that 41 percent of companies surveyed solicited contributions from employees through a short campaign once per year and that 50 percent of companies use incentive clubs (Public Affairs Council, 2019). Since administrative and fundraising expenses can be covered by the associated firm's treasury funds, a firm's overall size and size of its formal nonmarket strategy investments are defensible proxies for the intensity of a firm's employee mobilization efforts. As such, in our empirical analyses, we also control for the overall size of a firm's CPA to proxy for the likelihood that the firm is engaging in more explicit forms of employee political mobilization.

7.4.3 Independent Variables

Our key independent variables capture overall social reputation and domain-specific reputation for human relations. We use firm-level ratings provided by KLD, an extensively used proxy for firms' social reputations (e.g., McDonnell, King, & Soule, 2015; Werner, 2015). The

KLD measures reflect a proprietary data collection process that relies on a mix of publicly available information and privately collected data to compute annual ratings of firms' performance, including strengths and concerns, in seven categories. To construct our measure of *overall reputation*, we calculate the net composite score of the number of strengths minus the number of concerns in all seven major categories: community, corporate governance, diversity, employee relations, environment, human rights, and product. We recognize that the concept of a shared, generalized reputation is problematized somewhat by recent work that suggests that corporate social responsibility is politically contested (McDonnell & Darnell, 2022). Different corporate insiders may disagree about what corporate policies and practices are socially responsible, particularly within contested political domains (e.g., McDonnell & Cobb, 2020). However, the strengths and weaknesses as measured within the KLD components tend to avoid the most contentious issues (like policies related to immigration, guns, or trans-gender rights). Further, prior work has found that KLD performance is correlated with positive political outcomes regardless of the party in control of Congress, which supports its validity as a reasonably uncontested proxy for generalized corporate social responsibility (Werner, 2015).

Our measure of *employee relations reputation* reflects the net composite score for only the employee relations area. Since treating employees well often entails policies and procedures that increase a firm's costs (Qian et al., 2020) such as higher compensation or more generous benefits, employees are likely to be motivated to support their firm when they see more positive cues. In contrast, issues surrounding the treatment of employees may signal to employees that their firm prioritizes other goals or other stakeholders' interests over their own. In an effort to avoid temporal endogeneity, we lag reputation ratings by using the ratings of the year prior to the start of an election cycle.

7.4.4 Control Variables

We include several control variables that may be correlated with the rates of employee giving to their firm's corporate PAC. To account for differences in firm size, we control for the logged number of *employees*. Firms with more employees have a larger employee base from which to solicit Corporate PAC contributions. To capture firms'

market performance, we control for *Tobin's Q*, which is operational-
ized as the market value of assets divided by the replacement value of
assets, since it is less subject to possible manipulation by managers
making it a preferable measure in studies involving firm reputation
and nonmarket strategy (McDonnell et al., 2015). Controlling for
financial performance is also necessary because firms can cover PAC
expenses like staff salaries, fundraising, and administrative costs from
the corporate treasury, so financial performance may be correlated
with employee contributions to the PAC (FEC, 2018).

Based on recent contributions to our understanding of the influence
of employee political ideology on firm-level implementation of CSR
(e.g., Gupta et al., 2017), we also control for *employee ideology*. Using
a proxy of employees' personal political donations to political candidates and other PACs, we measure the ideology of a firm's employees
based on the conservative – liberal ideology axis used in political science and political psychology to capture the aggregate ideological orientation of a firm's employees. A research assistant manually searched
the Federal Election Commission website (www.fec.gov) to identify
political donations made by individuals who claimed one of the firms
in our sample as their primary employer. We aggregated all employees' individual political donations from the prior six years (three election cycles) and calculated the percentage of donations made to PACs
affiliated with Democratic politicians or liberal causes. Finally, we
subtracted .5 from this percentage to center *employee ideology* at 0
such that –.5 reflects all conservative donations and .5 reflects all liberal donations.

We also control for the partisanship of the corporate PAC's disbursements. Similar to the construction of the employee ideology
measure, we collected data on corporate PAC disbursements from the
FEC website for all firms and election cycles covered in our sample.
We measure *PAC partisanship* by calculating the percentage of corporate PAC disbursements made to PACs affiliated with Democratic
politicians or party committees over a two-year election cycle. We subtracted .5 from this percentage to center PAC partisanship at 0 such
that –.5 reflects that all PAC disbursements were made to conservative-
affiliated committees and .5 reflects all liberal-affiliated committees.

To control for differences in the likelihood that a firm actively tries
to mobilize its employees to engage politically on its behalf (Hertel-
Fernandez, 2018), we include two proxies to capture the intensity of

firms' overall political activity. Firms vary with respect to the energy behind their employee political mobilization efforts and because firms often simultaneously use complementary political engagement strategies (Ansolabehere, Snyder & Tripathi, 2002; Schuler et al., 2002), it is likely that employee mobilization occurs more frequently within firms with higher overall levels of political engagement. The presence of a Washington *DC office*, a formalized firm structure that "facilitates the practice of politics" (Hillman et al., 2004: 842) and higher *lobbying expenditures* are indicators of the intensity of firms' corporate political activities. We identified whether a firm maintained a DC office in a given election cycle by searching lobbying disclosure forms (lda.senate.gov). *DC office* is a binary variable that equals 1 if a firm had an active office and 0 otherwise. We gathered data on total lobbying expenditures from LobbyView (Kim, 2018) and aggregated to the election cycle. Since some firms do not engage in lobbying and this variable is highly skewed, we add 1 to the total of lobbying expenditures and take the natural log.

To account for variation in government regulations at the industry level and differences in industry structure, we include dummy variables for industry using the two-digit SIC code. All models also include two-year election cycle dummy variables to capture macroeconomic trends and changes in the domestic political environment that may affect corporate political activity. To avoid issues of multicollinearity, all explanatory variables are averaged or summed over the two-year election cycles and lagged by one cycle. We use OLS for all second-stage models and cluster standard errors at the firm. Our results are consistent when including random or fixed effects. While the Hausman test was rejected (*p*=.0192) suggesting that fixed effects models are preferable, we report the results of models including firm, industry, and time random (Models 1–3) and fixed (Models 4–6) effects for completeness.

7.4.5 Model Specification and Results

Results for all models can be found in Table 7.2. Before moving to the main results, we'll highlight several control variables that are significantly associated with employee contributions to their corporate PAC. Firm size and financial performance are positively related to employee contributions to their Corporate PAC. Maintaining a dedicated DC office is not consistently significant although higher engagement in lobbying is associated with higher levels of employee contributions. The positive signs of these coefficients supports the finding that firms often simultaneously deploy multiple CPA strategies (Ansolabehere, Snyder & Tripathi, 2002; Schuler et al., 2002; Walker, 2012) and that firms with larger overall CPA strategies may more actively solicit PAC contributions from employees.

The results of the between-firm or random effects models are shown in Models 1–3. Model 1 tests the first proposition, that employees within firms with better overall reputations would contribute more to their associated corporate PAC. Contrary to our expectations, a firm's general reputation is not significantly associated with their employees' mobilization to support the firm's political strategy. It is possible that employees, on average, are not aware of the full suite of their firm's investments in its informal nonmarket strategy, such as community-oriented or environmental initiatives. An alternative explanation is that employees are familiar with their firm's activities in these areas but that they don't enhance employee identification with the firm in the context of driving support for the firm's formal nonmarket strategy. Our null finding here complements the results of Burbano's (2021) field experiment which indicated that employees had no significant motivational response when their firm expressed a socio-political stance that they agreed with. Additional possible explanations for this result are explored further in the discussion section.

In Proposition 2, we hypothesized that a firm's domain-specific employee relations reputation is positively associated with employee contributions. As shown in Models 2 and 3 in Table 7.2, we find that the coefficient of Net Employee Relations is positive and statistically significant both on its own (Model 2) and when controlling for the other social reputation domains (Model 3). Thus, Proposition 2 is supported suggesting that firms with better employee treatment may facilitate employee support for a firm's formal nonmarket strategy. By parsing employee relations from the other reputation domains, we demonstrate that it may be the salience of a given set of issues to the focal stakeholder group that determines its motivating potential.

Proposition 3 hypothesized that a firm's reputation for human resources is more strongly associated with employees' support for the firm's CPA than a firm's social reputation in other domains. To test this proposition, we executed a Wald test comparing the coefficient

Table 7.2 Determinants of employee PAC contributions

	Random Effects			Fixed Effects		
	Model 1	Model 2	Model 3	Model 4	Model 5	Model 6
Net Social Reputation	0.007			0.009		
	(0.622)			(0.522)		
Net Empl. Relations		0.058*	0.061*		.050*	.050*
		(0.018)	(0.013)		(0.046)	(0.044)
Net Other Social Reputation			−0.008			−0.002
			(0.631)			(0.898)
Tobin's Q	0.256*	0.257*	0.248*	0.293*	0.290*	0.289*
	(0.014)	(0.012)	(0.012)	(0.015)	(0.013)	(0.012)
Employees (log)	0.522**	0.522**	0.524***	0.485**	0.482*	0.480**
	(0.001)	(0.001)	(0.000)	(0.009)	(0.010)	(0.009)
DC Office	0.345	0.322	0.310	0.377	0.353	0.352
	(0.092)	(0.112)	(0.127)	(0.104)	(0.123)	(0.131)
Lobbying Totals (log)	0.051**	0.051**	0.051**	0.048**	0.048**	0.048**
	(0.001)	(0.001)	(0.001)	(0.005)	(0.005)	(0.005)
Employee Ideology	−0.258	−0.269	−0.243	−0.378	−0.374	−0.374
	(0.541)	(0.526)	(0.563)	(0.385)	(0.389)	(0.388)
PAC Partisanship	−0.165	−0.237	−0.237	−0.142	−0.197	−0.196
	(0.831)	(0.759)	(0.760)	(0.852)	(0.798)	(0.799)
Constant	9.530***	9.432***	9.399***	9.328***	9.336***	9.344***
	(0.000)	(0.000)	(0.000)	(0.000)	(0.000)	(0.000)
Firm, Time, Industry Effects	Yes	Yes	Yes	Yes	Yes	Yes
No. of Obs.	543	542	542	543	542	542
R-squared	.11	.12	.12	.12	.12	.12

*$p<0.05$, **$p<0.01$, ***$p<0.001$.

of the Net Employee Relations and the Net Other Social Reputation variables in Model 3. The null hypothesis that the coefficients are equivalent was rejected at the .05 level ($p = .021$) providing additional evidence that employee relations issues may be more impactful in driving this stakeholder group's willingness to expand their firm's formal nonmarket influence than other reputational domains.

Models 4–6 report the results from the within-firm or fixed effects analyses. The results of these models are substantively similar, providing support for the theory that within-firm improvements in the treatment of employees are positively associated with increased employee support for the firm's formal nonmarket strategy. The Wald test comparing the coefficients of the Net Employee Relations and the Net Other Social Reputation supports Proposition 3 at the .10 level ($p = .065$).

7.4.6 Robustness Checks

While the main analysis was performed at the two-year Congress level, we replicated all analyses at the year level as a robustness check. The findings were consistent with the cycle level models such that the overall social reputation was not statistically significant but employee relations reputation was positively associated with employee contributions to their corporate PAC. The null hypothesis of the Wald test was rejected at the .05 level ($p = .027$) with random effects and fixed effects ($p = .048$) further supporting Proposition 3 that the reputation for employee relations is more strongly associated with employee contributions than all other social reputation domains.

We conducted additional robustness checks to mitigate concerns about a potential selection issue present in our context. Since our dependent variable is only observed during election cycles in which a firm operates a corporate PAC, we employed a two-stage Heckman selection model to account for these possible selection effects. The first-stage model is a probit regression estimating the likelihood that a firm in our sample has an active corporate PAC during a given cycle (Table 7.3). We include all firms that were a component of the S&P 500 at some point between 2008 and 2020. Following prior research (King, 2008; McDonnell & King, 2013), we included two selection instruments in the first stage: (1) the percentage of firms in an industry with a PAC (*Active PAC Pct*), and (2) whether a firm's industry

Table 7.3 *Determinants of a corporation having a PAC*

Industry PAC Pct	1.087***
	(0.000)
Gov Oversight	0.452***
	(0.000)
Revenue (log)	0.408***
	(0.000)
No. of Obs.	4710

$*p<0.05$, $**p<0.01$, $***p<0.001$.

is subject to oversight by a standing committee in the US House of Representatives (*Gov oversight*). These variables were selected because firm-level CPA has been positively associated with industry-level CPA and the industry's reliance on the government (e.g., Schuler et al., 2002). While both variables were highly predictive of whether a firm had an active corporate PAC during a cycle, neither was correlated with the dependent variable in the second stage of the analysis. In addition to the selection instruments, in the first stage model we also control for the firm's size (*Revenue (log)*) since a firm's financial resources are antecedents of CPA (Hillman et al., 2004). The second-stage models include the outcome of the first-stage probit regression referred to as the Heckman selection coefficient or the inverse Mills ratio. This ratio is derived from the first-stage model and its inclusion in the second-stage models controls for the likelihood that a firm has an active PAC during a given cycle, addressing potential selection bias.

With the inclusion of the inverse Mills ratio across all models tested, our results remain substantively similar to those reported in Table 7.2. In addition, the inverse Mills ratio was not statistically significant across any model, suggesting that selection is not a significant issue in this context.

In addition to firm-level variation in the extent to which firms actively attempt to politically mobilize their employees, states vary with respect to the legal protections granted to worker political speech and the prohibition of employer political coercion. As a final robustness check, we controlled for this state-level variation, which may affect employees' political contributions to their corporate PAC. We included a binary variable equal to 1 if the state in which a firm is headquartered has laws protecting employee political speech and/or laws that prohibit some type of employee political coercion (Hertel-Fernandez, 2018). We also included a control variable for state-level unemployment rates as a proxy for employee power to resist employer political coercion. Neither control variable was statistically significant nor did the results remain substantively similar to those reported.

7.5 Discussion

This chapter explores the effect of organizational reputation, as informed by informal nonmarket strategy, on stakeholders' support for their firms' formal nonmarket strategy. By recognizing and considering internal stakeholders' power over a firm's ability to engage in certain types of corporate political activity, we shed light on the potential for stakeholders' perceptions of a firm as a socially responsible actor to expand or constrain a firm's formal nonmarket strategy. Through increasing or decreasing contributions to the firm's PAC, employees signal their level of support for the firm's political influence. In particular, we focused on the impacts of a firm's overall social reputation as well as its reputation for employee relations and found preliminary evidence that a firm's overall social reputation is not associated, while its overall record on employee relations is positively associated, with employees' contributions to the firm's PAC. These results support our theory that signals of a firm's commitment to treating its employees well are more salient to employees than signals of a firm's prosocial activities in other domains and, therefore, are more clearly associated with employees' support for their firm's formal political activities.

More broadly, this chapter contributes to the growing body of research focused on the relationships between different aspects of a firm's overall nonmarket strategy (e.g., McDonnell & Werner, 2016; Werner, 2015). By considering the interplay between nonmarket activities targeting informal institutions, such as CSR, and those targeting formal institutions, such as CPA, we illustrate the complementary nature of different firm strategies encompassed by the umbrella of nonmarket strategy. Clearly conceptualizing such strategies as components of firms' portfolio of nonmarket strategies can help advance our nascent theoretical understanding of their underlying relationships and how their interactions drive informal and formal nonmarket performance.

Our findings also contribute to research focused on the strategic choices behind which types of political strategies firms employ. Firms often use a variety of tactics to engage politically (Ansolabehere et al., 2002), including a mix of more and less transparent strategies (Shanor et al., 2021). Future research could explore whether having a better reputation among employees and, in turn, stronger employee support for political engagement affects how firms choose to manage their formal nonmarket strategy. Firms with superior reputations might be able to support the use of more transparent tactics like corporate PACs since they are more effective at mobilizing employees to support their nonmarket activities than firms without equivalent reputational assets. In contrast, firms that lack employee support for their formal nonmarket activities may rely more heavily on less transparent forms of political engagement, such as lobbying or constituency building. As such, a firm's reputation, by way of its influence on stakeholders' support, may be an antecedent of the portfolio of nonmarket strategies available to firms and shape firms' nonmarket strategies in ways we do not yet understand.

We argued that because employee relations policies and practices are more proximate to the experience of employees than other contributing aspects of the firm's social reputation, these repeated cues of an employer's support, or lack of support, for improving their employees' wellbeing and careers is more closely related to employees' willingness to voluntarily support their firm's formal nonmarket strategy. Since the employer has demonstrated its commitment to supporting its employees, employees may be more likely to trust that the firm will act responsibly when engaging in government and promote issues that are also in the employees' best interests. In addition, employees may see their firm's formal nonmarket strategy as a way to expand their own prosocial impact. A 2019 survey of corporate PACs found that offering to match an employee's PAC contribution with a donation to charity was the most effective employee incentive (Public Affairs Council, 2019). This finding may further support our proposition that an employee's prosocial orientation may motivate them to support the firm's formal nonmarket strategy as the employee match program signals the firm's prosocial commitment and is a direct link between an informal and formal nonmarket strategy.

Although we found evidence supporting our theory that the motivating effects of more favorable employee policies and practices are stronger than signals of a firm's positive impact in other domains, several alternative explanations for this finding warrant further investigation. First, it is possible that in the context of employees' willingness to voluntarily support their employer's political activities, employees are less aware of their firm's informal nonmarket activities in nonemployee relations domains such as environmental protection or human rights. Alternatively, the lack of positive association between a firm's overall social reputation and employee support of the firm's PAC may be attributable to employees' expectation that firms with a more favorable reputation have superior access to nonmarket actors to begin with and, therefore, do not think the firm requires their support to engage politically. Employees may perceive that since their employer is already in a preferable position to influence policy, it is less imperative for them to bolster the firm's ability to engage through its PAC. Gaining a clearer picture of employees' awareness and perceptions of the relationship between firms' informal and formal nonmarket strategies as substitutes or complements would help improve our understanding of the underlying mechanisms at play in our analyses.

An additional explanation for the difference in effects between a firm's overall social reputation and its reputation for employee relations may be that some aspects of a firm's social reputation are politically contested, such that support for some issues is contingent on individuals' political ideology (McDonnell & Cobb, 2020; McDonnell & Darnell, 2022). For example, employee health and safety, compensation and benefits, and professional development are examples of specific issues embedded within employee relations that do not have a clear ideological bent. Firms that provide their employees with safe working environments, fair compensation, and opportunities for professional advancement are likely to be more universally perceived as good employers. Although *some* employees perceive their employer more favorably due to their employer's society-focused activities (Burbano, 2021), it may be that *most* employees perceive their employer as more trustworthy when they themselves are treated well. Therefore, a deeper dive into the effects of political ideology at the employee and corporate PAC levels will help clarify its potential impact on employees' support for the firm's formal nonmarket strategy. While Li (2018) found that at the individual level, political ideology alignment between the employee and their firm's PAC affected the employee's donation patterns, future research can help unpack how this dynamic may play out at the organization level. Historically, corporate PACs' decisions about which candidates to financially support were overwhelmingly determined by the firm's financial and regulatory goals and a candidate's position on social issues was irrelevant criteria (Public Affairs Council, 2019). But, the events of the 2021 presidential inauguration in the United States that led to widespread attention on PAC donations may fundamentally alter this dynamic.

Future research should further probe our initial findings regarding the association between net reputational scores and stakeholder support for the firm's formal nonmarket strategy by separately probing the effects of reputational strengths vs. concerns. Prior research in this area has found that negative cues are more impactful in updating people's prior beliefs. For example, Burbano (2021) found that only values misalignment between employees and their employer was demotivating while values alignment did not similarly motivate employees. She argued this finding may be attributable to the notion that because employees tend to assume their organization is already aligned with their values, receiving confirmatory information doesn't actually change their beliefs or behavior. In contrast, cues that their organization's values may not be aligned with their own challenges this assumption and has a bigger impact on employees' behavior. Follow-on work should consider whether negative perceptions of a firm's standing as a socially responsible actor may lead employees to withhold their support for expanding the firm's nonmarket impact while general positive cues of the firm's behavior may simply confirm their established beliefs about the firm.

Given that employee contributions to their firm's PAC are entirely voluntary and outside of their job responsibilities, ours may be a conservative test of the effects of a firm's reputation on employees' support for a firm's formal nonmarket strategy. Employees may also be motivated to support their firm's formal nonmarket strategy in other ways not captured in this analysis. Future research could explore whether a firm's reputation motivates employees to support the firm's CPA through other forms of employee mobilization (Hertel-Fernandez, 2018) such as volunteering to make calls for a specific campaign or voting in a key local election. By studying other ways employees support their firm's CPA, we could also improve the generalizability of our findings to firms without a corporate PAC.

During a time of increased public attention on corporate political activity, it is crucial for nonmarket strategy scholars to take a renewed look at the interplay between informal and formal nonmarket strategy. The connections between these aspects of nonmarket strategy are becoming clearer and represent an area of study with ever-increasing societal implications.

References

Aguilera, R., Rupp, D., Williams, C., & Ganapathi, J. (2007). Putting the S Back in Corporate Social Responsibility: A Multilevel Theory of Social Change in Organizations. *Academy of Management Review*, 32(3), 836–63.

Ansolabehere, S., Snyder Jr, J., & Tripathi, M. (2002). Are PAC Contributions and Lobbying Linked? New Evidence from the 1995 Lobby Disclosure Act. *Business and Politics*, 4(2), 131–55.

Benjamin, B., & Podolny, J. (1999). Status, Quality, and Social Order in the California Wine Industry. *Administrative Science Quarterly*, 44(3), 563–89.

Bode, C., Singh, J., & Rogan, M. (2015). Corporate Social Initiatives and Employee Retention. *Organization Science*, 26(6), 1702–20.

Burbano V. (2016). Social Responsibility Messages and Worker Wage Requirements: Field Experimental Evidence from Online Labor Marketplaces. *Organization Science*, 27(4), 1010–28.

Burbano, V. (2021). The Demotivating Effects of Communicating a Social-Political Stance: Field Experimental Evidence from an Online Labor Market Platform. *Management Science*, 67(2), 1004–25.

Dorobantu, S., Kaul, A., & Zelner, B. (2017). Nonmarket Strategy Research through the Lens of New Institutional Economics: An Integrative Review and Future Directions. *Strategic Management Journal*, 38(1), 114–40.

Eesley, C., Eberhart, R., Skousen, B., & Cheng, J. (2018). Institutions and Entrepreneurial Activity: The Interactive Influence of Misaligned Formal and Informal Institutions. *Strategy Science*, 3(2), 393–407.

Evers-Hillstrom, K. (2018). Democrats Are Rejecting Corporate PACs: Does It Mean Anything? *Open Secrets*, December 7.

Favotto, A., Kollman, K., & McMillan, F. (2023). Responsible Lobbyists? CSR Commitments and the Quality of Corporate Parliamentary Testimony in the UK. In T. Lyon, ed., *Corporate Political Responsibility*. Cambridge, UK: Cambridge University Press.

FEC (2018). Corporations and Labor Organizations Campaign Guide. Federal Election Commission, January.

Flammer, C. (2018). Competing for Government Procurement Contracts: The Role of Corporate Social Responsibility. *Strategic Management Journal*, 39(5), 1299–324.

Flammer, C., & Luo, J. (2017). Corporate Social Responsibility as an Employee Governance Tool: Evidence from a Quasi-Experiment. *Strategic Management Journal*, 38(2), 163–83.

Freed, B., Sandstrom, K., & Laufer, W. (2023). Targeting Private Sector Influence in Politics: Corporate Accountability as a Risk and Governance Problem. In T. Lyon, ed., *Corporate Political Responsibility*. Cambridge, UK: Cambridge University Press.

Grant, A. (2012). Leading with Meaning: Beneficiary Contact, Prosocial Impact, and the Performance Effects of Transformational Leadership. *Academy of Management Journal*, 55(2), 458–76.

Grant, A., Campbell, E., Chen, G., et al. (2007). Impact and the Art of Motivation Maintenance: The Effects of Contact with Beneficiaries on Persistence Behavior. *Organizational Behavior and Human Decision Processes*, 103(1), 53–67.

Greening, D., & Turban, D. (2000). Corporate Social Performance as a Competitive Advantage in Attracting a Quality Workforce. *Business & Society*, 39(3), 254–80.

Gupta, A., Briscoe, F., & Hambrick, D. (2017). Red, Blue, and Purple Firms: Organizational Political Ideology and Corporate Social Responsibility. *Strategic Management Journal*, 38(5), 1018–40.

Hadani, M., & Schuler, D. (2013). In Search of El Dorado: The Elusive Financial Returns on Corporate Political Investments. *Strategic Management Journal*, 34(2), 165–81.

Hall, R., & Wayman, F. (1990). Buying Time: Moneyed Interests and the Mobilization of Bias in Congressional Committees. *American Political Science Review*, 84(3), 797–820.

Hertel-Fernandez, A. (2018). *Politics at Work: How Companies Turn Their Workers into Lobbyists*. Oxford, UK: Oxford University Press.

Hillman, A., & Hitt, M. (1999). Corporate Political Strategy Formulation: A Model of Approach, Participation, and Strategy Decisions. *Academy of Management Review*, 24(4), 825–42.

Hillman, A., Keim, G., & Schuler, D. (2004). Corporate Political Activity: A Review and Research Agenda. *Journal of Management*, 30(6), 837–57.

Hirsch, L. (2021). Charles Schwab to End All Political Donations and Shutter PAC. *The New York Times*, January 13.

Kalla, J. L., & Broockman, D. E. (2016). Campaign Contributions Facilitate Access to Congressional Officials: A Randomized Field Experiment. *American Journal of Political Science*, 60(3), 545–58.

Keim, G., & Zardkoohi, A. (1988). Looking for Leverage in PAC Markets: Corporate and Labor Contributions Considered. *Public Choice*, 58(1), 21–34.

Kim, I. (2018). *LobbyView: Firm-level Lobbying & Congressional Bills Database*. Cambridge, MA: Unpublished manuscript, MIT.

Kim, J., & King, B. (2014). Seeing Stars: Matthew Effects and Status Bias in Major League Baseball Umpiring. *Management Science*, 60(11), 2619–44.

King, B. (2008). A Political Mediation Model of Corporate Response to Social Movement Activism. *Administrative Science Quarterly*, 53(3), 395–421.

Li, Z. (2018). How Internal Constraints Shape Interest Group Activities: Evidence from Access-Seeking PACs. *American Political Science Review*, 112(4), 792–808.

Lux, S., Crook, T., & Woehr, D. (2011). Mixing Business with Politics: A Meta-analysis of the Antecedents and Outcomes of Corporate Political Activity. *Journal of Management*, 37(1), 223–47.

Lyon, T., & Maxwell, J. (2004). Astroturf: Interest Group Lobbying and Corporate Strategy. *Journal of Economics & Management Strategy*, 13(4), 561–97.

McDonnell, M-H., & Cobb, J. (2020). Take a Stand or Keep Your Seat: Board Turnover after Social Movement Boycotts. *Academy of Management Journal*, 63(4), 1028–53.

McDonnell, M-H., & Darnell, S. (2022). Profiting from Protest: A Contingency Model of the Effects of Anti-corporate Activism. Working Paper.

McDonnell, M. H., & King, B. (2013). Keeping Up Appearances: Reputational Threat and Impression Management after Social Movement Boycotts. *Administrative Science Quarterly*, 58(3), 387–419.

McDonnell, M-H., & King B. (2018). Order in the Court: The Influence of Firm Status and Reputation on the Outcomes of Employment Discrimination Suits. *American Sociological Review*, 83(1), 61–87.

McDonnell, M-H., King, B., & Soule, S. (2015). A Dynamic Process Model of Private Politics: Activist Targeting and Corporate Receptivity to Social Challenges. *American Sociological Review*, 80(3), 654–78.

McDonnell, M-H., & Werner, T. (2016). Blacklisted Businesses: Social Activists' Challenges and the Disruption of Corporate Political Activity. *Administrative Science Quarterly*, 61(4), 584–620.

Mellahi, K., Frynas, J., Sun, P., & Siegel, D. (2016). A Review of the Nonmarket Strategy Literature: Toward a Multi-theoretical Integration. *Journal of Management*, 42(1), 143–73.

Microsoft Corporate Blogs. (2021). Transcript: Brad Smith's Remarks at an Employee Meeting Thursday. *Microsoft*, January 22.

Public Affairs Council. (2019). 2019 Corporate PAC Benchmarking Report. Public Affairs Council, October 9. pac.org/wp-content/uploads/2019-Corporate-PAC-Benchmarking-Webinar-1.pdf

Qian, C., Crilly, D., Wang, K., & Wang, Z. (2020). Why Do Banks Favor Employee-Friendly Firms? A Stakeholder-Screening Perspective. *Organization Science*, 32(3), 605–24.

Rindova, V., Williamson, I., Petkova, A., & Sever, J. (2005). Being Good or Being Known: An Empirical Examination of the Dimensions, Antecedents, and Consequences of Organizational Reputation. *Academy of Management Journal*, 48(6), 1033–49.

Scherer, A., & Voegtlin, C. (2023). MNCs as Responsible Political Actors in Global Business: Challenges and Implications for Human Resource Management. In T. Lyon, ed., *Corporate Political Responsibility*. Cambridge, UK: Cambridge University Press.

Schuler, D., Rehbein, K., & Cramer, R. (2002). Pursuing Strategic Advantage through Political Means: A Multivariate Approach. *Academy of Management Journal*, 45(4), 659–72.

Scott, W. R. (1995). *Institutions and Organizations: Ideas, Interests, and Identities*. Thousand Oaks, CA: Sage Publications.

Shanor, A., McDonnell, M-H., & Werner, T. (2021). Corporate Political Power: The Politics of Reputation & Traceability. *Emory Law Journal*, 71(2): 153–216.

Turban, D, & Greening, D. (1997). Corporate Social Performance and Organizational Attractiveness to Prospective Employees. *Academy of Management Journal*, 40(3), 658–72.

Walker, E. (2012). Putting a Face on the Issue: Corporate Stakeholder Mobilization in Professional Grassroots Lobbying Campaigns. *Business & Society*, 51(4), 561–601.

Werner T. (2015). Gaining Access by Doing Good: The Effect of Sociopolitical Reputation on Firm Participation in Public Policymaking. *Management Science*, 61, 1989–2011.

Werner, T. (2017). Investor Reaction to Covert Corporate Political Activity. *Strategic Management Journal*, 38(12), 2424–43.

Yue, L. (2015). Community Constraints on the Efficacy of Elite Mobilization: The Issuance of Currency Substitutes during the Panic of 1907. *American Journal of Sociology*, 120(6), 1690–735.

8 | Multinational Companies as Responsible Political Actors in Global Business

Challenges and Implications for Human Resource Management

ANDREAS GEORG SCHERER
AND CHRISTIAN VOEGTLIN

8.1 Introduction

Globalization can be understood "as the process of intensification of cross-area and cross-border social relations between actors from very distant locations, and of growing transnational interdependence of economic and social activities" (Scherer & Palazzo, 2008, p. 415). In their pursuit of profit, economic actors expand their operations beyond national borders and jurisdictions by directly investing in or sourcing from abroad. Some of these companies shift value chain activities to offshore locations or to countries with weak standards, oppressive regimes, violations of human rights, and failing governmental institutions with lax or nonexistent regulations and enforcement mechanisms regarding the externalities of business. As a matter of fact, some of the most preferred host economies for foreign direct investment (FDI) inflows (see UNCTAD World Investment Report, 2019) or of the top merchandize export nations (World Trade Organization World Trade Statistical Review, 2019) are listed in the "warning" categories of the annual "Fragile State Index," an index that measures the proper functioning of states along economic, political, and social criteria of good governance (Fund for Peace, 2019; Naudé et al., 2011; Scherer & Voegtlin, 2020).

As a result, a significant part of the world's goods are sourced or produced under conditions characterized by insufficient legal regulations and democratic control (see Scherer & Voegtlin, 2020, p. 178). This has negative side effects on the protection of human rights and the enforcement of social and environmental standards along supply chains (Scherer & Palazzo, 2011). The consequences on working conditions include poor health and safety standards, unclear or nonexistent employment contracts, suppression of unions and worker rights, discrimination, abuse, and even child labor, forced labor, or various forms of "modern slavery" (Crane, 2013; Schrempf-Stirling & Wettstein, 2017; Schumann, 2001). Multinational corporations (MNCs) are increasingly held responsible for the employment conditions both within their own firm boundaries and at their suppliers and sub-suppliers.

Business firms have responded to the growing pressure from nongovernmental organizations (NGOs) and have taken responsibility by closing governance gaps (Schrage & Gilbert, 2021) or joining corporate social responsibility (CSR) initiatives (Waddock, 2008) such as the UN Global Compact, the OECD Guidelines for Multinational Enterprises, the ILO Tripartite Declaration of Principles concerning Multinational Enterprises and Social Policy, as well as the Fair Labor Association or the Global Reporting Initiative. Companies have established CSR departments, drafted codes of conduct, and published CSR principles and reports that document their socio-environmental commitments. Yet, despite broad institutionalization of CSR principles, the actual level of implementation still seems limited as reports on violations of human rights and social standards and pertinent organizational misconduct and corporate scandals suggest (Greve, Palmer, & Pozner, 2010). The decoupling of firms' official policies and actual practices in socio-environmental issues seems endemic and is a matter of concern for academics, NGOs, and policymakers (Bromley & Powell, 2012; Wijen, 2014). Even worse, despite their public commitments many business firms continue to lobby for weak (or against stricter) regulation and enforcement of social and environmental standards in order to cut costs and increase returns and influence policymakers both in their home countries and in their host countries. They use a whole range of influence mechanisms on regulation in ways that benefit the firms' economic bottom line (Frynas & Stephens, 2015; on lobbying in the automotive industry see, e.g., Anastasiadis, 2014; Guerard, Bode, & Gustafsson, 2013), even though in many cases it is difficult to document what firms are actually lobbying for (Delmas & Friedman, 2023; Lyon & Mandelkorn, 2023).

This brief overview highlights the challenges of regulating labor issues, social standards and, in general, global business activities. In the absence of consistent global legal regulations or universal moral standards, corporations are increasingly confronted with the ethical challenge of deciding what is right or wrong in a given context and whether and if so how to responsibly influence their institutional environment via their political activities and relationships with policymakers. They are involved in national and global governance that determines whether and to what extent labor standards are defined and enforced to protect worker rights and human rights more broadly.

However, the implications of these ethical challenges on the human resource management (HRM) function in global business firms have been addressed only superficially (for exceptions see Budd & Scoville, 2005; Buller & McEvoy, 1999; Mirvis, 2012). This comes as a surprise, since we propose HRM can play an important dual role in shaping the political responsibility of firms vis-à-vis employees: in its *steward* role HRM can take responsibility for the wellbeing of the firm's own work force and the working conditions along the supply chain, and in its *enabler* role HRM can encourage employees to take responsibility for social, environmental, and political grievances by, for example, allowing employee involvement in social innovation projects for decreasing negative and increasing positive externalities, volunteering to resolve social and environmental issues or support third parties (Mirvis & Googins, 2018), or channeling employee activism (see, e.g., Gekeler, 2019; for examples from the United States, see Larcker, Tayan, & Miles, 2021; note that the Zicklin Model Code for CPA prohibits firms from pressuring their employees to take any sort of political action, see Freed, Sandstrom, & Laufer, 2023).

As a supporting function, HRM is greatly affected by the factors described above, as first, HRM is responsible for the deployment of a global workforce and thus, needs to tackle issues that relate to working conditions and employment within the company and beyond. In that respect HRM can be said to act as a *steward* of ethical working conditions along supply chains, especially in contexts where labor and human rights of workers are not sufficiently protected by national law (e.g., in fragile states). Second, HRM is crucial because it influences the attitudes, capabilities, and motivation of organizational members who support the corporate engagement with national or global governance and the production of public goods (Budd & Scoville, 2005;

Cohen, 2010). From this perspective HRM can be conceived of as an *enabler* of corporations (via their employees) that assume political responsibilities in national or international contexts to serve the public interest (Mirvis & Googins, 2018). The two HRM roles of steward and enabler apply to all HR functions (such as selection, appraisal, compensation, and development; see Stone, 1998) that can either support or impede employees' ability to shape the political engagement of corporations, to make ethical (rather than unethical) decisions, or to behave ethically (rather than merely instrumentally) on behalf of the corporation so that people are served and the planet is protected (Buller & McEvoy, 1999; Jabbour & Santos, 2008).

In this chapter we focus on the ethical challenges that globalization poses to the employment relationship and the resulting political engagement of MNCs. Ethics is concerned with the normative assessment of what *should* be considered right or wrong, including the evaluation of prevailing moral norms and practices in business (Steinmann & Löhr, 1994; Trevino & Weaver, 1994). In the discussion on the political role of MNCs the focus has been on the interface between business and society on a macro level of analysis (e.g., Chandler & Mazlish, 2005; Lyon et al., 2018; Matten & Crane, 2005; Scherer & Palazzo, 2011; Vogel, 2008). In these studies, business firms are treated as a "black box" and intra-organizational processes are largely neglected (for exceptions see, e.g., Maak & Pless, 2006; Mirvis & Googins, 2018; Scherer, Baumann-Pauly, & Schneider, 2013; Thompson, 2008; Voegtlin, Patzer, & Scherer, 2012). Edwards and Kuruvilla (2005) and Geppert and colleagues (2003) point out that MNCs can influence their institutional context by mobilizing power in order to determine public policy. Yet, they do not explore this issue and its implications for HRM in depth.

In the following, we combine insights gained from CSR, Corporate Political Responsibility (CPR), and HRM research to address the ensuing question: What are the implications of the emerging political role of MNCs for HRM? – We proceed as follows: First, we review approaches to the political role of the firm and assess their contributions and limitations. Second, using this discussion as a starting point, we engage with the role HRM plays in this regard and propose a framework of political HRM that takes account of the emerging challenges and political responsibilities of corporations. Our framework can be understood as a guideline for exploring the role of HRM in the political agenda of business firms and thus contributes to both Political CSR (PCSR) and CPR research.

8.2 The Emerging Discourse on the Political Role of MNCs: Four Approaches

For decades, the political role and significance of MNCs have been discussed in the literature. However, the literature is fragmented, and the various approaches build on different assumptions and draw competing conclusions on how MNCs should approach policymakers and the political system in general. A comprehensive review is beyond the scope of this chapter (see, e.g., Frynas & Stephens, 2015; Rasche, 2015; Scherer, 2018; Scherer & Palazzo, 2007, 2011). Instead, we focus in the following on a brief review of four main approaches that are relevant for our endeavor – corporate political activity, corporate citizenship, political corporate social responsibility, and, most recently, corporate political responsibility – before turning our attention to the implications for HRM.

Corporate political activity (CPA) is concerned with the various strategies and practices that companies employ to influence the political environment in their favor (Hillman, Keim, & Schuler, 2004; Lawton, McGuire, & Rajwani, 2013; Rajwani & Liedong, 2015). These influence mechanisms include financial strategies such as political action committees, "soft money" contributions or even forms of corruption, relational strategies that build on political connections, and informational strategies such as lobbying, petitions, or public comments (Rajwani & Liedong, 2015). The basic assumption of CPA research is that firms engage with the political system to increase their economic performance and to improve their competitive position (Baysinger, 1984; Hillman et al., 2004). Consequently, researchers study the factors that explain the CPAs of companies with the often more implicit than explicit goal to explore what influence strategies work best to enhance profits. As a result, this stream of research has tended to neglect the negative implications of CPAs, including regulatory capture (see, e.g., Carpenter & Moss, 2013) and the potential and actual negative effects on people and planet (Mantere, Pajunen, & Lamberg, 2009; Matten, 2009; Scherer, 2018; for exceptions, see, e.g., Fleckinger & Glachant, 2011; Lyon & Maxwell, 2004a, 2004b; Stigler, 1971). This is in so far problematic, as in a globalized world that is characterized by market failures, externalities, uneven distribution of power, and insufficient regulatory capacities of nation-states or global governance institutions, CPAs focusing on influencing policy to enhance corporate profits are likely to worsen institutional conditions further and to undermine public welfare (Scherer et al., 2016).

The underlying concept of politics in CPA research is a form of power politics, where corporations leverage their power to influence the institutional environment in their favor (Baron, 2003). Consequently, in the CPA approach corporations are not conceived of as possessing the motivation to contribute to public wellbeing, nor is there a demand that they should do so. Rather, seen through the CPA lens firms "attempt to further their interests by imposing their will on others" (Baron, 2003, p. 31) and by using their power they aim to "overcome the resistance of other actors" (Boddewyn & Brewer, 1994, p. 120). This implies that it is difficult to restrict corporate power by state regulations and domesticate it by means of democratic control in cases where states are unwilling or unable to do so (see, e.g., the Fragile State Index, Fund for Peace, 2019), but instead business is likely to capture the political system and to define the rules of the game in businesses' favor with potentially negative effects on public policy and social welfare.

Corporate citizenship (CC) and political corporate social responsibility (PCSR), by contrast, are complementary approaches that aim to develop a normative-ethical theory of the political role of corporations. These approaches emphasize the role of corporations in providing (global) public goods and in defining and enforcing public rules in cases where the state system, for whatever reason, is unwilling or incapable to establish restrictions and develop policies that effectively address public issues and serve the common good. CC is based on the idea of citizenship rights (Marshall, 1965), that is, social, civil and political rights of individuals. It defines the political role of business as "administering citizenship rights for individuals" (Matten & Crane, 2005, p. 173; Moon, Crane, & Matten, 2005) in situations where state agencies fail to do so. In these cases, corporations step in and fill the governance gap with a view on public wellbeing. Whereas the initial conception was largely descriptive (see Matten & Crane, 2005, p. 174), the aim was to further explore and justify the normative foundations of such an approach, that is, to study under what conditions political behavior of corporations can be considered legitimate.

PCSR is complementary to CC in this respect and aims to embed the corporate engagement with the political system in procedures of democratic authorization and control (Scherer & Palazzo, 2007, 2011), so that the legitimacy of corporate political engagement can be secured (Palazzo & Scherer, 2006). PCSR builds on the concept of deliberative democracy, which has become an eminent stream of conceptual and empirical research in the political sciences (see, e.g., Bächtiger et al., 2018; Dryzek et al., 2019; Fishkin, 2018; Habermas, 1998). Deliberative democratic theory is a normative theory that explores the legitimacy and efficiency of collective decision-making and develops procedures and criteria for criticizing procedures, institutions, and contexts that do not meet normative standards of democratic deliberation (Chambers, 2003). Deliberative approaches explore the argumentative processes that take place not only within, but also above and beyond institutionalized forms of representative democracy (i.e., elections, political parties, parliament, etc.), precede elections, and shape collective decisions. Deliberation is defined as "debate and discussion aimed at producing reasonable, well-informed opinions in which participants are willing to revise preferences in light of discussion, new information, and claims made by fellow participants" (Chambers, 2003, p. 309). Deliberative approaches take account of the contributions of non-state actors such as business firms, NGOs, or civil society groups in preparing collective decisions, providing public goods, or developing public policies that are efficient and legitimate. Deliberative approaches are normative in as far as they emphasize the quality of the public discourses in which collective decision-making is embedded. Consequently, the concept of politics in PCSR is tightly linked to this communicative approach and emphasizes three aspects: "(1) deliberations about collective issues, decisions and rules; (2) the production of public goods (and avoidance of public bads); and (3) the contribution to and impact on social welfare" (Scherer, 2018, p. 394).

Finally, corporate political responsibility (CPR) is a more recent discussion that was proposed as an alternative to the prevailing CPA approach, especially in the US context (Lyon et al., 2018). CPR builds on the observation that it might be too narrow to conceive of companies engaging with the political system only to serve their economic bottom line. Obviously, many business firms and firm leaders emphasize their responsibilities via people and planet, as for instance indicated by the recent statement on the purpose of a corporation by the Business Roundtable (https://purpose.businessroundtable.org). Even more so, many investors withdraw money from businesses that involve social and environmental risks and seek investments in sustainable businesses. The protagonists of CPR are deeply concerned about the prevailing lobbying activities of business firms, especially in the United States, and demand more transparency in corporate political engagements regarding financial implications and relational ties (Lyon et al., 2018; Lyon & Mandelkorn, 2023). The authors' general message is that businesses should serve the interests of shareholders but with a view on the public interest so that a balance between financial and public interests is achieved. Even more so, proponents of CPR emphasize that corporations are scrutinized and pressured by various stakeholder groups that aim to make their concerns heard and influence the corporate political agenda to align it with the public interest. However, CPR research has yet to sketch out in detail how such a balance between corporate and stakeholder interests, between financial and societal goals should be achieved, and what conceptions of democracy, politics and responsibility should guide the CPR approach in order to account for the different motivations of firms' political engagement and the variety of political interests they pursue (financial, social, environmental). This might also involve thinking beyond politics as a game of power to achieve particularistic outcomes, as is often the underlying assumption in the CPA approach, the approach CPR wants to set itself apart from.

Consequently, we propose to extend CPR research along three dimensions: first, by considering the implications of different institutional contexts on CPR. The initial research is mainly focused on the US context. Apart from studying the different arrangements and practices in different countries, this also implies to explore the conditions of a global environment as mentioned above, including situations of limited statehood (i.e., fragile or oppressive state contexts). Second, CPR research could open the black box of the company and take account of the organizational structures and procedures. As we argue, CPR, and CSR in general, should not be shouldered by the top management alone, should not be decided and implemented in a top down fashion, but needs to be conceived of as an organization-wide task to which potentially any organizational member (and stakeholders from outside the firm) can contribute. Consequently, employees (and other stakeholders) should be enabled and encouraged to participate, both in the formulation and the implementation of a corporate political agenda. Therefore, HRM is an important lever to steer CPR in an appropriate way. Third and finally, CPR research could further reflect on the concept of democratic politics in which any legitimate corporate political engagement is necessarily embedded. That would include defining the underlying conception of politics and to expose the conception of democracy in which corporate engagement with policymakers is situated (on alternative conceptions see Habermas, 1998, 2003). Whereas CPA's view on power politics is limited to "situations in which people attempt to further their interests by imposing their will on others" (Baron, 2003, p. 31), PCSR assumes a broader view related to an understanding of communicative politics as "the activity in which people organize collectively to regulate or transform some aspect of their shared social conditions, along with the communicative activities in which they try to persuade one another to join such collective action or decide what direction they wish to take it" (Young, 2004, p. 377). In the latter it is not power per se, that is, "the capacity of social actors to overcome the resistance of other actors" (Boddewyn & Brewer, 1994, p. 120), but the exchange of arguments and the willingness to revise preferences in light of those (Chambers, 2003; Habermas, 1998) that drive deliberations and determine the direction of collective decisions. The following elaborations on political HRM may be helpful in order to complement CPR research and eventually build bridges to the available research and approaches to PCSR.

8.3 Developing a Framework for Political HRM

We build on PCSR and propose a political perspective for theorizing on HRM with distinct characteristics and practices (see Table 8.1). Political HRM focuses on supporting the political engagement of the company in contributing to global governance, improving working conditions along the entire supply chain, and fostering proactive employee engagement via their political and citizenship behavior embedded in and facilitated by processes of democratic will-formation and control. This focus has far-reaching implications for the role of HRM that differ from mere instrumental or strategic HRM perspectives (for an overview of approaches to the link between CSR and HRM, see Voegtlin & Greenwood, 2016) and take account of the role of the employee as a citizen in society and politically active person

Table 8.1 *Political HRM characteristics and practices*

HRM characteristics and practices	Political HRM
Focus	Focus on how the corporation can contribute to global governance
	Focus on working conditions along the global supply chain
	Focus on employees' political and citizenship behavior
Role of HRM	Economic role amended through the proactive political role
	Contribute to global governance of working conditions
	Guarantee ethical working conditions for employees
	Enable employees to engage in CSR
Role of employee	The employee as citizen in a society (with rights and responsibilities)
	The employee as a politically active person
HRM practices:	
Selection	Create positions that promote political and social responsibility and staff them adequately
Appraisal	Honor employee traits such as creativity and the ability to exert and to accept criticism
Compensation	Reward economic, social and ecological innovations
Development	Develop political abilities, encourage economic and social entrepreneurship

with respective rights and responsibilities. MNCs can and should foster these rights and responsibilities via their HRM practices and aim to support these via the four generic HRM functions of selection, appraisal, compensation, and development (see Table 8.1).

Our framework of political HRM is depicted in Figure 8.1 and comprises four major elements: the challenges of globalization, the political role of HRM, its internal and external policy choices, and the contribution of political HRM to intra- and inter-organizational outcomes. The challenges arise from two factors: first, from the complex and heterogeneous institutional contexts in which MNCs operate around the globe; second, from the increasing sensitivity of stakeholders toward negative business externalities and awareness of the

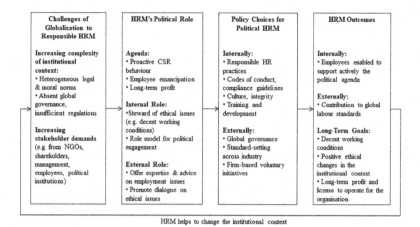

Challenges of Globalisation to Responsible HRM	HRM's Political Role	Policy Choices for Political HRM	HRM Outcomes
Increasing complexity of institutional context: • Heterogeneous legal & moral norms • Absent global governance, insufficient regulations **Increasing stakeholder demands** (e.g. from NGOs, shareholders, management, employees, political institutions)	**Agenda:** • Proactive CSR behaviour • Employee emancipation • Long-term profit **Internal Role:** • Steward of ethical issues (e.g. decent working conditions) • Role model for political engagement **External Role:** • Offer expertise & advice on employment issues • Promote dialogue on ethical issues	**Internally:** • Responsible HR practices • Codes of conduct, compliance guidelines • Culture, integrity • Training and development **Externally:** • Global governance across industry • Standard-setting • Firm-based voluntary initiatives	**Internally:** • Employees enabled to support actively the political agenda **Externally:** • Contribution to global labour standards **Long-Term Goals:** • Decent working conditions • Positive ethical changes in the institutional context • Long-term profit and license to operate for the organisation

HRM helps to change the institutional context

Figure 8.1 Framework of political human resource management.

positive contributions businesses can make to the wellbeing of people and the protection of the planet. The main challenge for HRM is to reconcile the commitment to organizational performance with the commitment to ethical business standards. The political role expands the responsibilities of HRM toward a proactive political engagement in not only establishing decent working conditions but also in shaping the institutional context in the public interest, providing public goods, and avoiding negative externalities. This political perspective is based on the insight that the political engagement of companies and its implications for HRM cannot simply rely on the benevolence of top-managers but must be embedded in and derived from processes of democratic deliberation, both within and outside the boundaries of the corporation so that the legitimacy and effectiveness of corporate policies are secured.

8.4 The Implications of Globalization and the Political Role of Business for HRM

HRM is itself a contested concept with debates around the institutions, discourses, and practices focused on the management of people within an employment relationship (Voegtlin & Greenwood, 2016). In this chapter, we focus on the generic and observable empirical practices of selection, appraisal, compensation, and development of employees usually associated with HRM as a supporting function in corporations (Batt, 2002; Paauwe, 2009; Stone, 1998). As an integral part of management, HRM is inevitably affected by the processes of globalization (Koontz & Weihrich, 2009). While globalization creates several business opportunities, it also creates tensions in areas that concern ethical issues related to employment, the deployment of the workforce and working conditions (Schoemaker, Nijhof, & Jonker, 2006; Schumann, 2001). These challenges can be summarized as the challenge of dealing with heterogeneous legal and moral norms, insufficient regulations in fragile states, the absence of universal standards on employment conditions, and an increase in (often conflicting) stakeholder demands.

Thus, HRM has to tackle the conflicting demands of ethics and efficiency; that is, the demands that result from the pressure to increase competitiveness and profitability on the one hand, and to take into account ethical considerations that relate to employment and working conditions on the other. Doing what seems ethically right or investing in CSR does not always enhance organizational performance, but may lead MNCs to redefine the profit motive and adapt it if ethical considerations make it necessary (Margolis & Walsh, 2003; Scherer & Palazzo, 2007). In global competition MNCs aim to increase profits, but at the same time need to deal with ethical issues that arise from gaps in global governance and from the heterogeneity of legal regulations, norms and values on a global scale. This affects HRM in various ways: HRM may have to resolve the question of how an MNC can guarantee a minimal living wage along its entire value chain, or to what extent it is justified to relocate work to countries where labor is less costly or regulations are lax compared to the home country. How can HRM contribute to global governance and the institutionalization of best practices that relate to global employment and other CSR issues and at the same time foster the competitiveness of the corporation? Corporations can conceive of their political role in an instrumental way – by building on their power and influence and lobbying governments to promote their economic interests – or in a more proactive political way, by shaping public policy so that the public interest is served. This may involve actively promoting human rights and global labor standards, or providing education, health services, and infrastructure to employees along the value chain of the corporation (Besley & Ghatak, 2007; Wheeler, 2005).

MNCs have to deal with competing legal frameworks of employment regulation, different institutional forces (such as the strength of labor unions), and (often only implicit) heterogeneous norms and values that underlie a company's relationship with its employees (Wheeler, 2005; Wright, Snell, & Dyer, 2005). These challenges of globalization apply to MNCs operating in developed as well as in developing countries. Even across developed countries there are considerable institutional and cultural differences (see, e.g., the results of cross-national comparative studies; Marler, 2012; Preuss, Haunschild, & Matten, 2009). Examples include the differences in union strength or employee representation in the supervisory board across developed countries, but also for instance, ethical considerations about what is considered as corruption: In Germany up until the late 1990s it was legally possible for a company to record bribes to foreign officials or representatives of foreign firms as business expenses that could actually be included as deductions in the company's tax statement (Gebhardt & Müller-Seitz, 2011).

Viewing corporations as political actors has certain implications for the role of HRM as well as for HR practices. We suggest that HRM can respond to the challenges of globalization in two ways: first, by improving working conditions and influencing the way in which the employment relationship is shaped (within and outside the corporation) (stewardship role of HRM); second, by promoting the participation of employees in CSR or CPR activities and providing the infrastructure for employee training and development to engage in CSR or CPR (enabling role of HRM). We will elaborate on these aspects in the following.

8.5 The Political Role of HRM and Its Policy Choices

8.5.1 *The Political HRM Agenda*

On the basis of the previous discussion on how HRM can help companies address the challenges of globalization we can outline a political agenda for HRM. This agenda includes (1) the effort to change the status quo and emancipate employees within the company and along the company' value chain, (2) ensuring the company's long-term survival and improving or maintaining its performance, and (3) contributing to the company's political responsibility agenda (see Figure 8.1).

On the basis of such an agenda, HRM serves as a facilitator of the company's political activities – for example, participating in global governance initiatives on human or labor rights (Fung, 2003), supporting social and environmental entrepreneurship both within the company and beyond (Ambos & Tatarinov, 2022; van Wijk et al., 2019), or channeling employee activism (Gekeler, 2019; Larcker et al., 2021). A political HRM agenda also supports companies in acting as corporate citizens, that is, in taking action in order to fill gaps in norms and regulations on the fair treatment of employees, and introducing or adjusting HR practices that enable employees to contribute to the improvement of working conditions and to become responsible citizens (Matten & Crane, 2005). For example, at Van de Velde, a Belgian textile company, the head of HR chaired the project on introducing the social responsibility reporting standard SA8000. The primary goal was to formalize (socially responsible) HRM procedures as a reaction to the internationalization of business (Preuss et al., 2009). Another example is AA Group, a French agro-food company, where top management and HR management launched a proactive CSR agenda that led to setting up "an international works council, which in the 1990s became formalized as a European works council, long before such a body became part of EU law" (Preuss et al., 2009, p. 962).

We distinguish two different functions for political HRM: first, it can be regarded as a steward of ethical issues and the long-term license to operate of the firm; second, it can be regarded as an enabler of employee' engagement in CSR and CPR. Stewardship offers "an alternative view in which organizational actors see greater long-term utility in other-focused prosocial behavior than in self-serving, short-term opportunistic behavior" (Hernandez, 2012, p. 172). In that sense, HRM functions as a custodian of ethical working conditions (Parkes & Davis, 2013) while also guaranteeing that employees fulfill their job descriptions and contribute to long-term organizational performance. Part of the enabling role is to encourage organizational members to participate actively in CSR (Mirvis, 2012) and to support the organization's engagement with global governance, the production of global public goods, or the facilitation of social and responsible innovations (see Mirvis & Googins, 2018; Scherer & Voegtlin, 2020). These two roles can be further differentiated with respect to the responsibility of HRM for the people who are directly employed by the organization

	Political HRM as steward	Political HRM as enabler
Externally (HR responsibility for non-contractual employees)	Safeguard ethical standards and the well-being of third-party employees along the supply chain	Encourage and assist corporate engagement in the global governance of working and environmental conditions
Internally (HR responsibility for contractual employees)	Safeguard ethical standards within the firm and the well-being of company employees	Encourage employee engagement in CSR

Figure 8.2 The political HRM agenda: HRM as steward and enabler.

(contractual employees), and for third-party employees the organization is held increasingly responsible for in a global business environment (non-contractual employees) (see Figure 8.2).

8.5.2 The Internal Role of Political HRM

The political agenda we propose means that HRM functions first of all as a steward of ethical behavior within the organization. HR managers can serve as positive role models for employees (Parkes & Davis, 2013), and HRM can help develop a basis of shared values by making these values explicit and by communicating them throughout the organization (Trevino et al., 1999), emphasizing transparency and dialogue as means of coping with ethical challenges and political responsibilities (Palazzo & Scherer, 2006). In that context, HRM representatives can encourage and participate in intra-organizational discourses with employees and top-management to address controversial issues.

In addition, HRM in its enabling role can provide opportunities for and encourage engagement with social entrepreneurial ventures and innovations (Jabbour & Santos, 2008). Regular dialogue with different stakeholder groups and important organizational constituencies can create the necessary room for responsible innovation (Scherer & Voegtlin, 2020; Voegtlin & Scherer, 2017). Including NGOs in decision-making can help the company focus on social and environmental innovation (Voegtlin et al., 2012). In this regard, HRM's enabling role also involves practices such as training employees, sensitizing them for political issues and providing them with the necessary autonomy for participating in the dialogue with different stakeholders.

HRM thereby shapes the CSR and CPR agenda of a corporation by either directly initiating CSR practices (e.g., initiating CSR reporting standards like the SA 8000 or corporate volunteering programs; Preuss et al., 2009) or by channeling employee concerns. Muller and colleagues (2014) argued that empathic reactions of employees toward human need are important drivers of corporate philanthropy. They emphasized the role of middle managers in translating these reactions into top management decision-making. However, we propose that HR management can play an even more central role in conveying employees' CSR and CPR concerns to top management, if it is conscious of its enabling role and facilitating a deliberative process on the political agenda of the corporation.

Further, aligning a company's HR practices to educate and encourage employees to engage in CSR activities, train them to cope with the challenges of globalization (e.g., show them how to cope with inadequate legal regulations on corruption), and promote social intra- and entrepreneurship are all means of supporting a corporation's proactive political agenda. Another way of supporting this agenda is to create internal positions that are designed to promote the social responsibility of the business firm and to use the process of personnel selection to fill these positions effectively. This may include, for instance, creating a CSR or sustainability department or emphasizing the need to tackle proactively issues of global governance when staffing the legal department or the compliance department.

Furthermore, having an HRM system that uses appraisal schemes (Chiang & Birtch, 2010) to foster traits such as creativity and the ability to exercise and accept criticism can encourage employees to engage in discourses on CSR and related political issues. This could also involve switching from a bonus system that rewards employees who achieve short-term profits to a system that rewards long-term sustainable decision-making and behavior. To support social entrepreneurial ventures, compensation could also include rewards for social and ecological innovations. The aim of such an HRM system would be to encourage employees to create wealth for the organization as well as for the society (Hitt et al., 2011). Finally, as part of that system, the company could provide opportunities for training and development to enable managers to participate in political processes and deliberations within their local environment (for instance, to negotiate for better working conditions with the suppliers or local government officials).

This may involve helping managers to develop communication skills (such as rhetorical and argumentative skills) and adopt a broader view of the interconnection of societal actors (see Table 8.1).

8.5.3 The External Role of Political HRM

Political HRM is also concerned with issues beyond the organization's borders, such as industry self-regulation, global standard-setting, and global governance (see Table 8.1). On the global level, empirical examples include the commitment to the UN Global Compact, to which over 10,000 companies are subscribed, having pledged to uphold human rights and to refrain from corruption (www.unglobalcompact.org). On the industry level there are public-private partnerships that work, for instance, on standards and product labels that help to ensure minimal wages or profits for producers (of, e.g., coffee or bananas) in developing countries (Waddock, 2008). In the apparel industry, where in the 1990s MNCs have been heavily criticized for the working conditions that many of their suppliers imposed on workers, currently several MNCs cooperate with NGOs to create "ethical" product labels. Such initiatives include Fairwear (www.fairwear.org) or the Clean Clothes Campaign (www.cleanclothes.org). In the private financial sector, Bank Track, the "global network of civil society organizations and individuals tracking the operations of the private financial sector [...] and its effect on people and the planet" (www.banktrack.org), is another example of the extent to which organizations that do not directly employ people who suffer the consequences of poor labor and employment standards are nevertheless held responsible for such injustices. This initiative monitors institutions such as banks, insurance companies, and pension funds that invest in ventures that are known to violate human rights of employees. Apart from monitoring, the voluntary disclosure of working conditions along a company's supply chain can improve transparency – an example is the GRI.

The above examples indicate the scope of a company's political HRM agenda, which is aimed at increasing employee awareness of ethical issues, helping managers to tackle human rights or labor issues (Budd & Scoville, 2005), promoting an MNC's self-regulating activities in this context and thus helping to define standards for the respective industry (Wheeler, 2005). Because political HRM means that a company assumes responsibility for the working conditions along the entire value chain, communicating with contractors, especially in developing countries, and ensuring that they comply with human rights standards and minimum labor standards (e.g., by not employing children) is essential (and an example of the "stewardship" described above). Transparency in the application of HR practices along the entire value chain of globally operating MNCs is also vital. Furthermore, a politically active HRM engages in deliberations between the company and internal or external stakeholders (employees, management, suppliers, competitors, NGOs, local governments, etc.) and encourages the company to contribute to the global governance of working conditions as well as employees to assume citizenship responsibilities for sustainable development (examples of the "enabling" role described above).

8.5.4 HR Outcomes

In the previous sections we discussed the implications of the political HRM agenda on the internal and external behavior of MNCs in relation to ethical issues. Here we would like to illustrate the political role of HRM and its outcomes with examples from business practice. The first example shows how service-learning and related HR practices could be used in the CSR education of employees. The Project Ulysses, which was set up by PricewaterhouseCoopers, is "an integrated service-learning program which involves sending participants in teams to developing countries to work in cross-sector partnerships with NGOs, social entrepreneurs, or international organizations" (Pless, Maak, & Stahl, 2011, p. 237). Pless and colleagues (2011) analyzed the impact of the program on the participants. They found evidence of important outcomes in learning areas like ethical literacy, cultural intelligence, and community building and suggest that such programs can be a "powerful experience in shaping the perspectives and capabilities of effective global leaders and sensitizing them to the wider social and ethical issues facing companies in an increasingly complex and interconnected world" (Pless et al., 2011, p. 250).

The second example highlights how globalization affects HR issues in MNCs, touching upon the tensions we have discussed, and shows how a company can foster decent working conditions while securing its license to operate. This example concerns the involvement of Levi Strauss & Co in child labor in Bangladesh (Pless & Maak, 2011). To start with, it is often difficult to judge the age of the workers, as many children born in Bangladesh are not issued with birth certificates. Another point is that working children are a vital source of income for their families, whose survival may depend on that income. Thus, when the management of Levi Strauss & Co discovered that contracting suppliers in Bangladesh employed children in their factories, it was faced with an ethical dilemma for which there was no easy solution. According to local norms and customs child labor is not unethical but, on the contrary, necessary. Moreover, if the company shifted production to regions with stricter regulations its labor costs would increase, posing the additional question of ethics versus efficiency. However, the representatives of Levi Strauss & Co thought they had to do something, especially as child labor was forbidden by the company's code of conduct. As a result, they started working together and engaged in deliberations with a range of stakeholders involved in this issue, including the suppliers, NGOs, the country's government, as well as the families of juvenile workers, in an effort to secure the company's economic interest, and at the same time find a political solution. Eventually they came up with a solution that involved abolishing child labor and at the same time enabled the children to go to school. Levi Strauss compensated the loss of income for the families while their children were in school, thus offering the children opportunities for their future and paying their families enough money to survive (Pless & Maak, 2011). This case points toward a politically proactive and imaginative way to manage human resources and to negotiate working conditions, as well as to demonstrate corporate citizenship behavior by the involved parties in providing public goods (like education) where legal regulations are insufficient.

Finally, there are examples of employee activism that was shepherded by companies. Ecosia is a German company that provides an internet search engine that has over 15 million active users (www.ecosia.org/). It subscribes to strong environmental values and invests a major part of its profit in climate action. The company recently decided to allow its employees to get involved in campaigns related to climate protection during their working hours, paying for the time employees spent in these activist activities. It even goes as far as tolerating civil disobedience as long as it is nonviolent, for instance, when supporting actions by the social movement Extinction Rebellion. The company's leadership declared that it is ready to bear all costs incurred if its employees run into legal problems. If they are arrested during an operation, the time they are held in prison is counted as working time (Gekeler, 2019).

Even if only a few have been as radical as Ecosia so far, other companies in Germany, including Naturstrom, Veganz, and the GLS Bank, have announced that they will allow their employees to participate in climate-related activities outside the firm with continued payment of their wages (Gekeler, 2019). In the United States there is also a growing number of companies that face bottom-up activism of their employees, among those Alphabet, Amazon, and WalMart (Larcker et al., 2021). We propose that political HRM can play an important role in supporting and channeling these growing political concerns by employees and relating them to the company's CPR agenda, by, for example, sensitizing employees on political debates, encouraging and training critical thinking, and facilitating deliberations on these issues both within the company and with external stakeholders.

8.6 Conclusion

With this chapter, we contribute to the emerging discussion on CPR by providing an overview of different approaches to the political responsibilities of corporations and by focusing on a key organizational function, that is, HRM. Our overview of the ethical challenges of globalization examines the macro-level effects that the changing environment in which many companies operate has on CSR, CPR, and HRM. Consequently, we proposed a framework of political HRM as a way to extend the discussion on CPR by, *first*, taking account of the broader (institutional) context of globalized business activities. We further argued that a single focus of corporate political engagement on influencing government agencies may be too limited for shaping the institutional environment in a responsible way, especially in fragile state contexts. Future research on CPR should explore the systematic links between CPR and the varieties of forms of governance, that is governance by the state, with the state, and without the state, in which MNCs engage in global business today to responsibly address issues of public concern or provide (global) public goods where state agencies are unable or unwilling to do so (see Matten & Crane, 2005; Scherer & Palazzo, 2011).

Second, CPR research can benefit from opening the black box of the corporation and studying the questions of who is and should be shaping and implementing the political agenda of corporations. There is ample evidence and growing awareness that employees, among other stakeholders, do want and can have a more active role in shaping the CPR agenda (see the examples of employee activism we referred to). Therefore, future research on CPR might want to explore the various forms in which employees (along with other stakeholders) participate in the endeavor of forming the corporate political agenda (see, e.g., Darnell & McDonnell, 2023; Scherer & Voegtlin, 2020). Our framework suggests that political HRM is an important theoretical lens that helps scrutinizing such a political role of employees.

And, *third*, by suggesting a definition of communicative politics that is rooted in the idea of deliberative democracy we propose a perspective that can help to address normative assumptions underlying CPR. Our elaborations can inform CPR research on suitable concepts of responsibility, politics, and democracy that have gained traction in PCSR literature (Scherer & Palazzo, 2007, 2011). Favotto and colleagues (2023) give a good example on how the deliberative approach to democracy can be leveraged in the context of responsible and deliberative lobbying (see Lock & Seele, 2016). They show this alongside empirical cases on corporate lobbying in the United Kingdom.

The political perspective we propose is an attempt to orientate research on CPR more generally, and HRM more specifically, to the idea that HRM can help shape the corporate political agenda by facilitating for instance MNCs' contributions to working conditions or human and labor rights and contribute to public discourses on such issues. We acknowledge that this perspective needs further refinement. This, however, will also provide avenues for future research.

The new role for HRM provides for instance opportunities for future research on antecedents, moderators, and outcomes that relate to political HRM aspects. Such research could start with the framework of political HRM we proposed, analyzing empirically the impact of the identified globalization challenges on HR practices and procedures or the influence of HR policy choices on intra- and inter-organizational outcomes. Further, it would be interesting to investigate the interaction between HRM, top management, the organizational culture, or the leadership climate in encouraging firms assuming political roles. Because HRM is part of the process of developing or reassessing corporate governance, it would also be worth exploring the impact of political HRM on the form and content of corporate governance (e.g., on whether stakeholders such as civil society groups are included; Scherer & Voegtlin, 2020). Finally, investigating the links between HRM, CSR, and CPR more closely, including the implications of the sociopolitical dimension therein merits future research (see, e.g., Mirvis & Googins, 2018; Shen & Benson, 2016; Voegtlin & Greenwood, 2016).

Another way to push the research agenda forward would be to conduct empirical research on changing conditions for HRM. This could include investigating existing or emerging global governance initiatives on working conditions, examining how firms co-develop global working standards, or to analyze cultural or national differences in HRM in relation to issues of social responsibility (Preuss et al., 2009). Further topics worth investigating include the voluntary disclosure of HRM activities (Holder-Webb et al., 2009) and the impact that joining initiatives such as the GRI has on the employment relationship and the diffusion of standards (Haack, Schoeneborn, & Wickert, 2012). Such research could be complemented with case studies of HRM practices and rhetoric within firms that have established themselves as corporate citizens. Overall, we hope that the political HRM agenda we propose here will stimulate a lively discussion that will yield new insights into this subject area and drive the search for ways of tackling the practical challenges of globalization and the political responsibilities of corporations.

Acknowledgment

The authors thank the editors for their encouragement, invaluable comments, and continuous support in this project. The Swiss National Science Foundation provided financial support for our research (project no. 10010_165699/1, "When individuals become social innovators").

References

Ambos, T. C. & Tatarinov, K. (2022). Building Responsible Innovation in International Organizations Through Intrapreneurship. *Journal of Management Studies*, 59(1), 92–125.

Anastasiadis, S. (2014). Toward a View of Citizenship and Lobbying: Corporate Engagement in the Political Process. *Business & Society*, 53(2), 260–99.

Bächtiger, A., Dryzek, J. S., Mansbridge, J. & Warren, M. E. (2018). *The Oxford Handbook of Deliberative Democracy*. Oxford: Oxford University Press.

Baron, D. P. (2003). Private Politics. *Journal of Economics and Management Strategy*, **12**, 31–66.

Batt, R. (2002). Managing Customer Services: Human Resource Practices, Quit Rates, and Sales Growth. *Academy of Management Journal*, **45**(3), 587–97.

Baysinger, B. D. (1984). Domain Maintenance as an Objective of Business Political Activity: An Expanded Typology. *Academy of Management Review*, **9**(2), 248–58.

Besley, T. & Ghatak, M. (2007). Retailing Public Goods: The Economics of Corporate Social Responsibility. *Journal of Public Economics*, **91**(9), 1645–63.

Boddewyn, J. J. & Brewer, T. L. (1994). International Business Political Behavior: New Theoretical Directions. *Academy of Management Review*, **19**, 119–43.

Bromley, P. & Powell, W. W. (2012). From Smoke and Mirrors to Walking the Talk: Decoupling in the Contemporary World. *Academy of Management Annals*, **6**(1), 483–530.

Budd, J. W. & Scoville, J. G. (2005). *The Ethics of Human Resources and Industrial Relations*. Ithaca: Cornell University Press.

Buller, P. F. & McEvoy, G. M. (1999). Creating and Sustaining Ethical Capability in the Multi-national Corporation. *Journal of World Business*, **34**(4), 326–43.

Carpenter, D. & Moss, D. A. (2013). *Preventing Regulatory Capture: Special Interest Influence and How to Limit It*. Cambridge, UK: Cambridge University Press.

Chambers, S. (2003). Deliberative Democratic Theory. *Annual Review of Political Science*, **6**(1), 307–26.

Chandler, A. D. & Mazlish, B. (2005). *Leviathans: Multinational Corporations and the New Global History*. Cambridge, UK: Cambridge University Press.

Chiang, F. F. T. & Birtch, T. A. (2010). Appraising Performance across Borders: An Empirical Examination of the Purposes and Practices of Performance Appraisal in a Multi-country Context. *Journal of Management Studies*, **47**(7), 1365–93.

Cohen, E. (2010). *CSR for HR: A Necessary Partnership for Advancing Responsible Business Practices*. Sheffield: Greenleaf.

Crane, A. (2013). Modern Slavery as a Management Practice: Exploring the Conditions and Capabilities for Human Exploitation. *Academy of Management Review*, **38**(1), 49–69.

Darnell, S. & McDonnell, M.-H. (2023). Licence to Give: The Relationship between Organizational Reputation and Stakeholders' Support for Corporate Political Activity. In T. P. Lyon, ed., *Corporate Political Responsibility*. Cambridge, UK: Cambridge University Press.

Delmas, M. A. & Friedman, H. L. (2023). Disclosure of Political Responsibility with Regard to Climate Change. In T. P. Lyon, ed., *Corporate Political Responsibility*. Cambridge, UK: Cambridge University Press.

Dryzek, J. S., Bächtiger, A. & Chambers, S., et al. (2019). The Crisis of Democracy and the Science of Deliberation. *Science*, 363(6432), 1144–6.

Edwards, T. & Kuruvilla, S. (2005). International HRM: National Business Systems, Organizational Politics and the International Division of Labour in MNCs. *International Journal of Human Resource Management*, 16(1), 1–21.

Favotto, A., Kollman, K. & McMillan, F. (2023). Responsible Lobbyists? CSR Commitments and the Quality of Parliamentary Testimony in the UK. In T. P. Lyon, ed., *Corporate Political Responsibility*. Cambridge, UK: Cambridge University Press.

Fishkin, J. S. (2018). *Democracy When the People Are Thinking: Revitalizing Our Politics through Public Deliberation*. Oxford, UK: Oxford University Press.

Fleckinger, P. & Glachant, M. (2011). Negotiating a Voluntary Agreement When Firms Self-Regulate. *Journal of Environmental Economics and Management*, 62(1), 41–52.

Freed, B., Sandstrom, K. & Laufer, W. S. (2023). Targeting Private Sector Influence in Politics: Corporate Accountability as a Risk and Governance Problem. In T. P. Lyon, ed., *Corporate Political Responsibility*. Cambridge, UK: Cambridge University Press.

Frynas, J. G., & Stephens, S. (2015). Political Corporate Social Responsibility: Reviewing Theories and Setting New Agendas. *International Journal of Management Reviews*, 17(4), 483–509.

Fund for Peace. (2019). *Fragile States Index: Annual Report 2019*. Washington, DC.

Fung, A. (2003). Deliberative Democracy and International Labor Standards. *Governance*, 16(1), 51–71.

Gebhardt, C. & Müller-Seitz, G. (2011). Phoenix Arising from the Ashes: An Event-Oriented Analysis of the Siemens' Corruption Scandal as Nexus between Organization and Society. *Managementforschung*, 21, 41–90.

Gekeler, S. (2019). Ecosia gibt Mitarbeitern frei für Klima-Aktivismus. www.humanresourcesmanager.de/news/ecosia-gibt-mitarbeitern-frei-fuer-klima-aktivismus.html, accessed December 9, 2021.

Geppert, M., Williams, K. & Matten, D. (2003). The Social Construction of Contextual Rationalities in MNCs: An Anglo-German Comparison of Subsidiary Choice. *Journal of Management Studies*, 40(3), 617–41.

Greve, H. R., Palmer, D. & Pozner, J. E. (2010). Organizations Gone Wild: The Causes, Processes, and Consequences of Organizational Misconduct. *Academy of Management Annals*, 4(1), 53–107.

Guerard, S., Bode, C. & Gustafsson, R. (2013). Turning Point Mechanisms in a Dualistic Process Model of Institutional Emergence: The Case of the Diesel Particulate Filter in Germany. *Organization Studies*, 34(5–6), 781–822.

Haack, P., Schoeneborn, D. & Wickert, C. (2012). Talking the Talk, Moral Entrapment, Creeping Commitment? Exploring Narrative Dynamics in Corporate Responsibility Standardization. *Organization Studies*, 33(5–6), 815–45.

Habermas, J. (1998). *Between Facts and Norms: Contributions to a Discourse Theory of Law and Democracy*. Cambridge, UK: Polity Press.

Habermas, J. (2003). *Truth and Justification*. Cambridge, MA: MIT Press.

Hernandez, M. (2012). Toward an Understanding of the Psychology of Stewardship. *Academy of Management Review*, 37(2), 172–93.

Hillman, A. J., Keim, G. D. & Schuler, D. (2004). Corporate Political Activity: A Review and Research Agenda. *Journal of Management*, 30(6), 837–57.

Hitt, M. A., Ireland, R. D., Sirmon, D. G. & Trahms, C. A. (2011). Strategic Entrepreneurship: Creating Value for Individuals, Organizations, and Society. *Academy of Management Perspectives*, 25(2), 57–75.

Holder-Webb, L., Cohen, J. R., Nath, L. & Wood, D. (2009). The Supply of Corporate Social Responsibility Disclosures among US Firms. *Journal of Business Ethics*, 84(4), 497–527.

Jabbour, C. J. C. & Santos, F. C. A. (2008). The Central Role of Human Resource Management in the Search for Sustainable Organizations. *International Journal of Human Resource Management*, 19(12), 2133–54.

Koontz, H. & Weihrich, H. (2009). *Essentials of Management: An International Perspective*, 8th edn. New Delhi: Tata McGraw Hill.

Larcker, D. F., Tayan, B. & Miles, S A. (2021). Protests from within: Engaging with Employee Activists. Harvard Law School Forum on Corporate Governance, https://corpgov.law.harvard.edu/2021/03/24/protests-from-within-engaging-with-employee-activists/, accessed December 9, 2021.

Lawton, T., McGuire, S. & Rajwani, T. (2013). Corporate Political Activity: A Literature Review and Research Agenda. *International Journal of Management Reviews*, 15(1), 86–105.

Lock, I. & Seele, P. (2016). Deliberative Lobbying? Toward a Noncontradiction of Corporate Political Activities and Corporate Social Responsibility? *Journal of Management Inquiry*, 25(4), 415–30.

Lock, T. P., Delmas, M. A., Maxwell, J. W. et al. (2018). CSR Needs CPR: Corporate Sustainability and Politics. *California Management Review*, 60(4), 5–24.

Lyon, T. P. & Mandelkorn, W. (2023). The Meaning and Measurement of CPR. In T. P. Lyon, ed., *Corporate Political Responsibility*. Cambridge, UK: Cambridge University Press.

Lyon, T. P. & Maxwell, J. W. (2004a). Astroturf: Interest Group Lobbying and Corporate Strategy. *Journal of Economics & Management Strategy*, 13(4), 561–97.

Lyon, T. P. & Maxwell, J. W. (2004b). *Corporate Environmentalism and Public Policy*. Cambridge: Cambridge University Press.

Maak, T. & Pless, N. (2006). Responsible Leadership in a Stakeholder Society: A Relational Perspective. *Journal of Business Ethics*, 66(1), 99–115.

Mantere, S., Pajunen, K. & Lamberg, J.-A. (2009). Vices and Virtues of Corporate Political Activity: The Challenge of International Business. *Business & Society*, 48(1), 105–32.

Margolis, J. D. & Walsh, J. P. (2003). Misery Loves Companies: Rethinking Social Initiatives by Business. *Administrative Science Quarterly*, 48(2), 268–305.

Marler, J. H. (2012). Strategic Human Resource Management in Context: A Historical and Global Perspective. *Academy of Management Perspectives*, 26(2), 6–11.

Marshall, T. H. (1965). *Class, Citizenship and Social Development*. New York: Anchor Books.

Matten, D. (2009). Review Essay: "It's the Politics, Stupid!" Reflections on the Role of Business in Contemporary Nonfiction. *Business & Society*, 48(4), 565–76.

Matten, D. & Crane, A. (2005). Corporate Citizenship: Toward an Extended Theoretical Conceptualization. *Academy of Management Review*, 30(1), 166–79.

Mirvis, P. (2012). Employee Engagement and CSR: Transactional, Relational, and Developmental Approaches. *California Management Review*, 54(4), 93–117.

Mirvis, P. & Googins, B. (2018). Engaging Employees as Social Innovators. *California Management Review*, 60(4), 25–50.

Moon, J., Crane, A. & Matten, D. (2005). Can Corporations Be Citizens? Corporate Citizenship as a Metaphor for Business Participation in Society. *Business Ethics Quarterly*, 15(3), 429–53.

Muller, A. R., Pfarrer, M. D. & Little, L. M. (2014). A Theory of Collective Empathy in Corporate Philanthropy Decisions. *Academy of Management Review*, 39(1), 1–21.

Naudé, W., Santos-Paulino, A. U. & McGillivray, M. (2011). *Fragile States: Causes, Costs, and Responses*. Oxford, UK: Oxford University Press.

Paauwe, J. (2009). HRM and Performance: Achievements, Methodological Issues and Prospects. *Journal of Management Studies*, 46(1), 129–42.

Palazzo, G. & Scherer, A. G. (2006). Corporate Legitimacy as Deliberation: A Communicative Framework. *Journal of Business Ethics*, 66(1), 71–88.

Parkes, C. & Davis, A. J. (2013). Ethics and Social Responsibility – Do HR Professionals Have the Courage to Challenge or Are They Set to Be Permanent Bystanders? *International Journal of Human Resource Management*, 24(12), 2411–34.

Pless, N. M. & Maak, T. (2011). Levi Strauss & Co. – Facing Child Labour in Bangladesh. In M. E. Mendenhall, G. Oddou and G. K. Stahl, eds., *Readings and Cases in International Human Resource Management*. London, UK: Routledge, pp. 446–57.

Pless, N. M., Maak, T. & Stahl, G. K. (2011). Developing Responsible Global Leaders through International Service-Learning Programs: The Ulysses Experience. *Academy of Management Learning & Education*, 10(2), 237–60.

Preuss, L., Haunschild, A. & Matten, D. (2009). The Rise of CSR: Implications for HRM and Employee Representation. *International Journal of Human Resource Management*, 20(4), 953–73.

Rajwani, T. & Liedong, T. A. (2015). Political Activity and Firm Performance within Nonmarket Research: A Review and International Comparative Assessment. *Journal of World Business*, 50(2), 273–83.

Rasche, A. (2015). The Corporation as a Political Actor–European and North American Perspectives. *European Management Journal*, 33(1), 4–8.

Scherer, A. G. (2018). Theory Assessment and Agenda Setting in Political CSR: A Critical Theory Perspective. *International Journal of Management Reviews*, 20(2), 387–410.

Scherer, A. G., Baumann-Pauly, D. & Schneider, A. (2013). Democratizing Corporate Governance: Compensating for the Democratic Deficit of Corporate Political Activity and Corporate Citizenship. *Business & Society*, 52(3), 473–514.

Scherer, A. G. & Palazzo, G. (2007). Toward a Political Conception of Corporate Social Responsibility: Business and Society Seen from a Habermasian Perspective. *Academy of Management Review*, 32(4), 1096–120.

Scherer, A. G. & Palazzo, G. (2008). Globalization and Corporate Social Responsibility. In A. Crane, A. McWilliams, D. Matten, J. Moon & D. S. Siegel, eds., *The Oxford Handbook of Corporate Social Responsibility*. Oxford, UK: Oxford University Press, pp. 413–31.

Scherer, A. G. & Palazzo, G. (2011). The New Political Role of Business in a Globalized World: A Review of a New Perspective on CSR and Its Implications for the Firm, Governance, and Democracy. *Journal of Management Studies*, 48(4), 899–931.

Scherer, A. G., Rasche, A., Palazzo, G. & Spicer, A. (2016). Managing for Political Corporate Social Responsibility: New Challenges and Directions for PCSR 2.0. *Journal of Management Studies*, 53(3), 273–98.

Scherer, A. G. & Voegtlin, C. (2020). Corporate Governance for Responsible Innovation: Approaches to Corporate Governance and Their Implications for Sustainable Development. *Academy of Management Perspectives*, **34**(2), 182–208.

Schoemaker, M., Nijhof, A. & Jonker, J. (2006). Human Value Management. The Influence of the Contemporary Developments of Corporate Social Responsibility and Social Capital on HRM. *Management Revue*, **17**(4), 448–65.

Schrage, S. & Gilbert, D. U. (2021). Addressing Governance Gaps in Global Value Chains: Introducing a Systematic Typology. *Journal of Business Ethics*, **170**, 657–72.

Schrempf-Stirling, J. & Wettstein, F. (2017). Beyond Guilty Verdicts: Human Rights Litigation and Its Impact on Corporations' Human Rights Policies. *Journal of Business Ethics*, **145**(3), 545–62.

Schumann, P. L. (2001). A Moral Principles Framework for Human Resource Management Ethics. *Human Resource Management Review*, **11**(1/2), 93.

Shen, J. & Benson, J. (2016). When CSR Is a Social Norm: How Socially Responsible Human Resource Management Affects Employee Work Behavior. *Journal of Management*, **42**(6),1723–46.

Steinmann, H. & Löhr, A. (1994). *Principles of Business Ethics [Grundlagen Der Unternehmensethik]*, 2nd edn. Stuttgart: Schaeffer-Poeschel.

Stigler, G. J. (1971). The Theory of Economic Regulation. *The Bell Journal of Economics and Management Science*, **2**(1), 3–21.

Stone, R. J. (1998). *Human Resource Management*. Brisbane: Wiley and Sons.

Thompson, G. F. (2008). The Interrelationship between Global and Corporate Governance: Towards a Democratization of the Business Firm? In A. G. Scherer & G. Palazzo, eds., *Handbook of Research on Global Corporate Citizenship*. Cheltenham, UK: Edward Elgar, pp. 476–500.

Trevino, L. K. & Weaver, G. R. (1994). Business ETHICS/BUSINESS Ethics: ONE FIELD OR TWO? *Business Ethics Quarterly*, **4**(2), 113–28.

Trevino, L. K., Weaver, G. R., Gibson, D. G. & Toffler, B. L. (1999). Managing Ethics and Legal Compliance: What Works and What Hurts. *California Management Review*, **41**(2), 131–51.

UNCTAD. (2019). *World Investment Report 2019: Special Economic Zones*. Geneva: United Nations.

van Wijk, J., Zietsma, C., Dorado, S., de Bakker, F. G. A. & Martí, I. (2019). Social Innovation: Integrating Micro, Meso, and Macro Level Insights from Institutional Theory. *Business & Society*, **58**(5), 887–918.

Voegtlin, C. & Greenwood, M. (2016). Corporate Social Responsibility and Human Resource Management: A Systematic Review and Conceptual Analysis. *Human Resource Management Review*, **26**(3), 181–97.

Voegtlin, C., Patzer, M. & Scherer, A. G. (2012). Responsible Leadership in Global Business: A New Approach to Leadership and Its Multi-Level Outcomes. *Journal of Business Ethics*, 105(1), 1–16.

Voegtlin, C. & Scherer, A. G. (2017). Responsible Innovation and the Innovation of Responsibility: Governing Sustainable Development in a Globalized World. *Journal of Business Ethics*, 143(2), 227–43.

Vogel, D. (2008). Private Global Business Regulation. *Annual Review of Political Science*, 11(1), 261–82.

Waddock, S. (2008). Building a New Institutional Infrastructure for Corporate Responsibility. *Academy of Management Perspectives*, 22(3), 87–108.

Wheeler, H. N. (2005). Globalization and Business Ethics in Employment Relations. In J. W. Budd & J. G. Scoville, eds., *The Ethics of Human Resources and Industrial Relations*. Champaign, IL: Labor and Employment Relations Association, pp. 115–40.

Wijen, F. (2014). Means versus Ends in Opaque Institutional Fields: Trading Off Compliance and Achievement in Sustainability Standard Adoption. *Academy of Management Review*, 39(3), 302–23.

World Trade Organization. (2019). *World Trade Statistical Review 2019*. Geneva: WTO.

Wright, P. M., Snell, S. A. & Dyer, L. (2005). New Models of Strategic HRM in a Global Context. *International Journal of Human Resource Management*, 16(6), 875–81.

Young, I. M. (2004). Responsibility and Global Labor Justice. *Journal of Political Philosophy*, 12(4), 365–88.

Responsibility: Corporate Political Responsibility and Climate

9 | Measuring Climate Policy Alignment
A Study of the Standard and Poor's 100

YAMIKA KETU AND STEVEN ROTHSTEIN

9.1 Introduction

Climate change demands robust public policy action if the hope to mitigate climate risks and manage the transition to a net zero emissions economy is to materialize. The latest climate science highlights that limiting global temperature rise to 1.5°C is necessary to avoid the most catastrophic outcomes, including climate-driven drought, floods, extreme heat, and poverty for millions of people (IPCC, 2021). Doing so will require bold global action to reduce greenhouse gas (GHG) emissions by nearly half by 2030 and to reach net zero GHG emissions by 2050. But as of 2021, global GHG emissions are not on track to meet the established deadlines. Current policies are estimated to keep the world on a path of 2.7°C warming; factoring in updated Nationally Determined Contributions (NDCs), net-zero commitments, and long-term targets brings warming down to 2.1°C, but it is still far from the aspirational goal of 1.5°C (Climate Action Tracker, 2021). Climate policy must align with climate science to effectively address the systemic nature of the climate crisis.

Corporate America is uniquely positioned to support efforts to address climate risks at a systemic level, and to assist with the creation of a stable policy environment enabling a shift to a clean energy economy. U.S. companies do not just power the country's economy, they also wield enormous influence both in the United States and globally, and are critical messengers on climate policy. Companies that align their lobbying efforts to support science-based climate policies are supporting the creation of a regulatory environment that best positions them for resilient growth. Lack of policy leadership on climate change from prominent businesses contributes to a fractured and uncertain regulatory environment that is costly to the economy and corporate bottom lines.

The policy engagement landscape, however, has shifted significantly since the Supreme Court's 2010 *Citizens United* ruling. Whereas

247

corporate money was once kept out of political elections, *Citizens United* has created an opaqueness around corporate political contributions, as explained by Lyon and Mandelkorn in Chapter 3 of this volume. Not only does this have negative implications for the democratic process, as average citizens are unable to match the outsized influence from corporations on issues like climate change, it also has detrimental impacts on business activity. Emerging research suggests that companies caught up in the political rent-seeking process are unable to focus their attention on the value creation and innovation side of the business. The consequences around this phenomenon are substantial in regard to fighting the climate crisis; companies that are distracted by lobbying against climate regulations are unable to capture the opportunities that a green economy would provide their business and are instead making themselves more vulnerable to financial and material risks (Lund and Strine, 2022). Furthermore, it is not uncommon for companies to be misaligned between their policy engagement and ESG policies, which is largely what this chapter intends to dissect.

The chapter will first discuss the recent history of corporate engagement on climate policy, how it has evolved to shape the current corporate landscape, and what actions companies are taking either in support of, or against, climate policy as evidenced by the findings in Ceres' Blueprint for Responsible Policy Engagement (RPE) Benchmark.[1] The second section will provide background on the Ceres' RPE Benchmark, summarizing the methodology and engagement process with the benchmarked companies, as well as the deployment strategy to alter corporate behavior. Finally, the third section explores whether meaningful changes in corporate lobbying on climate can be attributed to these efforts, and the future implications for effective engagement on this topic within an evolving policy environment.

9.2 Corporate Alignment on Climate Policy

Despite growing evidence that inaction on climate change will damage the economy and corporate bottom lines, corporate lobbying for science-based climate policies has historically been weak

---

[1] This reflects the data from the 2021 Ceres Responsible Policy Engagement report. Some of the company-specific comments would be different in the 2022 Responsible Policy Engagement. www.ceres.org/accelerator/responsible-policy-engagement.

(Flavelle, 2021). Even as more large U.S. companies are taking steps to address climate change in their own operations, including setting emissions reduction goals, their advocacy for climate change policies often does not match the ambition of their individual commitments, and even more often fails to match the ambition demanded by climate science. Additionally, in some instances, companies and their trade associations are lobbying directly and strenuously against the adoption of meaningful climate policies – undermining the very conditions that would enable companies to meet their climate goals.

The spectrum of corporate engagement on climate lobbying is broad, ranging from companies that have aligned their climate lobbying and targets, to companies that are unaware or refuse to take responsibility for their part in the climate crisis and actively lobby against climate policy. Companies also play both sides; they lead institutionally on climate but are misaligned in their lobbying efforts, advocating against climate policy either directly or indirectly through their trade associations. This phenomenon is further elucidated by the InfluenceMap graphics on pages 78 and 91 in Chapter 3 of this volume (Lyon and Mandelkorn, 2023).

Primary examples of companies along this spectrum include Apple, ExxonMobil, and General Motors. Apple, on the aligned end of climate lobbying, has stated its goal of becoming carbon neutral by 2030, and it plans to cut its emissions by 75 percent from 2015 levels to do so. While Apple has not conducted a comprehensive audit of its trade associations, it relinquished its membership of the Chamber of Commerce in 2009 due to the Chamber's position on climate. Apple specifically stated that a key reason for its departure was the Chamber's opposition to the Environmental Protection Agency's effort to limit GHG emissions, which Apple supported (Schwartz, 2009). General Motors falls somewhere in the middle. It has publicly supported the Paris Agreement and has voiced support for science-based climate targets, but it is still a member of the Chamber of Commerce as well as the Alliance of Automobile Manufacturers – two organizations that have unfavorable records on climate lobbying (Ceres, 2021a).

ExxonMobil's robust and effective campaign against climate policy has taken many forms over the decades but is consistent with its historical lack of operational leadership on climate, regardless of the sustainability claims made on its website (ExxonMobil, 2021; Grasso, 2019). A viral exposé from 2021 caught an ExxonMobil lobbyist openly admitting to undermining federal climate policy and joining organizations that would help the company do so (Brady, 2021). For example, the company donated $1 million in 2018 to the Americans for Carbon Dividends campaign, which advocated for a carbon tax. This is seemingly progressive on climate, and hence in conflict with the climate position of the fossil fuel giant, but hidden among its objectives was the elimination of a company's legal liability for climate change and the revocation of GHG emission standards under the Clean Power Plan (InfluenceMap, 2019).

9.2.1 Trade Associations

Trade associations provide helpful resources and networking opportunities to their company members on public policy engagement, with the goal of collectively representing the positions of their members on key issues. In the United States alone, there are roughly 23,000 trade associations with a combined annual revenue of roughly $46 billion, representing a broad array of companies and business interests. Climate change has long been an area of focus for trade associations. Renewable energy trade groups, such as the American Wind Energy Association (AWEA) and the Solar Energy Industries Association (SEIA), have played an important role in advocating for policies aligned with climate science.

Nevertheless, some of the largest and most influential trade associations in the United States have played an obstructionist role on climate policy. In 2019, the UK-based nonprofit Influence Map reported that some large U.S. trade associations were among the most negative influences on climate policy around the world, as illustrated in Lyon and Mandelkorn's chapter in this volume. The two most powerful trade associations advocating against climate policy, according to their report, were the U.S. Chamber of Commerce and the National Association of Manufacturers, both of which lobbied for the United States to withdraw from the Paris Agreement. Powerful sector groups such as the American Petroleum Institute, the American Fuel & Petrochemical Manufacturers, and the Alliance of Automobile Manufacturers were also identified as aggressive actors in opposing climate policy progress, winning regulatory rollbacks on methane emissions and automotive fuel economy standards in 2018 and 2019. These rollbacks were expected to result in the release of more than 200 million metric tons of additional GHG emissions each year, putting the United States on a path to increase average global temperature by 4° C (InfluenceMap, 2019).

9.2.2 Ceres' BICEP Network

Although the history of corporate climate lobbying is largely one of antagonism to climate policies, there have been notable exceptions. More than a decade ago, Ceres embarked on an effort to understand and foster the conditions under which constructive corporate engagement on climate policy is possible. The result was the founding of the Ceres Business for Innovative Climate and Energy Policy (BICEP) Network in 2009. The Ceres BICEP Network, made up exclusively of consumer-facing energy users (versus providers), provided member companies a community of like-minded peers and offered opportunities to stand out as leaders in driving positive change.

Since its founding, Ceres BICEP Network members have advocated for federal policies to advance renewable energy and fuel efficiency standards, implement sustainable transportation policies, invest in clean power sources, and achieve the goals of the Paris Agreement. At the state level, Ceres' BICEP Network members have played a critical role in passing some of the most ambitious climate laws in the country. The group has been a respected and credible voice across the political spectrum – contributing to key bipartisan climate victories in states across the country (Ceres, 2021b).

9.2.3 Direction of Corporate Engagement and Climate Policy

In recent years, expectations on whether – and how – companies should engage on climate change have evolved. Companies and investors now largely understand that climate change poses material financial risks to companies and industries across the economy. Climate change is now widely recognized as posing a systemic threat to financial markets as a whole, with significant potential for disruptive impacts on overall economic stability and the lives and livelihoods of tens of millions of people across the United States and globally (CFTC, 2020).

Despite the growing evidence that climate inaction represents a systemic threat to corporations, many influential companies have continued to lobby against climate policy measures, both directly and indirectly through their trade associations. The RPE Benchmark was conceived as a way to highlight this inconsistency, and to drive better alignment between climate science, corporate action, and corporate advocacy. Separate from the Ceres BICEP Network, which achieves constructive policy engagement through collective business advocacy, lawmaker education, and corporate leadership, the RPE Benchmark was aimed at benchmarking a representative set of large U.S. companies to identify laggards and create pressure for them to improve.

9.3 Identifying Best Practices: The Blueprint

The Blueprint for Responsible Policy Engagement on Climate Change (the Blueprint) was conceived as a mechanism for highlighting the risks inherent in misalignments between climate science, corporate actions, and corporate lobbying. In the Blueprint, climate science was defined as the recognition that, to avoid the worst impacts of climate change, businesses need to do their part to limit global average temperature rise to 1.5°C above pre-industrial levels. Corporate actions included statements supporting the Paris Climate Agreement and the adoption of Science-Based Targets.[2] Corporate lobbying encompassed both direct lobbying, either individually or through coalitions, and indirect lobbying through trade associations.

Through a literature review, company surveys, and interviews, the Blueprint authors identified best practice recommendations and examples in three areas – Assess, Govern, and Act – and they published them as a resource for both companies and investors pursuing greater alignment. This guidance is included below, along with the rationale behind key recommendations.

Assess – Given the systemic nature of climate change, companies should analyze the nature of its impacts on their business and devise strategies for mitigation and adaptation. Once a company understands the nature of its climate risk exposure, it should also assess the extent to which both its direct and indirect lobbying serve to address or exacerbate these risks.

---

[2] Science-Based Targets are as defined by the Science Based Targets Initiative (SBTi), which vets emissions reduction commitments to ensure they are aligned with commonly accepted standards such as net-zero company emissions by 2050 or sooner.

As a first step, companies should assess the scope and nature of their climate risk exposure by integrating climate change into the enterprise risk management (ERM) process. When conducting these assessments, a company should factor in the latest climate science, including projections on how the physical and transition risks from climate change could affect its operations, its value chain, the constituencies it engages, and its license to operate. The policy and regulatory environment within which a company operates is also a critical factor to consider as a part of these assessments, including assessments of how that landscape is likely to change in coming years as an increasing number of jurisdictions take climate action.

Companies should also consider their contribution to climate change. Given the systemic nature of the climate crisis, it is not possible to hedge against or externalize its risks and impacts. In 2018, the World Business Council of Sustainable Development (WBCSD) and the Committee of Sponsoring Organizations of the Treadway (COSO) released guidance on how to integrate environmental, social, and governance (ESG) risks within the traditional ERM process. The guidance explains how to reduce risk exposure by integrating climate and sustainability risks within corporate strategy deliberations, including how policies regulating ESG issues can be examined within a company's risk exposure assessment.

For the vast majority of companies, the nature of the risk posed by climate change is so significant that it rises to the level of being considered "material." The Sustainability Accounting Standards Board (SASB) considers climate risk to materially impact seventy-two out of seventy-nine industry sectors. When climate is identified as a material issue, it needs to be disclosed in the company's financial filings. In 2010, the U.S. Securities and Exchange Commission (SEC) issued interpretive guidance for public companies on existing SEC disclosure requirements as they apply to business or legal developments relating to the issue of climate change.

Many investors look for companies to provide details about the specific risks posed to them by climate change. These investors focus on what is material to the company within the context of emerging trends, ask for decision-useful quantitative and qualitative information, and want companies to disclose these risks in commonly available sources such as 10-Ks, proxy statements, annual reports, and investor relations websites.

> Example: Coca-Cola identified climate change as a material risk in
> its 10-K in 2021,[3] stating that climate risks posed potential long-
> term adverse impacts on its operations. The company cited scientific
> evidence that increased temperatures caused by GHG emissions
> would result in decreased global agricultural productivity and would
> exacerbate water scarcity and extreme weather, all of which could
> cause the company to experience supply chain disruptions.

Some 90 percent of the 2,400 North American companies reporting to the Carbon Disclosure Program (CDP) climate questionnaire
in 2019 (72 percent of the S&P 500) stated that they had integrated
climate-related issues within their business strategy. However, only
23 percent of the S&P 500 discussed ESG issues, including climate
change, in their 10-Ks. This suggests that the issue is still not regarded
as material, let alone systemic, by most companies.

The next step for companies would be to conduct an internal audit
of direct and indirect lobbying positions on climate change. Once a
company understands the nature of its climate risk exposure, including the consequences it faces from climate change as a systemic risk,
it should assess the extent to which its direct lobbying and indirect
lobbying serve to address or exacerbate these risks. Such audits should
cover both direct lobbying and indirect lobbying conducted on a company's behalf by the trade associations to which it belongs.

Indirect lobbying via trade associations is an area of particular concern due to a lack of transparency. Many companies do not publish
comprehensive lists of their trade association memberships, and many
trade associations themselves do not disclose their member lists or
their climate policy positions and lobbying efforts. Internal audits on
science-based climate policy alignment can help surface when companies may be "spending against themselves" and "spending against
climate mitigation." Climate lobbying audits can also allow companies to hold trade associations accountable for representing their best
interests.

It is important for companies to conduct such internal audits regularly, whether annually or otherwise, as the scope and context on what
is being assessed (climate policies, climate science, membership in
trade associations) evolve continuously. The results should be shared

---

[3] Source: Coca-Cola's 2021 10-K filing.

with the board of directors to allow proper oversight, and companies should identify steps and timelines to address any misalignments that may be identified through these audits.

Finally, companies should publicly disclose both the results of the audit and any planned steps to address policy misalignment. Such disclosure will demonstrate to investors and other stakeholders that companies recognize the risks associated with misaligned climate lobbying and are looking to assess and mitigate such exposure. It also makes clear to policymakers that the trade association positions do not necessarily represent that particular company, helping reduce confusion and perceived opposition to climate action.

> Example: Shell conducted an audit of its largest trade groups and disclosed the results, including noting where its position on climate change is misaligned from its associations and the actions taken. Other organizations that have conducted such internal audits and disclosed the results include BP and Total SA.

Govern – Once companies have assessed their exposure to the systemic risk from climate change, including through their direct and indirect lobbying, they need to engage relevant internal stakeholders across the enterprise on this risk, including those in legal, government affairs, risk, and sustainability departments. The board of directors should be kept informed and oversee the company's public policy efforts on climate change.

Systematizing decision-making on climate policy engagement is a crucial governance practice. Internal audits for science-based climate policy help companies identify their risks from lobbying that may be misaligned with climate science. Companies should supplement these audits by also establishing clear systems to drive forward-looking decisions on public policy engagement on climate change.

A cross-organizational group that includes government affairs, the chief legal counsel, the financial or risk management teams, and the sustainability team will be best positioned to discuss the company's position on the evolving regulatory and policy landscape on climate change and ensure that the company's position is aligned with climate science. This cross-functional group should bring relevant and important perspectives to the deliberations about how the company is involved with trade associations that may be engaging in climate policy. Chief Legal Officers (CLOs) have an especially important role to play, given their roles overseeing the company's disclosures, tracking risk exposures, and acting as key advisors to the C-suite and board of directors.

> Example: Adobe's Executive Vice President and General Counsel is the lead for government affairs and public policy, including sustainability policy and environmental and renewable energy policy advocacy. This role includes oversight of the company's climate-related issues, risks, and opportunities and approval of its policies, strategies, and financial disclosures.

Such a cross-functional team becomes particularly important when decisions on climate lobbying alignment are complicated by competing organizational priorities, such as when membership in a trade association provides other important benefits to the enterprise. A cross-organizational team involving government affairs, legal, risk, and the sustainability functions would bring insight into the range of issues and priorities the company grapples with and would be able to assist in breaking down silos to engage relevant internal and external stakeholders in making decisions. Such teams and systems can ensure a company's lobbyists are well versed on its latest climate priorities, that they regularly raise climate issues in their interactions, that they track climate-related legislation and decisions to ensure they are science-based, and that they are aware of policy misalignment.

> Example: Allstate's Sustainability Council, which reviews operational efficiency, climate change, and employee-focused sustainability initiatives, consists of representatives from key functions across the enterprise, including Law & Regulation, Government Affairs, Real Estate & Administration, Investments, Products, Supply Chain, and Risk Management. The council studies company policies and practices and their impact on the environment, reviews the policies and engagements of the trade organizations Allstate engages with, and evaluates issues related to climate change to ensure consistency with the company's overall climate change strategy. Should inconsistencies arise, the Sustainability Council addresses them with Allstate's Government Affairs division, housed within the company's Law & Regulation department, which owns Allstate's advocacy relationships.

Another essential step regarding governance is engaging the board. Given the systemic nature of the climate crisis and the growing investor understanding that this issue is material to most companies, boards should oversee climate change as a part of their oversight of corporate risk, strategy, and resiliency performance. Lobbying on climate change should also be regularly evaluated by the board, considering that a company's direct and indirect lobbying on climate change will either increase those risk factors or be risk mitigation factors. Further guidance on board governance and political spending can be found within the CPA-Wharton Zicklin Model Code of Conduct in Chapter 2 (Freed, Laufer and Sandstrom, 2023).

Corporate boards with an explicit mandate to oversee both climate change and public policy are best positioned to consider these issues and the overlap between them regularly and robustly. Where these responsibilities are in separate committees, the committees should work together to allow for the necessary integrated deliberations.

Example: Citigroup Inc.'s Nomination, Governance and Public Affairs Committee oversees the company's public and government policy efforts, as well as its memberships in trade associations that engage in lobbying activities or make independent expenditures. The committee is also responsible for overseeing Citi's sustainability policies and programs, including on the environment, climate change, and human rights. This committee's oversight of public policy efforts, trade association memberships, and climate change enables the board to have informed deliberations on how to conduct responsible climate lobbying in ways that can best address climate risk.

Some 89 percent of the 2,400 North American companies reporting to the CDP climate questionnaire in 2019 stated that their board oversees climate-related issues. However, the extent to which this oversight extends to public policy is not clear. To support boards, management should provide regular updates on the company's climate risk exposure, as well as on its opportunities to mitigate this exposure by engaging in public policy. Where the company has established a cross-functional group to systematize organizational decision-making on climate policy, this group should also regularly brief the board, including on the risks of staying silent or inactive if the company's direct or indirect lobbying on climate policy is misaligned with climate science. When a company has conducted internal audits assessing the alignment of lobbying efforts with climate science and identifying planned climate action and accountability, these audits should be discussed with the board.

Ceres' report *Running the Risk: How Corporate Boards Can Oversee Environmental, Social and Governance Risks* (Ceres, 2019) details how ESG risks, including climate change, fit within the risk oversight mandate of corporate boards. The report includes detailed recommendations on how boards can oversee risks posed by sustainability issues, including questions for directors to ask management throughout the risk identification, assessment, and mitigation processes.

Act – After the company has engaged internal stakeholders on science-based climate policy, it should take the necessary action to consistently demonstrate this alignment through its direct and indirect lobbying on climate change. Direct lobbying includes actions taken both individually and through coalitions, while indirect lobbying refers to actions taken by trade associations of which the company is a member.

One simple action a company can take is to publicly state that it supports science-based climate policies. As a fundamental step, companies need to unequivocally state their position that climate change is caused by human activity that has led to increases in GHG emissions and global average temperature. Companies should then affirm their understanding that the scientific consensus has shifted to 1.5°C as the ceiling for global average temperature increases, if we are to avoid climate change's worst impacts. These positions should be consistently expressed across all company statements on climate to protect the company from risks associated with having misaligned statements on climate on different platforms.

Example: Mars' "Climate Action Position Statement" affirms that humanity's GHG emissions have changed the climate and acknowledges that the world must contain global temperature increase to no more than 1.5°C to avoid the worst climate-related impacts. Further, the company outlines its assessment of its value chain GHG emissions and discloses targets to decrease emissions 27 percent by 2025 and 67 percent (from 2015 levels) by 2050 to stay within its "share" of the global carbon budget. The company is also an active member of the Sustainable Food Policy Alliance (SFPA) and has promoted the importance of worldwide wind power by launching a global advertising campaign.

An additional way for companies to act is by directly lobbying for science-based climate policies. This represents an important opportunity for companies to mitigate the climate risks they face in their broader operating environment. Companies can play a role in shaping public policy in the United States by openly supporting legislative and regulatory efforts in line with the latest climate science. The project team identified a number of science-based public policy proposals, at both the federal and state levels, that companies could consider supporting.

> Example: Microsoft has shown strong support for state, federal, and global policy efforts to spur clean energy generation and establish an economy-wide carbon tax. In its 2019 CDP report, Microsoft disclosed several examples of how it has actively engaged on climate policy, including forming the Advanced Energy Buyers Group to advocate for policies that provide more renewable and zero-carbon purchasing options. In 2018, the company also advocated for carbon tax legislation in Washington State through issuing statements from their President and Chief Legal Officer, providing Senate testimony, and making a formal endorsement during the Senate committee proceedings (Meyer, 2018).

It is important that companies also actively lobby against policies misaligned with climate science. For example, companies can state that they do not support the weakening of standards that help reduce U.S. GHG emissions.

> Example: In response to the Trump administration's proposal to weaken fuel economy and vehicle emissions standards, Ford, BMW, Honda, and Volkswagen, later joined by Volvo, effectively rejected the weakened standards and joined a compromise agreement with California. In a joint statement produced by the four automakers, they noted that "these terms will provide our companies much-needed regulatory certainty by allowing us to meet both federal and state requirements with a single national fleet, avoiding a patchwork of regulations while continuing to ensure meaningful GHG emission reductions." In contrast, GM, Toyota, Fiat Chrysler, and others intervened in litigation defending the Trump administration's revocation of state authority and its rollback of the standards.

In addition to lobbying for science-based climate policies in general, companies should also disclose their specific positions on key proposals and publicly share how they communicate these positions with policymakers, shareholders, and stakeholders. Disclosing details about the methods and goals of these engagements will allow a company to showcase the seriousness, breadth, and depth of its climate policy commitments. Whether their engagement includes active lobbying with state or federal legislators, direct political expenditures, offering testimony on the importance of climate policy, or participating in sign-on letters for strong science-based climate policies, companies need to be transparent about how they mitigate climate risks by advocating for such policies.

Lobbying for science-based climate policies can be done individually and through coalitions. Ceres' BICEP Network, as mentioned previously in the chapter, brings together more than seventy-five companies to advocate for strong climate and clean energy policies that will accelerate the transition to a net-zero emissions economy. Ceres' 2021 Policy Outlook highlights possible corporate engagement opportunities for businesses to help advance policies that create a net-zero emissions economy. These opportunities include calling for better corporate access to renewable energy; stronger state renewable portfolio standards and energy efficiency resource standards; the transformation of the clean transportation sector; and the overall growth of a clean energy economy. Similarly, America Is All is a coalition of businesses, cities, states, and other entities committed to realizing the goals of the Paris Agreement through societal mobilization, alongside federal climate action (Bloomberg Philanthropies, 2022).

A third method of action by corporations is engaging with trade associations to align their lobbying with climate science. Once a company has established that its commitment to science-based climate policies is a key element of its risk reduction efforts and has aligned its direct lobbying, it needs to take steps to align its indirect lobbying, conducted via trade associations, with this climate science. In the "Assess" section of Blueprint, we identify a process for companies to internally audit their direct and indirect lobbying efforts to ensure alignment with science-based climate policies and the goals of the Paris Agreement. When misalignments are identified, companies need to take corrective action with their trade associations.

As a first step, companies should engage their trade associations to fully understand their positions on climate change beyond what is publicly disclosed. Many trade associations do not provide easily accessible disclosure of their positions on key issues like climate change, nor on their efforts to influence regulatory and legislative proposals. Companies should encourage their trade associations to be more transparent in this regard, and they can do so either independently or collectively with other members of the association. If a company finds that it is a member of a trade association that is not aligned with science-based climate policy efforts, it should, at a minimum, publicly disclose this information. The company should also then provide a rationale as to why it remains a member of the association in question and outline its plans to engage the trade association on identified misalignment.

Example: PepsiCo disclosed that its climate goals and policy advocacy efforts are consistent with the goals of the Paris Agreement and has asked its trade associations to adopt a similar stance when engaging on climate policy. The company also annually reports on its trade association memberships and how each of its trade associations lobbies or holds positions on climate policy. PepsiCo updated its 2018 Political Activities, Political Contributions & Issue Advocacy policy with a section on lobbying practices related to climate change, specifically stating the company does not share the U.S. Chamber of Commerce's views on climate policy, including their lobbying efforts against legislation aimed at reducing GHG emissions.

Building on this approach, companies should look for opportunities to help trade associations evolve positions on science-based climate policies. Such engagement could take place either individually or through coalitions and could include a request for an association to put lobbying and making political contributions on particular issues on hold if there are unresolved misalignments between members and the association or members themselves.

Example: Unilever's CEO Alan Jope sent an open letter to its trade associations and business groups asking them to confirm that their current lobbying positions on climate policy are consistent with Unilever's positions, the 1.5°C goal, and the general Paris Agreement goals. Unilever also states that it supports the United Nations Global Compact's (UNGC) Guide to Responsible Engagement on Climate Policy, which calls for companies and their trade associations to ensure their lobbying aligns with their public positions on climate change.

Companies can also take steps to disclose disagreements with trade associations' stances on climate change through their Political Engagement Reports, which is discussed in more detail in Chapter 3 of this volume (Lyon and Mandelkorn, 2023).

Example: UPS disclosed that it does not support the U.S. Chamber of Commerce's opposition to the regulation of GHG emissions under existing laws, including the Clean Air Act. As a form of engagement, UPS management met with the Chamber's leadership to explain the company's position on climate and the steps it has taken to reduce its carbon footprint. UPS also joined the Chamber's energy and environment committee to assert its positions on climate as legislative opportunities arise. UPS then urged the Chamber to support a rule requiring government vendors to disclose whether they publish their GHG emissions. The Chamber agreed not to oppose the rule because of UPS's communication with the association, despite being urged by other members to oppose it.

If engaging with misaligned trade associations is unproductive, companies can consider leaving these associations. Companies should develop criteria to determine what degree of misalignment and what amount or timeline of unproductive engagement will cause them to leave. Companies also need to commit to disclosing these criteria and any decisions that result in their direct and indirect climate lobbying audits so that stakeholders can understand the particulars of such criteria and be informed of the decisions.

Example: Apple left the U.S. Chamber of Commerce in 2009 along with PG&E, PNM Resources, and several other companies. Each company stated that its reason for leaving centered around climate change policy differences with the Chamber. In 2018, Danone, Mars, Nestlé, and Unilever cited differences over climate policy as a key reason for leaving the Grocery Manufacturers Association to form the Sustainable Food Policy Alliance. The Chairman and CEO of Nestlé, Paul Grimwood, categorized this move as one toward greater transparency on the issues their consumers care about, including climate change.

Comprehensive and urgent corporate action on climate change is vital if we are to achieve a stable climate and mitigate the devastating impacts of average global temperature increase. But we cannot tackle climate change without strong, science-based climate policies. In today's deeply interconnected society, companies and their shareholders understand it is not just the actions of a company on climate policy that matter – it's also the climate actions undertaken on behalf of companies by their trade associations. Companies need to holistically and proactively assess all elements of their direct and indirect lobbying on climate policies to ensure they are acting in alignment with both climate science and with their own climate targets.

For each of the three types of alignment (Assess, Govern, Act), the Blueprint recommended specific frameworks and tools. These included climate scenario analysis for risk assessment, an internal audit of direct and indirect lobbying positions, the implementation of key board oversight mechanisms, and a set of engagement options for addressing misalignment issues with trade associations. The resulting publication, the Blueprint for *Responsible Policy Engagement on Climate Change* (Ceres, 2020), contains a greater level of detail and specificity than covered in this chapter.

9.4 The Private RPE Benchmark

As a part of the research and preparation for the Blueprint, the initial benchmarking was not made public. Instead, it was used as a tool for engagement with the companies it analyzed. This allowed the project team to confirm its methodology in the face of critical feedback, include any data that might have been overlooked, and, most importantly, give companies the opportunity to use the analysis to better understand their own lobbying misalignments and improve accordingly.

In this sense, the RPE Benchmark was different from a typical academic study in that the overarching goal was to change behavior, building on Ceres' decades of experience in the corporate sustainability domain. In late 2019, representatives of Ceres emailed contacts at all ninety-six companies, the text for which can be found in Appendix A. By keeping initial company assessments private and offering to discuss the results with representatives of the companies themselves, the Ceres team hoped to motivate companies to improve their practices.

During the first few months of 2020, the Ceres team conducted a total of twenty-four private dialogues as a result of this outreach. In some instances, companies were already aware of and involved with Ceres' advocacy more generally, and a number were members of Ceres' Company Network (a separate group from the BICEP Network). In other cases, this letter and the resulting dialogue were the first-time company contacts had engaged with Ceres on any topic.

Each private dialogue, conducted via phone or video call, offered companies an opportunity to see how they performed in the private benchmark, challenge any evaluations that the company believed were in error (e.g., by pointing to additional publicly available information), and ask questions in order to better understand the motivation and methodology behind these results. All companies were made aware that the benchmark would be updated after one year, and those results would be made public, which created an opportunity and incentive for companies to improve.

Based on these engagements, as well as on data availability, some adjustments were made to the benchmarking methodology prior to the 2021 update. Ceres also tracked changes in company performance following direct engagement and identified twenty improvements in benchmarked indicators that could be reasonably attributed to this interaction. Details about the company improvements will be discussed later in the chapter.

9.5 The Public RPE Benchmark

During the first few months of 2021, one year after the private benchmarking analysis was conducted, the Ceres team repeated its assessment of the ninety-six companies, with some adjustments in methodology based on learnings from the prior year. High-level changes to the alignment categories included a move to action-oriented language, reframing "Governance" as "Systematize," and dividing Act into direct lobbying ("Advocate") and trade association relationships ("Engage").

9.5.1 The New Assessment Comprised Fourteen Binary Indicators

9.5.1.1 Assess

• Whether the company's 10-K recognizes the physical risks of climate change as a material risk.
• Whether the company's 10-K recognizes the transition risks associated with climate change as a material risk.

9.5.1.2 Systematize

• Degree to which the board assigned formal oversight of climate change and/or sustainability to one or more standing committees.

9.5.1.3 Advocate

• Whether the company publicly affirms the science of climate change.
• Whether the company made statements supporting the need for ambitious climate policies.
• Whether the company publicly supports the Paris Agreement.
• Whether the company publicly joined a group of companies to advocate for specific science-based climate policies.
• Whether the company publicly and individually advocates for specific science-based climate policies.
• Whether the company has refrained from opposition to science-based climate policies.

9.5.1.4 Engage

• Whether the company has disclosed a list of its trade association memberships.
• Whether the company has conducted an audit of its trade associations for science-based climate policy alignment.
• Whether the company is a member of the U.S. Chamber of Commerce.
• If a member of the Chamber, whether the company has disclosed its understanding that the Chamber has a record of lobbying in misalignment with climate science.
• If a member of the Chamber, whether the company has disclosed its engagements to evolve the Chamber's climate change positions and lobbying.

Each company's scoring on all fourteen indicators was released publicly, and accompanied by media amplification efforts which focused on key findings – including the following:

• While large US companies are putting in place the right internal systems and processes to address climate risks, companies provide minimal insight on how they consider climate change policy as a part of the overall climate risk landscape.
• Ninety-two percent of the assessed companies plan to clean up their own operations by setting emissions reduction goals.

- Eighty-eight percent of companies formally charge their boards with the responsibility to oversee sustainability/climate change.
- Seventy-four percent of companies acknowledge that climate change poses a material risk to their enterprises.
- The majority of large companies assessed have not translated their broader statements on the importance of climate change policy into consistent advocacy in favor of specific climate policies.
- Seventy-six percent of assessed companies have publicly affirmed the science of climate change, and 57 percent supported the need for science-based climate change policies, but only 40 percent engaged directly with lawmakers.
- Twenty-one percent of assessed companies have lobbied in opposition to science-based climate policies. Yet, nearly all of these companies have set or committed to set emissions reduction targets.
- Most of the assessed companies are not holding the U.S. Chamber of Commerce accountable for its oppositional climate change track record or disclosing how they are engaging with the Chamber to support science-based climate policy.
- Seventy-three percent of assessed companies affirmed that they are members of the Chamber of Commerce.
- Nine percent have publicly acknowledged the Chamber's historic track record on climate change and the importance of science-based climate policies.
- Seven percent have disclosed that they have engaged with the Chamber to evolve its climate change position to align with climate science, and just one company (Apple in 2009) left the Chamber over its climate stance.

Ceres announced the 2021 RPE Benchmark with a press release that was shared with media contacts directly, resulting in media interviews with key Ceres experts. The Benchmark was covered in several news outlets, with more than a dozen press hits in publications such as Bloomberg, Grist, S&P Global, and Politico. News of the Benchmark was also shared with more than 30,000 subscribers to Ceres' email updates, resulting in over 5,000 unique opens. It was also shared on Ceres' social media, leading to over 70,000 impressions.

The RPE Benchmark itself was made public via a "microsite" (www.ceres.org/practicingRPE) hosted on the main Ceres website. The microsite contained background on the motivation for the project, methodology behind the indicators, company-specific results,

Table 9.1 *Voting on climate disclosure and lobbying resolutions, 2021*

	Delta	Exxon Mobil	Norfolk Southern	Philips 66	Sempra Energy	United Airlines
State Street	FOR	FOR	FOR	FOR	AGAINST	FOR
Blackrock	AGAINST	FOR	AGAINST	FOR	AGAINST	FOR
Vanguard	FOR	FOR	FOR	AGAINST	AGAINST	FOR

and analyses of the data with graphics to illustrate key findings. This enabled users to explore and download the data and read narrative text about the data's implications for practice. Six months after the launch of the microsite, it had garnered nearly 10,000 views.

Opportunities for private dialogue were once again offered to individual companies, both before and after the public benchmark was released. These conversations focused on helping companies understand their assessments and on providing recommendations for improvement. Contacts at the benchmarked companies were also invited to a Ceres-hosted webinar discussing the results and implications, giving them the chance to ask further questions about the RPE Benchmark.

In parallel to direct dialogue and media amplification, the RPE Benchmark was used to inform investor coalitions interested in pushing their portfolio companies toward better alignment. Sharing these results allowed investors to target low-performing companies with shareholder resolutions that asked for improved disclosure and alignment around climate lobbying. By providing investors with the data they needed to act, Ceres leveraged this key constituency to further amplify the pressure on companies in partnership with activist investors such as the Interfaith Center for Corporate Responsibility. During the subsequent proxy season, a total of six shareholder resolutions came to a vote at companies scoring poorly on the RPE Benchmark. Of these, five won majority votes, with large investors such as Blackrock, State Street, and Fidelity often adding their powerful voices to smaller activist investors. Details are provided in Table 9.1.

9.6 Measuring Change and Attributing Causality

It should be noted that the scale of corporate action needed on climate policy has yet to materialize. As mentioned in the previous section,

Figure 9.1 A general theory of change

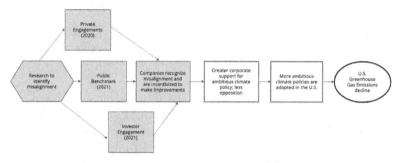

Figure 9.2 A theory of change for Ceres' responsible political engagement initiative

Wall Street investors have been dangling carrots but have yet to pull out the sticks to drive greater alignment on climate lobbying and corporate policy. The ideological change we are seeing is relatively recent and incremental, but it is also gaining momentum. As stated at the outset of this chapter, the goal of the RPE Initiative was to drive change toward greater alignment between climate science, corporate actions, and climate advocacy. Considering the initiative is only two years old, we are optimistic about its future ability to drive more outcomes on climate policy.

As an organization, Ceres focuses on articulating a "theory of change" for each organizational initiative, providing a description and illustration of why certain actions are expected to have their desired impacts. Figure 9.1 illustrates a general theory of change. Creating a theory of change involves mapping out a causal chain, which begins with actions that are under the organization's control. Those lead to outputs, which are work products that go out into the world. The outputs drive outcomes, or specific changes in external behavior. If the theory proves accurate, those outcomes have a broader impact, leading to progress toward a social or environmental goal such as climate stability.

In the case of the RPE Initiative, as illustrated in Figure 9.2, the project team theorized that identifying the misalignment between companies' words, actions, and advocacy (actions) and then documenting those as the RPE Blueprint guidelines, private company assessments, and a public benchmark (outputs), would lead companies to address certain misalignments that were unintentional, while also providing investors with the awareness and tools they needed to push their portfolio companies toward further alignment. Bringing policy actions into alignment at benchmarked companies (and driving media coverage intended to spur additional companies to do the same) would create the corporate support needed for ambitious climate policies to be approved and implemented in the United States, thereby reducing the greenhouse gas emissions of the country and contributing meaningfully to a lower-carbon future globally.

Measuring success in the context of a theory of change involves looking at key points in the causal chain, to understand if there is evidence of the expected relationship. In evaluating the impact of the RPE initiative, for example, Ceres tracked the following changes over time:

9.6.1 Relationship 1: Outputs Drive Awareness

Prior to publishing the 2021 Benchmark, Ceres notified all ninety-six companies that they were being evaluated, resulting in the following outcomes:

- Forty-six companies agreed to engage directly with Ceres on responsible policy lobbying.
- Post-release, three additional companies contacted Ceres to request a conversation.

While working to support companies publicly speaking out in support of science-based action, Ceres also engaged several of these to point out inconsistent policy positioning uncovered by the RPE Initiative – and pointed out the risks related to misalignment. Additionally, Ceres hosted two webinars focused on the findings of the RPE project during September 2021.

9.6.2 Relationship 2: Awareness Drives Alignment

During dialogues with benchmarked companies, many company representatives indicated a willingness to change their practices in line with the recommendations in the RPE Blueprint, resulting in a total of twenty specific improvements in benchmarked indicators. Examples include:

.

- Adobe and Facebook updated board committee charters to specifically and formally include board-level oversight of ESG.
- Southern Company updated public disclosure of its understanding of climate science and its support of the Paris Agreement.
- Netflix, which had not previously spoken out in support of science-based climate change positions, signed Ceres' Clean Energy Standard statement and publicly supported the climate provisions of the U.S. budget reconciliation bill.
- Ford released its first climate lobbying assessment in March 2021.
- General Motors publicly disclosed its Chamber of Commerce membership for the first time and committed to do a climate audit by the end of 2021.
- PepsiCo joined the Chamber of Commerce's Climate Solutions Working Group.
- Coca-Cola sent and publicly disclosed a letter to the Chamber asking them to align their position and lobbying with the Paris Agreement.
- Mondelez increased transparency of its Chamber of Commerce membership, publicly stated that the Chamber's position on climate is inconsistent with the company's own and disclosed that they are engaging with the Chamber to evolve its position.

There also seemed to be ripple effects from the changing conversation around corporate climate advocacy and the role of trade associations. Examples include:

- Two large global companies (LaFarge Holcim and Unilever) that Ceres works with, but were not benchmarked, left trade associations citing misalignment on climate positions.
- Logitech signed Ceres' Clean Energy Standard statement, and the CEO publicly supported the climate provisions of the U.S. Budget Reconciliation Bill.

9.6.3 Relationship 3: Investors Drive Alignment

In addition to a strategy of direct engagement with companies, Ceres provided benchmarking data directly to institutional investors who had expressed an interest in engaging companies on climate. During the proxy season that followed, shareholder proposals related to climate lobbying increased and received disproportionately high support compared to climate-related proposals in general, as shown in Table 9.2.

Table 9.2 *Votes on shareholder resolutions, 2019–2021*

	2019 vs. 2020 vs. 2021 Average Votes					
Meeting Year →	2019		2020		2021	
Working Group ↑	Average Votes	Record Count	Average Votes	Record Count	Average Votes	Record Count
Carbon Asset Risk Working Group	19%	4	33.20%	6	48.40%	2
Climate Action 100+ North America Working Group	48%	3	0.00%	0	0.00%	0
Shareholder Initiative on Climate and Sustainability	21%	6	0.00%	0	0.00%	0
Banking on Low Carbon	0%	0	24.80%	4	31.10%	1
Board Oversight of Climate & Sustainability	19%	5	25.90%	10	22.80%	8
Clean Energy and Transportation	0%	0	42.10%	2	0.00%	0
Food Waste	26%	1	32.00%	1	0.00%	0
GHG Goals	30%	8	45.80%	3	48.20%	11
Lobbying & Political Spending Disclosure	30%	10	32.70%	17	46.70%	13
Methane	35%	1	0.00%	0	0.00%	0
Proxy Voting	0%	0	14.30%	1	16.80%	1
Say on Climate	0%	0	0.00%	0	42.80%	6
Sustainability Reporting	28%	1	52.30%	1	0.00%	0
Sustainable Agriculture	3.20%	1	0.00%	0	0.00%	0
Utilities	24.80%	2	7.60%	1	0.00%	0
Waste Management	28.00%	6	21.60%	3	54.10%	3
Water	22.60%	2	14.10%	2	11.00%	1
Sustainable Forests	21.80%	3	42.50%	3	98.90%	1
Total	26.30%	53	30.80%	54	42.40%	47

In particular, investors affiliated with the Ceres Investor Network submitted six climate-lobbying shareholder proposals that went to vote in 2021. Of these five – or 80 percent – received majority votes at the annual general meetings. This represents an exceptionally high success rate for any kind of shareholder proposal and was driven in large part by the voting practices of large institutional investors (such as BlackRock, State Street Global Advisors, and Vanguard) who would have been aware of the RPE recommendations and results, given their engagement with Ceres.

9.6.4 Relationship 4: Alignment Drives Policy Adoption

It is difficult – if not impossible – to attribute policy adoption (or lack thereof) to specific company actions that may have resulted from the RPE Initiative. This is where the theory of change relies more on the strength of its logic than on empirical evidence. Namely, we assume that corporate interests are a major influencer of policy in the United States and that corporate support for ambitious climate policies will make a significant difference in whether those policies come into existence. To the extent that this is a reasonable assumption, data proving the relationship is less important to understanding the effectiveness of the RPE Initiative.

9.6.5 Relationship 5: Policy Adoption Drive GHG Emissions Reductions

An essential underlying assumption for all these efforts is that adopting strong climate policies in the United States will be effective in bringing down national GHG emissions and will contribute to reducing global GHG emissions – which, in turn, will help the world avoid the worst impacts of climate change. Evaluating whether this is true is well outside the scope of the RPE Initiative, but it is commonly accepted that policy solutions are necessary and can be effective in the fight against climate change, and that reducing U.S. emissions is particularly essential.

A summary of the expected relationships and their key indicators in the Ceres theory of change is presented in Table 9.3.

As we reflect on what we have learned and how we might improve our future methodology, key strategic questions include:

Table 9.3 *Expected relationships and key indicators*

Expected relationship	Key indicator	Data collected

Outputs drive awareness	- Private engagements
	- Media coverage
	- Webinar attendance
		- 46 companies engaged directly
		- As of 9/17/21:
		  12+ press hits
		  6,846 microsite visitors
		  5,079 unique email opens
		  64,722 social media impressions
		- Representatives of 14 benchmarked companies attended Ceres RPE webinars

Awareness drives alignment	- Governance improvements - Left trade association - Petitioned trade association - Private commitments	- 20 specific improvements in benchmarked indicators
Investors drive alignment	- Benchmarking data shared with investors - Shareholder proposals on lobbying and disclosure -Institutional investor support for proposals	- Greater disclosure leads to better alignment of lobbying with company purpose, mission and values
Alignment drives policy	- Bipartisan HFC phasedown - 2015 Paris Agreement	- Coalition of actors[4] - American Business Act on Climate Pledge
Policy drives GHG emissions reductions	- Overall U.S. emissions - Industry-specific emissions - Analyses of policy impacts	- Essential assumption

9.6.6 How Can a Benchmark Drive Change if Most Companies Are Laggards?

Benchmarks often serve to make companies in the bottom quarter uncomfortable – but what if the majority of companies are not

---

[4] https://news.bloomberglaw.com/environment-and-energy/major-climate-win-scored-with-quiet-diverse-lobbying-campaign?context=article-related

performing as desired? What motivation does a company have to improve if it is already better than average, yet failing to incorporate the expectations of the RPE Benchmark? Going forward, we are considering integrating examples from outside the set of benchmarked companies, to show what leadership looks like and raise the bar for a universe of companies that by and large is underperforming on climate but is celebrated in the corporate world.

9.6.7 How Can Investors Be Further Activated to Drive Corporate Lobbying Alignment?

Another way to drive action, when peer pressure may not be a strong motivator, is to activate investors to demand better alignment. We may build on previous efforts to inform investors by not just providing data from the RPE Benchmark, but also contextualizing it as part of a webinar or investor briefing to demonstrate and discuss the implications of the topic and argue that the status quo is unacceptable.

9.6.8 What Other Stakeholders Should We Be Taking into Consideration?

The 2021 Benchmark only considered the U.S. Chamber of Commerce due to two factors – the first being most of the S&P 100 companies were members, and second, resource constraints did not permit a more in-depth analysis of a wider range of trade associations. For future reports, the team intends to expand the scope of trade associations to other leading cross-sector organizations, like the Business Roundtable, in addition to benchmarking what pro-climate coalitions the companies are members of. There is also consideration being given to sharing this information with advocacy groups, in an effort to keep all stakeholders involved in the policymaking process informed.

9.6.9 Which Current Policy Debates Reveal Whether a Company's Advocacy Is Aligned with Climate Science?

One possibility is to look at how companies used their influence to support or undermine the climate provisions in the Build Back Better budget reconciliation package. Overall, the influence of corporate lobbying, especially through the U.S. Chamber of Commerce and Business

Roundtable, watered down an initially rigorous climate bill as corporations worked to remove key provisions – including corporate tax adjustments and the Clean Energy Performance Program. Even some of the best performers on the RPE Benchmark are members of the Business Roundtable and or the U.S. Chamber, so it will be interesting to look at whether and/or how they addressed that misalignment (Mullins and Glazer, 2021).

Another policy debate that has been playing out since the publication of the 2021 RPE Benchmark is around methane emissions, with new regulations being developed and companies being asked to weigh in on them. The RPE Initiative team may incorporate comments and other forms of influence on this topic, as methane is an extremely potent GHG.

The 2021 public indicators used for benchmarking were binary, with simply "yes" or "no" answers, but this tended to cover up some useful nuance. For instance, some companies with "conflicting" stances on climate were disproportionately obstructionist, others disproportionately supportive, but both were lumped together. For the future, the project team has considered a middle ground involving a 3-point or "stoplight" scale to add more gradation to the benchmark.

Statements, signatures, and trade memberships are not the only ways that companies engage in political advocacy, and these tools do not capture the influence of corporate donations to candidates, elections, and lawsuits. Going forwared, there may be a greater focus on how political spending is aligned with other aspects of climate influence. However, there are challenges in attributing donations to any one issue, given that each political candidate has stances on multiple issues. Funding specific lawsuits intended to undermine climate regulations may be clearer.

Concluding Thoughts

There are alternative methods to collecting data for the RPE Initiative that better conform to an academic study. But when the goal is to drive change, and there is a strong theory of change, data analysis can play a supporting role even where these challenges exist. If we can use data to test the causal linkages that we are less certain of and rely on the practicality of our theory where good data is sparse, then we can be reasonably confident that a certain set of actions are worth pursuing. If an advocacy organization like Ceres invests in a number of strategies, each "reasonably certain" to drive change, then chances improve that one or more of these will have a positive influence. Taking a few reasonable bets seems a better strategy than waiting for certainty in addressing an existential crisis like climate change. All things considered, analyzing different points on the chain can lead to insights and strategic adjustments as we learn from prior results and may, at times, uncover that something is truly fruitless. In the case of the RPE Initiative, there are strong indications that publication of the Blueprint and subsequently of the Benchmark is beginning to drive change, but the team will need to continually evaluate its effectiveness to allocate its advocacy resources effectively.

References

Bloomberg Philanthropies. (2022). *America Is All In*, www.bloomberg.org/environment/supporting-sustainable-cities/america-is-all-in/

Brady, J. (2021). Exxon Lobbyist Caught on Video Talking about Undermining Biden's Climate Push. *NPR*, www.npr.org/2021/07/01/1012138741/exxon-lobbyist-caught-on-video-talks-about-undermining-bidens-climate-push

CDP, 2019. World's Biggest Companies Face $1 Trillion in Climate Change Risks, www.cdp.net/en/articles/media/worlds-biggest-companies-face-1-trillion-in-climate-change-risks

Ceres. (2019). Running the Risk: How Corporate Boards Can Oversee Environmental, Social and Governance (ESG) Issues, www.ceres.org/resources/reports/running-risk-how-corporate-boards-can-oversee-environmental-social-and-governance

Ceres. (2020). Blueprint for Responsible Policy Engagement on Climate Change. www.ceres.org/resources/reports/blueprint-responsible-policy-engagement-climate-change#:~:text=The%20Ceres%20Blueprint%20for%20Responsible,indirect%20lobbying%20on%20climate%20policies.

Ceres. (2021a). Practicing Responsible Policy Engagement: How Large U.S. Companies Lobby on Climate Change, www.ceres.org/practicing RPE#assessments

Ceres. (2021b). Ceres Policy Network: Business for Innovative Climate and Energy Policy (BICEP), www.ceres.org/networks/ceres-policy-network

Climate Action Tracker. (2021). https://climateactiontracker.org/global/temperatures/

Commodity Futures Trading Commission. (2020). Managing Climate Risk in the U.S. Financial System: Report of the Climate-Related Market Risk Subcommittee, Market Risk Advisory Committee of the U.S. Commodity Futures Trading Commission, www.cftc.gov/sites/default/files/2020-09/9-9-20%20Report%20of%20the%20Subcommittee%20

on%20Climate-Related%20Market%20Risk%20-%20Managing%20
Climate%20Risk%20in%20the%20U.S.%20Financial%20System%20
for%20posting.pdf

ExxonMobil. (2021). https://corporate.exxonmobil.com/

Flavelle, C. (2021). Climate Change Could Cut World Economy by $23 trillion in 2050, Insurance Giant Warns. *New York Times*, www.nytimes.com/2021/04/22/climate/climate-change-economy.html

Freed, B., Sandstrom, K., & Laufer, W. S. (2023). Targeting Private Sector Influence in Politics: Corporate Accountability as a Risk and Governance Problem. In T. P. Lyon, ed., *Corporate Political Responsibility*. Cambridge, UK: Cambridge University Press.

Grasso, M. (2019). Oily Politics: A Critical Assessment of the Oil and Gas Industry's Contribution to Climate Change. *Energy Research & Social Science*, 50(4), 106–15. https://doi.org/10.1016/j.erss.2018.11.017

InfluenceMap. (2019). How the Oil Majors Have Spent $1Bn since Paris on Narrative Capture and Lobbying on Climate, https://influencemap.org/report/How-Big-Oil-Continues-to-Oppose-the-Paris-Agreement-38212275958aa21196dae3b76220bddc

Intergovernmental Panel on Climate Change. (2021). Climate Change 2021, the Physical Science Basis: Summary for Policy Makers, www.ipcc.ch/report/ar6/wg1/downloads/report/IPCC_AR6_WGI_SPM_final.pdf

Lund, D., & Strine, E. (2022). Corporate Political Spending Is Bad Business: How to Minimize the Risks and Focus on What Counts. *Harvard Business Review*, https://hbr.org/2022/01/corporate-political-spending-is-bad-business

Lyon, T. P., & Mandelkorn, W. (2023). The Meaning and Measurement of CPR. In T. P. Lyon, ed., *Corporate Political Responsibility*. Cambridge, UK: Cambridge University Press.

Meyer, R. (2018). Washington State Likely Rejects a Historic Carbon Tax: If Climate Policy Can't Win in the Evergreen State, Can It Win Anywhere? *The Atlantic*, www.theatlantic.com/science/archive/2018/11/washington-state-votes-down-i-1631-major-climate-bill/575131/

Mullins, B., & Glazer, E. (2021). Some Companies Sit Out the Fight over Democrats' Tax Increases: Supporters of Climate-Change Measures Aren't Lobbying against the Roughly $2 trillion Spending Package. *The Wall Street Journal*, www.wsj.com/articles/some-companies-sit-out-the-fight-over-democrats-tax-increases-11636367400

Schwartz, A. (2009). Why Did Apple Quit the U.S. Chamber of Commerce? *Fast Company*, www.fastcompany.com/1392665/why-did-apple-quit-us-chamber-commerce

10 | *From Kyoto to Paris*
Business and Climate Change
DAVID VOGEL

10.1 Introduction

This chapter explores the political role of business in influencing several important federal climate change policy initiatives over the last two decade. These include the Kyoto Protocol (1998), the Climate Stewardship Act (2003), the Climate Security Act (2007), the American Clean Energy and Security Act (2009), the Clean Power Plan (2015), and the Paris Climate Agreement (2015). In addition to describing lobbying by individual firms, trade associations, and business peak associations, it examines business participation in the nearly 100 alliances, councils, organizations, and ad hoc coalitions that have been established since the late 1990s to address climate issues (Cory, Lerner, Osgood, 2021).

The discussion of business policy preferences and lobbying explored in this chapter underlines a central theme of this edited volume – highlighted in the introductory chapter – namely the importance of corporate political responsibility or CPR (Lyon and Mandelkorn, 2023). A politically responsible firm is one that uses its political resources to support responsible public policies, such as regulations that mandate national reductions in emissions of greenhouse gases (GHG) (Lyon and Delmas, 2018; Lyon et al., 2018). However, as this chapter documents, while many companies have voiced support for federal policies to address the risk of global climate change, the motivations for their support, the conditions underlying their backing for particular policies, and the extent of their political advocacy vary considerably. Thus not all such firms can be considered (equally) politically responsible.

This chapter draws upon the data presented in "Disclosure of Political Responsibility with Regard to Climate Change" as well as in "Practicing Responsible Policy Engagement: How Large U.S. Companies Lobby on Climate Change" (Delmas and Friedman, 2023; Ketu and Rothstein, 2023). It also complements the research of Ed

Walker and Tim Werner on the dynamics of corporate disclosure of political activity (Walker, 2023; Werner, 2023).

10.2 Business Policy Divisions

Business opposition to public policies to reduce greenhouse gas emissions primarily reflects the economic interests of the energy suppliers and customers of carbon-intensive industries who would be disadvantaged by policies that discourage the use or raise the costs of fossil fuels. "These supply chain linkages create shared interests among a strikingly diverse array of producers, providing a motive force behind extensive collective efforts to oppose climate action among an extended carbon coalition" (Cory, Lerner and Osgood, 2021, p. 69). The important role played by such industries in the American economy – 79 percent of national energy comes from fossil fuels – explain why business opposition to federal regulations to mandate national reductions in carbon emissions has been so extensive.

However, a growing number of business firms have positioned themselves as "constructive partners in the effort to find solutions that can help mitigate climate change" (Vormedal, 2010, p. 265). Why, then, has business support for national public policies to address the risks of global climate change increased during the last two decades?

One reason has to do with economics. Most obviously, restrictions on carbon emissions can benefit firms that produce less carbon-intensive or renewable energy, or that market more fuel-efficient products. The market for such "green" business activities has grown steadily. The participation of many firms in voluntary carbon reduction programs, the growth of state-level regulations, and the decline in the costs of renewable energy have reduced the costs of compliance with fossil fuel reduction requirements for many companies. Moreover, some restrictions on carbon emissions can also advantage firms or industries whose adjustment costs are lower than those of their more carbon-intensive competitors (Kennard, 2020). "Environmental regulation can foster competitive advantages for greener firms that are capable of meeting the newly generated demands for environmental quality as a lower cost" (Delmas, Kim and Nairn-Birch, 2016, p. 179).

A second factor has to do with social pressures and business norms. Many corporations have embraced the principles and practices of corporate social responsibility, which includes a commitment to ameliorate their negative environmental impacts. For such companies, supporting climate change regulations is consistent with their corporate values. Moreover, as pressures from corporate stakeholders and the public to recognize the risks of climate change have grown, both the reputation benefits of recognizing the risks of global climate change warming and the reputation risks of opposing policies to ameliorate them have increased. An important role has been played by environmental groups, nonprofit organizations, and foundations, which have both encouraged companies to participate in voluntary climate reduction initiatives and to support government regulation (Lyon, 2010).

However, firms may also support climate regulations for strategic reasons (Grumbach, 2015). Thus they may back a particular policy in order to make its specific provisions more favorable to them. This is how Jim Rogers, then CEO of Cinergy, explained his company's support of a pro-active climate strategy: "if you are not at the table, you will become the menu" (Meckling, 2015, p. 23). Likewise, they may support a particular climate change policy proposal in order to preempt the enactment of a more stringent one.

This can make it difficult to distinguish between a firm's primary goal, which is often no regulation, and its secondary policy goal, which is to enact the least burdensome policy alternative. Moreover, many firms belong to business lobbies that have taken opposite positions on proposed federal regulations, making it even harder to identify their actual policy preferences (Meckling, 2015). To the extent that a company's endorsement of climate change regulations is strategic, its policy preferences are likely to shift, supporting regulations when their likelihood of enactment grows and then withdrawing its support when the political environment is less threatening.

The focus of business lobbying can also change over time, depending on, for example, whether companies are seeking to define the future policy agenda, such as by supporting or opposing an international environmental treaty or a market-based regulatory approach on one hand, or bargaining over the terms of a specific public policy proposal such as cap and trade on the other.

Finally, it is important to recognize that while the extent of business political support for climate change regulation has markedly and steadily increased since the late 1990s, the business opponents of climate regulation have been more successful. Thus the United States has neither ratified nor implemented the Kyoto or Paris international climate change agreements. None of the legislative proposals to reduce national greenhouse gas emissions has been passed (though Waxman-Markey did pass the House of Representatives), and the Clean Power Plan was never implemented.

While the federal government has enacted fuel economy and energy efficiency standards, alongside with tax incentives, subsidies for the production and purchases of renewable energy products, and funded research into clean energy technology, it has yet to adopt or implement comprehensive regulations to reduce the nation's GHG emissions or even to formalize national targets or goals for such reductions. The concluding section of this chapter seeks to explain how business political activity and policy preferences have contributed to this policy stalemate.

10.3 The Kyoto Protocol (1998)

During the 1980s, several countries began to negotiate international agreements to address what was clearly a global environmental problem. The possibility of American participation in a binding international agreement to reduce greenhouse gas (GHG) emissions led many business firms to politically organize to oppose any international commitment by the United States. In 1989 the Global Climate Coalition (GCC), an ad hoc business coalition, was established under the auspices of the National Association of Manufacturers (Mildenberger, 2020). Formed to represent the interests of the major producers and users of fossil fuels, its founding members included the major oil companies, as well as the American Petroleum Institute, the National Coal Association, the US Chamber of Commerce, and the American Forest & Paper Association. The Edison Electric Institute also joined the coalition.

All told, the GCC represented more than 230,000 business firms from a wide variety of industrial sectors including aluminum, paper, steel, transportation, power generation, petroleum, and chemicals. The Coalition gave political voice to those sectors of the economy that either produced fossil fuels or whose businesses were energy-intensive, both of whom would be disadvantaged by an international agreement that required the United States to restrict its GHG emissions.

In the lead-up to the negotiations to the third Conference of the Parties to the UN Climate Conference in Kyoto, several business organizations began to campaign against American endorsement of any binding agreement. The GCC funded a $13 million television campaign to highlight the economic costs of the proposed Kyoto targets, while the auto industry organized the Coalition for Vehicle Choice. The coal industry sponsored the Centre for Energy and Economic Development which joined with the United Mine Workers to oppose American signing of an international agreement. The Business Roundtable published newspaper advertisements signed by 130 chief executives arguing against the adoption of mandatory emissions reduction targets at Kyoto.

However, negotiators did agree to a binding 7 percent reduction of greenhouse gas emissions below 1990 levels by 2010 and the Kyoto Protocol was signed by President Clinton on November 12, 1998. Clinton never submitted the Protocol to Congress as there was no likelihood of Congress agreeing to adopt it. "Business opposition was critical to the blockage of Kyoto Protocol ratification" (Vormedal, 2011, p. 1).

But there were also business supporters of the Protocol. The American Business Council for Sustainable Energy urged American ratification. In addition to producers of natural gas and alternative energy, the Council's membership included manufacturers of energy saving equipment as well as some insurance companies which feared significant losses from increased global warming. According to its Executive Director: "We all know with confidence that appropriate steps to respond to climate chance – based on the efficient and clean use of energy – will lead to long-term economic growth" (Meckling, 2011, p. 89).

The energy firm Enron was a highly vocal business advocate of Kyoto, anticipating that it would increase the demand for natural gas, in whose marketing and distribution the firm had made considerable investments The company was a prominent supporter of the ad hoc alliance Business Challenge, which published a full-page ad in the *Wall Street Journal* calling on "the United States Government to exert strong leadership by promoting climate change policies that provide incentives to act quickly" (Meckling, 2011, p. 89). Also backing American ratification was a new ad hoc business alliance, the International Climate Change Partnership, whose membership included a few Fortune 500 companies, such as General Electric, DuPont, and ATT. These firms sought to shape the terms of American implementation of the Protocol.

In 1998, the Pew Center for Global Climate Change, an environmental nongovernment organization, established the Business Environmental Leadership Council. With an initial membership of thirteen global corporations the Council's objective was to increase the credibility of climate change science by making business support for regulation more visible. Its initial membership included British Petroleum and American Electric Power. While cautious in endorsing Kyoto, it did regard the agreement as a first step toward implementing a global market-based mechanism to reduce global carbon emissions (Meckling, 2011). By 2002, the organization had thirty-eight corporate members, including AEP, Sunoco, Boeing, Toyota, and Lockheed Martin.

In another sign of increased business openness to addressing climate change, in 2000 the World Wildlife Fund announced a partnership with six major corporations, including Johnson & Johnson and IBM, to establish a Climate Savers Program. Its goal was to demonstrate that companies could voluntarily achieve carbon reductions that equaled or exceeded those called for by the Kyoto Protocol. That same year, the Environmental Defense Fund began working with Pew, the Nature Conservancy, and several corporations to develop an international emission trading scheme under its Partnership for Climate Action program. Although not themselves forms of political advocacy, these programs and partnerships were designed to demonstrate the economic feasibility of reducing carbon emissions, and by doing so increase business support for government regulation (Layzar, 2007).

10.4 Shifts in Business Preferences

There were other signs of increased divisions within the business community. One such indication was the steady withdrawal of corporations from the GCC. The first company to leave was British Petroleum, followed by DuPont, both of which left in 1996. Following his firm's departure, in May 1997 BP's CEO John Browne made a widely publicized speech in which he dramatically broke with the rest of the oil industry by acknowledging the need for precautionary action to address the risks of climate change. After environmentalists embarrassed Shell by highlighting the inconsistency between the support of Shell's European based parent company for Kyoto and Shell's membership in the GCC, Shell USA withdrew in 1998.

Between 1998 and 2000, Texaco, American Electric Power, the Southern Company, General Motors, Chrysler, Ford, and Daimler-Chrysler all withdrew from the GCC. On leaving the GCC, a Ford official stated, "There is enough evidence that something is happening that we ought to look at this seriously" (Meckling, 2011, p. 97). The *New York Times* described Ford's departure as "the latest sign of divisions within heavy industry over how to respond to global warming" (Bradsherm, 1999). In addition to signaling disunity within the auto sector, these withdrawals also pointed to political divisions among oil and utility firms.

For its part, in 2000, the GCC was restructured as an association of trade associations, a decision that reflected the loss of several of its important corporate members. Following the 2001 decision of President George W. Bush to withdraw the United States from the Kyoto process, the Coalition disbanded, with ExxonMobil as its last major corporate supporter. Membership had become a reputation risk as "the outright rejection of carbon controls was slowly but steadily being considered illegitimate by policy makers" (Meckling, 2011, p. 97). However, business opposition to climate change policies continued in other forums, including through the US Chamber of Commerce and the American Coalition for Clean Coal Electricity.

In 2004, Cinenergy, responding to both shareholder resolutions that asked the firm to consider the potential implications of federal constraints on carbon emissions and its CEO's personal interests, announced its support for federal cap and trade emissions controls. Its CEO, Jim Rogers, testified before Congress that he believed his company could comply with such a regulation in a cost-effective matter. After Cinenergy merged with Duke, the new firm, Duke Energy, continued Cinenergy's advocacy for climate change regulation. It was shortly joined by another major utility, American Electric Power, which now voiced its support for "comprehensive, cost-effective public policies that facilitate prudent near-term emissions controls" (Meckling, 2011, p. 150).

General Electric became another prominent corporate supporter of a federal response to climate change. In 2005, the firm launched its Ecomagination initiative which committed substantial research funds to improve the energy efficiency of GE's products, the demand for which would be increased by restrictions on GHG emissions. Its CEO, Jeffery Immelt, stated: "the amount of CO_2 must be reduced

.... We think that real targets, whether voluntary or regulatory, are helpful because they drive innovation.... We believe in the power of market mechanisms to address the needs of the environment" (Meckling, 2011, p. 151). For their part, several major financial firms now realized the potential benefits of carbon trading. JP Morgan Chase voiced its support for "a market-based national policy on greenhouse gas emissions," while Goldman Sachs called upon the federal government to adopt "a strong policy framework that creates long-term value for GHG emissions reductions" (Meckling, 2011, p. 151).

In 2004, The Conference Board, a nonprofit organization with 2,000 corporate members, issued a public statement that noted the growing scientific consensus that humans were contributing to the warming of the planet and predicted increased pressures on corporate boards to address the issue. While acknowledging that its member had taken varying positions on federal regulations, it concluded that there was now a scientific perception "that climate change is an urgent priority that must be addressed through a variety of measures" (Layzar, 2007, p. 116).

In its 2005 annual report, a voluntary business initiative, the Carbon Disclosure Project, observed that "a sea change in corporate positioning on climate change is discernible.... Perceptions are changing most noticeably among U.S. based companies, many of which have publicly asked for greater regulatory certainty on greenhouse gas emissions" (Meckling, 2011, pp. 149–150). This assessment was echoed by Vormedal, who observed that by around 2005 "a tipping point in the business strategies started to materialize." He added, "The decline of the fossil fuel lobby had become unmistakably evident" while "the emergence and growth of a whole new field of more proactive business organisations..., indicates an overall shift in how prominent business groups approached the issue of GHG regulation" (Vormedal, 2010, p. 265).

10.5 Cap and Trade in Congress (2003–2005)

These expressions of business willingness to support appropriately designed regulatory policies, most notably through a cap and trade system, helped place global climate change back on the post-Kyoto policy agenda. In 2003, Senators John McCain (R-Arizona) and Joe Lieberman (D-CT) introduced legislation to explicitly limit greenhouse gas emissions. The Climate Stewardship Act of 2003 required major sectors in the economy to cut their GHG emissions to 2000 levels by 2010 and to 1990 levels by 2016. It would accomplish these objectives through emissions trading. This regulatory approach would benefit companies that had already reduced their emissions since they could then "sell" their credits to other firms. The legislation also allowed companies to offset their obligations with carbon sinks and overseas reductions.

Opposition was led by several powerful trade associations, including the American Petroleum Institute, the Alliance of Automobile Manufacturers, the National Mining Association, the American Iron and Steel Institute, and the American Chemistry Council. In urging that the legislation be defeated, several trade associations wrote: "our industries and many others have been active participants in voluntary greenhouse gas reduction programs for nearly a decade" (Layzar, 2007, p. 115).

Clearly, at this point, for many industries voluntary reduction programs had become a substitute for government regulation. "For fence-sitting senators, the divisions among their colleagues over voluntary versus mandatory emission reduction made support of the Climate Stewardship Act politically risky" (Layzar, 2007, p. 115). Even after the legislation's long-term emissions goals were weakened, it was defeated in the US Senate by a vote of 43–55.

Two years later, in 2005, the two senators reintroduced a modified version of their legislation in the form of an amendment to a Senate energy bill. Survey data reported that most Americans were now convinced that global warming was taking place and that they supported public policies to address it. At a government-sponsored conference on climate change in April 2005, executives from Exelon, Duke Energy, General Electric, Shell Oil, Wal-Mart, and other corporations urged Congress to approve a mandatory cap on US greenhouse gas emissions. However, the Senate decisively defeated the legislation by 38–60.

10.6 The U.S. Climate Action Partnership (2007)

In 2007, business support for climate change regulations became more organized. A core group of six corporations, Alcoa, BP America, Caterpillar, Duke Energy, Dupont, and General Electric, along with four major environmental organizations (the Environmental Defence Fund, the World Resources Institute, the Pew Center on Global Climate Change, and the Natural Resources Defense Council), established the U.S. Climate Action Partnership (USCAP). USCAP significantly shifted the tectonics of business advocacy in US climate change policies. For the first time in the history of US climate politics, an alliance of multinationals and environmental groups was demanding mandatory emissions controls though a cap and trade scheme (Meckling, 2011, p. 152).

In less than one year, the USCAP had more than doubled its corporate membership. By September 2007, it represented more than twenty-five of the world's largest corporations from several different sectors. Its corporate membership included Lehman Brothers, the Pacific Gas and Electric Company, and PNM Resources, along with Alcan, Boston Scientific, Conoco Philips, Deere & Company, Dow Chemical, General Motors, Johnson & Johnson, Marsh, PepsiCo, Shell, Siemens, Chrysler, and the Ford Motor Company.

Six of these firms had previously been contributors to GCC, while several others had belonged to trade associations which had been part of the GCC. Thus for many of the USCAP members from the coal, oil, electric utilities, automobile, and chemical manufacturing industries, their support for the new coalition marked an apparent reversal of their earlier direct or indirect anti-climate lobbying. This shift was particularly noticeable in the case of the Edison Electric Institute, the largest utility trade association. Earlier it had helped establish the GCC and described US support for the Kyoto Protocol as "economic suicide." But it now signaled an openness to federal regulation (Mildenberger, 2012, p. 29).

The motives of the large number of firms that chose to join USCAP or the sixty-five financial and investor groups that backed its call for market-oriented climate legislation varied. For some companies, such as GE, DuPont, and BP that had long been advocates of federal regulation, climate regulations represented a business opportunity: Early movers in developing less carbon-intensive products and production process, they would benefit from a cap and trade scheme that rewarded their initiatives. For financial service firms, carbon markets would increase the demand for their services while insurance companies and other financial investors had become increasingly concerned about the economic risks of climate change.

But for most USCAP members, especially those from more carbon-intensive sectors of the economy, their support for GHG regulation was strategic:

Many corporations felt that the level of uncertainty now signalled an end to business as usual. If they did not start promoting favourable regulation and take a seat at the table they would end up being worse off. They could be the victims of a badly designed and costly regulatory system, or they could work actively to push for business-friendly and cost-efficient regulation. (Vormedal, 2011, p. 18)

According to a founder of USCAP, "there is not a single USCAP CEO who did not consider future GHG regulation inevitable" (Vormedal, 2011, p. 17). Many USCAP members also preferred that climate regulations be written by Congress rather than the Environmental Protection Agency, as they anticipated that they would have more influence over the former. However, the American Petroleum Institute, the National Association of Manufacturers, and the Chamber of Commerce were highly critical of USCAP's more moderate industry voices, with a NAM official calling the cap and trade approach "fundamentally flawed" (Meckling, 2011, p. 156).

10.7 Business for Innovative Climate and Energy Policy

In November 2008 another business initiative in favor of climate change regulation was organized (Business, 2019). A project of Ceres, an environmental organization, Business for Innovative Climate and Energy Policy (BICEP) sought to enlist the broader business community in "advancing progressive climate and energy policies in order to promote the transition to a 21st century, lower carbon economy [that] will create new jobs and stimulate economic growth" (Business, 2019). Although USCAP had consisted primarily of firms that had an economic stake in climate change regulation, BICEP was intended to give consumer facing businesses a stronger voice in the policy process. It aimed to provide a broader spectrum of viewpoints for solving the climate and energy challenges facing America.

BICEP's four founding business members were Starbucks, Nike, Timberland, and Levi Strauss and Company. Subsequently forty-four additional firms joined. They included Ben and Jerry's, the Gap, Cliff Bar & Company, IKEA, Salesforce, Seventh Generation, and

Stonyfield Farms. For the most part, its membership consisted of firms with a highly visible public or consumer profile who also had strong CSR reputations. Restrictions on GHG emissions were unlikely to directly affect their businesses – either positively or negatively – while their public support for regulation to address the risks of climate change was important to their customers and employees, and their public reputations.

The coalition worked to secure a broad bipartisan consensus in Congress in order to enact legislation that would reduce greenhouse gas emissions 80 percent below 1990 levels by 2050. Its members expressed their willingness to support a broad range of policies, including aggressive energy efficiency regulations, the promotion of renewable energy, adjusting fuel subsidies, and appropriate carbon pricing to achieve this objective. While BICEP did not actively advocate for any particular policy, the coalition's formation demonstrated the increasingly broad base of business support for federal regulations to address climate change.

10.8 The Climate Security Act (2007)

Paralleling the formation of these two important pro-climate policy business coalitions, Congress re-engaged the issue of carbon reduction. Democratic Senator Lieberman of Connecticut and Republican Senator John Warner of Virginia introduced the Climate Security Act. It first stabilized and then progressively cut US greenhouse gas emissions, reducing them by 70 percent by 2050. This would be accomplished through a cap and trade system: 24 percent of total allowances would be auctioned, with their revenues to fund new climate technologies and other adoption measures, consumer energy assistance, and worker retraining. The remainder would be distributed for free to carbon emitters.

This legislation predictably met with strong opposition from the US Chamber of Commerce, the National Association of Manufacturers, and the coal industry's newly established lobby, the American Coalition for Clean Coal Electricity. Strikingly, it was also opposed by firms that had joined the USCAP. Most notably, Duke Energy stated that while it supported cap and trade in principle, it did not support this bill's version of it. All told, only six of USCAP's corporate members supported Lieberman-Warner. Those firms. which included GE,

PG&E, and Exelon, co-signed a letter with environmentalists endorsing the legislation. The rest joined Duke in opposition.

The political lobbying over this legislation revealed a substantial
gap between the official position of USCAP in favor of regulations to
address global climate change and the actual willingness of most of
its member firms to back a particular approach to doing so. The most
contentious issue involved allowances. What fatally weakened business support for the Climate Security Act was that only 76 percent
of the initial allocation of allowances would be distributed for free
while the number of auctioned permits would increase over time. This
proved to be a "deal-breaker" (Vormedal, 2011 p. 15). Duke Energy
estimated that under this approach, the company would be required
to spend $2 billion during the first year. Like the Climate Stewardship
Act and the amendment to the energy bill, this legislation failed to
advance in the Senate. Thus, through the end of the Bush administration in 2008, "US climate reformers had little to show for their
two-decade effort to enact climate change policies" (Mildenberger,
2020, p. 122).

10.9 The American Clean Energy and Security Act (2009)

With the Democratic Party now in control of both the presidency
and both houses of Congress for the first time since 1993–4, the stage
was set for a major climate change policy initiative. The prospects
for its passage appeared promising. Large and influential segments of
the business community – including the membership of both USCAP
and BICEP – had now publicly acknowledged the need for policies
to reduce national emissions of greenhouse gases. They represented
a potential business counterweight to the US Chamber of Commerce,
the National Association of Manufacturers, the Farm Bureau, and the
American Coalition for Clean Coal Electricity – all of whom remained
strongly opposed to federal climate change legislation. The Chamber
and the NAM had long been opposed to climate change regulation,
and the American Coalition represented the nation's coal burning utilities. For the Farm Bureau, restrictions on fossil fuels threated to raise
the costs of operating farm equipment.

Like its legislative predecessors, the American Clean Energy and
Security Act – which became known as Waxman-Markey, named
after Representatives Henry Waxman of California and Edward

Markey of Massachusetts – also featured a market friendly cap and trade approach to carbon reduction. The more greenhouse gases a firm emitted, the higher would be its costs, while firms that produced fewer such emissions could then sell their "surplus." Under their plan, total carbon emissions would be capped and would gradually decline between 2012 and 2050; by the later date emissions of all greenhouse gases would be reduced by 83 percent.

The terms of this legislation were modeled on the draft legislation proposed by the USCAP partnership. While USCAP did not officially endorse the legislation, it publicly welcomed it as a "strong starting point" (Meckling, 2011, p. 161). In fact, many of the legislation's key provisions, including its reliance on a market-based cap and trade model and the number of carbon permits to be distributed for free, were designed precisely in order to maximize support from the Partnership's member firms. The latter was particularly important to securing business support since at a minimum (reserve) price of $10 per ton of carbon set by the legislation, the potential cost of the seven billion tons of carbon emitted into the air in the United States annually was substantial. The legislation's proponents subsequently agreed to increase the number of free carbon permits to 85 percent of the total market, and to push back the phasing out of these free permits from 2016 to 2026 (Grumbach, 2015).

The Edison Electric Institute released a plan supported by eighty utility CEOs that supported the bill's long-term GHG reduction targets, though it wanted less stringent short-term targets as well as limits on compliance costs. The EEI also asked that its industry receive 40 percent of the bill's total allowances, proportional to the utility sector's contribution to carbon pollution. Following lengthy negotiations, the utility sector was provided with 35 percent of allowances for free, sufficient to cover 90 percent of its emissions. The EEI then endorsed the bill, as did many of its member firms (Downie, 2017).

Many of these electric utilities produced relatively few carbon emissions and thus would be in a position to profit by selling their pollution rights. For example, the utility Exelon was the nation's largest nuclear power generator, while PG&E, NextEra Energy, and Edison International all generated substantial power from renewable energy. But the EEI's endorsement provoked opposition from coal-dependent utilities in the Midwest whom emissions trading would disadvantage. They broke away from the industry trade association and formed their own Midwest Climate Coalition to oppose the legislation. A third category of utilities, including Duke Energy and American Electric Power, hedged their bets, supporting the legislation but also working to shape its provisions in order to minimize their compliance costs (Downie, 2019)

Business differences extended well beyond the utility industry. Within the oil industry, Shell and BP supported the legislation while ExxonMobil and Chevron, along with the American Petroleum Institute, opposed it. The American Council for Clean Coal Electricity (ACCCE) lobbied against the cap and trade bill, while two of its corporate members, namely Alcoa and Duke Energy backed it. The American Chemistry Council, while supporting emissions trading in principle, opposed the particular provisions of the Waxman-Markey bill. But two of its members, namely DuPont and Dow Chemical Corporation, lobbied for the legislation (Mildenberger, 2012, p. 27). All the coal producers, with the exception of Rio Tinto, opposed the legislation (Downie, 2019).

Aside from the ACCCE, and the American Petroleum Institute, the most extensive organized business opposition came from the peak business associations, the US Chamber of Commerce, the National Association of Manufacturers, and the National Federation of Independent Business. The Chamber is the nation's largest business association, while NAM represents manufacturing firms and the National Federation represents the nation's small and independent business firms. Each launched multimillion dollar public advertising campaigns to mobilize public opinion against the bill's passage. The Chamber was particularly active, not only leading a high-profile public campaign, but establishing the Institute for 21st Century Energy to contribute to the election campaigns of candidates who denied the science behind climate change. The Chamber devoted more resources than any other single organization in lobbying against climate change regulation, spending $60 million in 2008 (Delmas et al., 2016, p. 178).

All told, the lobbying on this legislation was extensive. More than 700 companies and interest groups hired an estimated 2,349 lobbyists, adding up to four lobbyists for each member of Congress (Lavellem, 2009). According to Kenneth Green of the American Enterprise Institute: "When Obama was elected, there was a wakeup call to all the groups that something might happen. Once they actually drafted legislation that opened up the floodgates." The director of strategic policy for the American Wind Institute added: "There is a lot of interest in this bill. Hopefully you state your case as best you can and work your allies" (Mulkern, 2009). Total business lobbying expenditures came to $700 million.

The most exhaustive study of corporate lobbying in support of the legislation found competitiveness concerns to be the key factor shaping corporate political positions.

Policies designed to mitigate carbon emissions shift market share toward firms with lower adjustment costs. Firms whose competitors are expected to bear high costs are significantly more likely to lobby in favor. Competition for market share drives firms to support climate change policies in order to impose costs on its domestic competitors (Kennard, 2020, pp. 1, 3, 4).

Accordingly, industries based in states that had imposed limits on greenhouse emissions, such as by passing climate change legislation, participating in the Regional Greenhouse Gas Initiative, and/or enacting a renewable portfolio standard were more likely to support the legislation, since it would provide them with a comparative advantage, while electricity producers and business consumers in states which continued to rely upon carbon-intensive fuels such as coal were more likely to oppose it as it would raise their relative costs. "Dirty firms lobby to maintain the status quo while clean firms view environmental regulation as an opportunity to gain firm-level advantages" (Delmas et al., 2016, p. 177). These economic or strategic preferences were reinforced by political considerations. "The utilities and other companies that are supporting climate change legislation tend to be based in more liberal parts of the country and believe that being viewed as environmentally responsible is a good marketing strategy" (Entine, 2009).

The legislation narrowly passed the House of Representatives by a vote of 219 to 212. But what has been described as a "1,400 page pork-filled bill" (Entine, 2009) had become substantially modified due to the concessions demanded by the legislation's business supporters, several of whom had only backed it for strategic reasons (Grumbach, 2015). The changes that had been made to secure support from Democratic legislators from coal-producing states had turned two of the major oil companies, namely ConocoPhillips and BP, against the legislation. They contended that the allocation of free permits had been unfair to their industry – though it was unclear if these companies would have supported the legislation in any event. In a further split within USCAP, Caterpillar, a major producer of mining and construction equipment, opposed the bill. Some environmental organizations also wound up opposing the House bill due to its permissive permit allocation provisions. Further eroding environmental support for the House bill was the legislation's generous offsets in agriculture and forestry. According to one analysis, these "meant that the bill would not require any actual emissions reductions for 18 years" (Karapin, 2016, p. 216).

When the bill came before the Senate, its advocates, led by Senators John Kerry, Lindsey Graham, and Joseph Lieberman, made a number of further concessions in order to secure sufficient business and thus Senate support (Lizza, 2010). These included supporting nuclear power, backing increased natural gas production, expanding offshore oil drilling, and reducing EPA's regulatory authority. To gain the support of the oil industry, which was responsible for nearly a third of all carbon emissions and which had spent millions attacking Waxman-Markey, the bill's supporters agreed to change the formula by which emissions of GHGs from transportation would be calculated. In exchange, the industry agreed not to publicly challenge the legislation while the bill was before the Senate.

Notwithstanding these concessions, achieving sufficient Senate support proved elusive. The climate bill never reached the floor of the Senate, thus ending one of the most substantive legislative initiatives to establish national limits on carbon emissions. Even more clearly than the 2007–8 Lieberman-Warner bill, the lobbying over Waxman-Markey revealed that for carbon-intensive firms – including those who had joined USCAP – their support for cap and trade was contingent on a permit allocation that did not "unfairly" burden them. However, in light of the significant number of permits that were given away for free and the delay in requiring that they be auctioned, there may well have been no circumstance under which these firms would have willing to support legislation that would have raised their costs in the long-run.

10.10 Responses to the Defeat of Waxman-Markey

The prominent role played by the Chamber of Commerce in the defeat of Waxman-Markey created a backlash that revealed further business divisions (Clark, 2009; Surowiecki, 2009). While previous business divisions were expressed through the creation of ad hoc coalitions, dissension had reached a level that created a schism within a major business peak association. To protest against the Chamber's position, Nike resigned from its board stating that it "fundamentally disagreed" with the Chamber's position and described climate change as an "urgent issue" (Clark, 2009). Apple, PG&E, PNM Resources, and Exelon also left the Chamber.

Apple "strongly objected to the Chamber's recent comments opposing the EPA's efforts to limit greenhouse gases," while PG&E stated, "We find it dismaying that the Chamber neglects the indisputable fact that a decisive majority of experts have said that the data on global warming are compelling" (Bagri, 2017). The firm went on to accuse the Chamber of "extreme rhetoric and obstructionist tactics." For its part, Johnson and Johnson asked the Chamber to stop making public pronouncements on climate change that failed "to reflect the full range of views of its members" (Clark, 2009).

Other large firms, including Costco, eBay, Hewlett-Packard, General Mills, Kellogg, Kraft Heinz, Mars, Mattel, Mondelez, Nestle, Starbucks, and Unilever, also left the Chamber (Bagri, 2017). General Electric publicly criticized the Chamber for being out of step on climate change, though it retained its membership. Duke Energy, while opposing the Chamber's position on climate change, retained its membership in that organization but withdrew from the National Association of Manufacturers. However, eight corporate members of the USCAP – namely, Chrysler, Deere, Dow Chemical, Duke Energy, GE, PepsiCo, PNM Resources, and Siemens – remained on the Chamber's board. According to a Chamber official, none of these firms sought to change the Chamber's environmental policy (Grumach, 2015, p. 646).

But at around the same time, a number of corporations also withdrew from the USCAP. Between 2010 and 2012, ConocoPhillips, BP, Xerox, Marsh, Caterpillar, John Deere, Ford, and GM all left the partnership. The departures of the two oil companies were public: It was explicitly linked to their disappointment with the burdens Waxman-Markey had imposed on the transposition sector, which had "left domestic refineries unfairly penalized versus international competition" (Grumbach, 2015, p. 653). For its part, Caterpillar announced that it had "decided to direct our resources toward the commercialization of technologies that will promote and provide sustainable development and reduce carbon emissions" (Mildenberger, 2012, p. 47).

So many firms began to leave USCAP that the organization became dormant – like the GCC a decade earlier, "For many of these companies, incentives to strategically accommodate US climate reform efforts faded as the policy threat weakened" (Mildenberger, 2020, p. 149). The collapse of the USCAP underscored the "second-order strategic nature of business support for contemporary US climate policy" (Mildenberger, 2012, p. 48). As soon as the threat of legislation passed, so did business participation in the USCAP, further demonstrating the fragility of the coalition the USCAP had established (Grumbach, 2015).

10.11 The Clean Power Plan (2015)

Conflict over climate policy now shifted to the executive branch. Faced with a legislative stalemate, in June 2014 the Environmental Protection Agency, acting under the authority of the 1990 Clean Air Act Amendments, proposed the Clean Power Plan (CPP). Officially released by the Obama administration in August 2015, this regulation specifically targeted electric power generation. It set state-specific emissions limits for CO_2 based on the GHG emissions of each state's electricity mix. Each state was required to submit an implementation plan to the federal government or to develop regional plans with other states that would enable them to meet its interim emissions reduction targets by 2020.

These states' targets could be implemented through a combination of reducing emissions from coal-burning power plants, increasing the use of less carbon-intensive generating power such renewable energy, and/or promoting energy efficiency conservation measures. The EPA estimated that state compliance with the CPP would reduce electricity GHG emission by approximately 25 percent below 2005 levels by 2020 and by 30 percent by 2030.

Ceres, a nonprofit organization that promotes corporate sustainability, released a letter in support of the CPP which was signed by 365 companies and investors (Prattico, 2017). The plan's business supporters ranged in size from local companies to Fortune 500 firms and included firms with headquarters and operations in all 50 states. Larger corporate signatories included EMC Corp, IKEA, KB Home, Kellogg, Levi Strauss, Nestle, Novartis, Sun Power, Symantec, Unilever, and VF Corporation. The letter stated: "Our support is firmly grounded in economic reality. Clean energy solutions are cost effective and innovative ways to drive investment and reduce greenhouse gas emissions. Increasingly, businesses rely on renewable energy and energy efficiency to cut costs and improve corporate performance" (Prattico, 2017).

Underlying the extent of business backing was the growing number of companies that were relying more on renewable energy, both to lower their own costs and to decrease their dependence on price-volatile fossil fuels – as well as to publicly demonstrate their "green" commitments. Most of the Fortune 100 firms had set their own clean energy targets and many had experienced considerable cost savings. According to Letitia Webster, senior director of global sustainably at VF Corporation, a North Carolina apparel company whose brands include The North Face and Timberland, "Having access to clean energy choices helps us manage our energy related costs while also reducing our environmental impact."

Webster added: "The Clean Power Plan will enable us to continue to invest in clean energy solutions and further advance our greenhouse gas reduction goals" (Webster, 2017). As the latter quote suggests, the Clean Power Plan was attractive to many firms because it would facilitate their own efforts – driven by both cost considerations and public pressures – to rely more on renewable energy as a power source.

Opponents of the plan countered by establishing a business coalition called Partnership for a Better Energy Future. Representing 200 coalitions across multiple industries, and comprising both national and state and local organizations from 33 states, the Partnership informed EPA: "All are united by a widespread concern that the proposed rule – as well as EPA's broader GHG regulatory agenda – presents a significant threat to American jobs and the economy" (Partnership, 2014).

As an alternative, the Partnership advocated an "all-of-the above energy strategy in order to insure the availability of reliable and affordable energy." Coal-reliant utilities, which would be disadvantaged by the EPA rule, were active in the Chamber of Commerce and the National Association of Manufacturers, both of which actively campaigned against the CPP.

Following the failure of Republicans in Congress to strip carbon from the Clean Air Act, which would have challenged EPA's legal authority, the battle over the CPP switched to the courts. Twenty-four states filed a suit in federal court, claiming that EPA lacked the legal authority under the Clean Air Act to issue the plan (Mugill, 2016).

Opposition also came from several utilities, whose dependence on coal meant that they would face higher adjustment costs, as well as from manufacturers who were major consumers of power derived from fossil fuels such as the metals industry and textile companies. In addition to Peabody, the nation's largest coal company, the railway Norfolk Southern, and the Municipal Electric Authority of Georgia joined the litigation challenging the Plan's legality. The suit was also supported by Caterpillar and CSR, a leading freight railway which that transported coal.

In response, supporters of the Plan filed a brief with the U.S. Court of Appeals for the DC Circuit. In addition to 18 states and 60 municipal governments, as well as 208 members of Congress, this brief was endorsed by 10 utilities, accounting for nearly 10 percent of the nation's total power generation (List of Supporters, 2016). They were joined by four of the nation's largest high-tech firms – Amazon, Apple, Google, and Microsoft – each of whom had already committed to and made substantial progress in reducing their own fossil fuel consumption. The brief was also backed by IKEA, Adobe, and Blue Cross/Blue Shield and endorsed by the American Wind Energy Association and the Solar Energy Association.

The nation's utilities were most directly affected by the Clean Power Plan, and they were the most politically engaged in either supporting or opposing it. Analysis of their respective political positions "supports the notion of a home-state effect. Electric utilities operating in states with more aggressive climate policies were more likely to support the CPP in court, while utilities operating in more lax policy environments were most likely to oppose it" (Meckling and Trachtman, 2020, p. 19). Utilities in states with laxer regulations would be financially disadvantaged by having to change their sources of power generation, while utilities in "greener" states would not "have to do anything beyond what they were already planning to do" (Meckling and Trachtman, 2020, p. 17).

Significantly, outside the utility sector, most larger corporations, including many of those prominently aligned with environmental groups, either took no position or were lukewarm in their endorsement of the CPP. A survey of fifty corporations that had worked with the Environmental Defence Fund, the Nature Conservancy, and the World Wildlife Fund – firms that "tout their sustainability efforts and celebrate their environmental partnerships" – reported that most had taken no position on the CPP (Gunther, 2015). These companies included IBM, Bank of America, Procter & Gamble, Coca-Cola, Monsanto, Xerox, AT&T, DuPont, KKR, McDonalds, and Walmart. Most justified their neutrality on the grounds that regulating power plant emissions fell outside the scope of their businesses, though in some cases, firms appeared reluctant to go against the position of the Republican leadership in Congress which had urged the nation's governors to refuse to enact the green power rules.

The reluctance of so many of their corporate allies to back the CPP was a major disappointment to the environmental community. The EDF had described the Power Plan as "the most significant step in US history toward reducing the pollution that causes climate change," while other activists saw it as a "make-or-break climate change initiative" (Gunther, 2015). The silence of so many corporations also served to strengthen the political voices of the plan's business opponents.

Due to judicial challenges, the Clean Power Plan had yet to be implemented when the Trump administration took office in January 2017. In October 2017, EPA Administrator Scott Pruitt announced that he planned to repeal the Plan. Pruitt explained that he had made this decision after "listening to the needs of business," adding that regulators "ought to work with folks all over the country and say, how do we achieve better outcomes by working with industry not against industry" (Samuels, 2017). Predictably, the US Chamber of Commerce, along with 166 state and local Chambers of Commerce, applauded his decision. According to the Chamber, the plan would have adversely affected rural communities whose utilities would be unable to afford the shift away from coal, leading to "economic disaster" (Samuels, 2017).

In fact, however, the majority of states, which represented a disproportionate share of the nation's economy, could have met the CPP's requirements through their existing efforts to reduce their carbon emissions; in effect, they were already in compliance with the proposed regulation, and it would have imposed no additional burdens on their business customers. But twenty-one states would have had to change their energy mix to comply with the Plan, most importantly by reducing their dependence on coal. The former states were more likely to be controlled by Democrats; the latter by Republicans, and it was the latter group of states who applauded Pruitt's decision.

10.12 The Paris Climate Agreement (2015)

In 2015, before the opening of the United Nations Framework Convention on Climate Change Paris (COP 21) eighty-one major corporations, including Google, Facebook, Apple, Hewlett Packard, Monsanto, Coca Cola, Walmart, and General Motors, signed a White House statement to "demonstrate their support for action on climate change and the conclusion of a climate change agreement in Paris that takes a strong step towards a low-carbon sustainable future." In welcoming their support for his administration's carbon reduction goals, President Obama stated that these companies had recognized that "consideration of climate change, energy efficiency, renewable energies are not only not contradictory to their bottom lines, but it can enhance their bottom lines" (McArdle, 2015).

In April 2016, President Obama signed the international Paris Climate Agreement on behalf of the United States. To achieve its goal of limiting the rise of global temperatures to no more than 2°C above preindustrial levels, the agreement established GHG reduction targets for each national signatory. For its part, the United States agreed to reduce its economy-wide GHG emissions 26 to 28 percent below their 2005 levels by 2025. The Center for Climate and Energy Solutions promptly released a statement signed by seventeen corporations, welcoming the progress that had been made in Paris and urging ratification of the Agreement that had been reached (Business Statement, 2017). However faced with Republican and business opposition, the emissions reductions the United States agreed to in the Paris Agreement were not implemented – either through legislation or through rule-making.

Attention now turned to the policies of the newly elected Trump administration. In April 2017, thirty-three companies wrote to President Trump stating that "US business interests are best served by a stable and practical framework facilitating an effective and balanced global response" to climate change and urged the United States to remain in the Paris Agreement. Signatories to the letter included Apple, BP, Dupont, Facebook, Google, HP, Intel, Morgan Stanley, Microsoft, Novartis, Salesforce, Shell, Unilever, and Walmart (Center for Climate and Energy Solutions, 2017).

Following the president's announcement in June 2017 that the United States would be withdrawing from the Paris Climate Agreement, twenty-five companies placed full-page ads in the *New York Times*, the *Wall Street Journal*, and the *New York Post* to voice their support for the Agreement and their disappointment with the president's decision (Victor, 2017). The CEOs of Facebook, Twitter, Square, IBM, Cargill, and Salesforce criticized the president's position, while the CEOs of Tesla and Disney both announced that they were resigning from the president's advisory council in protest.

Approximately fifty CEOs of major American corporations signed one or more letters or public statements expressing their support for the Paris Agreement – a list that included many firms that had not previously been engaged in climate change policies – while more than 1,000 firms with cumulative assets worth more than $3 trillion expressed their support for the Agreement, along with nearly 300 institutional investors with more than $17 trillion in assets (Chen, 2017).

Following the president's withdrawal announcement, more than 2,000 companies and investors signed a "We Are Still In" declaration. Its signatories pledged to work to ensure that the United States meets its commitment under the Paris Agreement, notwithstanding the administration's withdrawal from it. The organizations making this commitment included not only businesses but also states, cities, religious organizations and universities. Collectively they were responsible for more than half of US carbon emissions (Henderson, 2020).

In 2017, Climate Action 100+, an affiliation of more than 200 investors which collectively controlled nearly half of the world's investment capital, urged the world's 100 largest private sector carbon emitters to "cut the financial risk associated with [climate] catastrophe" (Henderson, 2020 p. 48). It specifically challenged these firms both to assess their climate-related financial risks and to put in place measures to bring them into compliance with the goals of the Paris agreement. Subsequently, Blackrock, with $7.4 trillion in assets under management, announced that the firm planned to pressure companies "to disclose plans for operating under a scenario where the Paris Agreement's goal of limiting global warming to less than two degrees is fully realized" (Mckibben, 2020). However these investors did not pressure firms to lobby for regulations or legislation that would require the United States to limit global warming to meet the Paris goals.

In January 2021, President Joseph Biden restored American participation in the Paris Agreement. Shortly afterward, 408 business firms and investors sent an open letter to the president indicating their support for a federal emissions reduction target to meet the goals of the Paris Agreement. In May 2021, eighty large firms and investors called upon lawmakers to "enact policies to mitigate climate risk and meet the federal climate target of cutting emissions by at least 50% below 2005 levels by 2030, on the path to net-zero emission by 2050" (Ketu and Rothstein, 2023). Remarkably, even the Chamber of Commerce greeted the Biden administration by now announcing its support for climate policies such as carbon taxes, carbon emissions caps, and other market-based policies.

The contrasts between business support for the Paris Climate Agreement and the Kyoto Protocol negotiated roughly two decades earlier are striking. Far fewer firms had supported the ratification of the Kyoto Protocol than had advocated continued American participation in the Paris Climate Agreement. While there was relatively little business backlash following Bush's decision to withdraw from the Kyoto Protocol, there was substantial business disapproval of Trump's decision to withdraw from the Paris Agreement. Finally, far more firms and investors expressed their commitment to "staying in" the Paris Agreement – regardless of what the US government did – than had pledged to voluntarily comply with the emission reduction goals of the Kyoto Protocol.

This outpouring of business support for the Paris Climate Agreement reflected "increased pressures and higher expectations from the rest of society" as well as a more widespread recognition of the science of climate change and the risks it posed to many businesses (Gitsham, 2019). But it is also important to note that in marked contrast to cap and trade legislation and the CPP, support for Paris Agreement does not have any actual policy consequences. Even had the United States remained in the Paris Agreement (and it has since returned to it) it would still be up to Congress or the EPA to develop policies that specified how the burdens and benefits of reducing national carbon emissions were to be distributed. Those distributive impacts would likely be substantial, challenging each company to decide how to respond: should it "oppose, support or hedge?" (Meckling, 2015). Because the Agreement has not been implemented, the actual policy commitments of many of the prominent business supporters of the Paris Agreement remain unclear.

10.13 Why So Little Progress?

Notwithstanding the steadily increasing number of companies and investors who have voiced their support for national policies to address the risks of global climate change, business interests opposed to government restrictions on carbon emissions have remained politically dominant. In contrast to other industrial countries and several American states, the federal government has yet to implement a comprehensive policy to reduce the nation's greenhouse gas emissions. While the balance of power within the business community is not the only reason for this policy outcome – in recent years increasing partisan differences have also played an important role – it is worth exploring. Why have the changes in business political preferences described in this chapter not have had more of a policy impact?

Part of the explanation is that the extent of actual business support for climate change regulations may be exaggerated; much of it may actually be rhetorical or strategic. It is one thing to publically recognize the science behind global climate change and the risks it imposes and to want the federal government to address them. But it is quite another to advocate for a specific rule or regulation that imposes additional costs. Supporting the Paris Climate Agreement, emissions trading, or a carbon tax in principle is not the same as actively supporting a legally binding law or regulation. In fact, business climate change advocates have yet to agree on the actual terms of a climate policy that they are willing to support. In contrast, business opponents have been much clearer about their policy preferences.

Another contributing factor is organizational. Both "sides" face the challenge of collective action (Olsen, 1965, 1971). Adopting or not adopting climate regulations are both collective goods. A firm or industry that would be disadvantaged by climate change regulations would benefit from a policy that maintained the status quo even if it did not actively campaign against such proposals. Likewise, a firm or industry that supports climate change regulation would benefit from its enactment even if did not lobby for it.

But opponents have had important organizational advantages which have lowered their costs of collective action. They have benefited from several well-established, well-funded, and politically sophisticated trade associations representing important sectors of the economy such as oil, mining, coal, autos, chemicals, and utilities. These are in addition to cross-sectoral business associations such as the Chamber of Commerce, the National Association of Manufacturers, and the Federation of Independent Business. These established business lobbies have also served as the organizational basis for broader business alliances such as the Global Climate Coalition and the Partnership for a Better Energy Future. While there have been corporate defections from each these associations, organization, and alliances, on balance they have remained important organizational resources for business opposition to federal regulations.

There are associations that represent business interests on the other "side." They include the American Clean Power Association, the Solar Energy Industries Association, and the Renewable Energy Buyers Alliance. But there are far fewer of them and their lack the political resources of the fossil fuel lobbies, which in 2019 outspent them by a ratio of 13:1 (Lexington, 2021). Moreover, the fact that established cross-sectoral business organizations tend to be dominated by firms and industries opposed to climate regulations has forced business advocates to rely more on a series of ad hoc alliances. Nearly a dozen of these have been organized since the late 1990s – many allied with environmental organizations. But they have often had a short-term policy focus, few have proven politically or organizationally resilient and many have had limited business membership.

In addition, many business initiatives have focused on promoting voluntary reductions in carbon emissions, encouraging firms to anticipate the risks of global climate change, or to plan for future restrictions on their carbon emissions. While these private initiatives may have reduced business opposition to climate change regulation, they may also displaced or become a substitute for corporate political support for regulation. By contrast, opponents of climate change regulation face no such organizational distractions; their single-minded goal has been to oppose any regulations that might burden them.

A third set of explanations has to do with the relative economic incentives of business supporters and opponents. To understand its political significance, it is important to recognize a distinctive feature of greenhouse gas emissions. For virtually all conventional pollutants, reducing those places firms at a competitive disadvantage. Thus no auto firm could add emissions reduction technologies to its products as that would raise its products' costs compared to those of its competitors. Nor could any utility install scrubbers if other utilities did not, but greenhouse gas emissions are quite different. For these air pollutants, it can make business sense for a company to reduce them, even if other firms do not so. Hence the large number of voluntary reduction programs, policies, commitments, and agreements, as well as the substantial business investments in "clean tech." Equally significantly, several states have adopted their own GHG emission reduction policies and programs, as have some cities (Schlager, Engel and Rider, 2011).

If reducing GHG emissions made firms, sectors, or states less well off, or placed them at a competitive disadvantage, then we would expect such firms, sectors, and states to actively support federal regulations in order to impose similar costs on their less green competitors – or states. But precisely because the absence of federal regulations have not placed firms or states that are reducing their GHG emissions, promoting renewable energy, or investing in clean technology at a competitive disadvantage, they may have less motivation to devote substantial resources to lobby for such regulations. Ironically, the economic case for investments that reduce emissions of greenhouse gases may have weakened the extent or intensity of business support for national regulations to require such reductions.

Certainly, depending on how they are structured, federal regulations to reduce national GHG emissions can financially benefit some business firms or sectors. But for most business supporters of climate change regulations, those advantages are not critical to either their business strategies or environmental commitments. Without national mandates they can continue to become "greener" – albeit at their own and possibly slower pace. By contrast, national restrictions on GHG emissions threaten the economic viability of the fossil fuel based sectors of the economy. Accordingly, a third reason for the relative political effectiveness of anti-climate change business lobbying is that the firms and sectors opposed to climate regulations have economically more to lose than its proponents have to gain.

This may help explain why "the vast majority of climate lobbying expenditures came from sectors that would be highly impacted by climate legislation" (Brulle, 2018, p. 301). Or why the "Big Tech" supporters of climate change regulations have devoted significantly less of their lobbying resources to supporting their enactment than the "Big Oil" firms have allocated to opposing them (Influence Map, 2021). It may also help explain why of the firms that have devoted the most lobbying resources to climate change between 2006 and 2009, nearly two-thirds are among the nation's largest emitters of carbon (Delmas et al., 2016, p. 176).

In the final analysis, the long-standing maintenance of the status quo may represent a kind of political/economic equilibrium. It does not financially disadvantage those firms, sectors, investors, or local governments that are working to reduce their GHG emissions. Nor does it disadvantage those firms, states, or sectors that are unwilling or unable to make such reductions. However, it does, of course, weaken the ability of the United States to adequately address the risks of global climate change.

References

Bagri, N. (2017). The Environment-Hating US Chamber of Commerce Is Losing the Support of the World's Biggest Companies. *Quartz*, November 19.

Big Tech and Climate Policy: An Influence Map Report (2021). *Influence Map*, January 1.

Brulle, R. (2018). The Climate Lobby: A Sectoral Analysis of Lobbying Spending on Climate Change in the USA, 2100–2016. *Climate Change*, 149, 285–303.

Bradsherm, B. (1999). *New York Times*, July 12.

Business for Innovative Climate and Energy Policy (2019). *Wikipedia*, September 17.

Business Statement. (2017). *Center for Climate and Energy Solutions*.

Center for Climate and Energy Solutions. (2017). Dear President Trump. *C2ES Advertisement*, May 9.

Chen, H. (2017). Companies Defend Paris Deal Because of Its Economic Benefits. *National Resource Defense Council*, June 1.

Clark, A. (2009). US Firms Quit Chamber of Commerce over Climate Change. *The Guardian,* September 29.

Cory J., Lerner M., & Osgood, I. (2021). Supply Chain Linkages and the Extended Carbon Coalition. *American Journal of Political Science*, 65(1), 69–87.

Delmas. M., & Friedman, H. (2023). Disclosure of Political Responsibility with Respect to Climate Change. In T. Lyon, ed., *Corporate Political Responsibility*. Cambridge, UK: Cambridge University Press.

Delmas, M., Lim, J., & Nairn-Birch, N. (2016). Corporate Environmental Performance and Lobbying. *Journal of Management Discoveries*, 2(2), 175–97.

Downie, C. (2017). Fighting for King Coal's Crown: Business Actors in the US Coal and Utility Industries. *Global Environmental Politics*, 17(1), 21–39.

Downie, C. (2019). *Business Battles in the US Energy Sector: Lesson for a Clean Energy Transition.* London: Routledge.

Entine, J. (2009). Why Climate Change Legislation Is Turning Corporate America Green. *Forbes*, October 2.

Gitsham, M. (2019). Why Climate Change and Other Global Problems Are Pushing Some Business Leaders to Embrace Regulation. Sustainability, October 19.

Grumbach, J. (2015). Polluting Industries as Climate Protagonists: Cap and Trade and the Problem of Business Preferences. *Business & Politics*, 17(4), 633–59.

Gunther, M. (2015). Corporate America's Position on the EPA Clean Power Plan. *The Guardian*, April 2.

Henderson, R. (2020). The Unlikely Environmentalists. *Foreign Affairs*, May/June, 47–51.

Karapin, K. (2016). *Political Opportunities for Climate Policy: California, New York, and the Federal Government.* New York, NY: Cambridge University Press.

Kennard, A. (2020). The Enemy of My Enemy: Why Firms Support Climate Change Regulation. *International Organization*, 2, 187–22.

Ketu, Y., & Rothstein, S. (2023). Practicing Responsible Policy Engagement: How Large U.S. Companies Lobby on Climate Change. In T. Lyon, ed., *Corporate Political Responsibility*. Cambridge: Cambridge University Press.

Lavellem, M. (2009). An Army of Lobbyists Readies for Battle on Climate Bill. *Yale Environment*, 360.

Layzar, J. (2007). Deep Freeze: How Business Has Shaped the Global Warming Debate in Congress. In M. Kraft and S. Kamieniecki, eds., *Business and Environmental Policy: Corporate Interests in the American Political System.* Cambridge: MIT Press, pp. 93–126.

Lexington (2021). Green on Brown. *Economist*, October 2.

List of Supporters of the Clean Power Plan in Court. (2016). *Environmental Defense Fund.* www.edf.org/sites/default/files/content/list_of_supporters_of_the_clean_power_plan_in_court.pdf

Lizza, R. (2010). As the World Burns. *New Yorker*, October 2.

Lyon, T., ed. (2010). *Good Cop Bad Cop: Environmental NGOs and their Strategies Toward Business.* Washington DC: Earthscan.

Lyon, T., & Delmas, H. (2018). When Corporations Take Credit for Green Deeds Their Lobbying May Tell Another Story. *The Conversation*, July 17.

Lyon, T., & Mandelkorn, W. (2023). The Meaning of Corporate Political Responsibility. In T. Lyon, ed., *Corporate Political Responsibly.* Cambridge: Cambridge University Press.

Lyon, T., et al. (2018). CSR Needs CPR: Corporate Sustainability and Politics. *California Management Review*, 60(4), 5–24.

McArdle, M. (2015). 81 Major Corporations – Including Google, Facebook, Coca Cola, General Motors – Sign WH Pledge to Back Global Climate Change Deal. *CNS News*, October 20.

McKibben, B. (2020). Wall Street Is Starting to Put Pressure on the Fossil Fuel Industry – Just Not Aggressively Enough. *Fortune*, March 16.

Meckling, J. (2011). *Carbon Coalitions: Business, Climate Politics, and the Rise of Emissions Trading*. Cambridge: MIT Press.

Meckling, J. (2015). Oppose, Support, or Hedge? Distributional Effects, Regulatory Pressure, and Business Strategy in Environmental Politics. *Global Environmental Politics*, 15(2), 19–37.

Meckling, J., & Trachtman, S. (2020). The Home State Effect on National Business Coalitions: Evidence from U.S. Climate Policies. Prepared for Annual Meeting of the American Political Science Association.

Mildenberger, M. (2012). The Politics of Strategic Accommodation: Explaining Business Support for US Climate Policy. Unpublished Paper.

Mildenberger, M. (2020). *Carbon Captured: How Business and Labor Control Climate Politics*. Cambridge: MIT Press.

Mugill, B. (2016). The Suit against the Clean Power Plan, Explained. *Climate Central*, April 12.

Mulkern, A. (2009). Lobbying Cash Paved Climate Bill's Road to House Floor. *New York Times*, June 16.

Olsen, M. (1965). *The Logic of Collective Action*. Cambridge, MA: Harvard University Press.

Partnership for a Better Energy Future. (2014). Air and Radiation Docket and Information Center U.S. Environmental Protection Agency, May 9.

Prattico, E. (2017). Why Business Supported the Clean Power Plan: It Makes Economic Sense. *BSR Blog*, October 18.

Samuels, A. (2017). The Myth That Business Hated Obama's Clean Power Plan. *The Atlantic*, October 10.

Schlager, E., Engel, K., & Rider, S. (2011). *Navigating Climate Change Policy: The Opportunities of Federalism*. Tucson, AZ: University of Arizona Press.

Surowiecki, J. (2009). Exit Though Lobby. *New Yorker*, October 12.

Victor, D. (2017). "Climate Change Is Real": Many U.S. Companies Lament Paris Accord Exit. *New York Times*, June 1.

Vormedal, I. (2010). States and Markets in Global Environmental Governance: The Role of Tipping Points in International Regime Formation. *European Journal of International Relations*, 18(2), 251–75.

Vormedal, I. (2011). From Foe to Friend? The Tipping Point and U.S. Climate Politics. *Business and Politics*, 13(3), 1–29.

Walker, E. (2023). What Drives Firms to Disclose Their Political Activity? In T. Lyon, ed., *Corporate Political Responsibility*. Cambridge: Cambridge University Press.

Webster, L. (2017). Why the Clean Power Plan Is Good for Business. *GreenBiz*, September 13.

Werner T. (2023). Promise and Peril: Lessons from Shareholder Reactions to Corporate Political Activity Disclosure. In T. Lyon, ed., *Corporate Political Responsibility*. Cambridge: Cambridge University Press.

11 | Disclosure of Political Responsibility
The Case of Climate Change

MAGALI A. DELMAS AND HENRY L.
FRIEDMAN

11.1 Introduction

Firms have several channels through which they can influence public policies, including campaign contributions, lobbying, meetings with regulators, and sponsored research. Among these channels, lobbying is one of the most direct and documented conduits that firms can use to shape policy. Annual lobbying reports, whose dollar values are aggregated in Figure 11.1, show that direct lobbying expenditures in the United States run between $3 billion and $4 billion annually. This figure is approximately 12.7 times the amount corporations spend on political action committees (Drutman, 2015, p. 16).

Lobbying is often defined as an attempt to influence government action through either written or oral communication.[1] The activities associated with lobbying include providing information or background materials to decision-makers, monitoring ongoing activities in the policy arena, and providing expertise and knowledge to influence media and decision-makers' perceptions of a policy issue (Brulle, 2018; Drutman, 2015). However, because lobbying practices are

---

[1] For example, the European Commission defines lobbying as involving solicited communication, oral or written, with a public official to influence legislation, policy or administrative decisions (European Commission, 2006). According to the Green Paper of the European Transparency Initiative "lobbying means all activities carried out with the objective of influencing the policy formulation and decision-making processes of the European Institutions." The Green Paper defines lobbyists "as persons carrying out such activities, working in a variety of organizations such as public affairs consultancies, law firms, NGOs, think-tanks, corporate lobby units ('in-house representatives') or trade associations," https://op.europa.eu/en/publication-detail/-/publication/1e468b07-27ba-46bc-a613-0ab96fc10aa9.

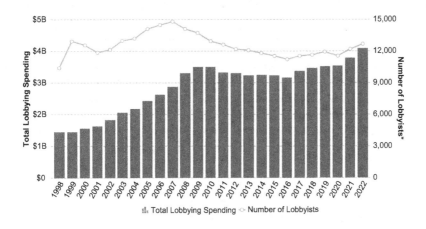

Figure 11.1 Total lobbying spending and number of lobbyists[2]

deeply embedded in a country's democratic and constitutional setting, there is no single legal definition of lobbying across countries
(OECD, 2006).

Climate change is one of the greatest ecological and social challenges of the twenty-first century, and climate legislation has often
been the focus of intense lobbying. In some industries, climate lobbying expenditures might be consistently reported as one of the issues
lobbied, such as in the mining, quarrying, and oil and gas extraction sector (see Figure 11.2). Figure 11.2 reports for the 2006–2013
period the percentage of lobbying expenditures where climate was
identified as one of the issues lobbied and compares it to lobbying
expenditures where climate wasn't mentioned (see methodology in
Appendix A).

Brulle (2018) provides an empirical estimate of lobbying expenditures related to climate change by organizational type and industry
sector over the time period 2000–2016. He estimates that during this
time period, over $2 billion was spent on this activity, constituting 3.9

---

[2] Numbers on this figure are calculations by OpenSecrets based on data from the
Senate Office of Public Records. Data for the most recent year was downloaded
on April 30, 2021, and includes spending from January 1 to March 31. Prior
years include spending from January through December. www.opensecrets.org/
federal-lobbying.

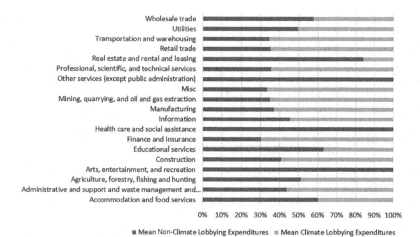

Figure 11.2 Share of expenditures from filings with climate identified as an issue[3]

percent of total lobbying expenditures. He identifies the industries with the highest percentage of lobbying on climate change as the electric utility industry (26.5 percent), the fossil fuel industry (17.7 percent), and transportation (12 percent).

There is increasing concern about the role of political lobbying over climate policy (Meng & Rode, 2019). Meng and Rode calculated that lobbying lowered the probability of enacting the Waxman-Markey bill by 13 percentage points, representing an expected social cost of $60 billion (in 2018 US dollars).

One explanation is that much of business lobbying, rather than being in the public interest, is "special interest" lobbying which seeks to gain an advantage for a particular business or industry group or its stakeholders (Hamilton & Hoch, 1997). Often, corporate interests are at odds with public policies seeking to mitigate climate change or environmental impacts, as firms bear private costs of activities such as carbon mitigation that provide public benefits such as reduced warming and disaster risk. Their political activity can thus encourage policies aligned with only some of their stakeholders, and push policies away from the public interest. As such,

---

[3] Based on data from for the years 2006–2013. Delmas, M., Lim, J., & Nairn-Birch, N. (2016). Corporate Environmental Performance and Lobbying. *Academy of Management Discoveries*, 2(2), 175–97.

there are both private (e.g., investor) and public (e.g., voter) concerns over corporate political activity related to climate. Despite these concerns, limited disclosure of lobbying allows only a highly incomplete understanding of firms' climate-related political activities and hampers an open debate based on scientific information. In this chapter, we develop recommendations for enhanced disclosure of political activity as it relates to climate and other issues relevant to sustainability more broadly.

Our discussion is organized as follows. We first describe the existing disclosures of political activity. We note shortcomings related to difficulty in inferring corporate positions on policies and the limited degree to which existing disclosures capture the broad swath of potential activities. We next describe initiatives aimed at increasing disclosure or facilitating the use of disclosures. These initiatives come from investors and asset managers, NGOs, public institutions such as the EU, nonprofits, and academics. Our last section discusses potential improvements to mandatory disclosure of climate-related political activity, including consideration of content, timing, disclosure channels, users, potentially relevant US regulators, and the value of third parties in aggregating, interpreting, and disseminating information gleaned from disclosures. In the conclusion, we offer a summary and suggestions for future research.

11.2 The Problem with Lobbying Disclosure

Empirical evidence indicates that lobbying on climate change is mostly conducted by big corporations and trade associations that oppose climate regulation. Indeed, the renewable energy sector and environmental organizations were minor players in lobbying for legislation focused on climate change. From 2000 to 2016, Brulle (2018) estimates that neither of these sectors accounted for more than 5 percent of total lobbying spending. Specifically, climate lobbying expenditures by environmental organizations constitute only 3 percent of total lobbying expenditures (Brulle, 2018).[4] He concludes that the vast expenditures

---

[4] This figure does not count volunteer lobbying activities, such as those conducted by nonprofit organizations (Brulle, 2018). Brulle furthermore concludes that actions conducted by nonprofits are often one-time, short-term mobilizations. This is in opposition to professional lobbying organizations, which are a permanent presence on Capitol Hill.

of professional lobbyists representing industry limit the impact of climate advocates from environmental organizations.

Despite this apparent unbalance, however, it is difficult to assess specifically what corporations are lobbying for. It is possible that corporations in the same sector might have divergent lobbying strategies, or that their focus changes over time. However, because lobbying is an activity conducted away from the public eye, researchers and the public can't access information on firms' current lobbying activities at the issue level. There is no record of the discussions that take place behind closed doors between professional lobbyist and government officials. Hence, this lack of open debate might hamper the communication of accurate scientific information. Furthermore, firms can take various pathways to lobby that are often difficult to track. Indeed, firms can lobby via their own in-house lobbyists, hire external lobbyists, or use trade associations to lobby Congress and federal agencies. Furthermore, firms can use complementary strategies to influence regulation. In addition to information strategy (i.e., providing information to regulators) through lobbying, firms can use constituency-building strategies that attempt to influence decision-makers indirectly by first obtaining voter support. By disclosing information related to environmental strategies and performance, dirty firms can suggest to voters and policymakers either that they are clean (i.e., through greenwashing; Lyon & Maxwell, 2011) or their intention to mitigate environmental harm and actions taken to this end (Clark & Crawford, 2012; Kolk & Pinkse, 2007). By doing so, they send the message that government intervention is redundant. At the same time, exemplarily performing companies convey to voters an achievable environmental standard to which competing firms should be held (Denicolo, 2008; Reinhardt, 1999). All these factors make it difficult for the public to identify clearly the position of a corporation on specific issues.

Current disclosure rules don't require firms to disclose their political positions on specific legislation. In the United States, for example, companies must disclose the subject of their lobbying, but do not have to disclose the position that they are lobbying for. Under the 1995 Lobbying Disclosure Act (LDA), all organizations that spend money on federal lobbying efforts are required to fill out quarterly lobbying reports. Specifically, lobbying firms that serve other individuals or entities and that earn (or expect to earn) more than $3,000 for three months of lobbying activities on behalf of a client and organizations whose own employees engage in lobbying on its behalf and that expend (or expect to expend) more than $10,000 for such activities during a three-month period must register with the Secretary of the Senate and the Clerk of the House of Representatives. Lobbying reports have been electronically coded since 1998 and are available for download on the Center for Responsive Politics' website. However, the limited reporting requirements hamper stakeholders' ability to understand firms' positions on specific issues. For example, lobbying disclosure rules don't require firms to provide a dollar value to a specific issue, but rather to disclose all the issues that were lobbied during a quarter associated with an aggregate spending amount. This hampers the precise identification of lobbying spending on specific issues, unless the firm reported only on a single issue for that quarter.

There are other issues that further limit citizens' ability to figure out firms' positions on specific issues that are not addressed by the current version of the LDA. These include shadow lobbying (individual is paid to engage with public officials but doesn't register as lobbyist); grassroots lobbying (attempts to persuade government decision-makers and influence policy outcomes by shifting public opinion and motivating citizens to take action), and the revolving door (when federal employees leave the government for employment in the private sector or the government hires former private sector employees for government jobs) (Congressional Research Service, 2015; Thomas & LaPira, 2017).

In sum, one cannot find out what lobbyists are saying about an issue by consulting the reports available through the LDA. Instead, one must engage in extensive independent work analyzing a host of outside sources to find out where a company stands.[5] But even such costly inquiry is imperfect as we describe below.

11.3 Attempts to Approximate Firm Lobbying Positions on Specific Issues

Researchers have tried to approximate the different positions that firms take on specific issues. The prevailing view is that climate regulation

---

[5] See Favotto, Kollman, and McMillan (2023) for an example that involves inferring lobbyist positions based on content analysis of transcripts of testimony before UK Parliamentary committees.

threatens industry, so most firms lobby against regulations and green firms don't lobby, having little interest in the outcome. However, the reality is much less monolithic. For example, Kim et al. (2016) show that firms in the electric utility sector might have different lobbying positions on climate change regulation. The authors link lobbying disclosure reports to detailed data on the fuel choices of all electric utilities in the United States along with socioeconomic, institutional, and political data from the states where the utilities operate. They argue that some utilities have strong incentives to lobby for the Waxman-Markey climate bill. As another example, Meng and Rode (2019) approximated firm lobbying positions, using market prices of publicly listed firms that lobbied on Waxman-Markey to infer which ones were expected to gain or lose value from the policy and by how much.

Delmas et al. (2016) examined the relationship between carbon emissions and climate lobbying expenditures of 1,141 firms between 2006 and 2009. The authors were able to focus on lobbying related to climate change by examining the issue descriptions that are filed with lobbying reports. They searched the issue descriptions for words that are related to climate change, such as "climate," "global warming," and "greenhouse," as well as the names and numbers of climate-related bills; if they found climate-related key words, bill names, or bill numbers in the issue description, they coded the amount as climate lobbying spending. If the authors found the search term in the issue description, then the entire amount (for the quarter to which the report refers) was coded as climate lobbying. This approach, however, likely overestimates the amount spent on climate lobbying as firms often lobby on multiple issues, and it is impossible to isolate the climate lobbying amount from other lobbying. It is also difficult to focus solely on those that only lobby on climate issues, since many firms lobby on multiple issues. This would severely limit sample size.

The authors estimated that between 2006 and 2009, 14 percent of firms lobbied on climate-related bills and issues. In the data, the usual suspects were most active in climate lobbying: Companies in the automobiles and parts sector spent an average of approximately $1.8 million lobbying climate change-related regulations per year, followed by the utilities sector ($1.1 million), oil and gas sector ($0.8 million), and basic resources sector ($0.8 million).

Their analysis shows that both higher than average greenhouse gas–emitting firms and lower than average greenhouse gas–emitting firms are active in lobbying climate change, challenging the stereotypical view that browner firms are most likely to lobby. Meanwhile, companies that had average levels of emissions didn't spend as much, having less to gain or lose from potential changes in laws. They find a U-shaped curve, in which both low and high carbon-emitting corporations lobbied extensively on climate legislation, and firms with intermediate carbon emissions spent relatively little on climate lobbying. Firms that stood to either gain or lose a great deal from climate legislation due to their levels of carbon emissions perceived that substantial interests were at stake, and thus invested heavily in lobbying efforts. Firms in between, with intermediate levels of carbon emissions, perceived that this legislation would not impact them greatly, and so did not invest heavily in lobbying. While confirming the stereotype that dirtier firms are more politically active, the findings suggest that greener firms also vie for political influence.[6] As an illustration, a scatterplot of the GHG emissions and climate lobbying expenditures for the basic resources and utility industries is shown in Figure 11.3a and 11.3b. InfluenceMap, which scores companies based on their positive and negative engagement toward climate policy, also shows important differences among firms within the same sector (InfluenceMap, 2021).[7]

Ackerman (2007) investigated the position of electric utilities from 2001 to 2005 on climate change regulation. She used publicly available literature published by each firm, sent out questionnaires, and personally met with lobbyists. She found tremendous variability in the positions of electric utilities as related to the support of voluntary mechanisms to reduce emissions and on subsidies for cost-effective low-emission technologies versus mandated reductions. She also found variability in the amount that each company voluntarily chooses to reveal about its positions on nine key issues under active debate.

Vogel (2023) argues that it is difficult to distinguish between a firm's primary goal, which is often no regulation, and its secondary policy goal, which is to enact the least burdensome policy alternative. This

---

[6] Lobbying by green firms still plausibly represents "special interest" political activity, as green policies can create barriers to entry or impose costs on brown competitors, benefiting green incumbents.

[7] https://lobbymap.org/site//data/000/861/CA100_AuditReview_April2021.pdf

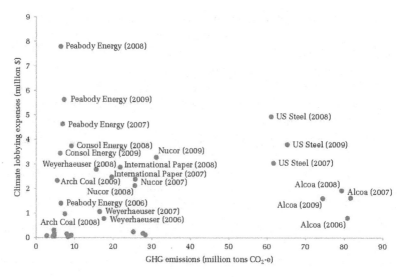

Figure 11.3a Lobbying expenditures associated with climate versus GHG emissions in the basic resources industry[8]

might explain why some companies may back climate policies in order to include provisions that are more favorable to them. Likewise, they may support a particular climate change proposal in order to preempt the enactment of a more stringent one. In addition, firm preferences over a regulation can shift over time depending on the likelihood of the enactment of the regulation (Rivera et al., 2009). A firm might initially oppose a regulation and, when it is likely to be adopted, start to bargain over its specific terms.

Others have shown that some corporations are contradictory in their actions, expressing concern about the threat of climate change in some venues – such as company websites, Securities and Exchange Commission (SEC) filings, annual reports, or statements to Congress – while working to weaken policy responses to climate change in others. For example, Grumbach (2015) shows that polluting firms joined the U.S. Climate Action Partnership (USCAP) coalition in pursuit of a national cap and trade policy, and appeared

---

[8] From Delmas et al. (2016). Reproduced with the permission of the Academy of Management.

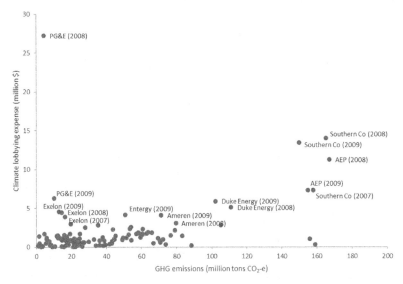

Figure 11.3b Lobbying expenditures associated with climate versus GHG emissions in the utilities industry[9]

to support climate legislation while providing resources in order to prevent the proposal's passage.[10] As another example, Cho et al. (2018) contrast the sustainability discourse via corporate reports to corporate political donations via Political Action Committee (PAC) contributions within a sample of US oil and gas firms. They use the context of the passage of the American-Made Energy and Good Jobs Act, also known as the Arctic National Wildlife Refuge (ANWR) Bill. The ANWR Bill was designed to allow oil exploration within the most sensitive environmental areas in the Refuge but failed to

---

[9] From Delmas et al. (2016). Reproduced with the permission of the Academy of Management.

[10] Alternatively, firms may support green policies that have low chances of success, potentially to mitigate the potential impact of moderate policies that, while more moderate, are against the firm's direct economic interests and more likely to pass. As an example, Exxon Mobil voiced public support for a carbon tax while one of its lobbyists was secretly on record saying that Exxon Mobil only supported the tax because it would be impossible to implement (www.bloomberg.com/news/articles/2021-08-06/exxon-mobil-suspended-from-international-conservation-alliance, accessed August 9, 2021).

become law. The bill was vigorously debated in the US Congress in 2005 and 2006. In the ANWR context, the primary interest of the US oil and gas firms is to be granted the rights to exploit the oil reserves of the wildlife refuge. The authors expect that lobbying spending will be used to promote the firms' interests, that is to say, to be able to drill in the Refuge. Their results suggest that the firms' sustainability discourse on environmental stewardship and responsibility contrasts sharply with their proactive political strategies targeted to facilitate the passage of the ANWR Bill. Their research documents the deceptive nature of the discourse contained in standalone sustainability reports.

While in the case of the ANWR bill it seems reasonable to assume that oil industry corporate lobbying should be in favor of drilling, the literature cited above shows that in most cases there is no direct correspondence between lobbying positions and entire sectors of the economy. Within any sector, there can be variances among corporations in the nature and extent of their support of or opposition to climate legislation. Furthermore, it might also be possible that firms appear to lobby on one issue while supporting the opposite view.[11]

11.4 Demand for More Transparency

The perception among the general public is that the wrong incentives are driving policy decisions at the expense of the public interest. There is the hope that transparency could potentially rebuild faith in the system, especially among millennials, who have increased distrust of nearly all political institutions.[12] This idea is shared by lobbyists and legislators. In surveys by the Organization for Economic Co-operation and Development (OECD), 74 percent of lobbyists and 68 percent of legislators agreed that transparent lobbying would increase citizens' trust in the decision-making process.

Fortunately, investors are banding together and pushing for transparency. For example, the CDP (formerly the Carbon Disclosure Project), an organization that works to promote disclosure of climate

---

[11] Ketu and Rothstein (2023) discuss the frequent conflict between corporations' stated concerns over climate change and pursuit of emissions reductions, on the one hand, and opposition to science-driven climate policy, on the other.

[12] www.thecrimson.com/article/2013/5/2/millenials-distrust-government/

performance of major corporations, is backed by investors and asset managers representing more than $100 trillion in assets. Recognizing that lobbying is an important part of a company's sustainability strategy, the CDP has recently added more detailed questions regarding engagement with policymakers. This includes lobbying, but also extends to engagement through trade associations and funding of research organizations – information that is not available under the Lobbying Disclosure Act. This information can illuminate an otherwise invisible firm political strategy.

Furthermore, some shareholder proposals are asking firms to provide more comprehensive disclosure of their lobbying activities. For example, the Interfaith Center on Corporate Social Responsibility (ICCR) has issued shareholder proposals requesting that the target company prepares a single report updated annually with information about all of its lobbying activities, direct and indirect. Specifically, the proposal asks for an annual report that provides disclosure on yearly federal and state lobbying expenditures, as well as indirect lobbying such as disclosure of memberships in trade associations and "social welfare" organizations (501(c)(4) organizations that make political expenditures and lobby), and membership in or contributions to any tax-exempt organization that writes and endorses model legislation.[13] ICCR cites Eastman Chemical as an example of a company that provides disclosure in all or nearly all of these areas. On its website, Eastman currently provides information about its PAC contributions, Lobbying and Participation in Trade Associations and Business Organizations, and Eastman LDA Filings.[14] For a more thorough discussion of political engagement reports see Lyon and Mandelkorn (2023) and Walker (2023).

Large asset managers have published recommendations for disclosure of corporate political activity and guidelines for how they approach shareholder proposals related to corporate political activity. Statements from BlackRock and Vanguard encourage firms to disclose political contributions, lobbying policy, management and board responsibilities, whether the company has a PAC, how PAC spending

---

[13] www.iccr.org/sites/default/files/resources_attachments/lobbying_disclosure_best_practice_examples_dec._2016.pdf
[14] www.eastman.com/Company/investors/Corporate_Governance/Political_Activity/Pages/Political_Activity.aspx

aligns with corporate objectives, and trade association membership.[15] They also call for statements regarding firms' political activity philosophy and board oversight, with an eye toward monitoring and mitigating material risks to long-term shareholders.

Similarly, the Global Reporting Initiative (GRI) requires disclosure on lobbying and participation in public policy development, as well as the total value of financial and in-kind contributions to political parties, politicians, and related institutions.[16]

Disclosure guidance provided by the Taskforce on Climate-related Financial Disclosure (TCFD) of the Financial Stability Board is targeted at helping firms in "disclosing clear, comparable and consistent information about the risks and opportunities presented by climate change" (TCFD 2017 "Final Report," page i). TCFD guidance is organized into four elements: governance; strategy; risk management: and metrics and targets. Although the TCFD guidance does not explicitly reference lobbying or political activity, corporate disclosures on these under the TCFD umbrella could fall reasonably into any of the four elements. Similarly, disclosure under the Sustainability Accounting Standard Board's (SASB) disclosure standards could incorporate information on lobbying and policy influence related to climate if such activities might have effects that are plausibly material to investors.

While these initiatives driven by investors are a step in the direction of more disclosure, they are still inadequate to push a large number of firms to voluntarily adopt comprehensive political activity disclosure.

11.5 Worldwide Initiatives to Improve Lobbying Disclosure

As a response to demands from citizens for increased transparency and integrity in lobbying, the OECD issued ten principles to provide decision-makers with directions and guidance to foster transparency

---

[15] See, for example, BlackRock and Vanguard statements regarding the evaluation of corporate political activities at www.blackrock.com/corporate/literature/publication/blk-commentary-perspective-on-corporate-political-activities.pdf and https://about.vanguard.com/investment-stewardship/perspectives-and-commentary/INVSPOLS_032021.pdf, respectively (accessed August 1, 2021).

[16] www.globalreporting.org/standards/media/1030/gri-415-public-policy-2016.pdf

and integrity in lobbying. Furthermore, the European Parliament, Commission, and Council have developed a Transparency Register, which tracks interactions between organizations or individuals and EU institutions involved in policy-setting and rulemaking. Researchers within academia and beyond are also developing initiatives to further lobbying transparency.

11.5.1 The OECD Framework

The OECD principles focus on four main areas: (1) building an effective and fair framework for openness and access; (2) enhancing transparency; (3) fostering a culture of integrity and (4) mechanisms for effective implementation, compliance, and review.[17]

The OECD framework emphasizes that core disclosure requirements should elicit information that captures the intent of lobbying activity; identifies its beneficiaries, and points to those offices and institutions that are its targets. They argue that disclosure requirements should ask lobbyists to identify the interests being represented by naming their clients and beneficiaries, as well as providing details on the objectives of lobbying activities. Furthermore, they detail the importance of timely registration and periodic reporting of lobbying activities to provide credible and up-to-date information on what takes place in the world of lobbying. Finally, mechanisms should be put in place for effective implementation to secure compliance. However, the public right to know should be balanced with avoiding excessive disclosure costs.

11.5.2 EU Regulations

The European Transparency Register tracks interactions between organizations or individuals and EU institutions involved in policy-setting and rulemaking. At the time of writing, participation in the Transparency Register is voluntary for organizations, although some activities (e.g., speaking at EU conferences) are limited to registrants. Across the EU, member countries vary in whether they lobbyists are required to register, though some provide incentives for registration

---

[17] www.oecd.org/gov/ethics/oecdprinciplesfortransparencyandintegrity inlobbying.htm

where it is voluntary.[18] The EU also tracks lobbying spending, with LobbyFacts.eu providing a platform through which users can access data. Notably, the EU regulations focus on lobbying EU institutions, rather than lobbying in general. Similar to the United States, lobbying at lower jurisdictional levels (member states, provinces, districts, etc.) is not broadly captured in the central repository.

Separate from the Transparency Register, the European Commission is in the process of updating mandatory reporting of nonfinancial information, via a review of the Non-Financial Reporting Directive (NFRD) and the adoption of a proposal for a Corporate Sustainability Reporting Directive (CSRD).[19] Under the CSRD, which is wide-ranging, publicly listed and large private companies would be required to provide audited information according to EU sustainability reporting standards to a central repository in a tagged, machine-readable form. The European Financial Reporting Advisory Group (EFRAG), tasked with developing the sustainability standards, provided an extensive set of reports and appendices in early 2021.[20] Besides requiring disclosures of impacts on the environment and people, EFRAG calls for governance disclosures that include lobbying activity, under a business ethics sub-topic.[21] However, they do not specifically highlight the need for disclosure of climate-related political activity.

11.5.3 Research Initiatives within Academia and Beyond

In addition, there have been several research initiatives within academia and beyond to help increase access to lobbying data. They either help by downloading the complex lobby data and communicating it in a more useful manner or by providing linked identifiers to aggregate the data with other databases.

---

[18] See www.europarl.europa.eu/news/en/headlines/eu-affairs/20180108STO 91215/transparency-register-who-is-lobbying-the-eu-infographic, accessed July 30, 2021, which reports "environment, research and innovation, and climate action" as the most popular topics of interest for organizations in the Transparency Register.

[19] See https://ec.europa.eu/info/business-economy-euro/company-reporting-and-auditing/company-reporting/corporate-sustainability-reporting_en, accessed July 30, 2021. The target date for standard adoption is October 2022.

[20] "Proposals for a relevant and dynamic EU sustainability reporting standard setting," available at https://ec.europa.eu/info/publications/210308-efrag-reports_en, accessed July 30, 2021.

[21] See page 101 of the report referenced in footnote 20.

For example, Delmas et al. (2016) developed a methodology to download the lobby data regarding climate change and posted the data online.[22] Lobbying reports must include one or more general issue areas lobbied, chosen from a list of seventy-nine issue areas. Each issue area listed in the report is accompanied by a more specific description of the issue. For instance, a report may list a general issue area such as environmental/superfund, and further elaborate its specific lobbying issue by naming the bills lobbied, "S. 2191, America's Climate Security Act of 2007." Alternatively, it may give a brief description of issues, for example, "Contact with members of Congress and congressional staff with regard to proposed climate change legislation." In order to determine whether lobbying pertains to climate change, the authors searched through the issue descriptions for key words, bill numbers, and bill names. The key words they searched for were "climate," "global warming," "greenhouse," "GHG," and "GHGs." Additionally, they included the more prominent climate bills: the Waxman-Markey Bill (in 2009–2010) and the lesser known Lieberman-Warner cap-and-trade bill (2007–2008). Before 2007, climate bills were less prominent. For the Waxman-Markey Bill, they searched for terms: "H.R. 2454," "Waxman-Markey," "American Clean Energy and Security Act," and "ACES." For the Lieberman-Warner Bill: "S. 2191," "S. 3036," and "Lieberman-Warner." Both S. 2191 and S. 3036 were iterations of the Lieberman-Warner Bill.

However, this methodology was limited since when the authors found the search term in the issue description, then the entire amount (for the quarter to which the report refers) was coded as climate lobbying amount. This is because specific issues cannot be isolated, and this likely overestimates the amount spent on climate lobbying as organizations often lobby on multiple issues.

As another example beyond climate change, in 2018 In Song Kim launched LobbyView,[23] a publicly available online database where researchers, journalists, and others who are interested in politics can search political activities that have been filed and reported. LobbyView includes identifiers that can be matched to common financial datasets, such as Compustat and CRSP, which in turn can be linked to additional

---

[22] See Appendix A for the full methodology. The full data presented in their article is available at www.ioes.ucla.edu/project/climate-change-lobbying-dataset/

[23] www.lobbyview.org/

data on governance, investor attention, ESG performance or ratings, voluntary corporate disclosure, coverage by financial analysts, and more. Outside of Academia, InfluenceMap,[24] a for-profit company, has developed a systematic approach to tracking, assessing and scoring companies and industry groups on their climate policy engagement. The objective of InfluenceMap is to produce a detailed analysis of corporate climate policy engagement at the company level. InfluenceMap combines data from the company website, social media, responses to the CDP questionnaire, legislation consultations, media reports, CEO messaging, financial disclosures, and information in the E.U. register. As stated on the InfluenceMap website, the InfluenceMap system does not account for hidden and undisclosed information relating to activities such as private meetings and money flows. Therefore, while the system does reveal a comprehensive account of corporate and industry group behavior based on publicly available data, there are still possibilities that corporations argue for different positions in closed-door meetings.

While these initiatives provide helpful information for researchers and the community, they are still limited by the current lobbying disclosure rules.

11.6 What Better Mandated Disclosure Could Look Like

In the United States, all the LDA requires in terms of disclosure of the content of lobbying communications (other than the names of active lobbyists) are the general issue area, the "specific" issue, and the House of Congress or federal agency lobbied. We argue below that there is also the need to provide information on the lobbying entity position on a specific issue. Furthermore, this information needs to be provided in a timely manner, and there should also be information on the officials who are lobbied.

11.6.1 Provide Information on Firm/Lobbyist Position

The first element to improve lobbying transparency is to mandate the disclosure of the positions that lobbyists take on specific issues. There are two main reasons for this disclosure. First, shining a light on the positions of lobbyists allows responsible and intelligent policymaking

---

[24] https://influencemap.org/

(Ackerman, 2007). Lobbying can be legitimate if all sides present their case and a decision is made through democratic processes on the basis of maximizing benefits, respecting rights and ensuring a just distribution. Statements made in public by lobbyists can be scrutinized by others and challenged with competing facts and arguments (Favotto et al., 2023; Scherer and Voegtlin, 2023). The resulting public debate is consistent with a healthy political process (Johnson, 2006). However, the current lack of transparency on lobbying doesn't provide the ability to probe or dispute statements made by lobbyists.

Second, the public will become distrustful if a firm's public pronouncements on an issue appear to diverge sharply from its lobbyists' positions. Transparent lobbyist positions are therefore important in order to further effective discourse, increase trust in American democracy, as well as to provide the incentives for firms to adopt consistent positions across their corporate sustainability reports and lobbying activities. Indeed, as described above, without transparency on lobbyists' positions, firms might carefully design "backstage" lobbying strategies that might sharply contrast with the "front stage" discourse contained in their corporate sustainability reports (Cho et al., 2018). In such cases, firm stakeholders such as investors, consumers, employees, and the community might not have a clear picture of firm positions on specific issues.

11.6.2 Timing of the Disclosure: Provide Information in a Timely Manner

In addition, the timing of the report is important (Ackerman, 2007). One of the chief objections to disclosure regimes is that the information often comes too late (Johnson, 2006). In the LDA, the current reporting, which is required twice a year, isn't enough to allow other actors to comment and respond to the arguments provided by lobbyists in a timely manner. By the time someone reviews the data, decisions have often been made about the underlying issues and public debate has moved on to other subjects (Johnson, 2006). Timeliness issues are partially resolved in public comment processes if agencies post comment letters in real time. However, linking comment letters to lobbying activity would facilitate a more informed public deliberation, because lobbying can enhance the influence of some comment letters relative to others. A lack of timely disclosure of lobbying thus mitigates the value of timely disclosures of comment letters. This could be addressed via a brief questionnaire on lobbying activity required when public comments are provided.

If the information on lobbyists' positions is provided on the internet, it can be available to everyone including the public, Congress members, and other stakeholders (Drutman & Mahoney, 2017). It will also help better understand at what stage of the regulation is lobbying implemented. Indeed, corporate political strategies might differ depending on the stages of the political process. For example, in the legislative stage, political leaders create new laws responding to the issue; while in the implementation stage, administrative agencies flesh out the details of the new legislation, and regulators, police, and the courts enforce it. Firm political positions and strategies might vary depending on the stage of the political process, with increasing resistance as the policy process moves from initiation to selection and growing cooperation thereafter (Rivera et al., 2009).

11.6.3 Provide Information on Officials Lobbied

In addition to disclosing the lobbyist position on a specific issue, disclosure on with whom the position is discussed should be mandated (Luneburg, 2008). Luneburg argues that this is because public officials represent the public interest, and it is important to learn who public officials are speaking to, and what content was presented to them in order to allow the public to respond to possibly false, misleading, skewed, incomplete, or simply different views and information. He describes how one of the lobbying bills introduced in the 110th Congress requires somewhat more detailed reporting with regard to lobbying communications than does the current LDA. In this proposed bill, which applied only to the executive branch, it was proposed that each record made, and each report filed, under subsection (a) shall contain: (1) the name of the covered executive branch official; (2) the name of each private party who had a significant contact with that official; and (3) for each private party so named, a summary of the nature of the contact, including: (A) the date of the contact; (B) the subject matter of the contact and the specific executive branch action to which the contact relates; and (C) if the contact was made on behalf of a client, the name of the client.[25]

---

[25] H.R. 984, 110th Cong. § 2(a) (2007). This bill did not progress beyond introduction and markup. See www.congress.gov/bill/110th-congress/house-bill/984, accessed August 5, 2021.

11.6.4 Provide Information on Political Activities beyond Lobbying

Firms can use many different strategies to influence the climate regulation they face. Beyond lobbying activities directed at influencing policymakers directly, firms can influence the rules and regulations they face using contributions to political campaigns, endorsements of politicians, contributions to politicians' pet projects or affiliated charities, public influence campaigns, sponsored research, and the provision of expertise (de Figueiredo & Richter, 2014). Each of these can also be done through trade associations, industry bodies, or special topic interest groups. Firms with significant employment or investment footprints also can use the allocation of their human, physical, and financial capital investments to garner concessions.[26] This is a particular concern if concessions in one jurisdiction have externalities on others, as is broadly the case for carbon emissions linked to climate change. Therefore, to provide a comprehensive view of firms' political activities, firms should disclose information on the broad range of their corporate political activity.

Existing political disclosure requirements capture a portion of lobbying and campaign contribution expenditures, largely at the federal level, although some states have more demanding disclosure rules. However, these requirements leave information about many of the other activities either undisclosed or provided only tangentially. Firms do not, in general, disclose meetings between their agents and regulators. The provision of help in the drafting of rules or standards goes largely unrecognized. Charitable contributions and public influence campaigns, in contrast, are recognized as financial expenditures. However, there is no effort that we know of that attempts to differentiate between expenditures in these categories undertaken in the pursuit of influence over public policy rather than other goals (e.g., donations to improve local communities or advertising directed at gaining market share).

---

[26] For example, in early 2020, a German court sided with Tesla over environmentalists, allowing Tesla to resume clearing trees as part of preparation for construction of a factory. The environmentalists characterized the trees as part of a forest habitat, while Tesla characterized the trees as a pine plantation. See www.dw.com/en/tesla-wins-court-approval-to-build-gigafactory-by-clearing-forest-in-germany/a-52454649, accessed July 29, 2021.

Additional disclosure requirements for publicly traded companies mandate the provision of information potentially relevant for understanding firms' influence activities. Specific categories include legal proceedings and risk factor disclosures in the annual report and, relatedly, contingent losses, which are either recognized in financial statements as liabilities or described in the notes to financial statements. Firms are required to disclose legal proceedings, and expressly instructed to disclose proceedings arising from environmental infractions.[27] Material risk factor disclosures are also mandated. Firms are required to explain how specific risks, potentially including regulatory or climate risks, might affect the business.[28] In the financial statements and notes, firms provide information about contingent liabilities or losses, that is, losses that depend on circumstances that are uncertain at the time of reporting but will be resolved in the future. Loss contingencies are an accounting treatment of risks, including those arising from legal proceedings. Firms are required to recognize liabilities for contingent losses that are measurable and probable, and must discuss contingent losses that are reasonably possible in the notes to financial statements. For each of these disclosures – legal proceedings, risk factors, and contingent losses – firms could provide information about their actions to mitigate the consequences of legal proceedings, material risks, or contingent liabilities. Such actions plausibly include political activity.

To provide a comprehensive view of firms' influence activities, firms should disclose information broadly. This would include disclosures of lobbying and contributions already mandated at the federal level, expanded to disclosures of similar activities and expenditures at the state, municipality, and international levels. Disclosures by jurisdictions or by jurisdictional aggregates would be helpful, and is already done for financial reporting of income tax expenses and firms' geographical segments, where applicable. Beyond lobbying and

---

[27] 17 CFR § 229.103 – (Item 103) Legal proceedings. Accessed at www.law .cornell.edu/cfr/text/17/229.103 on July 29, 2021.

[28] 17 CFR § 229.105 – (Item 105) Risk factors. Accessed at www.law.cornell .edu/cfr/text/17/229.105 on July 29, 2021. SEC Chair Gary Gensler indicated an upcoming proposal of mandatory qualitative and qualitative climate risk disclosure rules in a July 28 speech at the Principles for Responsible Investment (www.sec.gov/news/speech/gensler-pri-2021-07-28, accessed August 5, 2021).

contributions, firms should also disclose the influence activities their agents undertake, including political endorsements, involvement in policy-writing and implementation, and lawsuits to either support or hinder the enforcement of regulation. Separate reporting of charitable and advertising expenditures targeted at policy influence may also be relevant for some firms. Overall, understanding the role that a firm has in shaping its regulatory environment requires significant information across a number of levers through which firms can exert influence over environmental policy.

Similar to the measurement of emissions across a firm's value chain (i.e., scopes 1, 2, and 3), it is important to capture firms' political impact through both their own activities and the activities of organizations they sponsor, control, contribute to, or support via membership. Industry associations, PACs, and Super PACs in particular have the potential to engage in significant political activity. Disclosures should "pierce the veil" to attribute their activities to their sponsors and members, regardless of whether the second parties are required to disclose activities themselves. This can be complicated for employee PACs that may be technically independent, even though administered by corporate executives.[29]

11.6.5 Disclosure for Whom?

There are several potential stakeholders at which disclosure of climate-related political activity can be targeted. We group these broadly into four categories: voters, investors, non-investor stakeholders, and community-members.[30]

---

[29] See, e.g., the Employees of Northrop Grumman Political Action Committee (ENGPAC), which is "governed by a Steering Committee comprised of company executives and is funded solely from the voluntary personal contributions it receives from eligible employees" (www.northropgrumman .com/investor-relations/political-contributions/, accessed August 2, 2021).

[30] Firms are also interested in governmental activities. GovPredict, which was acquired by Phone2Action, "provides legislative, regulatory and issue monitoring, as well as campaign finance intelligence." Phone2Action provides grassroots advocacy software to firms, industry associations, and interest groups. Phone2Actions's CEO lauded the merger as allowing the firm to offer "an advanced suite of solutions to enable government relations and public affairs professionals to track and influence the policies that impact their work" (www .businesswire.com/news/home/20201102005838/en/Phone2Action-Acquires-GovPredict-to-Provide-the-Most-Comprehensive-Solution-for-Government-Affairs-and-Grassroots-Advocacy-Teams, accessed August 2, 2021).

Voters are key decision-makers in any democracy. Disclosures of firms' political influence activities can help voters better understand the means and motives behind both policy proposals and elected representatives. While much of the existing disclosure focuses on firms' influence of elected representatives, direct democracy via ballot initiatives provides an important channel though which firms can exert significant influence on policies.[31] Voters more informed about the origins and support for policies and representatives should be better placed to make decisions more aligned with their interests and preferences, consistent with inherent goals of representative and direct democracy.

Investors are interested in how firms acquire and engage their capital, be it human, physical, or financial.[32] Political influence activities can mitigate policy risks and help firms avoid unforeseen costs. Climate change in particular imposes both transition and physical risks on companies. For many firms, these risks are no less important than risks related to competition, access to capital, commodity price fluctuations, or demand shocks. As such, firms' management of these risks is plausibly material to investors as they make capital allocation decisions. Extractive firms and utilities in particular face risks involving future regulatory interventions and stranded assets. Disclosure of political influence activities can help investors understand how firms are managing their exposure to climate-related risks. As of the time of writing, the SEC is in the process of updating guidance and potentially issuing new rules on climate-related corporate disclosure. Their request for comments, while not explicitly requesting consideration of lobbying or political influence activities, did ask for input on "how disclosure rules could elicit meaningful discussion of the registrant's views on its climate-related risks and opportunities," which are likely to depend to varying degrees on climate-related policies and regulation.[33]

---

[31] As an example, DaVita "spent $68 million ... to defeat a union-backed California ballot measure to more strictly regulate dialysis centers." Ostrov, B.F. (2021), Will DaVita's indictment alter its big political spending in California? Accessed at https://calmatters.org/health/2021/07/dialysis-california-davita/ on July 29, 2021.

[32] See statements cited in footnote 15.

[33] See Acting SEC Chair Allison Herren Lee's March 15, 2021 statement, "Public input welcomed on climate change disclosures" (www.sec.gov/news/public-statement/lee-climate-change-disclosures, accessed January 2, 2022).

Non-investor stakeholders are customers and suppliers, including labor-supplying employees. Customers, in their purchase decisions, may be concerned about the use of the proceeds or the potential for their purchases to be viewed as implicit support for firms' actions broadly defined. Several boycott movements have emphasized customers' wallet power as a means of persuading firms to change strategies or operations, for example, to avoid unfair or oppressive labor practices.[34] Suppliers and employees are likely to have similar concerns as customers, though focused on their business relations rather than purchases. Employer reputation is plausibly important, and employees may gain or lose from association with the influence activities their employers undertake (Darnell & McDonnell, 2023). Additionally, both employees and customers may be directly affected by the policies a firm supports or opposes, as even environmental policies can affect product safety (e.g., contaminant content in food) and workplace conditions (e.g., air quality at a production facility) (Scherer & Voegtlin, 2023). As such, both customers and employees stand to benefit from disclosures that facilitate a better understanding of firms' political influence activities.

We use "community members" to refer to additional parties potentially affected by firms' influence over environmental policies. Their plausible interest in disclosures about firms' influence activities derives from costs imposed or benefits provided by such activities. Narrowly, this includes directly affected households, such as landowners whose water sources may be affected by pollutants, conservation mandates, or climate change. Broadly construed, community members can be viewed through a global lens given the worldwide implications of climate change.

11.6.6 Should Agencies or Firms Disclose?

Our breakdown of stakeholders above suggests several potential channels through which disclosures of political activities might be

---

[34] For example, a "study by Kantar UK reveals that 77% of UK grocery shoppers have, in the past 12 months, switched, avoided or boycotted buying certain products, or would consider doing so in the future, based on brands' environmental policies" (www.talkingretail.com/news/industry-news/consumers-boycotting-brands-environmental-policies-kantar-reveals-04-12-2019/, accessed August 2, 2021).

promulgated. Society has a general interest in informed, thoughtful voters. A focus on voters is consistent with political activity disclosure mandates imposed by federal law (e.g., related to campaign contributions and lobbying expenditures). Securities regulators, such as the SEC, could mandate corporate disclosures for registrants targeted at investors. Notably, as of late 2021, they are proceeding toward issuing new rules on disclosure related to climate change, albeit with little emphasis on climate-related lobbying. SEC rules, however, typically apply only to firms that have issued publicly traded securities or large entities with significant ownership or activity in public markets. Regulators focusing on employee or customer welfare (e.g., agencies under the Departments of Labor and Commerce) could mandate disclosures, though their mandates would focus on implications for their constituents. Finally, environmental regulators, such as the EPA or agencies under the Department of the Interior, could set up and enforce disclosures regarding political influence over policies that affect various communities.

The diversity of potential stakeholders interested in firms' climate-related political activities intersects with the patchwork regulatory framework in place in the United States. Because firms can pursue political influence across a variety of channels, no single regulator seems well placed to provide a comprehensive disclosure framework. Regulators can impose disclosure mandates targeted at benefiting their constituents or within their regulatory remit, and can provide information about firms' influence activities with the specific regulator. The federal government can also centrally report some activities, such as comment letters or meetings with regulatory agencies.[35] Geographical stratification (e.g., state versus federal versus international) is also relevant here, since different jurisdictions may impose different disclosure requirements, even within a given stakeholder-focused silo.

---

[35] See, for instance, comment letter tracking at regulations.gov, and summaries of the Federal Reserve's communications with the public regarding rulemaking and implementation of the Dodd-Frank Wall Street Reform and Consumer Protection Act of 2010 at www.federalreserve.gov/regreform/communications-with-public.htm

Effective use of broad information on firms' political activities requires the information to be accessible. A concern arises that information relevant to various stakeholders will be dispersed, particularly if firms are required only to provide information through a generally available channel such as a corporate website. To avoid this potentiality, disclosure mandates can require standardized reporting via existing platforms, such as SEC EDGAR and EPA ECHO.[36] This can be done above and beyond posting on corporate websites, as is common practice with SEC filings that appear on both EDGAR and investor relations webpages. Common identifiers would significantly facilitate linking data disclosed across platforms. Additionally, look-through identifiers that link parents to subsidiaries, sponsors (in the case of affiliated research organizations or PACs), and memberships (e.g., for industry associations) seem necessary to gain a holistic view of a firm's activities.

Many firms already provide information on their political activity on their corporate websites, partially driven by investor demand. The information provided often consists of narrative descriptions of the firm's guiding principles in lobbying and influence activities, supplemented by the provision of information available in mandatory reports filed with relevant regulators.[37] Shareholder proposals for enhanced corporate reporting of political activity are increasingly common and garnering heightened support. Furthermore, SEC commissioners have discussed the potential for investors to benefit from increased political activity disclosure.[38] Consistent with much of the mandatory disclosures, voluntary disclosures of aggregate activity at the firm level tend to focus on amounts and general issues (or proposed legislation/bills), rather than providing clarity on policies supported, outcomes, or activity not already reflected elsewhere in mandatory reports.

[36] SEC EDGAR is available at www.sec.gov/edgar/search-and-access. EPA ECHO can be accessed at https://echo.epa.gov/
[37] See, for example, Novartis disclosures at www.novartis.com/our-company/corporate-responsibility/reporting-disclosure/transparency-disclosure/public-policy-advocacy/novartis-responsible-lobbying-disclosures, accessed July 30, 2021.
[38] See www.jdsupra.com/legalnews/political-activity-disclosures-a-hidden-3132494/, accessed July 30, 2021.

11.6.7 Consolidate Information in a Central Repository

Aggregation of climate-related political activity reports dispersed across governmental repositories is likely to require a third party. Such a third party could gather the relevant information onto a single platform searchable by interested stakeholders. Already, the Center for Responsive Politics (CRP) operates opensecrets.org, which aggregates and makes available data from campaign contribution and lobbyist filings.[39] Good Jobs First gathers information on tax breaks, subsidies, and violations of federal and state regulations and makes these available via their platform at www.goodjobsfirst.org/. InfluenceMap, discussed earlier, provides investor-targeted information specifically on "how corporations influence policy needed to address climate change," but focuses on voluntary filings and does not make their data accessible for separate access in an easily downloadable format. A platform for data on climate-related political activity, based on either of these, would help interested stakeholders access relevant information in a single place. Notably, the platform could follow Good Jobs First's example in aggregating disclosures across both federal and state levels and including a field capturing the corporate parent, as political activity directed at state-level environmental policies is plausibly important for many stakeholders, some state-level policymakers (e.g., the California Air Resources Board) set policies that are relevant outside their borders, and firms can spread their activities – or violations – across subsidiaries. A centralized data platform would also facilitate additional analysis by interested parties, including academics, journalists, asset managers, proxy advisory firms, and corporate rating agencies.[40]

Besides the availability and accessibility of information, stakeholders would also benefit from the information being reliable, consistent across time, and comparable across firms. Already with ESG

---

[39] CRP data is available at www.opensecrets.org/. LobbyView, available at www.lobbyview.org/, also makes available data on lobbying and contributions. They perform additional analyses on political influence filings and provide identifiers that allow linking across databases (e.g., Compustat GVKEY).

[40] Drutman and Mahoney (2017) suggest a central repository hosted by the Library of Congress for advocacy groups to post their policy positions and activities.

disclosures, firms often choose which measurement and disclosure standards (if any) to use when preparing impact reports. Their choices differ considerably in the cross section, and can change over time.[41] This makes benchmarking across firms or measuring relative performance difficult. It is reasonable to expect that demand for information about climate-related political activity, if not mandated, will be met with voluntary disclosures characterized by significant heterogeneity and, potentially, a lack of reliability due to firms' opportunistic use of reporting flexibility. As such, we view the standardization of disclosure requirements as crucial, even if there is heterogeneity across regulators with regard to the information that is required to be disclosed (e.g., material information for investors versus workplace safety for employees).

11.6.8 Potential Issues Associated with Full Disclosure

There are notable costs of additional disclosure. First, there are nontrivial costs of gathering, classifying, and reporting relevant information. These costs can be particularly substantial for smaller firms or firms that are complex relative to their size. As with upcoming mandatory corporate sustainability reporting in the EU, it seems reasonable to organize disclosure requirements around thresholds that depend both on listing status and, for privately held firms, potential impact as proxied by size.

Second, disclosures can serve as coordinating mechanisms between parties external to the firms. Firms can face pressure from targeted interest groups based on disclosed political activity. This can lead to conflict between public pressure and decision-makers' fiduciary duties to the firm. Though hard to measure precisely, this effect can introduce frictions or additional costs into the market for corporate executives or directors. Difficulty in sourcing effective leaders can inhibit growth, and this effect is likely to be significant when the business's

---

[41] For an extensive discussion of existing sustainability-related standards, see "Appendix 4.2: Stream A2 Assessment Report – Possible Input from Existing Initiatives," available at www.efrag.org/Assets/Download?assetUrl=%2Fsites %2Fwebpublishing%2FSiteAssets%2FEFRAG%2520PTF-NFRS_A2_FINAL .pdf (accessed August 2, 2021). This document is one of six appendices to EFRAG's "Proposals for a relevant and dynamic E.U. sustainability reporting standards-setting."

activities rely closely on government decisions, such as in defense, forestry, transportation, or extractive industries.[42]

Third, disclosures can allow for coordination between firms themselves. Although firms frequently coordinate political activity via lobby groups (Friedman & Heinle, 2020), additional implicit coordination outside of formal associations remains feasible (Duso & Jung, 2012), and could be further aided by service providers that incorporate public information into guidance on firms' political strategies (e.g., GovPredict).[43] Such coordination might increase political influence in certain areas. Furthermore, it could allow firms to economize on influence efforts in crowded areas, allowing them to better target their efforts and spending. This is potentially problematic given that environmental issues, particularly climate change, are often characterized by private benefits and social costs.

Fourth, extensive disclosure can be excessive. The costs to acquiring, processing, and incorporating information into decisions can be significant.[44] The targeted users of the information can be overloaded, leading to a reduction in the usefulness of the information provided. Important information can be buried within extensive and possibly boilerplate disclosures, which is a frequent concern for narrative disclosures targeted at investors.[45] The potential for excessive disclosure emphasizes the value of informational intermediaries who can help various users make informed decisions or facilitate research on climate-related policy influence.

Fifth, disclosures can play a role in shifting norms, expectations, or benchmarks applied to firms' political activities. Extensive disclosure, while potentially facilitating external pressure to reduce activity associated with negative externalities, can lead some stakeholders to question whether firms are doing too little, relative to their peers.

---

[42] See, e.g., the Conference Board press release from March 21, 2021, at www .conference-board.org/press/Corporate-Political-Activity, accessed July 30, 2021.
[43] GovPredict, and their parent firm, Phone2Action, are discussed in footnote 30.
[44] For a review and discussion of disclosure processing costs, see Blankespoor et al. (2020).
[45] See, e.g., SEC Chair Mary Jo White's October 15, 2013 speech titled "The Path Forward on Disclosure," accessed at www.sec.gov/news/speech/ spch101513mjw on July 30, 2021.

Sixth, disclosure can make firms reluctant to engage in communication with policy-makers or regulators. This can be particularly problematic when policy decisions require expertise and expertise is concentrated in firms engaged in the relevant activities. A chilling effect on communication can lead to less informed policies, which may be technically infeasible, prohibitively costly, or inefficient in mitigating climate change.

11.7 Conclusion

Government policies, such as emissions limits and green subsidies, are one of the most important aspects of the global response to climate change. This makes understanding the determinants of climate-related policies particularly important. In this chapter, we focus on corporate disclosures of climate-related political activity. We describe the current landscape, note existing limitations, and suggest potential improvements. We take a global perspective, but focus mainly on US institutions given the history of regulated and, to some degree, consolidated disclosure.

Much of the existing information about corporate political activity derives from mandated disclosures of lobbying activity under the Lobbying Disclosure Act. Additional information is available via public comment letters submitted to regulatory agencies and discretionary disclosures that firms can choose whether to make, for example, related to political philosophies. However, the current disclosure regime allows for significant uncertainty regarding corporate political activity, particularly on activity related to environmental and climate policies.

One serious deficiency with Lobbying Disclosure Act data is that it doesn't include whether a company lobbied for or against a specific regulation. We only know how much was spent and on which topics. It is possible that firms lobby for climate change regulations while giving even more to block them – enabling them to advertise misleading descriptions of their sustainability activities. Lobbying disclosures do not capture other means of political influence, including activities pursued through affiliates such as quasi-independent research organizations or trade associations. Nor do they capture the content of meetings between corporate representatives and regulators or legislators. The lack of comprehensive disclosure facilitates political activities that can lead to policies that reflect special interests rather than public interests. With climate policies, such a tilt can have devastating consequences (e.g., increased risk from natural disasters).

We recommend a shift toward comprehensive and timely disclosures of climate-related political activities, though our recommendations might also apply to political activities more broadly. First, firms should disclose their positions above and beyond their lobbying expenditures and the broad topics at which the lobbying was targeted. Disclosures should extend beyond expenditures to capture meetings with legislators and regulators and information on a broad set of activities that might influence policy, including grassroots organization, public influence campaigns, sponsored research, and activities pursued by affiliates. The disclosure should be provided in a timely fashion, so that participants in regulatory and legislative deliberations can understand and respond to the distribution of special-interest influence. In this setting, voluntary disclosure is unlikely to be comparable across firms and may be inconsistent, suggesting a role for additional mandatory disclosure.

Given the patchwork regulatory framework in the United States, disclosures of different types of activities might be mandated by different regulators. Investor-focused disclosures regarding material risks might be mandated by the SEC, while other disclosures might fall under the jurisdiction of the EPA or Departments of Labor, Interior, and Justice. The dispersion of regulations suggests that disclosure might be similarly dispersed, which would make it harder for stakeholders (e.g., voters, investors, customer, employees, and community members) to acquire comprehensive information and incorporate it into better decisions. As such, we recommend that firms provide disclosures on their websites that reflect the broad range of activities undertaken, consolidating disclosures required by different agencies and jurisdictions. Several firms are already doing this with existing mandatory disclosures, due in part to investor demand.

Broad disclosure on corporate websites can assist stakeholders interested in specific firms, but does not go far enough in facilitating corporate benchmarking and research on political influence. Third-party data aggregators are likely to become even more important as the extent of political disclosure expands. Nonprofit and academically focused aggregators, such as OpenSecrets and LobbyView, make their data broadly available and, where possible, are transparent about their methodologies. In contrast, for-profit information intermediaries in general do not make their data widely available and rely on proprietary algorithms to index or score firms. While potentially useful to investors and asset managers who can afford them, data from for-profit intermediaries are unlikely to help stakeholders who are dispersed and small (e.g., individual voters, customers, or employees). Notably, investors, asset managers, and NGOs are encouraging companies to provide additional disclosure of corporate activities, while regulators in the United States and EU are moving toward broader, but still centralized, disclosure of political activity and climate-related risks.

There are ample opportunities for future research in this area. There is potential value in amalgamating data on political activities, broadly defined, and inferring policy positions or influence at specific stages in a legislative, regulatory, or enforcement process. Novel methodologies for extracting, parsing, and interpreting multimedia disclosures (i.e., via text, speech, and video) can facilitate analysis of comment letters, public statements, advertising, sponsored research, and so on. These can be linked to data capturing firms' incentives to engage politically on climate as well as related policy outcomes. Additional research could explore the degree to which disclosure of climate-related political activity facilitates spillovers to other firms or political stakeholders. That is, does disclosure facilitate coalition building or opposition? From a user perspective, what makes disclosures more or less relevant to various stakeholders? These questions provide potentially important inputs when thinking about how to create a policy environment that addresses and mitigates global risks, such as climate change.

Appendix

Climate Lobby Data Coding

Data coding used in Delmas, M., Lim, J., & Nairn-Birch, N. (2016). Corporate Environmental Performance and Lobbying. *Academy of Management Discoveries*, 2(2), 175–97.

Data on corporate lobbying are available online from the Senate Office of Public Records (SOPR). The Center for Responsive Politics (CRP), which runs the Open Secrets website, provides a more accessible version of the data that has standardized organization names and identifies the parent company of the firms. We chose to use the CRP dataset as it is richer and easier to work with. The CRP data required cleanup: Some observations were split across multiple lines and delimiters were sometimes inconsistent, but it was not a common occurrence. We describe below how we coded the data for use in this paper.

There are two kinds of lobbyists: lobbyist firms (which earn income from and lobby on behalf of clients) and in-house lobbyists (which incur lobbying expenditures). The Lobbying Disclosure Act requires both to file reports every quarter. Before 2008, the reports were required semiannually. These reports contain information of lobbying income or expenditure, general issue areas, and more detailed descriptions of specific issues.

Lobbyist firms must file a separate report for each client detailing income from the client. Organizations employing in-house lobbyist file one report for all lobbying activities detailing expenditure. This amount includes employee compensation, office overhead, and payment to lobbyist firms. If the organization pays membership dues to another organization, its reported lobbying expenditure must also include the portion of membership dues that goes toward lobbying. Thus, the expenditure reported by an organization that hires in-house lobbyists should be more than the total of the reported income of lobbyist firms that have it as a client. All amounts of less than $5,000 are reported as <$5,000 and coded as $0, and amounts of $5,000 or more are rounded to the nearest $10,000.

Reports must include one or more general issue areas lobbied chosen from a list of 79 issue areas. For instance, the five most popular issue areas in 2008 were: budget/appropriations, taxation/ internal revenue code, health issues, defense, and energy/nuclear. Each issue area listed in the report is accompanied by a more specific description the issue. For instance, a report may list a general issue area as environmental/superfund, and further elaborate its specific lobbying issue by naming the bills lobbied, "S. 2191, America's Climate Security Act of 2007." Alternatively, it may give a brief description of issues, for example, "Contact with members of Congress and congressional staff with regard to proposed climate change legislation. "

In order to determine whether lobbying pertains to climate change, we searched through the issue descriptions for key words, bill numbers, and bill names. The key words we searched for were "climate," "global warming," "greenhouse," "GHG," and "GHGs." Additionally, we included the more prominent climate bills: the Waxman-Markey Bill (in 2009–2010) and the lesser known Lieberman-Warner cap-and-trade bill (2007–2008). Before 2007, climate bills were less prominent. For the Waxman-Markey Bill, we searched for terms: "H.R. 2454," "Waxman-Markey," "American Clean Energy and Security Act," and "ACES." For the Lieberman-Warner Bill: "S. 2191," "S. 3036," and "Lieberman-Warner." Both S. 2191 and S. 3036 were iterations of the Lieberman-Warner Bill. We did not search for the name of the bill, "America's Climate Security Act," because our keyword search for "climate" would have picked that up.

We designed a relatively flexible algorithm to determine whether a word, phrase, or bill number was contained in the issue description that minimized false positives and false negatives. For instance, in searching for H.R. 6, the algorithm would have to pick up all its variations (e.g., "HR6," "H R 6," "H.R. 6," and "hr6") but not "H.R. 60." To make this easier, we first standardized the issue descriptions. We first replaced all non-alphanumeric characters with spaces to avoid issues with punctuation. We also replaced all white space characters, such as tabs and carriage returns, with a space. To correct likely typographic errors, we inserted a space any time a letter was adjacent to a number. For instance, "HR6House Energy Bill" would become "HR 6 House Energy Bill." Lastly, we replaced every instance of double spaces with single spaces, eliminated leading and trailing white space, and converted the issue description to lower case. This made issue descriptions into one long line in which each word was separated by one space.

We minimized false positives by requiring a full word match. For example, if we were looking for H.R. 6, we needed to distinguish "HR6," from "HR60." To do that, we split our issue description along spaces to get a list of words, and required a complete match for the word. For instance the sentence "we lobbied on HR6 and HR60" would become a list of six words. The algorithm would produce a match on the fourth word ("HR6") but not the sixth word ("HR60"), because it requires the full word to match.

Next, we ensured that the algorithm would be able to handle different spacing. For instance, we need to be able to recognize "HR6," "HR 6," and "H R 6." Consider a two-word phrase "HR 6"; we searched for two-word phrases in two steps. In the first step, we searched for pairs of adjacent words that produced an exact match: "we lobbied on HR6 and HR 6" would produce a hit on the sixth word but not the fourth word. In the second step, we then also searched for the two-word phrase combined into one word, "HR6," which would produce a hit on the fourth word. The search for the three-word phrase "H R 6," proceeded similarly: we searched for three adjacent words that produced exact matches, then performed two-word searches on the two possibilities "HR 6" and "H R6," and lastly performed a single word search on "HR6." Note that this still requires the individual words to be intact: a search for "H R 2454" would not produce a hit on the term "HR 24 54"; this was done to avoid false positives.

Lastly, in order to ensure that search terms and bill numbers were complete, we examined a sample of the data to find typical names. For instance, the Waxman-Markey Bill, American Clean Energy and Security Act is often abbreviated as ACES. Senate bills are usually denoted by a preceding "S." but searching through the data revealed that they are also preceded by "S.B.," "Sen.," "Senate Bill," and "S. R." Similarly, House bills are most often denoted by "H.R.," but are also sometimes denoted by "H.R. Bill," "H.," "H.B.," and "House Bill."

False positives are possible, although we visually inspected the data and adjusted our algorithm. For example, "climate" might not refer to climate change; similarly, "Waxman Markey" might refer to a different bill also sponsored by Representatives Waxman and Markey. We did not see any such examples, but that remains a possibility and it would be prohibitively time consuming to check every single entry.

False negatives from typographical errors might also be an issue because lobbyists likely find filling in the reports to be a hassle. For instance, "climte" almost certainly means "climate" but would not be picked up by our search. Fortunately, the search terms and bills occur in clusters, mitigating the problem: for instance, "s. 2191, america's climte security act of 2007," would not match "climate" but would still match "S. 2191."

If we found the search term in the issue description, then entire amount (for the quarter to which the report refers) is coded as climate lobbying amount. This likely overestimates the amount spent on climate lobbying as organizations often lobby on multiple issues. However, it was the most consistent method. It is impossible to isolate the climate lobbying amount from other lobbying. Assuming a proportion is also difficult because the organizations vary widely in how they report their lobbying issues areas and describe specific issues. We also considered relying on organizations that only lobby on climate issues; however, because many organizations lobby on multiple issues, this method would have severely limited our sample size. The climate lobbying amount for each year is added up for each organization. The lobbying amount by subsidiaries is added to the lobbying amount of its parent (as identified by the CRP). If the subsidiary's parent company did not exist in our greenhouse gas database but the subsidiary itself did, used the subsidiary's amount.

The CRP also codes the data to prevent double-counting. Double counting can happen if the organization files more than one report for the same quarter. Double counting might also happen if the organization employs in-house and outside lobbyists, and both file reports. (Recall that organizations that employ in-house lobbyists are required to report total expenditure, including expenditures paid to outside lobbyists.) Lastly, double counting can occur when the parent files a report that includes its subsidiaries' expenditures and its subsidiaries also file reports. The CRP identifies such cases and codes them to prevent double counting, and we relied on the CRP's coding.

In order to code whether the lobbyist is an outside (instead of in-house) lobbyist firm, we compared the name of the registrant with the name of the client and the name of its parent company. If the name of the registrant was not equal to either its client or its client's parent company, we considered those as outside lobbyists. With the coding for outside lobbyists, we use the same method as before to determine outside climate lobbying amount.

Open Secrets Data Description

Below we include a description of the CRP variables we used and how we used them.

Variable	CRP definition	How we used the variable
File: lob_lobbying.txt		
Uniqid	Corresponds to a particular report from SOPR	Used as an identifer when merging lobbying data and to double check original SOPR reports
Registrant	Standardized registrant	Party that filed the report; combined with client and ultorg variables to identify whether lobbyist was in-house
Client	Standardized Client	Party that registrant is lobbying on behalf of
Ultorg	Parent company to the client	Used to determine how much a firm spent lobbying (by aggregating data on parent company) and to merge with other data
Amount	Lobbying income/expenditures	Used to determine how much a firm spent lobbying on any issue; combined with issue coding to determine how much a firm spent on climate lobbying
Use	To indicate if this report should be used or ignored. The general method is to use the latest report.	Used to avoid double-counting when more than one report is filed by the same registrant in one quarter
Ind	To indicate if the amount on this report should be included to calculate industry totals.	Used to avoid double counting (1) when the firm employs in-house and outside lobbyists and both file reports and (2) when the parent files a report that includes its subsidiaries' expenditures and its subsidiaries also file reports.
Year	The year.	Used to merge with other data

File: lob_agency.txt

Uniqid	Corresponds to a particular report from SOPR	Used as an identifier when merging lobbying data and to double check original SOPR reports
Agency	The government agency lobbied	Used to identify which agency was lobbied

File: lob_issue.txt

Uniqid	Corresponds to a particular report from SOPR	Used as an identifier when merging lobbying data and to double check original SOPR reports
SpecificIssue	The specific issue	Used issue description to code whether lobbying was considered climate lobbying
Variable	CRP definition	How we used the variable

File: lob_lobbying.txt

Uniqid	Corresponds to a particular report from SOPR	Used as an identifier when merging lobbying data and to double check original SOPR reports
Registrant	Standardized registrant	Party that filed the report; combined with client and ultorg variables to identify whether lobbyist was in-house
Client	Standardized Client	Party that registrant is lobbying on behalf of
Ultorg	Parent company to the client	Used to determine how much a firm spent lobbying (by aggregating data on parent company) and to merge with other data
Amount	Lobbying income/expenditures	Used to determine how much a firm spent lobbying on any issue; combined with issue coding to determine how much a firm spent on climate lobbying

(cont.)

Variable	CRP definition	How we used the variable
Use	To indicate if this report should be used or ignored. The general method is to use the latest report.	Used to avoid double-counting when more than one report is filed by the same registrant in one quarter
Ind	To indicate if the amount on this report should be included to calculate industry totals.	Used to avoid double counting (1) when the firm employs in-house and outside lobbyists and both file reports and (2) when the parent files a report that includes its subsidiaries' expenditures and its subsidiaries also file reports.
Year	The year.	Used to merge with other data
File: lob_agency.txt		
Uniqid	Corresponds to a particular report from SOPR	Used as an identifier when merging lobbying data and to double check original SOPR reports
Agency	The government agency lobbied	Used to identify which agency was lobbied
File: lob_issue.txt		
Uniqid	Corresponds to a particular report from SOPR	Used as an identifier when merging lobbying data and to double check original SOPR reports
SpecificIssue	The specific issue	Used issue description to code whether lobbying was considered climate lobbying

Data Coding References

Center for Responsive Politics (CRP). 2014. Lobbying data. www.opensecrets .org/resources/create/data.php. Accessed 8/12/14.

Center for Responsive Politics. OpenSecrets Data Definitions for Lobbying Data. www.opensecrets.org/resources/create/data_doc.php. Accessed 8/12/14.

Secretary of the Senate and Clerk of the House of Representatives. 2013. Lobbying Disclosure Act Guidance. http://lobbyingdisclosure.house.gov/ldaguidance.pdf. Accessed 9/17/14.

References

Ackerman, S. (2007). What Are Lobbyists Saying on Capitol Hill-Climate Change Legislation as a Case Study for Reform? *Environmental Law*, 37, 137.

Blankespoor, E., deHaan, E., & Marinovic, I. (2020). Disclosure Processing Costs, Investors' Information Choice, and Equity Market Outcomes: A Review. *Journal of Accounting and Economics*, 70(2–3), 101344.

Brulle, R. J. (2018). The Climate Lobby: A Sectoral Analysis of Lobbying Spending on Climate Change in the USA, 2000 to 2016. *Climatic Change*, 149(3), 289–303.

Cho, C. H., Laine, M., Roberts, R. W., & Rodrigue, M. (2018). The Frontstage and Backstage of Corporate Sustainability Reporting: Evidence from the Arctic National Wildlife Refuge Bill. *Journal of Business Ethics*, 152(3), 865–886.

Clark, C. E., & Crawford, E. P. (2012). Influencing Climate Change Policy: The Effect of Shareholder Pressure and Firm Environmental Performance. *Business & Society*, 51(1), 148–175.

Congressional Research Service (2015). *The Lobbying Disclosure Act at 20: Analysis and Issues for Congress*. Analyst on the Congress.

Darnell, S., & McDonnell, M-H. (2023). License to Give: The Relationship between Organizational Reputation and Stakeholders' Support for Corporate Political Activity. In T. Lyon, ed., *Corporate Political Responsibility*. Cambridge, UK: Cambridge University Press.

De Figueiredo, J. M., & Richter, B. K. (2014). Advancing the Empirical Research on Lobbying. *Annual Review of Political Science*, 17, 163–185.

Delmas, M., Lim, J., & Nairn-Birch, N. (2016). Corporate Environmental Performance and Lobbying. *Academy of Management Discoveries*, 2(2), 175–197.

Denicolò, V. (2008). A Signaling Model of Environmental over Compliance. *Journal of Economic Behavior & Organization*, 68(1), 293–303.

Drutman, L. (2015). *The Business of America Is Lobbying*. New York, NY: Oxford University Press.

Drutman, L., & Mahoney, C. (2017). On the Advantages of a Well-Constructed Lobbying System: Toward a More Democratic, Modern Lobbying Process. *Interest Groups & Advocacy*, 6(3), 290–310.

Duso, T., & Jung, A. (2012). Product Market Competition and Lobbying Coordination in the US Mobile Telecommunications Industry. *Journal of Industry, Competition and Trade*, 12(2), 177–201.

Favotto, A., Kollman, K., & McMillan, F. (2023). Responsible Lobbyists? CSR Commitments and the Quality of Corporate Parliamentary Testimony in the UK. In T. Lyon, ed., *Corporate Political Responsibility*. Cambridge, UK: Cambridge University Press.

Friedman, H. L., & Heinle, M. S. (2020). Influence Activities, Coalitions, and Uniform Policies: Implications for the Regulation of Financial Institutions. *Management Science*, 66(9), 4336–4358.

Grumbach, J. M. (2015). Polluting Industries as Climate Protagonists: Cap and Trade and the Problem of Business Preferences. *Business and Politics*, 17(4), 633–659.

Hamilton, J. B., & Hoch, D. (1997). Ethical Standards for Business Lobbying: Some Practical Suggestions. *Business Ethics Quarterly*, 7(3), 117–129.

InfluenceMap. (2021). The A-List of Climate Policy Engagement 2021: An InfluenceMap Report. October. https://influencemap.org/report/The-A-List-of-Climate-Policy-Engagement-2021-b3ac0399b2dc640 56cee06e3d6324e6f

Johnson, V. R. (2006). Regulating Lobbyists: Law, Ethics, and Public Policy. *Cornell Journal of Law and Public Policy*, 16, 1.

Ketu, Y., & Rothstein, S. (2023). Practicing Responsible Policy Engagement: How Large U.S. Companies Lobby on Climate Change. In T. Lyon, ed., *Corporate Political Responsibility*. Cambridge: Cambridge University Press.

Kim, S. E., Urpelainen, J., & Yang, J. (2016). Electric Utilities and American Climate Policy: Lobbying by Expected Winners and Losers. *Journal of Public Policy*, 36(2), 251–275.

Kolk, A., & Pinkse, J. (2007). Multinationals' Political Activities on Climate Change. *Business & Society*, 46(2), 201–228.

Luneburg, W. V. (2008). Anonymity and Its Dubious Relevance to the Constitutionality of Lobbying Disclosure Legislation. *Stanford Law & Policy Review*, 19, 69.

Lyon, T. P., & Maxwell, J. W. (2011). Greenwash: Corporate Environmental Disclosure under Threat of Audit. *Journal of Economics & Management Strategy*, **20**(1), 3–41.

Lyon, T. P., & Mandelkorn, W. (2023). The Meaning and Measurement of CPR. In T. Lyon, ed., *Corporate Political Responsibility*. Cambridge, UK: Cambridge University Press.

Meng, K. C., & Rode, A. (2019). The Social Cost of Lobbying over Climate Policy. *Nature Climate Change*, **9**(6), 472–476.

OECD (2006). *Governance Arrangements to Ensure Transparency in Lobbying: A Comparative Overview*. Internal Coworking Document, Public Governance and Territorial Development Directorate. Paris: OECD.

Reinhardt, F. (1999). Market Failure and the Environmental Policies of Firms: Economic Rationales for "Beyond Compliance" Behavior. *Journal of Industrial Ecology*, **3**(1), 9–21.

Rivera, J., Oetzel, J., DeLeon, P., & Starik, M. (2009). Business Responses to Environmental and Social Protection Policies: Toward a Framework for Analysis. *Policy Sciences*, **42**(1), 3–32.

Scherer, A. G., & Christian Voegtlin, C. (2023). MNCs as Responsible Political Actors in Global Business: Challenges and Implications for Human Resource Management. In T. Lyon, ed., *Corporate Political Responsibility*. Cambridge, UK: Cambridge University Press.

Thomas, H. F., & LaPira, T. M. (2017). How Many Lobbyists Are in Washington? Shadow Lobbying and the Gray Market for Policy Advocacy. *Interest Groups & Advocacy*, **6**(3), 199–214.

Vogel, D. (2023). From Kyoto to Paris; Business and Climate Change. In T. Lyon, ed., *Corporate Political Responsibility*. Cambridge, UK: Cambridge University Press.

Walker, E. (2023). What Drives Firms to Disclose Their Political Activity? In T. Lyon, ed., *Corporate Political Responsibility*. Cambridge: Cambridge University Press.

Implementing Corporate Political Responsibility: Opportunities and Challenges

12 | Practitioner Views of Corporate Political Responsibility
Toward a New Social Contract

ELIZABETH A. DOTY

12.1 Introduction

One of the most notable recent trends in US public life has been the sharp increase in attention to business's involvement in societal, civic, and political issues. As demonstrated in countless headlines in 2020–2021, scrutiny of companies' political contributions, lobbying activities, public communications, and philanthropic giving has been intensifying (Washington and Spierings, 2021). Gaps or contradictions are viewed as hypocrisy or greenwashing, heightening reputational risk and sparking employee, customer, or investor backlash (Hacker and Pierson, 2021; Preventable Surprises, 2021). In addition, employees, customers, investors, and other stakeholders are pushing companies to take a more active role in solving society's most pressing challenges, from climate change to racial equity, inequality, LGBTQ rights, AI, privacy, toxic political polarization, voting rights, election integrity, free speech, and the peaceful transfer of power (Edelman, 2021; World Economic Forum, 2020). Many companies and CEOs have responded to these calls with commitments to upgrade internal operations, increase charitable giving, and, sometimes, revise their approaches to political or civic influence. Others have opted to "stay out of the fray," arguing that this is beyond their remit (Sorkin, 2021). Both strategies have resulted in criticism, with some accused of "woke capitalism" (Wall Street Journal Editorial Board, 2021) – pandering to employees, customers or investors rather than demonstrating genuine concern – and others accused of abdicating their responsibilities to their values or society (Livni, 2021). As a result, many executives are left feeling caught in the crossfire of an increasingly antagonistic and polarized society, expending countless management hours reacting to the issue of the moment, unsure of expectations or what "corporate political responsibility" means in practice (Lyon et al., 2018).

As scholars and activists explore strategies for improving the transparency, accountability, and responsibility of corporate political influence, they will be well served to consider practitioner perspectives, motivations and challenges, for at least three reasons. First, arguments for CPR may be viewed as proposing normative elements of a new (or renewed) political and economic social contract. According to recent scholarship, any discourse to shape a society's social contract must include deliberation with those affected – including business practitioners – if it is to achieve the benefits of legitimacy, acceptance, trust, and cooperation (Donaldson and Dunfee, 1999; Scherer and Palazzo, 2006; Scholz et al., 2019). Second, to achieve a substantive shift in mainstream business practices requires engaging practitioners in the spirit and not just the letter of CPR. Without active engagement with business leaders, efforts to define corporate political responsibility will come across as just another requirement "lobbed over the wall" to corporate staffs, eliciting compliance at best and active resistance at worst. Third, any attempt to advance CPR via public policy or regulatory frameworks will have to contend with business's current level of political influence.

This chapter relates learnings from a university-based effort to engage with practitioners around CPR, with the goal of showcasing early wins and highlighting pitfalls that must be surmounted if CPR is to achieve its full potential.

12.2 The Launch of the Corporate Political Responsibility Taskforce

In early 2021, the Erb institute at the University of Michigan launched the Corporate Political Responsibility Taskforce (CPRT) to engage practitioners in advancing CPR for members and across the private sector. We designed the program to provide "forums, foresight and frameworks to help companies better align their political influences with their commitments to purpose, values, sustainability and stakeholders."[1] We launched with a series of interactive public programs

---

[1] erb.umich.edu/corporate-political-responsibility-taskforce/. Last accessed 12/21/21.

to engage executives, academic experts, business students, and stake-holder advocates, while beginning individualized outreach to poten-tial members. Specifically, we were looking for individual, officer-level executives from 6 to 12 companies (a) who were US-based, if at all possible, (b) whose firms had taken some action that demonstrated a commitment to responsible political influence, (c) whose name would make a difference to other firms considering CPR actions, and (d) who faced at least one pressing CPR issue. These members were invited into a year-long process with five steps, including (1) selecting a focal issue; (2) listening to diverse views; (3) drafting CPR principles; (4) drafting a firm-specific CPR strategy for the focal issue; and (5) implementing, embedding, and articulating CPR principles and strategy at their firm.

The process of forming the taskforce provided a unique opportu-nity to hear how company executives were responding to calls for CPR. Through our outreach to potential members and our produc-tion of public educational programs, we spoke with over 40 senior executives in government affairs; sustainability; diversity, equity, and inclusion (DE&I); brand, or governance roles in large US-based com-panies; 30 former executives from similar roles; 15–20 consultants to major firms; and leaders of over 15 business networks. These contacts included executives working in apparel, automotive, chemicals, con-sumer goods, energy, financial services, food and beverage, hospital-ity, materials science, professional services, technology, and utilities. Although the vast majority of these contacts were US-based, some were housed in Europe and concerned with CPR practices internationally. Most discussions were with leaders from public companies, though several involved large private firms and partnerships. In addition, we have spoken with executive audiences about CPR during at least ten interactive presentations and workshops, all with opportunities for open discussion and at least four under Chatham House Rule.[2] One of these was a two-hour workshop in October 2021, at a national con-ference for sustainability professionals where we were able to gather input on a current case study and feedback on draft CPR principles.

Finally, we have spoken with leaders from business networks and stakeholder advocates who regularly engage with companies on CPR-related topics such as "corporate political accountability" and

---

[2] erb.umich.edu/corporate-political-responsibility-taskforce/. Last accessed 12/21/21.

"corporate civic responsibility," who shared themes from their conversations and provided feedback on our initial framing of the topic.

These conversations provided a rare look into the views of business practitioners in key CPR-related roles, especially as they responded to the dramatic events of 2020–2021, including the murder of George Floyd and rising concern over racial inequity, disputes over the outcome of the 2020 presidential election, polarization, and disputes in the workplace over vaccination and mask mandates amid the COVID-19 pandemic, the insurrection of January 6, changes to voting rights in dozens of states, the COP26 climate meeting in Glasgow, proposed legislation to curb climate change, and so on. In this chapter I present perspectives shared firsthand by practitioners in government affairs, senior leadership, sustainability, or DE&I roles, as well as comments shared by "insiders" such as business network leaders, consultants, or former senior leaders. Although the themes do not reflect the views of all the practitioners we have spoken with, they are representative of the range of responses we have heard, which could inform future quantitative research or engagement with businesses.

To support that process, I have summarized practitioner motivations, interests, barriers, and challenges related to engaging in conversations about CPR, as well as committing or acting to improve CPR. Quotes are anonymous and paraphrased, based on notes from the calls or presentations. Following the summary, I present implications for engaging practitioners in exploring CPR and acting to improve it, as well as for future research.

12.3 Findings

12.3.1 Motivations and Interest in Discussing CPR

When talking with practitioners, we briefly introduced the concept of corporate political responsibility as including three levels (Lyon et al., 2018), the definition of political activities and the elements of a CPR Framework, using the visual shown in Figure 12.1. The prompt for the conversation was generally related to heightened public scrutiny and pressure on companies to engage more actively on societal, civic and political issues.

Overall, practitioners tended to respond comfortably to the concept of corporate political responsibility and began using it in conversation

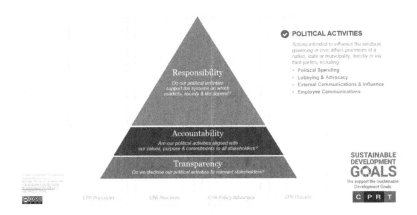

Figure 12.1 Corporate political responsibility
Reproduced with the permission of the Erb Institute and Leadership Momentum

without much preamble. Indeed, many practitioners told us they were missing places to discuss CPR beyond the "issue of the day." "The need is 'dead on,'" said one VP of Public Affairs, "Companies are looking for guidance on criteria, authority and motivation. Trade associations could be the place, but they tend to be least common denominator by definition." To be meaningful, potential members told us, it was critical to ensure discussions were neutral, to include more firms than the "usual suspects," and to involve a diverse range of geographic regions, industries, perspectives, and functions. For example, when network leaders viewed the detailed outline of avenues of corporate political influence that is presented in Chapter 1 of this volume, executives told them they found it more useful than some others because it was more value neutral. In addition, taking a long-term view was appealing to practitioners. "Watch out for narrowing down the taskforce's focus to a short-term issue," a Fortune 500 executive advised us. "The 'social contract' element of this project is critical."

When we asked practitioners about what specific issues they wanted to discuss, most were interested in CPR as it relates to social justice and inclusion, or climate and the environment, with others mentioning strong civic institutions or long-term shareholder value. A poll conducted during our virtual launch session in March 2021 illustrates the range of interests (see Figure 12.2).

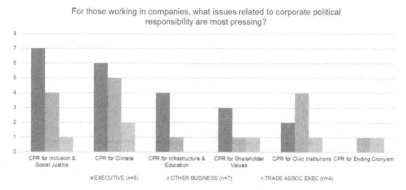

Figure 12.2 Practitioner poll results on pressing issues involving CPR

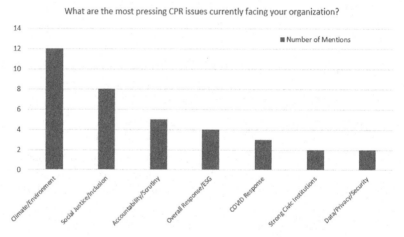

Figure 12.3 Analysis of practitioner poll on pressing issues involving CPR

During mid- and late-2021, we heard increasing interest in civic institutions, as state-level legislation over voting and elections gained public attention. At our workshop in October 2021, climate and environment came to the foreground, as shown in Figure 12.3, most likely because the conference where we presented the workshop was focused on sustainability, and climate was attracting attention due to the upcoming COP26 meeting in Glasgow and concurrent legislative proposals to address climate.

Staff availability was the single biggest barrier to discussing CPR. Several potential taskforce members declined due to the volume of company initiatives they had underway, some of which were in response to societal, civic, or political crises. "We value the work and would like to support it in other ways," said one diversity, equity and inclusion officer. Unfortunately, one consequence of this challenge was that executive attention to CPR became somewhat "episodic" as issues hit the headlines and then receded. In addition, some leaders declined to schedule an exploratory call about the taskforce, telling us, "We don't do politics," or "We are not going to get involved in these kinds of issues." Some leaders participated in initial calls about CPR and the taskforce, but later became nonresponsive. Finally, several of those who have engaged consistently have reported that the topic is "scary" or "treacherous" and some are careful to distinguish their views from their company's and prefer conversations where they can speak "off the record."

In reviewing these conversations, I noticed that practitioners tended to start out with one of two assumptions about what CPR means in practice. Some assumed it would involve companies more actively stepping forward – playing a more active role in addressing civic, societal, and political issues, while others assumed it implied stepping back – curtailing their involvement in civic or political spheres. These assumptions could lead some to decline to engage in discussions about CPR as inappropriate for their business or unnecessarily constraining of their political voice. (It is also possible that these assumptions lead some to dive in to advocate CPR uncritically, assuming greater business intervention in political and civic processes is an unqualified good, and neglect to explore the risks of undue business influence in civic process.) In addition, there was a frequent tendency among practitioners to equate corporate political influence with corporate PAC spending or political spending more broadly, without considering the other avenues of influence outlined in Chapter 1. Given these tendencies, working on CPR probably requires communicating explicitly about definitions and the need for nuanced conversations that do not presume solutions at the start.

12.4 Motivation and Interest in Improving CPR Overall

In addition to assessing interest in joining forums to discuss CPR, our early conversations also helped us understand leaders' motivations for considering actions to improve CPR, generally and on each of three

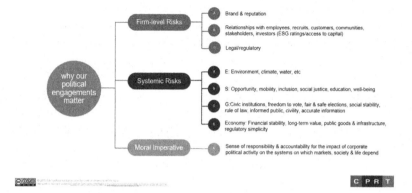

Figure 12.4 Why CPR matters
Reproduced with the permission of the Erb Institute and Leadership Momentum

levels outlined in Figure 12.1. Below is a summary of responses that indicated interest and motivation to improve CPR overall.

At a high level, we might hypothesize three major categories of motivation for firms to be interested in improving CPR in practice: (1) Firm-level Risks and Opportunities, (2) Systems-level Risks and Opportunities, and (3) Moral Imperatives, as summarized in Figure 12.4.

When we shared this overview, we found that firm-level risks were top of mind for most practitioners. A poll taken during our virtual launch on March 3, 2021, shown in Figure 12.5, is illustrative. For nineteen officer-level executives in government affairs, sustainability, operations, brand, governance or stakeholder engagement functions (mostly in large public companies), threats to brand and reputation, and potential damage to employee, investor, or customer relationships were the most important risks related to misaligned corporate political influence. Violation of purpose and values were also reported as a concern. By contrast, larger systemic risks resulting were less top of mind, which is discussed in more detail later. Though the sample size for this poll was extremely small, the results reflect much of what we heard in one-to-one conversations, conferences, and presentations.

To flesh out these themes, here is a bit more detail related to motivation to improve CPR overall.

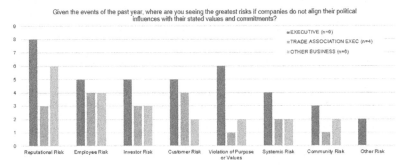

Figure 12.5 Practitioner poll results – why CPR matters

12.4.1 Firm-Level Risks

We can't put our reputations at risk Leaders were highly aware of the potential damage from news headlines that show misalignment between a companies' stated commitments and its political influence. One C-Suite executive told us, "If you are not aligned or not authentic, you face reputational risk." Reputational risk was mentioned as impacting recruiting, employee engagement, share price, costs of capital, customer retention, and public sentiment. Some mentioned watching friends and colleagues at other companies suffer over perceived contradictions, saying they felt "sad" to hear how their firms had resumed donations to election objectors and suffered a measurable drop in share price as a result. Still, in managing reputational risk, many worried about the risks of both action and inaction and struggled with having to "choose sides" among political factions amid intensifying polarization.

Responses to an open text question about brand risks from current civic, societal, or political issues during our October 2021 workshop echoed these concerns about misalignment, reputational risk, backlash, and responding to shifting expectations (see Figure 12.6). As mentioned above, though the sample size is extremely small, the results echo themes from private conversations.

Our employees (and customers) are pushing us to take a stand Practitioners frequently mentioned rethinking their political engagements in response to concerns voiced by employees or potential employees. For example, one head of government affairs reported in January 2021, "I can't tell you the number emails I've received from colleagues

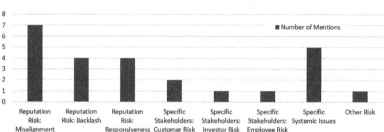

Where are you seeing the greatest brand risks and challenges related to current civic, political or societal issues?

Figure 12.6 Analysis of practitioner poll on brand risks and challenges related to CPR

after the Capitol attack, asking, 'What are we doing, associating with some of these folks?'" Several had implemented processes for engaging employees in whether and how to respond to voting rights and election-related legislation. "It has been very important to listen to our employees on these issues," said one VP of government affairs. And, just as with reputational risk, responding to stakeholder groups presented challenges. Several struggled with polarization among employees, or divergence between employee and customer views.

Investors are paying more attention to CPR Finally, several practitioners predicted that the rise of ESG would lead to greater focus on CPR as a key factor in investor relationships and minimizing the cost of capital.

12.4.2 Systems-Level Risks

Business cannot thrive without an inclusive, stable, civil and sustainable society As far as systemic motivations for CPR, we heard a general sense that business benefited from an inclusive, prosperous economy, cultural civility, and environmental sustainability. They were also inspired by the idea that business could contribute to solving society's most challenging issues, such as climate change or inequality. There was generally less discussion of how lack of CPR might undermine inclusion, prosperity or sustainability, and eventually harm the environment for business (AAA Framework for Climate Policy Leadership, 2019; Gehl and Porter, 2020; Henderson, 2020; Preventable Surprises, 2021).

12.4.3 Moral Imperatives

CPR is part of fulfilling our company purpose Practitioners were often proud of their companies' commitment to a stated purpose or proactive engagement on ESG – and recognized that CPR would be involved in following through on those intentions. "Now, we are a purpose-driven company – we have new leadership, new branding, a new awakening and more transparency. And that means we need to stand for something. This civic crisis is a movement. We are not just responding; we will lead," said a member of a project team with a financial services firm inquiring about CPR.

12.5 Motivation and Interest in Improving the Three Levels of CPR

In addition to asking about interest in discussing CPR and improving CPR overall, we also invited comments about the three levels of CPR conceptualized in Figure 12.1. By far, the level that made the most sense to practitioners was Accountability, which we described as "aligning political influences with commitments to purpose, values, sustainability and stakeholders." That said, practitioners did value Transparency, at least in principle, and many mentioned a sense of Responsibility arising out of their firm's values, societal trust in business, and for some, a dependence on systems sustained by civil society. Here are a few specific themes indicating motivation or interest (though not necessarily a commitment to action).

12.5.1 Motivation and Interest in Transparency

Transparency is good, in principle Practitioners generally valued transparency and several mentioned being proud of their company's practices. "We've led with transparency for over 20 years," one government affairs officer told us. A few worked for companies that produced Political Engagement Reports. Several people mentioned that they were not familiar with their firm's approach to political influence, and wanted to know more. "I had no idea how our PAC was setting priorities, yet I was sending my check every year. I had to stop until could find out." Still there was some hesitation when it came to implementation. For example, those working in private firms mentioned that it was not necessary or appropriate to mandate disclosure as they could simply report internally to key stakeholders. This recognition of the need for Transparency echoes the account shared in Chapter 2 of this volume, that firms are adopting greater disclosure to avert reputational, legal and regulatory risk (Freed, Sandstrom and Laufer, 2023).

CPR will likely be part of reporting on the "G" in ESG As part of the investor interest mentioned above, there was a sense that CPR would eventually be relevant to ESG reporting. One leader asked, "How should we talk about the lobbying that we do? What do our investors and external stakeholders want to see?" This echoes the theme in Chapter 4 of this volume (Walker, 2023), highlighting investor pressure for greater disclosure of political influence, and in Chapter 9 which emphasizes rising investor interest in climate policy lobbying (Ketu and Rothstein, 2023).

12.5.2 Motivation and Interest in Accountability

We need to do what we said we would Over and over, leaders described how their company's reputation, the power of their purpose to attract, retain and engage employees, their brand value with customers, strong ESG ratings and a low cost of capital were all contingent on following through on their commitments – including commitments to contribute to solutions to systemic societal issues. Many expressed a strong aversion to "greenwashing," "zero-washing," or "ESG-washing." "I have to know our political influence is aligned with the values of the kind of company I would want to work for," said one C-Suite executive. Indeed, several contacts asked for more information when a headline or report mentioned contradictions at their company, and nearly all recognized the value of cross-functional, proactive, and principled approaches, with strong oversight. (Several actually told us this had been a condition of their taking on their current role.)

When we led the workshop in October 2021, this focus on integrity and genuine action based on values became very apparent. We introduced a case study based on a well-known company that had committed not to contribute to members of the US Congress who had refused to certify the electoral college results ("election objectors"), had then quietly resumed contributions sometime later. In response to a news report on this resumption of contributions, the company issued a statement defending their decision. When that response was criticized, they finally returned to their policy of not contributing to the objectors. When we asked participants if they agreed with the company's ultimate decision, twenty-four of twenty-seven respondents did. Most of those who agreed with the decision (nineteen of twenty-four) did so based on principles or values, while the remainder referenced responsiveness to stakeholders, business impact, or transparency. Sample reasons given in the freeform text format included, "This issue goes beyond differing views and threatens the principles of democracy itself," and "There is a line after which it's not politics, it's harmful." A few of the comments were more pragmatic, such as, "They needed to unplug to avoid turning off a significant portion of their customer base." One comment that stood out, in particular, highlighted a strictly business view of the engagement and would be worth exploring further: "Corporations need to get legislators in place that support their business model."

I'm so glad we don't make contributions! A notable subset of practitioners felt it was important that their company did not make political contributions, which made it easier to avoid contradictions. "I love that we do no political giving," said one. Another told us, "We don't do any election donations, we never have. My friends over at XYZ company do, and it takes a lot of their time." Three also said it was a significant part of why they felt comfortable taking a government affairs role. "I only took this job because we don't do political spending," said one, and another echoed, "I don't want to do that *@! I was in government for years, and that aspect is not attractive."

12.5.3 Motivation and Interest in Responsibility

We need to engage based on our values When asked about when business should step forward to address societal issues or systemic challenge, most practitioners cited their company's values or purpose as the touchstone. Indeed, those that had developed internal processes for selecting issues and determining their positions often referenced their company purpose, values, or employee input as the impetus for taking a stand. There were several that echoed the comments of one CEO who spoke about his company's approach in a public webinar, "We have a responsibility to speak up on business issues to avoid harm to society and when our teammates are concerned – but not to engage in politics for own sake."

We have an obligation to help solve society's most challenging issues As mentioned above, many practitioners mentioned an affirmative responsibility for business to step forward on challenging issues, often citing polls showing that business is more trusted than government or media, and viewed as more competent (Edelman, 2021). Companies translated this sense of trust into a responsibility to promote civic engagement, accelerate innovation, or address systemic issues such as climate or inequality. "Our CEO has argued repeatedly that we cannot solve climate without clear, stable federal policy," said one government affairs leader. A smaller subset articulated an affirmative responsibility to support foundational civic institutions. One government affairs leader told us, "We are very focused on underlying challenges to the process and institutions of democracy, as a baseline issue to the specific policy areas we work on." Immediately after the January 6 Capitol attacks, another head of government affairs argued:

Very few institutions have as much influence as the ones where we work. We have the benefit of access and the ability to influence for stakeholders, shareholders and other interests, and that means we have a higher obligation than just moving our agenda forward. If we wish to preserve or create the kind of country we claim to be, business leaders all have an obligation to engage.... If we wish the current destructive patterns to stop, we have to act.

We need to be sure we are not part of the problem Finally, a much smaller share of practitioners actively questioned business's role in current systemic issues. "Business is frustrated with the gridlock, partisanship and antagonism. Do they think they have nothing to do with that?" asked an officer in a financial services firm. This group referenced the potential for corporate political influence to exacerbate classic market failures such as externalities, monopoly power, or information asymmetries, through rent-seeking or "crony capitalism." "If you have resources, you can play the game, which enables you to influence policy based on self-interest," said one C-Suite executive. Some focused on political spending, explaining that "Corporate political spending is a small portion of the total, but it raises the question, 'What are you buying?' Overall, that has a significant corrosive effect on trust, and it exposes companies to being shaken down by politicians." Finally, a few pointed to the United States as an outlier in current corporate political influence practices. For example, executives in a global professional services firm explained, "The questions you are asking about CPR are very US-centric. Those practices are not even legal in Europe."

12.6 Challenges and Barriers in Improving CPR

As part of our conversations, we frequently asked about barriers to improving CPR. Drawing on my prior practitioner experience (Doty & Kouchaki, 2015) and a recent WRI report, "Seven Barriers to U.S. Climate Policy Leadership and How to Break Them Down," we hypothesized five types of challenges would inhibit CPR, as outlined in Figure 12.7.

Here is a summary of major barriers mentioned by practitioners, organized by CPR level.

12.6.1 Challenges and Barriers to Transparency

We are drowning in scorecards Many leaders echoed one government affairs officer, who told us, "The last thing we need is another scorecard." Executives in sustainability and government affairs reported being buried under the "alphabet soup" of ESG ratings and reporting requirements, and scorecards posted by a range of "unelected stakeholder groups" who can create a "fire drill with a single article or tweet" that threatens the company's brand. There was visible frustration related to the reporting burden added by each new metric or framework. Practitioners often told us they had never heard of

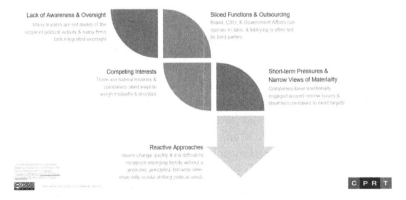

Figure 12.7 Barriers to CPR
Reproduced with the permission of the Erb Institute and Leadership Momentum

stakeholder groups whose data on corporate political influence was used by reporters and policymakers – even when their firm had been featured for drastic improvement.

ESG reporting expectations are unclear As we said earlier, there was a sense that CPR would be included in global ESG reporting standards at some point. Yet the specific expectations were murky, where "no one knows what the S and G will entail," especially as they "harder to define than climate," which is "more settled, with more visible effects." These conversations tended to focus on meeting the reporting expectations of external and internal stakeholders, rather than driving changes in company behavior.

Our statements are misinterpreted In addition to the reporting burden, practitioners found increasing disclosure to be risky because it could easily be misinterpreted. "Companies worry about disclosure because it means they lose control of the narrative," said a business association leader. This perceived risk was higher when reporting was not uniform and universal. "XYZ is getting skewered in the headlines, because they are the one that discloses," said one reporter. "Why would we subject ourselves to all of that scrutiny, if we don't have to?" asked one executive. Some professionals were critical of the ways other companies communicated their decisions related to political influence. For example, in reviewing the case study discussed during our October 21 workshop, participant raised concerns about ambiguity and vague language. One person said, "The response was so agonizingly 'corporate neutral' that it ended up saying almost nothing."

12.6.2 Challenges and Barriers to Accountability

We struggle with siloes and reactive processes Despite their value on coordination, many practitioners struggled to develop or implement cross-functional approaches. Leaders mentioned lacking adequate processes and frameworks, increasing the risk of reactive, fragmented approaches, reputational risk, and political blowback when they "wander into topics without a compass." "The word 'political' prompts people to think, 'Let government affairs figure this out,' which perpetuates the siloed approach," one officer told us. Our contacts also cited tensions across functions around priorities and metrics. "Historically, sustainability officers have not exercised as much influence with executive teams," explained one leader. "This is partly due to their traditional association with philanthropy." This echoes more broadly the finding in Chapter 9 of this volume, that companies often do not take an integrated approach to their climate policy influence (Ketu and Rothstein, 2023). Finally, we heard repeated accounts that C-Suite and Board oversight were not as consistent as they could be, due to historical inattention, siloed thinking, and lack of reporting, similar to the assessment in Chapter 2 of this volume (Freed, Sandstrom and Laufer, 2023). While a few companies had already developed internal guidelines and processes, many leaders described an urgent need for principles or a "decision tree" to help them determine when to engage in societal, civic, or political issues, guide them in formulating and articulating their firm's positions, reduce management time and attention required, and avoid partisan politics. Another challenge in developing an integrated view was consistency over time. Indeed, several firms going through leadership changes wondered if their firm would sustain a long-term view of its political influence. Finally, some firms struggled with time delays, as getting alignment and taking substantive action on an issue slowed them down. "We need to know we can follow through, so we might not respond to every issue that stakeholders want us to and might not meet the timeframe needed by society in a politicized environment."

Reactivity also raised questions about a firm's actual commitment to values or purpose (Paine, 2003). For example, eighteen of twenty-seven respondents to the case study during our October 2021 workshop expressed concern that the company's focus on responding to stakeholders meant they were not actually holding true to their values – even though these respondents agreed with the substance of the decision (not to fund election objectors). Several comments illustrate this concern, including, "They need to let their north star guide them, not the whims of the loudest group," and "They should have a back[bone] and stick to their decision, not be so reactive." Interestingly, this critique echoes some skepticism of "woke capitalism," reported by network leaders, who said that declarations of support on current societal issues were driven by cheap attempts to advance a brand reputation, rather than genuine belief (Wall Street Journal Editorial Board, 2021).

We are dealing with difficult political realities Many practitioners felt their critics did not understand the political realities that drove their engagement, and the need to have a "seat at the table" for important decisions (Novet, 2021). In particular, they felt the public did not fully grasp how important it was for them to cultivate allies who understood their industry and issues in Congress and the state legislatures, especially with those in leadership positions on committees or in the political parties. "We have relationships to uphold," said one leader. Not surprisingly, executives were reluctant to be held accountable for every position or action a candidate has taken. "Our issues are complex, and we have to drive big things," said another. "We don't want scrutiny for every single action and one-time events, when there has been trust, character and collaboration over an entire career." One network leader said she heard similar comments from members, who told her, "There are so many members of Congress in positions of leadership who are strong on our company's issue. How do split hairs for every member?" In addition, practitioners frequently described the pragmatic need to be cross-partisan. "we have to contribute to both parties," one officer told us, "And, in Georgia, that means you are going to contribute to an election objector."

Don't hold us accountable for what our trade associations do As outlined in Chapter 9, trade associations are a major factor in the slow progress around coherent, stable climate policy in the United States (Kelly et al., 2022). Yet, generally, executives we spoke with did not feel they should be branded based on the actions of their trade associations. "Stakeholders should measure us for what we do, not our trade associations," one government affairs officer told us. Several explained that they did not agree with every position their associations took but were working to elevate certain issues and considered many priorities when making membership decisions. Several executives and trade association leaders described associations as inherently oriented toward the "least common denominator," functioning almost as "bodyguards," that could "kill" or block legislation to protect a firm or industry. Several trade association insiders reinforced this assessment, and described their organizations as less accustomed to developing proactive, forward-thinking strategies. Finally, one leader described being on a committee and reviewing trade association positions. "We met twice a year to review the detailed position playbook," he told us. "They would take about 5 minutes to explain their recommendation and ask what we thought, then invite us to send in comments. I honestly can't say I know who was writing the positions or who had access to them before these reviews."

Our core business has to come first Finally, practitioners described the need to protect their business or industry as their top priority, frequently mentioning the threat of "bad policy." This might mean supporting candidates or trade associations who understood and took a favorable view of their industry's issues but might not align with the company in terms of broader societal issues. For example, in weighing a firm's position on legislation that bundled corporate tax increases with climate policy, we heard from network leaders that CSOs were not included in the discussions, because their tax policy teams were making the decision.

12.6.3 Challenges and Barriers to Responsibility

We are exhausted! Many practitioners reported sheer fatigue, as executive teams struggled with reactive, disjointed responses to the "issue of the day," "zig-zagging" from issue to issue. "There are so many requests, we cannot possibly sign on to all of them," said a Sustainability manager. "These issues need to be integrated into existing frameworks." Some worried that business was being dragged into the fray of a dysfunctional political system for partisan purposes, asked to "weigh in on issues that are not fundamental to our business." "We weighed in after George Floyd, based on our values, and now we are on the hook for engaging in many more public debates," said one financial services executive. As part of this, practitioners worried that they were reacting to the "squeakiest wheel" without considering where they could and should really weigh in.

Business should stick to its "swimlane" As a corollary to the need for the core business to come first (under Accountability), many practitioners expressed reluctance for businesses to get involved in issues outside of their firm, industry or general business interest. Some worried about neglecting the health of their business and their primary fiduciary duty to shareholders. Others felt it was beyond their legitimate role to prioritize among competing societal interests or factions. "Who am I to make tradeoffs on social issues, weighing policies that focus on LGBTQ+ issues and racial equity?" asked one PAC manager. Some questioned the sincerity of efforts to speak out on social issues and viewed current trends as a "fad." Executives were also very uncomfortable weighing in on issues related to civic institutions or societal issues and did not feel they had the expertise to have a meaningful opinion on specific legislation. "We don't know about elections; how can we weigh in?" said a sustainability manager in pharmaceuticals. For these reasons, as well as the risks of criticism, there seemed to be a common assumption that engaging was optional for business leaders, and that there were strong arguments for "staying out."

We can't win, whatever we do Some practitioners were unconvinced that there was any common ground or expectations they could meet. The phrase, "we are damned if we do and damned if we don't," came up repeatedly, as companies felt they were punished by one side for not getting involved and then faced retaliation when they did. Many complained about kneejerk vilification and anti-corporate sentiment, where certain watchdogs "exist to attack us, no matter what we do." One officer explained, "Corporate political spending is a very small share of the total, but it is used to generate an enormous share of public distrust." Another leader in Government Affairs told us, "We are being exploited by each side. It's in their interest to drag us into this, and it puts us in the crosshairs," and a CEO explained, "They are using our own money against us, to create constituencies who view us as an enemy." For these reasons, addressing CPR issues was viewed as risky and caused "nervousness among CEOs." For example, one network insider reported that several admired CEOs were hesitant to tackle misaligned trade association lobbying on climate policy, arguing, "We are already out ahead of the pack; this pushes us too far." Some worried that they might face a similar fate to a CEO who had been sacked by his Board because he was paying "too much attention to non-financial issues." In response to this and related examples, many agreed that "CEOs need cover" to help them "tread into areas that are challenging to them" and where "the incentives are all wrong" when it comes to acting on values and enlightened self-interest. This is one reason metrics were viewed as critical. Generally, leaders were discouraged by the "dysfunctional political situation" in the US, and the use of political influence for private gain. As one chairman summarized, "Normally, crony capitalism doesn't go too far, because Congress is there to adjudicate, to ensure a broad, long-term focus on the well-being of the country. But there is currently a complete breakdown of effective government. And that problem is well beyond crony capitalism!" In particular, they were concerned that political polarization was affecting their employees, leading to "fights in the cafeteria" as people returned from COVID-19 lockdowns, and got them "pulled into the fray" between factions, and led to regulatory instability with the political pendulum oscillating more often. Generally, these leaders seemed exasperated with government gridlock and inability to generate workable solutions to current challenges but were unsure that anything could be done. "Has it always been this way?" asked the chairman mentioned above. "Maybe it has."

Those issues don't really apply to us In many conversations, systemic issues such as climate, social justice, strong civic institutions or healthy markets seemed more abstract and less vivid or actionable to practitioners, than firm-level or even moral issues. Compared to stakeholder advocates, consultants, and former executives, practitioners were less detailed and specific when referring to the direct business impacts of systemic issues such as climate change, inequality, erosion of civic institutions or short-termism. This echoes the findings outlined in Chapter 9 of this volume, highlighting that few businesses have fully accounted for the systemic nature of climate risk (Ketu and Rothstein, 2023). Practitioners were also less likely to reference ways that business might be contributing to systemic risks in their core operations and activities (and, therefore, has the opportunity for high leverage influence). Unfortunately, this seemed to contribute to the perception that engaging with CPR is an optional activity, and firms could wait out the difficult periods if they chose.

There were two specific areas where we found practitioners generally less aware of their impact on systems than academics and stakeholder advocates. First, a very few were deeply familiar with the risks of classic economic market failures, negative externalities, or the potential for market activity to destroy value, though these have been described in some recent business reports (KPMG, 2014) (World Business Council for Economic Development, 2021). Focusing on business's "swimlane" in political influence was generally viewed as unproblematic, though there were a few references to cronyism. In general, most business leaders seemed to equate financial performance with real value creation and, by implication, societal welfare, though they acknowledged that this performance might fall short of societal goals or focus too much on short-term goals at the expense of long-term investment.

If my interpretation is accurate, this gap in practitioners' lexicon could have two major negative side effects. First, it could hamper or misdirect business's efforts to address societal challenges, increasing the chances that some business political influence will unintentionally exacerbate the very systemic issues businesses are attempting to address, and which, in the aggregate and over the long-term, harm the business environment (Gehl and Porter, 2020; Henderson, 2020; Ramanna, 2020). In addition, it is likely to increase the risk of communication breakdowns with various stakeholders, potentially contributing to polarization, distrust and the vilification of business. For example, if activists and investors assume business leaders are versed in the risks of externalities and other market failures, they may be more likely to view business advocacy of "market-based" solutions that do not address externalities as hypocritical and disingenuous. Similarly, some conservative practitioners we have spoken with view those advocating for a price on carbon or support for de-carbonization as seeking government favors and cronyism, rather than a correction for externalities, contributing to their distrust.

The second major potential gap is that practitioners did not seem broadly aware of the drivers of deteriorating trust in civic institutions, or business's contribution as one of multiple factors. Bolstered by recent data on trust in business, practitioners tended to focus on whether and how much to help fix an ineffective government (Edelman, 2021). They were less cognizant of data that show public distrust in government is affected by its responsiveness to the interests of entities with economic power and unresponsiveness to the interests of ordinary citizens (Gilens and Page, 2014). Few were aware of the relatively recent and dramatic rise of industry- or firm-specific lobbying for favorable economic rules or the contribution of these trends to declining public trust in government, decreased government effectiveness, populism and polarization (Friedman and Rinehart, 2019; Rainie et al., 2019). With the exception of several very old companies that referenced their own precedents in influencing politics for the greater good, very few referenced historical trends, prior eras when political influence for narrow gain was considered distasteful or the potential for business to exercise undue influence in political or civic processes (Drutman, 2015; Mizruchi, 2013).

Overall, practitioners tended to focus on how firms that "did the right thing" could differentiate themselves with employees, customers and investors, with fewer of them focused on the need to address systems as a whole. Yet, as outlined in Chapters 4, 5, and 7 in this volume, neither transparency nor managing reputational risks nor stakeholder relationships at the firm level are likely to be sufficient in driving CPR or addressing systemic issues on their own (Darnell and McDonnell, 2023; Walker, 2023; Werner, 2023). Indeed, it is difficult to imagine how even courageous, values-driven leaders would be motivated to advocate for a more elevated playing field for all without a coordinated, pre-competitive approach.

What exactly IS our responsibility? Finally, for some executives, the escalating frequency, intensity, and number of issues demanding business involvement led to deeper inquiries into shifting expectations for business's role in society. For example, one line leader mused, "We are working internally to ensure we improve diversity, equity and inclusion, but our industry has had a major impact on inequity in society. What is our responsibility to act beyond our walls?" A communications officer recounted, "In the past few years, we have had to weigh in on so many issues we would never have touched historically. We want to respond in an authentic, action-oriented way, not just being a mouthpiece. But it is unclear exactly what IS our responsibility." A few used these questions as a prompt to look at a broader context. For example, one CEO said, "As systems break down, more and more grievances and problems will be laid at business' feet. It will continue to be overwhelming until we fix the systems."

One of our goals for the Taskforce is to outline principles that help businesses recognize and act on their responsibilities related to civic, political and societal processes. During the October 2021 workshop for sustainability professionals, we shared a rough first draft set of principles and asked for feedback from the sustainability professionals who attended. Specifically, we asked them to share which values related to CPR most aligned with their views and to assess where their firm seemed to be strongest in practice. Figure 12.8 provides a summary of participant responses based on the core values listed in the draft principles.

The high priority and perceived follow-through on the Public Good dimension fits both the motivation described in 4f above around contributing to solving society's most challenging problems and the focus of sustainability professionals. The high priority on Integrity and Transparency reflects the motivations describe above in 4c and 4a, and the challenges of delivering in practice, including the challenge of siloes in 5d and firm policies on transparency that are likely to be out of the control of sustainability professionals. Finally, the perception

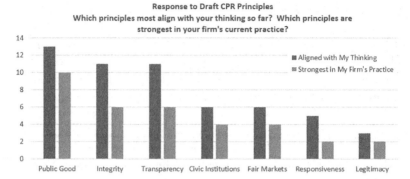

Figure 12.8 Analysis of practitioner poll in response to draft CPR principles

that Civic Institutions and Fair Markets are less relevant reinforces the interpretation that practitioners are less aware of larger trends and risks related to deteriorating trust in US civic institutions, externalities and other market failures, outlined in 5I above.

12.7 Conclusions and Possible Pathways for Improving CPR

Drawing on the motivations and interests above, several possible pathways seem promising for raising the bar on CPR as a new norm for business. Here are a few potential avenues for leveraging common ground, while addressing the challenges, barriers, and gaps identified above.

12.7.1 Consider Starting Internally with Accountability

Because practitioners were genuinely committed to honoring commitments, it seems possible that focusing on Accountability might be a useful starting point as a focus for CPR initiatives within firms (and, perhaps, challenges from external actors). First, it taps a sense of urgency in the face of employee concerns and investor, customer or stakeholder questions, awareness of coordination gaps, and espoused values around integrity (Doty and Kouchaki, 2015). Second, it provides a focal point for proactive work, encouraging companies to craft policies and develop more holistic governance and engagement processes to minimize the risk of contradictions, regardless of whether they view CPR as about companies stepping up or stepping back. Linking

CPR to enterprise risk management, strategic planning, scenarios, or planning in advance of future disclosures and reporting could help overcome the tendency to episodic attention. These processes can provide a practical opening for learning about the socio-political context, weighing competing priorities and thinking more systemically about the firm's impacts and interests, without the pressure and antagonism of concerted criticism or attack. Third, processes can be tailored for each company, drawing on the firm's own purpose, values or commitments, without super-imposing external standards or norms (at least as a starting point). And, finally, this approach can help prepare firms for greater Transparency or Responsibility over time, as disclosure expectations change and larger values around systems and institutions are debated.

One downside of this approach is that without external pressure, corporate attention to CPR processes will likely fade. In addition, companies may set the bar too low, applying only their stated company purpose, values or commitments, without considering their actual impact on larger systems, civic institutions or societal issues.

12.7.2 Sustain External Pressure for Transparency

Though other authors in this volume have argued that Transparency is likely insufficient as a driver of CPR, credible pressure for increased disclosure and reporting may be important in helping to sustain attention to Accountability as outlined in 6a above (Darnell and McDonnell, 2023; Walker, 2023; Werner, 2023). According to our conversations, questions from stakeholders – especially employees and investors – are a major factor in pushing companies to investigate and address contradictions, especially given executive values around accountability and integrity. Thus, it seems critical to sustain external pressure on Transparency, even as executives express concerns about misinterpretation. In addition, external pressure may provide "cover" for leaders facing conflicting interests internally, enabling them to take more proactive action to minimize reputational risk. As they exert this pressure, NGOs and stakeholder advocates may be able to intensify their impact by simplifying and aligning their expectations among themselves, addressing practitioner perceptions that there is "no way to win." The AAA Framework is an interesting example, where multiple NGOs collaborated to align on specific climate policy areas they believe companies need to prioritize for responsible policy engagement (AAA Framework, 2019; Ketu and Rothstein, 2023). NGOs may also find it more effective in the short run to focus on surfacing contradictions rather than imposing externally driven standards.

12.7.3 Strengthen Awareness of Systems, Especially Related to Externalities and Civic Institutions

At a very general level, practitioners seem to be responding to systemic challenges when called to by specific stakeholders but are less vividly aware of their dependence on those systems directly. This is particularly true around the risk of exacerbating market failures or undermining civic institutions through their business-as-usual influence activities. Thus, to foster Responsibility, it will likely be helpful to make systemic issues more vivid and immediate and elevate the importance of the concepts of externalities and market rules. It will also likely help to provide more historical and international context regarding civil society, CPR, and business's involvement in shaping the environment for business. This has implications for business education at the undergraduate, graduate, and executive levels, as well as communications strategies. In particular, it will be helpful to develop new tools and terminology for exploring externalities and other market failures in more everyday language. The good news is that many business leaders are being mobilized personally out of concern for civic institutions, which creates an opening for executive education and communications to put current pressures in context.

12.7.4 Reframe CPR Discussions as Part of a Larger Dialogue around Society's "Social Contract"

Lastly, I would like to introduce a pathway that could help practitioners and stakeholders develop more coherent strategies and address challenges related to overload, unclear expectations and conflict among stakeholders over the longer term. Outlining the advantages of this strategy will require some additional background.

As we have seen, responding to issue-by-issue pressure for CPR amid polarization is overwhelming to managers and contributes to a sense that there is "no way to win," increasing the risk that companies will disengage from dialogue about CPR unless stakeholder advocates escalate pressure even further. With many substantive CPR-related issues looming on the horizon, what can be done to enable coherent, integrated, effective responses? One option could be to approach CPR discussions more explicitly and directly as part of a broader renegotiation of the "social contract" between citizens, government, business, and civil society.

As summarized in Carroll et al. (2012), philosopher John Locke argued that individuals should have a "social contract" with government, in which "each respects the rights and responsibilities of the other." According to this tradition, a society's social contract involves unwritten shared understandings about what individuals have a "right to expect" and what actions are viewed as legitimate, emerging through "ongoing public conversation between people and the institutions they create" (p. 25). Gradually, the concept of a social contract has expanded beyond government to include business, the media, and civil society (Carroll et al., 2012; d'Agostino et al., 2011; Donaldson and Dunfee, 1999; Gunningham et al., 2003). For example, in explaining her support for the Business Roundtable Statement on the Purpose of the Corporation, then-CEO of IBM Ginny Rommetty explained, "Society gives each of us a license to operate.... It's a question of whether society trusts you or not. We need society to accept what it is that we do" (Murray, 2019; Wheeler, 2019). Over time, these implicit social contracts have adapted and changed. For example, Milton Friedman's 1970 argument that business's rightful obligations should be limited to shareholder financial returns and the resulting body of scholarship and practice reflecting this, can be viewed as a shift in the Western social contract away from the post-WWII period of the "good corporation" where business responsibilities were conceived of more broadly (Carroll, 2012; Mizruchi, 2013). Though the concept of a social contract raises complex questions about who shapes them, we can see that the idea of an implied "contract" is operative by the fact that certain actions are viewed as violations or breaches of trust, generating intense emotional reactions of outrage and cynicism.

Evidence suggests that many Western political economies are now in the midst of a major renegotiation of the social contract between civil society, government, business, and the media. Data shows widespread distrust and dissatisfaction with many foundational institutions (Edelman, 2021; Friedman and Rinehart, 2019; Gallup, 2021; Rainie et al., 2019; Repucci and Slipwitz, 2021; Transparency

International, 2020). Fundamental premises and previously accepted sources of legitimacy are being challenged, including the presumed economic benefits of capitalism, the sufficiency of adhering to local laws or cultural norms, the inevitability of the shareholder value maximization model, and the basis for trustworthy news (Scherer and Palazzo, 2006). This turmoil is not just a matter of adapting to new, mostly agreed-upon standards. As noted in our conversations, stakeholders, employees, customers, investors, and the public actively disagree on what should be expected from various actors. The current debate over stakeholder capitalism versus shareholder value maximization is at the center of this negotiation. Though 20–30 years of multi-stakeholder engagement and initiatives by leading companies have led to increasing convergence around the meaning of "corporate social responsibility," there is still an active debate over whether these new approaches belong in mainstream business practice or the core curricula of most business schools (Carroll et al., 2012; Ramanna, 2020).

Unfortunately, neither proponents of stakeholder capitalism nor shareholder value maximization have addressed CPR explicitly and directly thus far. This is somewhat surprising, given the fact that influence by special interests, including business, is a major driver of declining public trust, and that business's political influence has increased over the past forty years (in the United States) (Friedman and Rinehart, 2019; Lyon et al., 2018; Rainie et al., 2019; Scherer and Palazzo, 2006; Winkler, 2018). Indeed, though there have been several significant communications aiming to articulate new understandings of business's role in society, none of these has yet fully engaged the larger question underlying recent crises and ongoing public concern: "On what legitimate basis does business influence society's civic and political processes?" (Business for Social Responsibility, 2020; Schwab, 2019; Strine, 2019; United Nations, 2021; Wheeler, 2019).

Given this historical omission, it may be possible to help practitioners navigate current contentiousness by adopting a more direct and deliberative approach to the underlying tensions related to CPR. According to Scherer and Palazzo (2006, 2007), the answer to questions about business's role in civic and political processes requires public processes of "deliberative democracy." A relatively new form of governance applied to civic decision-making and conflict resolution, deliberative democracy is a process of moral debate, where those affected by a norm or decision exchange and weigh "good reasons," arguing for the validity of their views and considering the reasons behind opposing views, potentially changing their opinions in the process. The process builds on a desire to advance mutual understanding and shared goals without manipulation or threat (Chambers, 2003; Gilbert and Benham, 2009; Scherer and Palazzo, 2006). Through these processes, early experimenters have found it is possible to arrive at shared understandings across partisan divides, even on highly contentious issues (Fishkin et al., 2021).

For our purposes, approaching conversations about CPR as part of a deliberative process of social contract formation would open up several new options in practice:

Experiment with Deliberative Democracy Methods Internally

When engaging employees on CPR-related issues, companies could support and model deliberative approaches that promote genuine listening, sharing and weighing of reasons, engaging tradeoffs and dilemmas together, testing one's opinions, changing perspectives, problem-solving, learning about the broader context, and responding to others' concerns, while minimizing the influence of power and status. For example, rather than polling employees for their position on a current issue, firms might invite employees to reason together about how their firms' values apply or explore the broader basis for legitimate business influence in civic and political processes. As Favotto, Kollman, and McMillan describe in Chapter 6 of this volume, firms that are already strong in corporate social responsibility tend to be familiar with these practices and can simply deepen them. Others may choose to invest in them to support employee civic participation (Favotto, Kollman, and McMillan, 2023).

Support Deliberative Approaches with Stakeholders and Other Business Actors

When stakeholders disagree with each other, one option is to encourage them to engage with each other (and bring more voices to the table), using deliberative methods to weigh reasons and consider tradeoffs. For example, business leaders might prompt civil society organizations to adopt more coherent and aligned expectations among themselves, as recently demonstrated by the AAA Framework for Climate Policy Leadership (AAA Framework, 2019).

Identify and Apply Existing "Justified Hypernorms" for CPR

According to Integrated Social Contract Theory (ISCT), managers can think about social contracts as a foundational set of "hypernorms" or universal principles against which they test the norms of a specific community (Donaldson and Dunfee, 1999). Recently, Gilbert and Benham (2009), and Scholz et al. (2019) have proposed modifying this approach by ensuring that such hypernorms have been "justified" through multi-stakeholder deliberative processes and are truly universal and responsive. Fortunately, according to Scholz et al. (2019), there are already several sets of such hypernorms that have passed through such deliberative processes, and to which many companies have already publicly committed, including ISO 26000, the Caux Round Table Principles, the Ruggie Principles, the United Nations Global Compact. This provides managers with a valid, readily accessible source of guidance in weighing and articulating specific CPR issues and decisions building on prior deliberative processes.

Develop New CPR Hypernorms While Responding to Urgent Issues

Finally, to support alignment on more stable and coherent expectations for CPR, practitioners could engage internal and external stakeholders and other business actors beyond the specific issue at hand. One way to do this without hampering near-term responsiveness is to include some time in any deliberative process to exploring the hypernorms or principles that are relevant to that issue.

None of these strategies is simple or guaranteed to address all the challenges of implementing CPR. They may elevate calls for significant changes in political influence practices, stakeholders, and other actors may not choose to engage in deliberative processes proposed, and conflicts and misinterpretations may persist (Scherer and Palazzo, 2006). Still, they seem worth considering because they promise several likely advantages: (1) they enable practitioners to begin internally, (2) they address several underlying drivers of current overload and pressure, (3) they engage other actors in harmonizing expectations rather than leaving each business to reconcile conflicts on their own, (4) they empower business to take a proactive role in developing shared principles, (5) they can be applied even amid debate over stakeholder capitalism and shareholder value maximization, and finally (6) they help build capacities that are starting to work in civic contexts to reduce toxic polarization and foster civic participation.

12.8 Possible Additional Research

Beyond experimenting with the pathways above, there are several areas of research that could inform future efforts to engage practitioners in CPR, including:

- Assessing CPR practices longitudinally, to test whether beginning with Accountability accelerates or advances progress on Transparency or Responsibility
- Experimenting with ways to deepen practitioner understanding of externalities and market failures, civic health, climate, or other systemic issues, without resorting to jargon
- Clarifying which CPR practices build stakeholder trust and which erode it
- Studying the impact of deliberative processes for the development of "justified hypernorms" for CPR, internally, with external stakeholders and among business actors
- Exploring whether and how CPR can be articulated and applied effectively in firms with left-leaning, right-leaning and mixed executive teams

In summary, our preliminary conversations with practitioners suggest that the concept of CPR is easily accessible, many managers are interested in addressing it as a vehicle for engaging employees, meeting customer expectations, responding to investor ESG interest, and delivering on their stated purpose and values. Though bandwidth and skepticism about the ability to fulfill stakeholder expectations are major barriers, managers' commitment to the elements of Accountability – especially the need to eliminate contradictions – suggests a positive basis for building capacity that may later improve Transparency and Responsibility. Overall, our initial findings reinforce the need for forums to engage practitioners in deliberative processes and methods for increasing the vividness and salience of systemic issues in management decisions related to CPR as complements to external pressures and standards.

References

AAA Framework for Climate Policy Leadership. (2019). *AAA Framework for Climate Policy Leadership.* www.aaaclimateleadership.org/

Business for Social Responsibility. (2020). The Business Role in Creating a Twenty-First Century Social Contract, June 24.

Carroll, A.B., Lipartito, K., Post, J.E., & Werhane, P.H. (2012).*Corporate Responsibility: The American Experience.* Cambridge, UK: Cambridge University Press.

Chambers, S. (2003). Deliberative Democratic Theory. *Annual Review of Political Science*, 6(1), 307–326.

D'Agostino, F., Thrasher, J., & Gaus, G. (2011). Contemporary Approaches to the Social Contract. *The Stanford Encyclopedia of Philosophy*, Winter.

Darnell, S. & McDonnell, M.H. (2023). License to Give: The Relationship between Organizational Reputation and Stakeholders' Support for Corporate Political Activity. In *Corporate Political Responsibility.* Cambridge, UK: Cambridge University Press.

Donaldson, T. & Dunfee, T.W. (1999). *Ties That Bind: A Social Contracts Approach to Business Ethics,* Boston, MA: Harvard Business School Press.

Doty, E. & Kouchaki, M. (2015). Commitments, Disrupted: Understanding and Addressing Commitment Drift in For-Profit Enterprises. Working Paper.

Drutman, L. (2015). *The Business of America Is Lobbying: How Corporations Became Politicized and Politics Became More Corporate.* New York, NY: Oxford University Press.

Edelman. (2021). Edelman Trust Barometer 2021.

Favotto, A., Kollman, K., & McMillan, F. (2023). Responsible Lobbyists? CSR Commitments and the Quality of Corporate Parliamentary Testimony in the UK. In T. Lyon, ed., *Corporate Political Responsibility.* Cambridge, UK: Cambridge University Press.

Fishkin, J., Siu, A., Diamond, L., & Bradburn, N. (2021). Is Deliberation an Antidote to Extreme Partisan Polarization? Reflections on "America in One Room." *American Political Science Review*, 115(4), 1464–1481.

Freed, B., Sandstrom, K., & Laufer, W.S. (2023). Targeting Private Sector Influence in Politics: Corporate Accountability as a Risk and Governance Problem. In T. Lyon, ed., *Corporate Political Responsibility.* Cambridge, UK: Cambridge University Press.

Friedman, W., & Rinehart, C. (2019). The Fix We're In: What Americans Have to Say about Opportunity, Inequality and the System They Feel Is Failing Them. *Public Agenda.*

Gallup. (2021). Confidence in Institutions. *Gallup.*

Gehl, K.M. & Porter, M.E. (2020). Fixing U.S. Politics. *Harvard Business Review*, July–August.

Gilbert, D.U. & Benham, M. (2009). Advancing Integrative Social Contracts Theory: A Habermasian Perspective. *Journal of Business Ethics*, 89, 215–234.

Gilens, M. & Page, B.I. (2014). Testing Theories of American Politics: Elites, Interest Groups, and Average Citizens. *Perspectives on Politics*, 12(3), 564–581.

Gunningham, N., Kagan, R.A., & Thornton, D. (2004). Social License and Environmental Protection: Why Businesses Go Beyond Compliance. *Law & Social Inquiry*, 29(2), 307–341.

Hacker, J. & Pierson, P. (2021). Conflicted Consequences. *The Center for Political Accountability*, July 13.

Henderson, R. (2020). The Business Case for Saving Democracy. *Harvard Business Review*, March 10.

Henderson, R. (2020). *Reimagining Capitalism in a World on Fire*. New York: Public Affairs Press.

Ketu, Y. & Rothstein, S. (2023). Practicing Responsible Policy Engagement: How Large U.S. Companies Lobby on Climate Change. In T. Lyon, ed., *Corporate Political Responsibility*. Cambridge: Cambridge University Press.

KPMGInternational. (2014). A New Vision of Value: Connecting Corporate and Societal Value Creation.

Livni, E. (2021). On Voting Rights, It Can Cost Companies to Take Both Sides. *New York Times*, June 5.

Lyon, T.P., et al. (2018). CSR Needs CPR: Corporations, Sustainability and Politics. *California Management Review*, 60(4), 5–24.

Mizruchi, M. (2013). *The Fracturing of the American Corporate Elite*. Boston, MA: Harvard University Press.

Murray, A. (2019). America's CEOs Seek a New Purpose for the Corporation. *Fortune*, August 19.

Novet, J. (2021). Microsoft President Brad Smith Explains How Political Contributions Really Work. *CNBC*, January 22.

Paine, L.S. (2003). *Value Shift: Why Companies Must Merge Social and Financial Imperatives to Achieve Superior Performance*. New York: McGraw-Hill, 2003.

Preventable Surprises. (2021). Corporate Lobbying Alignment Project (CLAP). *Preventable Surprises*.

Public Affairs Council. (2021). Taking a Stand: How Corporations Engage on Social Issues. *Public Affairs Council*.

Rainie, L., Keeter, S., & Perrin, A. (2019). Trust and Distrust in America. *Pew Research Center*, July 22.

Ramanna, K. (2020). Friedman @50: Is It Still the Social Responsibility of Business to Increase Profits? *California Management Review*, 62(3), 28–41.

Repucci, S. & Slipowitz, A. (2021). Democracy under Siege. *Freedom House*.

Scherer, A.G. & Palazzo, G. (2006). Corporate Legitimacy as Deliberation: A Communicative Framework. *Journal of Business Ethics*, 66, 71–88.

Scherer, A.G. & Palazzo, G. (2007). Toward a Political Conception of Corporate Responsibility: Business and Society Seen from a Habermasian Perspective. *Academy of Management Review*, 32(4), 1096–120.

Scholz, M., de los Reyes Jr., G., & Smith, N.C. (2019). The Enduring Potential of Justified Hypernorms. *Business Ethics Quarterly*, 29(3).

Schwab, K. (2019). Why We Need the 'Davos Manifesto' for a Better Kind of Capitalism. *World Economic Forum*, December 1.

Sorkin, A.R., et al. (2021). The C.E.O.s Who Didn't Sign a Big Defense of Voting Rights. *New York Times*, April 14.

Strine, Jr., L.E. (2019). The 2019 CPA-Zicklin Index of Corporate Political Disclosure and Accountability: Foreword. *The Center for Political Accountability*, 7–8.

Transparency International. (2020). Corruption Perceptions Index 2020. *Transparency International*, January.

United Nations. (2021). United Nations Global Compact Website. *United Nations*

Walker, E.T. (2023). What Drives Firms to Disclose Their Political Activity? In T. Lyon, ed., *Corporate Political Responsibility*. Cambridge, UK: Cambridge University Press.

Wall Street Journal Editorial Board. (2021). The Price of Woke Corporate Politics. *Wall Street Journal*, May 19.

Washington, P. & Spierings, M. (2021). Under a Microscope: A New Era of Scrutiny for Corporate Political Activity. *The Conference Board*.

Werner, T. (2023). Promise and Peril: Lessons from Shareholder Reactions to Corporate Political Activity Disclosure. In T. Lyon, ed., *Corporate Political Responsibility*. Cambridge, UK: Cambridge University Press.

Wheeler, K.J., et al. (2019). Statement on the Purpose of a Corporation. *The Business Roundtable*.

Winkler, A. (2018). *We the Corporations: How American Businesses Won Their Civil Rights*. New York, NY: Liveright Publishing.

World Business Council for Economic Development. (2021). Time to Transform. *Vision 2050*, March.

World Economic Forum. (2020). Measuring Stakeholder Capitalism: Towards Common Metrics and Consistent Reporting of Sustainable Value Creation. *World Economic Forum*, September 22.

Index

Printed in the United States
by Baker & Taylor Publisher Services